The Antitrust Enterprise

The Antitrust Enterprise

Principle and Execution

Herbert Hovenkamp

HARVARD UNIVERSITY PRESS

Cambridge, Massachusetts

London, England

2005

Library of Congress Cataloging-in-Publication Data

Hovenkamp, Herbert, 1948–
    The antitrust enterprise : principle and execution / Herbert Hovenkamp
        p.   cm.
    Includes bibliographical references and index.
    ISBN 0-674-01897-4 (alk. paper)
    1. Competition—United States.   2. Antitrust law—Economic aspects—
United States.   I. Title.

HF1414.H68 2005
343.73′0721—dc22   2005050362

Contents

Preface

The operating principles of every discipline must periodically be reexamined. Too much mischief results when the everyday rules of the law lose connection to their foundations and acquire a life of their own. This book originated in many law school and economics classes and seminars devoted to the effective administration of the antitrust laws. More than any other forum, classroom encounters have challenged me to identify antitrust's most fundamental and realistic aspirations.

I have too many intellectual debts to list here, but I must mention one. Phillip E. Areeda was my senior coauthor for nearly fifteen years prior to his untimely death in 1995. He helped me to understand and make order out of this discipline, to appreciate its significant limitations, and to articulate and define its rules. His life's work, the multivolume *Antitrust Law* treatise that he and Donald F. Turner began in the 1970s, has now become my life's work as well.

I am also indebted to the University of Iowa—and particularly to the two deans under whom I have served, N. William Hines and Carolyn Jones—for ample support of my research. Finally, and gratefully, I dedicate this book to my father, Bert Hovenkamp.

Introduction

After decades of debate, today we enjoy more consensus about the goals of the antitrust laws than at any time in the last half century. By contrast, antitrust's rules for decision making remain unfocused and imprecise. Few people dispute that antitrust's core mission is protecting consumers' right to the low prices, innovation, and diverse production that competition promises. Articulating the means to achieve this end is a different matter. Policy makers continue to dispute questions about the robustness of markets; about the extent to which strategic business behavior exists and whether antitrust can do much about it; about where the most protection is needed and what form it should take; about the special role of antitrust in regulated or deregulated industries; and about the proper relationship between antitrust and innovation.[1]

The modern debate over basic antitrust goals began during the era when Earl Warren was Chief Justice of the Supreme Court (1953–1969). Under Warren antitrust cases became relatively easy for plaintiffs to bring and win, and they were highly likely to go to jury trials unless fearful defendants settled out of court. But too often the protected class seemed to be small business rather than consumers. Indeed, many Warren-era decisions condemned conduct precisely *because* it reduced costs or generated more desirable products.[2] Such practices harm rivals unable to match them, but they benefit consumers. On top of that, Warren Court antitrust was highly distrustful of markets, suspicious of innovation and the intellectual property laws, and convinced that aggressive antitrust remedies would make the economic world a better place. The result, wrote Robert H. Bork, the most influential critic of Warren-era

1

antitrust policy, was a mélange of incoherent policies that confused competition with small business protection and was probably worse than no antitrust policy at all.[3]

The antitrust counterrevolution of the 1970s and 1980s challenged every one of these values. The procedural limitations placed on plaintiffs became severe, and far fewer antitrust cases go to trial today. The only articulated goal of the antitrust laws is to benefit consumers, who are best off when markets are competitive. But the definition of "competitive" has changed as well. The Warren Court defined "competitive" as a market containing many firms, the small ones having a "right" to compete with the bigger ones. Today antitrust policy generally defines "competitive" in the economic coin of low prices, high output, and maximum room for innovation. The academic lawyers and economists of the Chicago School, who were responsible for much of the counterrevolution, sometimes conceded that firms could engage in anticompetitive strategic behavior. But outside of remedies for collusion, they found little promise in antitrust cures. Rather, they believed that markets are generally robust and tend to correct themselves, and that government intervention is as likely to make things worse as better.

A few things seem clear about this dramatic switch in perspective. *First,* in the 1960s and 1970s the Supreme Court went overboard in protecting small business from larger firms, often at the expense of consumers. However, the Supreme Court had no clear vision about how much society should be willing to pay for such protection, or exactly who the beneficiaries should be. *Second,* the rise of the Chicago School in the 1970s was a much needed corrective, restoring rigor that had been lost, and identifying a protected class—consumers—and some rules for assessing how they could best be protected.

But, *third,* at least some parts of the counterrevolution went too far. Historically, the Chicago School tended to regard only price-fixing and large mergers as within the competence of the courts. While more complex forms of behavior might be anticompetitive, the courts generally were thought to lack the ability to develop rules for these problems without doing more harm than good. At the same time much of so-called "post-Chicago" antitrust, discussed in Chapter 2, has wandered too far to the opposite extreme, identifying problems and solutions that are beyond the competence of the court system to comprehend and correct.

Fourth, during the mid-twentieth century United States policy was deeply suspicious of patents and other intellectual property rights. We tended to see intellectual property as inherently monopolistic and in need of control. Antitrust policy responded not merely by creating severe limits on anticompetitive abuses of intellectual property rights, but also by imagining threats to competition where none existed. The result was silly rules that often deprived creative entrepreneurs of their innovations even when they posed no competitive threat. And the outcome of limiting intellectual property rights in haphazard, unforeseeable ways is a reduced incentive to innovate. In the last two decades, however, this pendulum has swung to the opposite extreme. Congress has continuously expanded the scope of patent and copyright, and we have become much more tolerant of practices that were routinely condemned a few decades ago. A strong case can be made that today we overprotect at least certain intellectual property rights, perhaps severely so. This problem is in the first instance not one for the antitrust laws, but it necessarily shows up in the attitude that antitrust takes toward intellectual property practices that are alleged to be anticompetitive. In evaluating such claims the first job for antitrust is to determine that competition really has been threatened.

Fifth, the transition from regulatory to antitrust control of deregulated industries has gone far more smoothly in some markets than in others. During the New Deal the United States embarked on top-to-bottom regulation of many industries, including electricity and natural gas, communications, banking, insurance, securities, land use, and interstate transport, including airlines, railroads, and trucking. Government agencies often specified the prices that regulated firms could charge (through tariffs filed by the firms themselves), restricted the entry of newcomers, and required firms to justify any expansion into a new territory or product. Along with regulation came various degrees of antitrust immunity, most generally under the theory that the regulatory agency should oversee anticompetitive abuses. But much of this regulation was an economic failure. Regulation is costly, produces haphazard results, is not good at making firms minimize their costs, and impedes innovation. Furthermore, agencies are too frequently "captured" by the very firms they are supposed to control. Only a few markets work so badly that elaborate price and entry regulation is worth these substantial costs.

Under "deregulation," which emerged in the 1980s, regulation was relaxed in each of these industries, competition was restored, and antitrust given a new role. But antitrust's record in these formerly regulated markets has been mixed. It has succeeded in markets where regulation was never appropriate in the first place, such as trucking; and in markets where changes in technology have facilitated competition among numerous rivals, such as long-distance telecommunications. It has largely failed in markets that require hardwired networks, such as local telephone service or retail electricity. Where deregulation has worked well, antitrust has slipped in rather easily to fill the void. But where deregulation has worked poorly, the role of the antitrust laws remains highly uncertain, and they are often misapplied. In some cases we have simply replaced regulation-by-agency with regulation-by-antitrust-trial, which is far worse.

Sixth, confidence in the federal courts as principal administrator of the antitrust laws is higher than it was two decades ago. Nevertheless, the overall record of the federal courts remains spotty. Lack of adequate Supreme Court supervision has led to many divisions among the federal courts of appeal. Jury trials continue to produce indefensible outcomes. The remedies system is badly designed. The courts rely excessively on experts engaged by the parties, often with unacceptable results. In general, although the courts have become better at identifying problematic market *structures*, they have not done so well in dealing with complex anticompetitive *strategies*, where they continue to permit juries to make decisions that the judge feels incapable of making.

Dealing with these problems is not easy. Often their roots are systemic, originating in the Constitution or inherent in the structure of the antitrust laws themselves, which assign the overall power of interpretation to generalized federal courts. The Seventh Amendment provides for a jury trial upon demand in damage actions, and the antitrust laws contain a liberal provision of threefold (treble) damages for prevailing plaintiffs. Jury trials in front of intelligent but nonspecialist judges is a truly miserable way to make economic policy, but federal courts do it all the time in the guise of enforcing the antitrust laws. The current phenomenon of greatly overused private enforcement leads to the closely related problem of unprincipled experts, whose skills at persuading an untutored jury are often much greater than the quality of their economic or market analysis. The courts have responded to these problems by developing a remarkably expansive doctrine of "summary judgment," or the judge's power to decide a case without a jury trial. Judges also have broad power to limit and exclude the testimony of expert witnesses. Unfortunately, having the power to exclude expert testimony is one thing; exercising it sensibly has proven to be extraordinarily difficult.

Antitrust Policy and the Rehnquist Court

The problem of well-articulated principles but poorly designed rules is severe because in the short run rules weigh much more heavily than principles. Judges do not rewrite antitrust ideology in every case, or even in every decade. Most of the time it matters little what the judge or anyone else thinks about the likelihood and social cost of strategic behavior. To be sure, the rules that courts develop are related to the values they believe antitrust should further. If we think copyrights are packed with anticompetitive potential, then we might respond with a rule that presumes that their owners are monopolists. Several decisions have done just that.[4] But rules generally perform a much subtler function. They reflect concerns about the competencies of courts as much as our substantive concerns about whether and when firms do anticompetitive things. For example, the rules governing expert testimony and summary judgment have to be applied in nearly every significant antitrust case.

The rules problem has been exacerbated by a reduction in the Supreme Court's supervisory role and by a growing amount of conflict among the lower federal courts. In theory, federal antitrust law is unitary. The federal district courts make law at the trial level. Their decisions are reviewed by the Circuit Courts of Appeal, and the fact that most appellate review is mandatory means there is fairly close intracircuit consistency in antitrust law making. The United States Supreme Court sits on top of the circuits, and its traditional role has been to supervise their work and resolve conflicts. The potential for conflict is substantial because there are thirteen federal circuits deciding antitrust cases. These include the First through Eleventh Circuits, plus the D.C. Circuit and the Federal Circuit, which decides patent cases, some of which contain antitrust issues.[5]

One of the remarkable phenomena of the Rehnquist Supreme Court is the degree to which it has denied review in antitrust cases, leaving conflicts to simmer and not correcting clear errors. Robert Bork's *The Antitrust Paradox*, written in 1978, was aimed entirely at the United States

Supreme Court, because at that time that court made virtually all of the important antitrust law. But today the task of making antitrust rules largely befalls the federal courts of appeals, which typically decide between fifty and eighty important antitrust cases per year, very few of which are reviewed by the Supreme Court. This is a significant number, although splits in the circuits tend to reduce their authoritativeness.

The decline in Supreme Court antitrust supervision is partly a consequence of the dramatically reduced docket of the Rehnquist Court from its recent predecessors. In its later years the Rehnquist Court issued a little over half as many decisions per year as the Burger Court (1969–1986) did.[6] Correspondingly, the number of granted petitions for review has declined from approximately 20 percent just after World War II to roughly 2–3 percent today. One explanation for the reduction is that the Court intentionally set out to take fewer cases so that it could write "bigger" decisions—making up for reduced numbers by increased breadth or importance. If that was the strategy it has largely failed. The Rehnquist Court has also been ideologically divided and, perhaps because each Justice is assigned fewer opinions, the number of concurring and dissenting opinions has increased significantly. Instead of speaking more decisively, the Court has often simply generated more confusion by issuing decisions that reveal deep divisions among the Justices.

A review of the Supreme Court workload discloses that the number of reviewed cases in the area of antitrust has declined dramatically. For example, if one compares the 1983–1985 terms, during the tail end of the Burger Court, to the 1993–1995 terms, the number of antitrust cases declined from eleven to one.[7] The Supreme Court issued one antitrust decision per year in 1996, 1997, 1998, and 1999. It issued none in 1995, 2000, 2001, 2002, and 2003. The result is an increasingly balkanized antitrust policy dominated by the circuit courts, even though we nominally have a single set of statutes that cover the entire United States. The Court issued three decisions in 2004, and will issue at least three in 2005. This is a welcome upturn that we hope will continue into subsequent years.

Coupled with this decline in annual antitrust review is the Supreme Court's repeated warning that the lower courts should not anticipate that the Supreme Court will reverse an outmoded precedent, but must let the Supreme Court perform that task for itself.[8] Outmoded and simply bad rules tend to "cling" because the Supreme Court does nothing about them and the lower courts are helpless to make the changes themselves.

Clear Goals but Deficient Rules

Antitrust is a more defensible enterprise today than it was three and four decades ago, when the Supreme Court produced decisions that were calculated to benefit small business at the expense of consumers. Antitrust has not merely moved to the right, as the federal judiciary has in general. It has also become more coherent, more identifiable with a single economic model, and more trusting of the market to solve most competitive problems. Part of the credit for this lies with a federal judiciary that became increasingly sophisticated about economics in the 1980s and 1990s. Part of it lies also in the scholarship of the "Chicago School" and the more centrist "Harvard School" of antitrust. While these two schools of antitrust thought have diverse origins and historically diverse ideas about the complexity of the economy and the appropriate role of government, they have also converged on a number of important points.

Antitrust is a far humbler enterprise today than it was several decades ago. Those administering the antitrust laws are generally more aware that antitrust is a form of regulation—a type of market intervention in an economy whose nucleus is private markets. Furthermore, intervention is the exception rather than the rule. Market intervention must be justified and the justifications by and large are not moral ones. Punishing unfair behavior is not antitrust's role. Its purpose is to make markets perform more competitively, and intervention is justified only when it moves us toward that goal.

Administrability is key because antitrust is a justifiable enterprise only if court intervention can make markets work better. The sad fact is that economists are often convinced that a certain practice can be anticompetitive, at least part of the time. However, antitrust is forced to leave the practice alone because it has not developed rules that can reliably distinguish anticompetitive results or remedy them effectively.

By appreciating its own limitations antitrust today produces fewer "false positives," or instances when courts condemn predominantly procompetitive behavior. In the process it also produces more false negatives, or situations where it declines to remedy behavior that is very likely anticompetitive. Ironically, part of the problem of false negatives lies with the very aggressiveness of the antitrust laws themselves, which provide for attorneys' fees and treble damages, and broadly pronounce that "any person" who is injured by an antitrust violation may sue. The result of these broad provisions is a natural attempt by lawyers to turn every conceivable tort and contract dispute into an antitrust action, on a wide range of marginal or even outlandish theories. The equally natural reaction of the federal courts is to trim private antitrust enforcement with rules that narrow the scope of liability, make individual elements of a violation more difficult to prove, and narrow the range of plaintiffs who can sue.

As a historical matter, we probably would have been better off with a less aggressive set of antitrust prohibitions accompanied by a set of procedural and substantive rules that make violations easier to prove. For example, concerns about the excesses of treble damages suits produced the highly underdeterrent indirect purchaser rule considered in Chapter 3. The result is that many firms that have committed antitrust violations never pay a penalty sufficient to deter their conduct. Likewise, concerns about jury speculation and the willingness of courts in the mid-eighties and earlier to infer conspiracies from circumstantial evidence have led to harsh rules that fail to detect many harmful agreements among competitors.

Perhaps most seriously, it has become something of a commonplace that rule of reason antitrust violations are almost impossible to prove, particularly in private plaintiff actions. The rule of reason inquiry remains undisciplined—a problem that the Supreme Court only exacerbated by its 1999 *California Dental* decision, discussed in Chapter 6. Unfocused explorations of restraints generally turn up something that appears beneficial; and as long as plaintiffs have the burden of proof, complexity favors defendants. But rational administration of the antitrust laws requires more focused inquiries and a hard look for less anticompetitive alternatives when a restraint seems both competitively harmful and not essential to the socially beneficial functioning of a joint enterprise.

Not all the errors remaining in the antitrust enterprise are false negatives. Plaintiffs' lawyers continue to push the envelope in their presentation of expert testimony, often crossing the line into "junk" science. The screening rules developed by the Supreme Court have provided only a partial, highly imperfect repair. A great part of the difficulty lies with a system that regards technical expert testimony as a "question of fact," which means that it falls within the province of the jury. But questions such as whether an expert's multiple regression analysis should have excluded a particular outlying data point, or should have employed more or fewer variables, are "fact" questions only in a highly idiosyncratic sense. Nevertheless, too often the judge who feels unqualified to assess the basic rationality of an expert's methodology hands the job off to the one decision maker in the courtroom who is even less qualified than he is, namely the jury. Fundamentally, we take "questions of law" away from the jury because we distrust jurors' ability to engage in technical interpretation of statutes or legal doctrine. Expert testimony is at least as technical and its jargon just as specialized.

Finally, strategic behavior itself poses a problem. In the 1960s and 1970s the Supreme Court and lower court judges were apt to be suspicious of firms and distrustful of markets. They tended to see a large amount of behavior as strategic, and, moreover, to believe that strategic behavior was anticompetitive. Often they did this with insufficient inquiry into power or even the basic rationality of plaintiffs' claims. At the opposite extreme, Bork's *The Antitrust Paradox,* from the perspective of 1978, saw very little room for anticompetitive strategic behavior other than the formation of cartels. He was inclined to see virtually all single-firm actions, vertical practices, and even most horizontal agreements as procompetitive or competitively harmless simply because strategic opportunities seemed to him to be so few.

The so-called "post-Chicago" antitrust of the 1980s and 1990s reclaimed a concern with strategic behavior, put more rigor into its definition, and tried to raise the level of antitrust concern. Nevertheless, the most visible impact of that movement remains the Supreme Court's 1992 *Kodak* decision, which held that a nondominant firm can have antitrust market power vis-à-vis its "locked in" buyers. Chapter 5 argues that *Kodak* has probably been the most useless and harmful antitrust decision of the Rehnquist Court, which typically has not been expansive in its interpretation of the antitrust laws.

The strategic behavior question divides into two subparts: first, does strategic behavior exist that antitrust doctrine has failed to acknowledge? And second, assuming that it does exist, can antitrust do anything about it? The answer, which some keepers of the faith are loathe to hear, is yes to the first, but often no to the second. Anticompetitive pricing and exclusion strategies may exist far beyond our institutional capacity to identify them accurately and remedy them effectively. As a result we must frequently conclude that although anticompetitive behavior is probably occurring, antitrust can do nothing about it. Creating any test at all for identifying the practice threatens too many false positives and deficient remedies that are more costly than any social benefits they produce.

Antitrust is an economic, not a moral, enterprise. Nor is its goal compensation for competition's victims, albeit the competitive process produces many. Antitrust is a defensible enterprise only if intervention into the market is economically justified. That entails that the market be "bigger" in some sense as a result of intervention—whether "bigger" is measured by higher output, improved quality, lower prices, or more innovation. Furthermore, the increase must be enough to justify the high cost of operating the antitrust machinery.

Lest these conclusions sound too pessimistic, one must remember that antitrust is not the only way that government manages the economy. Rather, antitrust is the residual regulator, filling in the lacunae among other regulatory and property regimes. For example, while at this writing antitrust seems to have been unequal to the task of managing the Microsoft monopoly, other solutions remain and are likely to be more effective. These possibilities are considered in Chapter 12.

This book is organized into three parts. The first considers the institutional enterprise of antitrust, looking at its history and ideology, its tendency to create overly complicated rules, the numerous problems attending private enforcement, and the uses and misuses of experts. Part II then looks at substantive antitrust doctrine as developed in "traditional" markets. Finally, Part III considers the role of the antitrust laws in regulated industries and networks, as well as the intersection between antitrust and the intellectual property laws.

I

LIMITS AND POSSIBILITIES

The most fundamental problem antitrust confronts is dealing with complex market information through institutions whose competence is limited. Part I considers antitrust's surprisingly simple core economics, its disconcerting special interest origins and divergent schools, and the institutional scheme we have created for enforcing the antitrust laws. Antitrust's overly ideological history, as well as our failure to appreciate the limitations of the litigation process, has served to make antitrust more complex than it needs to be.

1

The Legal and Economic Structure
of the Antitrust Laws

The antitrust laws are concerned with maintaining competition in private markets. "Competition" refers to a state of affairs in which prices are sufficient to cover a firm's costs, but not excessively higher, and firms are given the correct set of incentives to innovate. "Innovation" in turn is a market-driven concept. It refers not only to new technology, but to any novel product, service, or method of distribution that increases sales.

The antitrust laws are only one among many legal regulators of competition and innovation. Intellectual property laws and market-specific regulations for such areas as telecommunications or electric power also pursue the same ends. Furthermore, these alternatives come not only from the federal government but also from state and even local governments. One good way to think of antitrust is as a "residual" regulator; its purpose is to promote competition to the extent that market choices have not been preempted by some alternative regulatory enterprise. Much of antitrust decision making is concerned with the proper allocation of regulatory power between the antitrust laws and other legal regimes, such as the intellectual property laws, federal telecommunications law, state regulation of public utilities, or municipal regulation of land use.

While we often think of antitrust as troubled by high prices, it is better to think of antitrust's main concern in terms of restrictions on output. Competition is injured when a firm or group of firms is able to reduce output in some market, and "output" can be measured by either quantity or innovation.[1] A restraint on output, such as a cartel, forces prices up because the same number of customers must chase fewer goods. A restraint on innovation forces customers to accept an inferior good, service, or method of distribution when an unrestrained market might produce something better.

Using the law to create competitive incentives is a tall order. Speaking very generally, one would describe the market circumstances that facilitate *price* competition as several firms in the market, unrestricted entry, product homogeneity, good information held by both producers and consumers, and strong rules against price-fixing. But as soon as innovation is thrown into the mix, the story becomes more complicated. Innovation—and also the intellectual property laws that protect it—can produce market power, and even monopoly in extreme cases. Furthermore, the set of market structures that produces aggressive price competition is often quite different from the structures that encourage significant innovation. Much, perhaps most, profitable innovation occurs in relatively concentrated markets with a relatively small number of firms producing distinguishable products. Optimal pricing may require firms to compete with each other, but optimal innovation may require a more complex mixture of competition and cooperation. And patents and copyrights sometimes constitute formidable barriers to entry.[2]

So antitrust rules for protecting competition cannot simply encourage regimes of hundreds of tiny firms forced to compete against one another. Firms in such a market will compete, but products could still be expensive and the economy could lose much of the innovation it is capable of producing. In short, the general prescription that antitrust must "maximize consumer welfare" gives us very little guidance for developing specific antitrust rules that will facilitate the proper balance between competitiveness and progress.

Fortunately, antitrust is not a positive administrative enterprise such as the regulation of retail electricity, where a government agency sets rates, decides when plants need to be built or modernized, and determines how much should be invested in developing new technologies. Opting to have antitrust at all entails a belief that in most cases the market will produce the correct amount of competition and innovation. All antitrust must do is see to it that the market functions reasonably well. This requires the creation of a few second-order incentives to develop the proper market structures and to discourage anticompetitive practices.

By "second order" I mean that antitrust is largely reactive—for example, it never decides when firms should merge or create internal distribution systems; but it may pass judgment on the legality of such decisions once private firms have made them on their own. As far as innovation is concerned, antitrust's main job is not to stand in the way, trusting that the market will generally take care of things, yet intervening when a significant restraint threatens to limit the avenues of innovation.

Antitrust's Model of Consumer Harm

The neoclassical model of economic welfare provides antitrust with many of its general principles. The term "neoclassical" refers to neoclassical economics, which has been the dominant economic ideology in the United States and most other places for more than a century. The first great modern school of economics in the Anglo-American tradition were the classicists, whose best-known representative is Adam Smith. Classical political economy gave western civilization far too many ideas to summarize here, but among the most important is capitalism's confidence in unregulated markets. We are indebted to Adam Smith for the thesis that the uncontrolled, apparently chaotic, and completely self-interested behavior of businesspersons actually produces more welfare than government command and control.

What the classical political economists did not give us, however, was a usable theory of costs or prices, or normative ideas about what the optimal price and output should be. More seriously, classicism did not provide much useful theory about how people and business firms make decisions. For the classical political economist, determining costs was largely a matter of averaging past expenses. The firm computed its costs by taking everything it purchased and dividing the total by the amount it produced. A rational businessperson determined how much to produce and what price to charge by looking at these historical averages.

The great intellectual dividing line between classical political economy and what we now call "neoclassical economics" was the development of the concept of marginalism and the construction of the marginal cost curve, which represents the cost of the next unit that a firm produces. Just as American antitrust policy was originally being formulated, the first great neoclassicists such as William Jevons and Alfred Marshall began to argue that rational actors make decisions not by averaging the things that had happened in the past, but rather by assessing the cost and value of the next choice to be made.[3] For most decision-making purposes the relevant "cost" of something is the cost of the next unit to be produced. The value of something is the amount that some consumer is willing to pay for the next unit. To be sure, historical costs and values are an essential part of the information any economic decision maker must collect, but the values themselves are forward- rather than backward-looking.

The neoclassical revolution was both profound and pervasive, upsetting economic thinking on nearly every issue. For example, under the classical "wage fund" theory of employee compensation, wages were determined by the profits that a firm had previously earned and were thought to be available as a "fund" to pay employees. If wages rose higher than this historical fund, then the firm would be driven into bankruptcy. By contrast, under the neoclassical "marginal value" theory of wages, a firm's manager looked forward, considering how much additional value a worker was likely to contribute to the firm. Any wage below that marginal value would make the firm better off.[4]

Neoclassicism gave economics the important insight that demand curves slope downward: as people purchase goods, their willingness to pay for yet one more unit declines. In the aggregate, willingness to pay for the next unit decreases as more is produced. Furthermore, a business firm produces at a rate at which the marginal cost of producing— that is, the cost of producing the next unit—just equals the anticipated price. For example, if the farmer anticipates that corn will sell for $3 per bushel, she will produce on any field whose anticipated production costs are less than $3, but not on fields whose costs are greater than $3. Neoclassical economists were able to show that under perfect competition, where price equals marginal cost, market output tends to be highest and market prices lowest. They were also able to show that perfectly competitive markets maximize the short-run value of society's resources.[5] And they were able to give us important insights into the destructive power of cartels and monopolies.

The welfare model of competition and monopoly is illustrated by Figure 1.1. The market demand curve D slopes downward, and we have made it a straight line for convenience. Making the line straight does not change the analysis but simplifies the mathematics. We have also drawn the firm's marginal cost curve (*MC*) so that it is upward sloping in the relevant range of output, which means that costs are rising. This is typically the case, although marginal cost curves can also be constant over a fairly wide range.

A perfectly competitive firm maximizes its profits by producing at a rate, Q_c, at which the marginal cost of the next unit is just equal to the market price, or P_c. For example, the farmer planning corn production for next year and anticipating a price of $3.00 per bushel will bring her lowest-cost land into production first, then the next lowest, and so

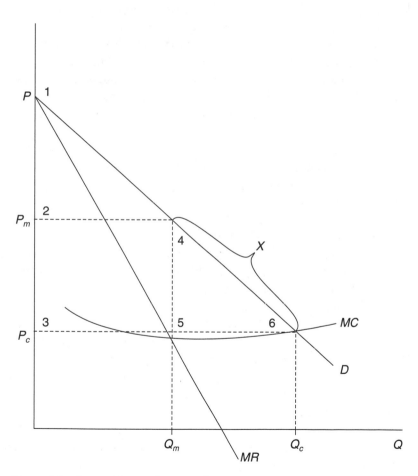

Figure 1.1. Competition and monopoly

on until the cost of producing an additional bushel hits $3.00. If the farmer's last unit of production costs $3.10, then she would be ten cents richer by not producing that unit. If her last unit of production was $2.90 and the next bushel promises to be about the same, then she could earn ten cents more by producing that additional bushel. Her output decision would hover around an equilibrium in which the last unit of production equaled the market price.

Production at the competitive rate of output maximizes the farmer's personal profits, but it is also the socially efficient output. In a competitive economy the money that it costs Farmer Brown to produce a bushel of corn represents the market costs of those resources, or the cost to society of mobilizing them. If Farmer Brown is able to take resources that society values at $2.75 and turn them into a $3.00 bushel of corn, society is twenty-five cents richer (it does not matter whether the twenty-five cents go into the pocket of the farmer or others, such as suppliers or customers). But if she requires $3.25 to produce that same bushel of corn, then society would be twenty-five cents better off if she did not produce it.

Monopoly is a different matter. A monopolist in Figure 1.1 produces at output Q_m and charges price P_m. The reason for this is that the monopolist, unlike the competitor, obtains a higher price as it reduces output. Price is not affected by the competitor's individual output decision. If Farmer Brown decides to grow 300 acres of corn next year rather than 400, the market will not care, for Brown's output is trivial in relation to the entire market. But when the monopolist, or only firm in the market, produces less, its output "clears" at a higher point on the demand curve. For example, if entire market output went from 400 to 300 bushels, the price would rise.

The neoclassical model recognizes the monopolist's control over price with the marginal revenue curve (*MR*), which reflects the fact that the market price changes as the monopolist produces less or more. For example, suppose the demand curve indicates that the monopolist's output decreases from ten to nine as its price increases from one dollar to two. The demand curve thus falls from ten units to nine units, or one unit. However, the monopolist must sell both the first and the second units at the lower price, so its revenue will be ten at a price of one and eighteen (9×2) when the price is two. "Marginal" revenue, or the change in revenue as the monopolist increases the price, goes from ten to eight, or two units. In sum, the marginal, or additional, revenue that the monopolist receives as it increases output falls faster than the demand curve falls. Indeed, it can be shown mathematically that if the demand curve is linear, the marginal revenue curve will be precisely twice as steep, as Figure 1.1 illustrates. If demand as the monopolist raises prices goes in the progression 10, 9, 8, 7 . . . , its marginal revenue goes in the progression 10, 8, 6, 4 . . .

The all-important difference between the competitor and the monopolist is that the competitor maximizes its profits by equating its marginal cost with the demand curve. The monopolist does so by equating its marginal cost with the marginal revenue curve, which is the point at which the additional revenue from a sale just equals the additional cost. Beyond that point each additional unit will produce more in incremental costs than in incremental revenues, so the monopolist will not produce them. After locating the intersection of *MR* and *MC*, we draw a vertical line showing that the monopolist's output will be Q_m, and by going up to the demand curve we see that the monopoly price will be P_m. Significantly, the monopoly price is higher than marginal cost, telling us that resources are being wasted. Consumers are expected to pay more for the monopolist's output than the cost of the resources used in producing it. As a result they are either poorer or else they make inefficient substitutions, which are substitutions that they would regard as "inferior" if their first choice were competitively priced. Triangle 4-5-6 represents the traditional "deadweight loss" that monopoly causes. The consumers located along this portion of the demand curve, which is under bracket *X*, would be willing to pay the competitive price. However, they refuse to purchase at the monopoly price and make an inefficient substitution for something else. Since the monopolist earns nothing on unmade sales, this triangle represents a loss to both consumers and the monopolist, and thus a net social loss as well.

Rectangle 2-3-5-4 is traditionally thought to represent a "wealth transfer" from consumers to the monopolist. This consists of overcharges on sales that the monopolist makes to consumers at higher prices. As a result the monopolist is richer and consumers are poorer by precisely this amount. There is good reason to believe that the traditional "deadweight loss" triangle understates the cost of monopoly. Two other sets of costs must be included, and both can be considerable. *First,* the wealth transfer (rectangle 2-3-5-4) represents a significant value to a monopolist, and a firm will spend substantial sums in order to acquire it. If the expected value of having a monopoly is $1,000, a firm would be willing to spend any amount up to that figure to have it. Some of this "rent seeking" behavior is efficient, such as research and development leading to a market-shifting innovation. But some of it is socially harmful. A firm might consume the entire expected value of its monopoly in socially harmful activities such as predatory pricing or making fraudulent patent claims.[6]

Second, the creation or maintenance of monopoly by exclusionary practices also imposes costs on immediate victims—such as the firm whose investment is lost because it is victimized by predatory pricing or wrongfully brought patent infringement suits. This is a special case of the general proposition that a social cost of harmful activity is the cost of defending or preventing such activity as well as the collateral costs of the victim. For example, a theft of $100 is not merely a wealth transfer if the robber shoots or clubs his victim, who will now also have medical or burial plus other costs. And part of the social cost of theft is the hundreds of millions of dollars spent each year on burglar alarms and other loss prevention devices. In some cases these costs far exceed the value of the wrongful conduct to the violator.[7]

The Antitrust Statutes and Harm to Competition

When Congress drafted the antitrust laws, its members were not thinking of the model for consumer harm just developed, although some of the ideas might seem implicit. The principal antitrust laws of the United States are the Sherman Act of 1890 and the Clayton Act of 1914. The Clayton Act was significantly amended in 1936 and 1950. Over the last century these statutes have been amended several additional times, but their substantive "core" remains remarkably as it was initially passed, taking up only two or three pages of text.

Even this handful of sentences may be more than we need. The case has been made that antitrust policy would be cleaner, simpler, and more effective if the legislation were radically simplified. Close parsing of the statutory language has led to many complicated and quite useless antitrust doctrines. An antitrust statute that read simply, "Unreasonable restraints on competition are hereby forbidden," would do all the work that our current antitrust laws do without all the doctrinal baggage that has been developed along the way.[8] Such a provision would reach both unilateral and multilateral practices and would rely on the courts, advised by experts, to develop rules for determining when practices were unreasonably anticompetitive.

This book does not contemplate such a radical amendment, but is dedicated to making the best use of what we have. And what we have is a series of overlapping provisions that reach most anticompetitive practices with overdeterrence to spare, and a few practices that are not even arguably anticompetitive. Very briefly, the main substantive antitrust provisions are these:

- *Sherman Act, §1:* cartels and market division agreements; boycotts; vertical restrictions, typically imposed by an "upstream" firm, such as a manufacturer, on a "downstream" firm, such as a dealer; historically, mergers. What all these practices have in common is that they require an "agreement" between two or more actors.
- *Sherman Act, §2:* "monopolization," or exclusionary practices, which are practices by which a dominant firm, acting unilaterally, seeks to keep others out of its market. These practices can include some of those listed under §1, including mergers.
- *Clayton Act, §2, as amended in 1936 by the Robinson-Patman Act:* a competitively harmful provision that often operates to limit a supplier's use of wholesale pricing to make the distribution of its product more efficient.
- *Clayton Act, §3:* "tying" and "exclusive dealing," two vertical practices by which a supplier limits the range of products that its dealers can sell, although tying law has been expanded into other contexts as well. All the practices prohibited by this provision are also addressed by §1 of the Sherman Act, making §3 of the Clayton Act very close to superfluous.
- *Clayton Act, §4:* providing treble damages and attorneys' fees to prevailing antitrust plaintiffs.
- *Clayton Act, §7:* mergers.

Other than the Robinson-Patman Act, which is not generally addressed to restraints on competition at all, the antitrust laws try to detect and prosecute anticompetitive output restraints by grouping them into three classifications: (1) multilateral, horizontal restraints; (2) unilateral exclusionary practices; and (3) vertical practices, both unilateral and multilateral.

Horizontal Restraints

Figure 1.1 above illustrates the logic of anticompetitive restraints. In order for a group of firms to raise their collective price, they must reduce market output from competitive level Q_c toward monopoly level Q_m. Note that the restraint need not be perfect: it can be highly profitable to the cartel and do considerable social harm if it succeeds in reducing output only a portion of the distance from Q_c to Q_m. All cartels are imperfect to one degree to another, but new ones are constantly created, indicating that they are profitable.

As the bracket marked X illustrates, the cartel's output reduction entails that there are many consumers along the demand curve who are willing to pay more than a marginal cost (i.e., competitive) price but are out of the market at the monopoly price. In order for the cartel to succeed, the consumers represented by bracket X must be kept out of the market, and this illustrates the two problems that the cartel faces and the restraints that are designed to solve them. The cartel first must restrain its *own* members' output. For the single-firm monopolist this is ordinarily not a problem because the monopolist loses money whenever it charges less than its own profit-maximizing price. But each cartel member has an incentive to "cheat" by producing more than its allocated share. The Sherman §1 law concerned with collusion addresses restraints whose purpose is to enable cartel members to keep their collective output down. For example, in *NCAA* the Supreme Court struck down an NCAA rule that placed severe limits on the number of times an NCAA football team could have its games televised. The NCAA was fixing the price it was paying for TV advertising, and in order to do so had to impose the output limitation on its members. But an individual member of the NCAA, the University of Oklahoma (the plaintiff in this instance), could earn more by televising more of its own games.[9]

But the output increment designated by bracket X can also come from firms who are not members of the cartel. In addition to suppressing its own members' output, the cartel must keep the output of others out of the market. The Sherman Act law of *exclusion,* or boycotts, is concerned with restraints designed to exclude others from coming into the market, or suppressing the output of noncartel members. For example, *Eastern States Lumber* condemned an agreement among lumber retailers that they would not purchase from any wholesaler who was also engaged in retailing.[10] The retailers were probably fixing prices. The wholesalers responded by entering retailing themselves, hoping to avoid the retailer cartel's high markups. The retailers in turn responded with an agreement intended to keep the output of these new retailers out of the market by destroying their wholesale business, thus forcing market output back to Q_m.

All horizontal restraints, including some horizontal mergers, can be explained in terms of this model. Unfortunately, §1's requirement of a "contract," "combination," or "conspiracy" has been interpreted to require a fairly explicit agreement among the parties, making §1 a poor tool for dealing with implicit agreements. That topic is addressed in Chapter 6.

Agreements among rivals are not necessarily anticompetitive, even when they serve to regiment output or exclude others from the market. One good illustration of procompetitive agreements that serve both to limit members' output and to exclude nonmembers is standard setting. Trade associations, professional associations, and other industry groups often set standards for those wishing to sell in their market. Suppose, for example, that the American Medical Association passes a rule requiring graduation from an accredited medical school and a multiyear residency before one is admitted to practice. This rule serves both to restrict the number of people who can practice and to keep a large set of potential practitioners out of the market. Nevertheless, the public benefits from reasonable rules requiring professionals to be qualified. Furthermore, the people best qualified to make such rules are typically the professionals themselves, even though their incentives might be anticompetitive.

Unilateral Exclusionary Practices

The prohibition of monopolization in Sherman §2 reaches exclusionary practices, and Figure 1.1 explains them as well. In order to earn monopoly profits a dominant firm must also succeed in reducing output from Q_c to Q_m, or at least part of the way toward Q_m. Unlike the cartel, the monopolist need not be concerned about maintaining its *own* output reduction. But it does have to keep other firms from entering the market for the customers located along bracket *X*. Section 2 of the Sherman Act is addressed to the dominant firm's "exclusionary" practices, which are practices reasonably capable of facilitating that result.

Antitrust is more cautious about condemning a single firm's exclusionary practices than the practices of a group of collaborators, and for good reason. A cartel can be created very quickly. For example, the *NCAA* rule limiting televised games might have been passed at a single meeting. By contrast, dominant firms typically come into existence slowly and with great difficulty, most often by welfare-enhancing practices such as innovation or low prices. These practices "exclude" just as much as anticompetitive exclusionary practices, and distinguishing pro- from anticompetitive exclusions is often very difficult. Finally, exclusionary agreements among multiple firms are easily recognized unless they are kept secret. Such agreements are also somewhat idiosyncratic, in the sense that most firms act without them. In sharp contrast, every act that a monopolist undertakes is its own. Unilateral acts are essential to the conduct of any firm's business. This difference is particularly prominent when the practice in question involves pricing. For a group of firms to agree with each other on a pricing scheme that injures a rival is a visible act that requires an explanation. By contrast, no single firm, including the monopolist, can sell without setting a price.

Vertical Practices

A business relationship is said to be "vertical" when it involves the coordination of two stages of production or distribution. A firm might integrate vertically by new entry, as when Chrysler as manufacturer builds its own windshield plant or opens its own wholly owned car dealership. A firm might also integrate vertically by contract, as when Domino's Pizza enters into a long-term agreement with a franchisee. Or a firm might integrate by merger, as when Ford acquired Autolite, a maker of spark plugs, or when DuPont, a large maker of automobile paints and seat covers, acquired a significant interest in General Motors.[11]

Over history both Congress and the courts have been highly suspicious of vertical practices. That probably explains why every single substantive antitrust provision has been used to condemn them under one theory or another. Sherman §1 reaches vertical contractual restraints, including resale price maintenance, nonprice vertical restraints, tying, and exclusive dealing, as well as vertical mergers. Sherman §2 also reaches all of these when imposed by a dominant firm. Clayton §2, the Robinson-Patman Act, is concerned mainly about how an upstream firm such as a manufacturer prices to its distributors or dealers. Clayton §3 is concerned with tying and exclusive dealing; Clayton §7 reaches vertical mergers. Nevertheless, as Chapter 8 develops, very few vertical practices are anticompetitive, and during the last quarter century the Supreme Court has backed off considerably from many, many years of overdeterrence.[12]

Antitrust Treatment of Efficiencies and Innovation

The set of lines in Figure 1.1 explains the difference between perfect competition and monopoly, but does not say anything about the role of efficiencies and innovation. Perfectly competitive firms always have a short-run incentive to reduce their costs, but they may not have the resources necessary for the kinds of efficiency gains that show up only after a long period of investment. Research and development (R&D) is typically quite costly, and often promises returns only after several years. At the other end of the spectrum, monopolists are likely to have the resources to engage in R&D, but they do not always have sufficient competitive incentives to do so.

Every efficiency gain is an innovation of sorts. To be sure, the person who obtains an efficiency may not be able to patent it, perhaps because the innovation is sufficiently obvious that the government will not issue a patent. So innovations include the electronic calculator, which replaced the electric adding machine and slide rule. But they also include a firm's decision to use plastic bags rather than paper, because plastic bags are cheaper and easier to handle, or to give its delivery drivers cell phones so they can respond to order changes while they are on the road.

For antitrust purposes it is also useful to distinguish between innovations that are the result of collaboration from those that are wholly internal to the firm. When a firm innovates entirely on its own, without agreeing with any other firm about anything, then the innovation rarely violates the antitrust laws. About the only exceptions are a small number of "predatory" acts by monopolists, such as strategically creating a product so as to make a rival's technology incompatible and worthless.

The principal acts of innovation that concern antitrust are collaborative, involving mergers, joint ventures, and a few vertical practices. Nevertheless, the great majority are welfare-enhancing as well. Consider these examples:

- A merger might enable a firm to organize its production more efficiently by specializing its plants. Prior to the merger each firm had only one plant, which produced both Alpha product and Beta product. After the merger the firm has two plants, and it shifts all of Alpha production to one and all of Beta production to the other. This enables the firm to take advantage of economies of scale in production.
- One merging firm may have state-of-the-art production facilities but be weak in research and development. The other may have older production facilities but a strong R&D department. A merger of the two could make the postmerger firm stronger in both areas.
- A half-dozen pediatricians may join forces in order to create "Pediatric Associates," a partnership that enables the pediatricians to (a) share expensive durable equipment; (b) centralize office management services such as scheduling, billing, and dealing with insurers; and (c) take turns being "on call" so that patients always have a pediatrician available but individual partners can get some rest.
- Two manufacturers of specialized aircraft may combine their efforts to develop a more efficient avionics system that would work in both their aircraft.

Each of these combinations of actors promises significant efficiency gains, but at least some of them raise the potential for harming competition by reducing the number of firms in a market or facilitating price-fixing. So there may be cases in which efficiency gains and injuries to competition must be traded off against each other before we can determine whether a union of competitors is beneficial or harmful. Unfortunately, if efficiency gains and competitive losses have to be quantified and "balanced" in a reasonably close case, the antitrust courts lack the measurement tools necessary for the job.

The welfare trade-off model that antitrust uses most often was developed in the 1960s by economist Oliver E. Williamson. The model is illustrated by Figure 1.2, which is probably the most frequently reproduced graph in all of the antitrust literature.[13] The figure illustrates what happens when a union (merger, joint venture, or other collaboration) transforms a market from perfect competition to perfect monopoly but also produces cost savings that result from some innovation or efficiency, such as the examples given above. The savings result in lower marginal costs.

Shaded triangle *A* in the illustration shows the "deadweight loss" that results when the market moves from competition to monopoly. By contrast, shaded rectangle *B* consists of efficiency gains that occur when the costs of the firms' output drop from MC_1 to MC_2, reflecting whatever efficiencies this union produces. Generally speaking, this union is economically efficient if rectangle *B* is larger than triangle *A*. Note that this could happen even if the collaboration causes prices to rise. For example, consumers might be injured by $100 as the price rises from $1.00 to $1.10, but the union might also produce $125 in efficiency gains. In this

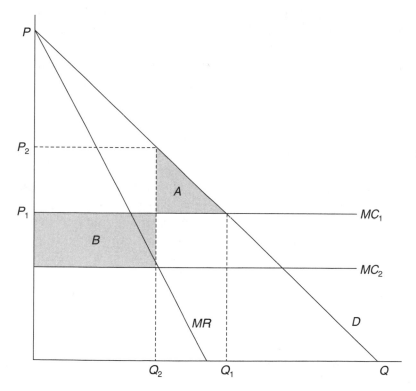

Figure 1.2. The welfare trade-off model

case the merger or other union is efficient on balance, but the efficiency gains show up as increases in producer profits rather than lower prices.

Williamson's model predicted that relatively small gains in efficiency would be sufficient to offset rather large amounts of monopoly profit. As a result antitrust should be particularly sensitive to efficiency gains and leave efficiency-producing collaborations alone, even if they threaten significant amounts of monopoly.

That said, the Williamson model is a rather severe oversimplification of reality. For example, it does not distinguish between immediate savings in production costs, which show up instantly in the market price, and long-run savings whose benefits will not accrue until much later. These differences can be significant for antitrust policy because our assessment of the social cost of monopoly is driven heavily by factors of time and uncertainty. For example, a merger of the two dominant firms in a market would very likely produce a monopoly price increase immediately. The merger might also promise increased R&D that could have significant results ten years down the road. In such a case an antitrust court might be asked to "balance" immediate competitive harm against the prospect of innovation gains that are far in the future and may not occur at all.

Furthermore, the Williamson model assumes that prior to the collaboration in question the market was competitive but afterward was monopolized. As a result the efficiency gains apply across the entire market. But that is rarely the story. For example, mergers and joint ventures are most frequently condemned because they are thought to facilitate collusion between the uniting parties and other firms in the market. Suppose a market contains five firms of roughly equal size and two of them merge, reducing the total number to four. Any collusion facilitated by this merger would raise the prices of *all four,* causing a marketwide deadweight loss. In contrast, the only firms that could claim the efficiencies would be one or both of the partners to the merger. This qualifier swallows up many of the cases. Most merger and joint venture challenges occur where the union involves fewer than all of the firms in the market, and often fewer than half as measured by market share. Consequently, the Williamson model can significantly overstate efficiency gains, a fact that Williamson himself realized.[14]

Finally, the balancing model applies only if there is something to trade off. Nothing needs to be traded off if (1) the union creates no market power to begin with; (2) the union creates no efficiencies; or (3) while some efficiencies might result, they could have been obtained by alternative means. These three possibilities have strong implications for antitrust policy. *First* and foremost, if the practice under consideration does not threaten competition at all, then any efficiency gain, no matter how small, confers a social benefit. Even if there is no gain, antitrust has no business condemning harmless practices.

Second, and at the opposite extreme, when likely anticompetitive effects are established, antitrust need not be detained by unions that create no or only modest efficiencies. As we shall see in our discussion of horizontal mergers, while the theoretical case for an "efficiencies defense" is appealing, the practical case is weak because measurement problems are so extreme. Rather, we use fairly underdeterrent substantive rules that do not permit antitrust courts to interfere in the market unless the threat to competition is strong. Then we ignore all but the very strongest and most compelling efficiency claims. In the case of mergers, strong and credible efficiency claims are not all that common.

Joint ventures are another matter because they come in such a variety. A few ventures, such as the blanket licensing venture in the *Broadcast Music (BMI)* case, create such extraordinary efficiencies that the market as we know it could not exist without them.[15] *BMI* involved an arrangement under which thousands of owners of performance rights in recorded music gave nonexclusive licenses to BMI, which then issued "blanket licenses" to radio stations and others who wished to have immediate access to large and diverse collections of music. Under these blanket licensing arrangements a radio station or other purchaser paid a fixed fee and was then entitled to perform without independent prior approval any song in BMI's library. The alternative—individual negotiation with copyright holders for each recording—would impose unimaginable transaction costs and make many types of radio and other programming impossible.

Sports leagues are another set of highly efficient joint ventures. Coordination among teams is essential to organized sports. For example, the members of the NFL must agree with each other on when and where to play, which is a market division agreement; similarly, they must agree on how many games to have in a season and how long each game should be, both of which are output limitation agreements. If revenue is to be shared, they may even have to agree on some prices, such as that for television advertising. To be sure, an alternative universe might exist in which a single very large firm such as General Motors owns the entire NFL. But in the world that we live in, with separately owned teams, joint arrangements are essential to making this market work.

Third, a union of competitors with a significant anticompetitive potential is justified by efficiencies only if the particular union is necessary to create them. Many efficiencies are readily created by less restrictive alternatives. Firms do not have to merge or even coordinate their production in order to benefit from joint research; they need only do the research together and agree to license the results to one another. Often ventures can be structured in alternative ways that permit the efficiencies to be obtained but with smaller threats to competition. In the *BMI* case, for example, the individual rights holders gave BMI *non*-exclusive rights to perform their compositions. The significance of nonexclusive rights is that BMI had no power to reduce market output even if it wanted to. If it attempted to charge a higher price than rights holders could obtain individually, the radio stations could always go directly to the performance rights holders and get their own licenses from each one. In this particular case the court did not have to impose nonexclusivity because the parties had already built it into their contract. In a case involving firms with significant market power but also a significant efficiency potential from the sharing of intellectual property rights, judicially mandated nonexclusivity might preserve the efficiencies while eliminating most of the competitive concerns.

Antitrust generally attempts to deal with these problems *not* by balancing efficiency gains against competitive harms—"balancing" is simply not something the courts can do unless the difference in weights is fairly obvious. Rather, antitrust proceeds by asking first if the restraint threatens competition. If the answer is no, the inquiry is aborted. If the answer is yes, it asks whether significant efficiency gains are likely and if the restraint is reasonably necessary to achieve them. If the answer to either question is no, then the restraint is condemned. Otherwise, if "balancing" is required and the case is at all close, antitrust stands aside, trusting that the market rather than the government will strike the right balance.

2

The Design of Antitrust Rules

Judges have spoken of antitrust law as a "consumer welfare prescription" for so long that the phrase seldom produces anything but yawns. The consumer welfare model was first articulated in Chicago School writings in the 1950s and 1960s, and received widespread currency when it was popularized by Robert H. Bork in 1978.[1] The rhetoric of "consumer welfare" is very powerful. A statute declaring protection of consumers to be the goal of antitrust would probably pass Congress by a unanimous vote. But that would have been true even during the 1950s and 1960s, when anticonsumer decisions were antitrust's stock in trade.

Nevertheless, we cannot identify appropriate rules without considering the meaning of underlying ideologies and slogans, and "consumer welfare" is rhetorically the most powerful of these. The principal antitrust ideologies are the Chicago and Harvard Schools and the "post-Chicago" alternative. Although it may once have been otherwise, today these schools no longer articulate different *goals*. By and large, all three agree that protection of consumer welfare is antitrust's ultimate purpose. The remaining dissimilarities lie in their views about how antitrust can best achieve that end. Their divisions reflect contrary assumptions about the complexity and robustness of markets, as well as divergent assessments of the abilities of courts and other government agencies to correct market failures. The most extreme Chicago School vision is dedicated to the twin propositions that markets are relatively simple and tend naturally toward competitive outcomes. By contrast, government institutions are feeble instruments for improving on what markets can ordinarily accomplish on their own. To one degree or another, the other schools disagree with or qualify both of these propositions.

The Chicago School

The economists and legal scholars who began teaching and writing at the University of Chicago in the 1950s developed the most unified and sustained critique ever of antitrust policy. The Chicago School offered an elegant, pro-market, and largely anti-interventionist vision of antitrust.[2] Building on neoclassical economics, Chicago School antitrust writers argued that in the long run markets tend to correct their own imperfections; that the history of aggressive judicial intervention has produced many indefensible results; that courts have often condemned suspicious-looking business practices without understanding them, and when these practices were understood they were shown to have benign or procompetitive explanations. As a result tribunals should study business practices much more thoroughly before deciding that intervention is appropriate.

The members of the Chicago School also argued that effective competition demands far fewer firms than once believed. Such competition does not require dozens of little firms, and in most cases three or four is sufficient. Therefore, the Supreme Court's hostility toward mergers in unconcentrated markets in the 1960s and 1970s was seriously over-deterrent. Furthermore, even when competition is imperfect, most attempts at monopoly pricing will be undermined by new entry, which is highly likely to occur in well-functioning capital markets. One of the biggest differences between Chicago School antitrust and its predecessors was the Chicago School's confidence that entry by new firms would solve most competitive problems. By contrast, antitrust law in the seventies and earlier routinely condemned poorly understood practices in markets where entry barriers seemed practically nonexistent.[3]

Chicago School writers also believed that many of the practices identified in the case law and literature as "exclusionary" in fact reflected aggressive competition or innovation. These practices were either not exclusionary at all, or else they excluded rivals only because competing with an efficient firm is difficult. Chicago School writers argued that nearly all vertical practices, price discrimination and most strategic pricing, many patent practices, and business torts were rarely or never anticompetitive.

A correlative tenet of Chicago School antitrust was its misgivings about government. While private markets generally work themselves pure, government intervention can almost never make that claim. The one type of entry barrier that Chicago School economics heartily embraced was the government-created barrier,[4] such as regulatory requirements that gave firms monopolies or raised the costs of new entry, or absolute entry restrictions such as the licensing requirements placed on broadcasters[5] or the "certificate of need" that a new hospital must have before it can build.[6] This distrust of government also extended to the courts, producing the belief that court-ordered antitrust fixes actually make markets less rather than more competitive, or injure consumers for the benefit of competitors. As a result the best antitrust policy is one of doing as little as possible, intervening only in the case of blatant practices such as naked price-fixing or market division.

Chicago School scholarship served antitrust policy well by pointing out the economic nonsense undergirding so many antitrust decisions. One example is the explosion of the "leverage" theory of vertical integration. The leverage theory condemned vertical practices such as tying arrangements by assuming that a monopolist in one product could use tying to create a second monopoly in a tied product, thus earning two monopoly profits while destroying competition in the tied product. In *Carbice* (1931), Justice Brandeis condemned the maker of a patented ice box whose license agreement required users to purchase their dry ice from him as well. Justice Brandeis wrote that this requirement permitted

> the patent-owner to "derive its profit, not from the invention on which the law gives it a monopoly, but from the unpatented supplies with which it is used" [and which are] "wholly without the scope of the patent monopoly" . . . . If a monopoly could be so expanded, the owner of a patent for a product might conceivably monopolize the commerce in a large part of the unpatented materials used in its manufacture. The owner of a patent for a machine might thereby secure a partial monopoly on the unpatented supplies consumed in its operation.[7]

Brandeis's theory reflects the belief, then current, that monopoly is ubiquitous and easily spread by the simple device of contracts tying monopoly to nonmonopoly products. It also reveals the period's deep distrust of patents. Justice Brandeis apparently believed (1) that the patent on the ice box automatically gave its owner a "monopoly," (2) that the patentee then had the power to expand that monopoly indiscriminately by contracts obliging people to take additional products in order to get the patented product, and (3) that this "leveraging" of ordinary commodities (dry ice) enabled the firm to enlarge its monopoly profits and exclude rivals. These views arose from a broad distrust of bigness—but bigness really meant vertical integration, or the fact that a firm operated in numerous interrelated markets. The reason Carbice could "expand" its ice box "monopoly" was because it also sold dry ice.

The Chicago School's demolition of the leverage theory showed that a monopolist's profit-maximizing price depends on the price of complementary products. For example, the price people are willing to pay for a bolt depends on the price that they must pay for a nut, assuming they need both. Thus a firm charging its most profitable price for bolts when nuts were priced competitively could raise the price of nuts only by offering a compensating reduction in the price of bolts. To see this more easily, if two retailers were charging $100 for a pair of shoes, one could not obtain your trade by telling you that his price was only $30 for the left shoe and $70 for the right one, while the other retailer was charging $50 for each. The only price of significance is that for the pair. Once we understand this extraordinarily simple proposition about the relationship between complementary products (such as ice boxes and ice, right and left shoes, hardware and software, toasters and bread, automobiles and gasoline), we lose many of our fears about firms that operate in two or more markets.[8]

Chicago School economists identified other, equally serious, problems with then-existing antitrust theory. For example, pre-seventies policy was often built on exaggerated notions of market dominance and monopolization that too often failed to ask whether the defendant controlled anything capable of being monopolized. The same policy overstated the pernicious effects that flowed from competitor agreements while minimizing or often ignoring their procompetitive effects.[9] And it condemned mergers under a variety of "leverage" or "deep pocket" theories that emphasized the competitive advantages that merging firms obtained, while ignoring that most of these advantages resulted from lower costs or superior products. Courts ended up condemning mergers because of, rather than in spite of, efficiencies.[10]

But the Chicago view of antitrust was oversold. Many markets very likely are messier than Chicago theory assumes. People often lack good information. Often they are stuck by virtue of previous investments and face large "switching costs." As a result investment may not flow toward competitive solutions as freely or as quickly as we hope. While the leverage theory never recovered very much from the Chicago critique, it also became clear that the Chicago School assumed fairly simple markets in which the only consideration was whether the firm could enlarge its monopoly price by relating two markets together. When the concerns are stated more broadly, the Chicago analysis loses much of its force. For example, our fear when Microsoft ties the platform market (Windows) to the Internet browser market (Internet Explorer) is *not* that Microsoft will be able to extract a double monopoly profit from bundling two products together, like *Carbice's* ice box and dry ice. Rather, the concern is that Microsoft can use its dominant position in the platform market to restrain innovation in the browser market and prevent the emergence of rival platforms. The plausibility of that theory, discussed in Chapter 12, survives the Chicago critique.

The Harvard School

The Harvard School began in a much different place than the Chicago School but also has diverged much more from its historical roots.[11] Traditionally Harvard School economics was heavily "structuralist," which meant that it was apt to view markets as noncompetitive whenever they deviated from what were thought to be basic competitive conditions. For example, as the number of firms in a market became fewer and more diverse, or as products became more differentiated or entry became more difficult, Harvard School economists tended to see significant opportunities for noncompetitive performance. To oversimplify, while the Chicago School emphasized the ways that firms would continue to compete notwithstanding imperfect structures, the Harvard School emphasized the ways that firms could avoid competing.[12]

Harvard School structuralism developed out of a strong commitment to Cournot oligopoly theory. A French economist of the mid-nineteenth century, Augustin Cournot's principal contribution to economics, which formed the basis of both neoclassical industrial organization theory as well as modern game theory, was the idea that each firm in a market maximizes its own profits by accepting the output of all other firms as given and computing its profit-maximizing price based on that assumption. The orthodox Cournot theory is mathematically elegant but it is also perfectly "structural" in the sense that its conclusions about market performance are a strict function of such factors as the number of firms in the market, their relative costs or size differentials, and the degree of product differentiation. For example, if all firms in a market are identical, the Cournot theory produces formulas that can predict the relationship between the oligopoly price and either the competitive or the monopoly price, or the relationship between the oligopoly output and competitive output. One who knows the extent to which the firms have different costs can draw conclusions about their market share, with lower-cost firms having larger shares. The distribution in firm size also says something about price. For any given number of firms price is minimized when all of the firms are of the same size, and becomes greater as the disparity in firm size increases. The mathematics of Cournot is a complex and seductive thing.[13]

The result of the Harvard School's strong commitment to Cournot theory was that it was much more concerned with structural manifestations of oligopoly, such as fewness of firms or product differentiation, and tended to see structure as problematic at lower concentration levels than the Chicago School did. Harvard School merger policy was historically more aggressive, condemning mergers on lower market shares and in less concentrated markets. The Harvard School was also much more concerned about entry barriers than the Chicago School, and generally presumed that new entry would not discipline anticompetitive practices in concentrated markets. For this reason the Harvard School was also more suspicious of various forms of vertical integration, whether by merger or long-term contract practices such as exclusive dealing, tying arrangements, or distribution restraints. These were all seen as increasing entry barriers and thus facilitating monopoly pricing.

Harvard School economists were among the most important contributors to the so-called Structure-Conduct-Performance (S-C-P) paradigm. The S-C-P paradigm was based on a fairly rigid theory of Cournot oligopoly behavior. Stripped to its essentials, the paradigm held that a given market structure dictated certain types of conduct, and that this in turn dictated performance. For example, in a market containing only three or four firms, oligopoly behaviors were simply natural, or inherent in the structure itself. These behaviors included excessive product differentiation and advertising, extravagant innovation along frivolous lines, reluctance to cut price, and artificial attempts to restrict new entry. The result was noncompetitive performance.

An important tenet of the S-C-P paradigm was the basic principle of logic that if S entails C and C entails P, then S entails P. As a result C can drop out. In the *S-C-P* theory, conduct analysis became relatively unimportant as an independent basis for understanding anticompetitive threats. A certain structure made certain types of conduct inevitable, so antitrust should be directed mainly toward anticompetitive industry structures. This led to an aggressive merger policy, which placed a premium on preventing markets from becoming too concentrated, and which simply assumed that most of the consequences that flowed from mergers in concentrated markets were anticompetitive. It also explains the Harvard School idea, discussed in Chapter 7, that the government should be empowered to break up durable monopolists even if they had not engaged in any unlawful conduct.

But the Harvard School underwent a significant transformation in the late 1970s. Indeed, the term "Harvard School" today is used mainly to refer to the writings of a collection of economists and antitrust scholars who wrote from the 1930s through the 1960s, not to the Harvard approach to antitrust that is characteristic of the last three decades.[14] An instrumental factor in the Harvard School's antitrust metamorphosis was the unacknowledged conversion experience of Donald F. Turner, whose writing in the influential *Antitrust Law* treatise in the late 1970s bears little resemblance to his earlier work. The first volumes of *Antitrust Law,* published in 1978–1980, departed significantly from Harvard orthodoxy although they did not fully embrace the Chicago position either. Those volumes reflect a greatly diluted concern with entry barriers, dismissed most of the claims that vertical integration was inherently anticompetitive, and proposed greatly relaxed merger standards. They also largely abandoned the view that anticompetitive conduct was a necessary consequence of structure, and aligned themselves with the Chicago School position requiring closer examination of conduct.[15]

This new Harvard position is the one most consistently advocated in this book, and it is the position most followed by the federal courts today. However, the latter point should be read in context. Most of the Chicago School writing was contained in economics journals and law review articles, as well as polemical works by Richard A. Posner, Robert H. Bork, and others.[16] By contrast, the new Harvard position is presented in a multivolume legal treatise aimed mainly at antitrust judges and lawyers, although it has a wide academic readership as well.[17] Legal treatises are generally much less polemic than academic writings, and they are also more likely to reflect rather than criticize the law.

In sum, while antitrust decision making has moved considerably to the right since 1980, it has not moved as far as the orthodox members of the Chicago School wished it to move. Rather, it has adopted middle-of-the-road positions more reflective of the current Harvard position than any other. That position finds markets to be far more robust than the old Harvard position did, although not as robust as the Chicago School proclaimed, at least in its heyday. Today the Harvard School is modestly more interventionist than the Chicago School, but the main differences lie in details.

"Post-Chicago" Antitrust

"Post-Chicago" antitrust grew out of economic theory that found Chicago models to be too simple to take real-world phenomena into account.[18] Like the Harvard School, post-Chicago theory believes that markets are messier and more complex than the Chicago School acknowledged. But post-Chicago is hardly a return to the structuralism of the Harvard School. Rather, post-Chicago theory typically models strategic behavior by use of game theory, with alternatives that reach far beyond the conventional Cournot oligopoly analysis.

The post-Chicago economic literature argues that certain market structures and types of collaborative activity are more likely to be anticompetitive than Chicago School antitrust writers imagined. For example, when the proportions of inputs can be varied, vertical integration can be socially harmful.[19] When information is not evenly balanced, anticompetitive strategic behavior is possible.[20] If a market has economies of scale and firms have specialized assets, then strategic pricing even at prices significantly above cost can be anticompetitive.[21] Post-Chicago scholars developed a fairly robust theory of "raising rivals' costs," under which dominant firms or cartels adopt strategies that impose higher costs on rivals, thus creating a price umbrella for the strategizing firms.[22] They argued that mergers in product-differentiated markets pose unique threats to competition that are not captured by traditional merger review.[23] Even firms that lack dominant positions can charge high prices if consumers are "locked in" to their aftermarket parts or service.[24] Finally, in network markets such as those for computer operating systems or telecommunications, dominant firms can obtain decisive advantages that enable them to exclude superior technologies from the market. This is explained by the high degree of "path dependence" in network markets: previous decisions tie users to a particular technology not because it is superior, but because compatibility is essential and so many others use the established technology as well.[25]

Just as Chicago School antitrust policy became oversold, post-Chicago antitrust has been oversold as well. The real value of post-Chicago economics is its renewed recognition that markets are more varied and complex than the orthodox Chicago School was willing to admit. Thus the number and variety of anticompetitive practices are unknown and open-ended, particularly in relatively new markets.

The biggest danger presented by post-Chicago antitrust economics is not that the variety and likelihood of anticompetitive practices are exaggerated, although that too has happened. Rather, the complexity of post-Chicago theories would force the federal courts to confront problems that they are not capable of solving. Antitrust is a defensible enterprise only if it can make markets more competitive—that is, if antitrust intervention produces lower prices, larger outputs, or improved product quality. Developing antitrust rules that reliably increase wealth is a daunting task that courts can perform with confidence only if they are applying theories that are within their grasp.

An Unhelpful Legislative History

One way to select among competing visions of antitrust policy is to consider what the framers had in mind. After all, policy makers in a democratic society have a duty to pay more than lip service to statutory design and intent. The antitrust laws do not suffer from a shortage of legislative history. Fully collected, the debates and congressional reports stretch across some eleven fat volumes.[26] But much of the legislative history is useless. It gives no support for any of the three described views of basic antitrust ideology. Indeed, the legislative history tends to favor a view that most people today find unacceptable.

The consumer welfare principle for antitrust is so well established that most people simply assume that it was Congress's principal design all along. In the 1960s Robert H. Bork attempted to ground a version of that principle in the legislative history of the antitrust laws,[27] as though the neoclassical economic values espoused by the Chicago School's antitrust policy were what the framers of the Sherman Act had in mind. Already in 1890, Bork argued, the members of Congress had adopted the goals of perfect competition, high output, and low prices, and protection for innovators and low-cost producers, just as neoclassical economists were first articulating these goals in print.[28] Bork collected all the sentences and phrases in the debates and reports that spoke of the evils of high prices, and that distinguished between oppressive and innovative monopolies. He believed that these all added up to a Chicago School vision of antitrust policy in which big business was not perceived as bad in and of itself, but only if it led to higher prices or reduced innovation.

To someone familiar with the Chicago School today, Bork's argument rings hollow. While Chicago School advocates may believe that economic efficiency should be the goal of legal policy generally, they also tend to distrust legislation and usually find that it favors special interests rather than the common good. Certainly, the 1890 Congress was not known for its insulation from interest group pressure. Indeed, the McKinley Tariff, which was passed in the same year, is one of the most regressive, protectionist pieces of federal legislation in American history, designed to insulate high-cost domestic producers from low-cost imports at consumers' expense.[29] Moreover, writings by the Chicago School and its sympathizers in the 1980s and after have generally concurred that the antitrust laws were passed as special interest legislation.[30]

Moderates and liberals also took issue with Bork's interpretation of the legislative history. Robert Lande argued that the principal value that Congress articulated was aversion to transfers of wealth from consumers to business firms.[31] The real bite of Lande's position occurs when a cartel or monopolist does something that both increases its efficiency *and* raises its prices. Bork argued that Congress favored net efficiency gains regardless of who captured them. As a result Congress approved even restraints that increased consumer prices, provided that the gains to the defendant were greater than the losses imposed on consumers and no one else was affected. In contrast, Lande read the legislative history as disapproving any restraint that transferred wealth from consumers to producers, whether or not overall gains exceeded losses. That position, incidentally, has been expressly incorporated into some policy statements by the government enforcement agencies. For example, the Justice Department and Federal Trade Commission Merger Guidelines permit an "efficiency defense" to mergers, but *only* if the cost reductions from increased efficiency are sufficient to offset any price increase that the merger might otherwise cause.

The legislative record as a whole is very difficult to harmonize with either the economic efficiency theory or the wealth transfer theory. Although writers heaped scorn upon Warren Court antitrust policy in the 1960s for its protection of small business, that policy was probably the most faithful to Congress's goals in passing the Sherman Act. To one degree or another, all of the antitrust laws passed from 1890 through 1950—virtually every substantive antitrust provision—were special interest legislation. Furthermore, the special interest that most members of Congress had in mind was small business. Consumers did not fare particularly well under any of these statutes.

While the rhetoric that accompanied the passage of the antitrust laws often spoke of high prices, the real villains in the legislative history were guilty of precisely the opposite. Most of our substantive federal antitrust laws were passed in four years: 1890 (the Sherman Act), 1914 (the Clayton and Federal Trade Commission Acts), 1936 (the Robinson-Patman Act), and 1950 (the Cellar-Kefauver Act, which significantly amended the antimerger provision).

The Sherman Act's legislative history makes the best case for any "efficiency" view, but even the Sherman Act has a highly dubious political history. In addition to the small business protectionism illustrated by the McKinley Tariff, the 1880s experienced steeply declining rather than increasing prices. Indeed, the aggregate decline was an unprecedented 7 percent in the consumer price index, as market output expanded dramatically.[32] Most of this was a consequence of the great technological revolution in production methods that followed the Civil War, but these methods required significantly larger firms because the technology required high rates of output. Firms that did not or could not adopt the new technology were squeezed to the point of bankruptcy, and they made their case to Congress. Most of the wrath of the Sherman Act's framers was directed at two large firms, the Standard Oil Company and the sugar trust. However, from 1880 through 1890 the price of refined petroleum fell by 61 percent and output increased fourfold. Refined sugar prices fell by more than 18 percent.[33] The iron and steel industry, another target of the Sherman Act's proponents, had witnessed price declines of about 20 percent, and railroad rates were also in rapid decline. Finally, the decade of the 1880s was one of rapid economic growth, with the real gross national product increasing by about 24 percent.[34]

This context makes it highly improbable that Congress would have picked 1890 to intervene in the economy with an antitrust statute designed to protect consumers from high prices. In fact, Senator John

Sherman of Ohio was the cat's paw of the well-organized Ohio petroleum producers, dominated by small firms that Standard Oil had driven out of business with a combination of lower costs and anticompetitive practices.[35] The vast majority of contemporary economists were opposed to the Sherman Act.[36] They believed that the emergent "trust," or large business firm, was efficient and would result in higher output and lower consumer prices, but that the antitrust law would interfere with their development.

So the Sherman Act was very likely passed at the behest of small businesses, injured by a technological revolution that left them on the sidelines. They were also well organized politically, and had long been effective in making their case to legislative bodies. Various labor organizations also lobbied Congress, but their principal concern seems to have been that new technology would steal jobs.[37] Although the Sherman Act included provisions for private lawsuits, nearly everyone who spoke on the issue believed that *consumer* lawsuits would be ineffectual. When the congressmen spoke of private lawsuits, they were thinking of competitor suits,[38] adding further support to the argument that the welfare of small business rather than consumers was foremost on the mind of the Sherman Act's framers.

As one moves from the Sherman Act to later antitrust legislation, the consumer interest story becomes even less supportable. The Clayton Act and the Federal Trade Commission Act of 1914 were passed by the small business-oriented Wilson administration at the height of the Progressive Era. The principal concern was protecting small firms from aggressive pricing, technology-induced mergers, and overly expansive uses of intellectual property rights. In addition, the Clayton Act gave us our first antitrust immunity for labor union organizing. The Robinson-Patman Act of 1936 was expressly pointed at the buying practices of large chain stores, which were making it very difficult for small family-owned retailers to compete. And the protected class in Congress's collective minds in 1950 when the merger statute was amended were small businesses injured by mergers that streamlined production and distribution, creating large vertically integrated firms that undersold their rivals.[39]

The Abiding Case for the Consumer Welfare Principle

What should one make of this discomfiting legislative history? The best answer is not very much. We certainly cannot find much support for the consumer welfare principle in the legislative history of the antitrust laws; but outside of Bork's argument in the 1960s, the success of that principle has never depended on a reading of the legislative history. The best justifications for ignoring the anticonsumer, pro-small business thrust of the legislative history are these: (a) the spare, malleable, and generally "economic" statutory language; (b) a century of case law; and (c) the need to make administration of the antitrust laws a rational enterprise.

Concerning the first of these, while the legislative history of the antitrust laws is dominated by a concern with small business welfare, the statutory language is not. The Sherman Act refers only to "restraints of trade" and "monopolization," without giving those terms any meaning. The Clayton Act requires a showing that the restraints it covers (predatory pricing, exclusive dealing, tying, and mergers) are unlawful only when they "substantially lessen competition," without giving that phrase any meaning. The 1950s amendments to the merger law do the same thing. Only the Robinson-Patman Act expressly articulates a goal of protecting one set of wholesale customers from the lower prices obtained by other wholesale customers. So whatever one makes of the legislative history, the statutory language is in fact much more benign and at least consistent with the consumer welfare principle. And particularly in the case of special interest legislation, the statutory language is what governs; the legislative history is not what is enacted into law.[40]

Of course, this argument is a little beguiling. Terms such as "monopolization" and "competition" have meant different things to different people. Today the term "competition" means, roughly, a state of affairs in which prices are driven to cost and constraints on business firm expansion and innovation are minimized. The legislative history makes clear that when Congress spoke of competition it had something different in mind, namely, a market with many little firms that should be enabled to survive against larger, more aggressive rivals.

But Congress picked economic words and chose not to tie its own idiosyncratic meanings to them. This is well illustrated by §1 of the Clayton Act, which contains the basic glossary of terms for the antitrust laws. The glossary defines what the "antitrust laws" include, as well as the meaning of "commerce" and "person" (so as to include corporations). To be sure, clarity of meaning for these terms is essential. But the glossary never defines such terms as "competition" or "monopoly" in a statute that repeatedly condemns practices whose effect "may be to substantially lessen competition or tend to create a monopoly."[41] The interpretation of these terms was left entirely up to the courts, with no guidance from the statutory language.

A second reason we should not feel bound by the legislative history of the antitrust laws is that the very spareness of the statutes has invited the courts to create a kind of "common law" of antitrust that has ranged far from anything explicit in the statutory language. The common law is nothing if not flexible, and it is uniquely able to evolve with changing ideological and economic views. Indeed, that is why the common law has remained a powerful institution in the United States notwithstanding the proliferation of statutes. Modern conceptions of economic efficiency have infiltrated the law of contracts and torts just as they have entered antitrust. At its best this common law quality enables judges to make decisions relatively free from the grosser influences of interest group politics, although one never wants to push this point too far. Even judges are the product of politics, and Congress can always respond to common law decisions it does not like by legislating differently. But this last statement is itself a powerful defense of the consumer welfare principle as it has developed in antitrust case law over the last quarter century: although Congress always has the power to overrule annoying judicial decisions, it has chosen not to do so.

The final consideration is the question of administrability. Whatever one thinks of neoclassical economics as a foundation for legal policy, it does provide a coherent vision of how the economic world should work. That point having been made, one must also allow that even the most elegant models leave many unanswered questions, and economics is certainly no exception. But if we read the spare language of the antitrust laws as a kind of small business welfare prescription, applying it would put us completely out to sea. Should we condemn every cost-reducing practice by a firm, simply because it injured smaller rivals who could not adopt the practice? Would we enjoin every efficiency-creating merger that made life harder for smaller firms, and let consumers be damned in the process? Would we preclude every assertion of a patent or copyright that prevented a rival from taking advantage of a valuable product or process? Taking such proscriptions literally would drive the American economy back to the Stone Age. We would not want to do that without the clearest possible directive from Congress.

Of course, we might come up with a softer set of prohibitions. For example, we might say that cost-reducing practices should be condemned only when they injure rivals "unnecessarily," or only when it can be shown that at least one small firm was driven out of business by the practice. Or we might want to condemn aggressive but nonpredatory pricing only when "most" of the rivals in the market cannot earn a reasonable profit while matching the defendant's price.

None of these rules has anything to be said in its defense. They certainly cannot be justified by the statutory language or even the legislative history. There is certainly no reason to think that any of them would be healthful for the economy generally. While small business protection may be a worthy goal, it is not one that the courts can readily administer in a common law fashion. As a general rule, the common law is an effective guarantor of the efficiency of markets for legal entitlements, but it is a very bad wealth redistribution device, and small business protection is ultimately a policy about how wealth should be distributed. That is best done through such things as congressionally created tax breaks or incentives directed at specific markets, and with detailed regulations describing who qualifies and who does not. A statute that simply condemns "contracts in restraint of trade" or those who "monopolize" provides absolutely no guidance for such protectionism.[42]

The Need for Simple (and Often Underdeterrent) Antitrust Rules

Antitrust seeks to apply rules of microeconomics to government policy concerning business competition. The rules that antitrust develops must be administrable, meaning that the court can implement them with reasonable accuracy. They must also be robust, which means that they improve market performance in the intended way.

Markets are complex and diverse institutions. The fields of microeconomics and industrial organization are dedicated to determining how markets work and the conditions under which noncompetitive behavior might occur. Even in their traditional, or neoclassical, versions these subdisciplines of economics are technical, and have become even more so with the incorporation of game theory.[43]

Economic theories are not only complex, but often they are insufficiently robust to be useful for antitrust purposes. We generally think of empirical testing as rigorous exclusion of alternative hypotheses, thus proving that a given explanation is correct.[44] However, a frequent complaint about post-Chicago economic theories in particular is that they are not testable in the conventional scientific sense. That is, often all that economists can do is produce data that are consistent with the theory, but cannot rule out alternative explanations.[45] As a result there are far too many instances when a particular kind of business conduct has more than one explanation, and no one can completely rule out alternatives. This is particularly true in areas such as merger policy, where we are asked to predict the competitive consequences of a merger that has not yet occurred; or strategic pricing, where an expert will be asked whether a particular price cut or discounting practice is anticompetitive. Often there are sensible explanations pointing in both directions.

These critiques can prove fatal to rational antitrust administration. Courts are far worse than economists in ruling out alternative explanations. Economists often select markets for study because data gathering in them is particularly easy or other characteristics of the market tend to simplify economic analysis. By contrast, the markets for antitrust litigation are selected by plaintiffs, who pay scant attention to their complexity or may even regard it as advantageous.

Furthermore, the court does not come close to having the analytic or fact-finding power that the econometrician has. The judge is typically a well-educated generalist trained mainly in law, as are counsel for both sides. If a trial is needed and the plaintiff is seeking damages, fact issues will be decided by a jury whose degree of education and sophistication in business or economics is no greater than that of the general population. Often the jury will sit through testimony by experts for the two sides, offering opposing explanations that seem about equally plausible. The most persuasive factors frequently are rhetorical—favoring the expert with the best communication style, the ability to speak with clarity and apparent sincerity, or the best set of graphs or other visual aids.

For her part, the judge will try to exclude improper testimony—more on that in Chapter 4—but the judge suffers from some of the same disadvantages as the jury. She is unlikely to know whether failure to exclude an outlying data point makes a statistical study unreliable, or whether one behavioral assumption is better than another for describing conduct in a particular market. The judge then compensates for her own ignorance by doing the worst possible thing: handing the decision off to the jury, which is even less qualified.

This picture of antitrust decision making in a federal court may be overly pessimistic, and not all cases are equally hard. Nevertheless, there is relatively little disagreement about the basic proposition that often our general judicial system is not competent to apply the economic theory necessary for identifying strategic behavior as anticompetitive. This makes the development of simple antitrust rules critical. Antitrust decision making cannot consider every complexity that the market presents.

In order to justify government intervention against a firm that has been successful in the market, a court must be able to do better than merely observe conduct that is consistent with an anticompetitive explanation and then let a jury decide the issue by a "preponderance" of the evidence. If antitrust policy goals are to be furthered, the anticompetitive explanation must be substantially more robust than alternative, more benign or procompetitive explanations. Failing this, antitrust policy will operate so as to chill procompetitive conduct.

This is implicit in the Supreme Court's *Matsushita* decision, which held that conduct that is no more than equally consistent with the existence of an anticompetitive agreement cannot be presented to a jury.[46] *Matsushita* has proven to be very powerful, for one factor limiting the court's ability to confront complex behavior is the jury system. But juries are hardly the only problem. As noted earlier, judges are not always well versed in economic concepts either, and too often seem unaware of the severe fact-finding limitations inherent in the institutions they oversee. They are tempted to believe that if a jury question can be formulated and the jury forced to answer it, then the answer is rational.

When a particular form of behavior is too complex for reliable analysis, then the only defensible antitrust rule is to let the market rather than the courts control. Of course, Congress can always intervene, and further development in our tools of analysis may permit more definite conclusions later. But a court is in hazardous territory when it assumes that it can make society wealthier by condemning a practice whose competitive effects are poorly understood. The basic rule should be nonintervention unless the court is confident that it has identified anticompetitive conduct and can apply an effective remedy.

Antitrust is not good at transferring wealth, and cannot be defended on that basis in any event. Nor does it have any moral content of its own, and is not well designed to provide rules of business ethics. To be sure, we may wish the jury's values about fairness to trump the harsher business judgments made by firms in competition. But the whole purpose of antitrust is to make markets work better, and "better" means more efficiently. Furthermore, antitrust as an enterprise is dedicated to the proposition that markets work tolerably well as a general matter, and enduring failures are the exception rather than the rule. So intervention must be justified. If the judge does not hear a fairly robust theory explaining why certain behavior is anticompetitive, and some relatively unambiguous facts supporting application of that theory, then intervention is not justified. As a result the rather tolerant Chicago School rule may be the best one for policy purposes even though substantial anticompetitive behavior goes undisciplined, simply because we cannot recognize and remedy it with sufficient confidence.

Thus one implication of antitrust's lack of moral content is a reduced role for the jury. Juries perform two useful functions in our legal system. The first is to determine whether a witness is speaking truthfully, although there is plenty of reason for believing that judges accomplish this better than juries. The second function of the jury is to define the community's moral boundaries. Juries decide whether the defendant acted improperly when "improperly" means the same thing as "unethically" or "immorally." But the morality of business behavior is not properly a subject of antitrust concern, although it may be in other areas of business law, such as some business torts and consumer protection. Antitrust law presumes that firms maximize profits and asks whether in doing so they acted anticompetitively. The term "anticompetitive" is defined by technical rules.

In the American federal court system this requires that a relatively high percentage of antitrust issues be decided "as a matter of law" by the judge. Although we ordinarily say that juries decide matters of fact while judges decide matters of law, the line between fact and law actually is indistinct, and the difference between them is a matter of policy rather than science. In part, this policy is driven by concerns over institutional limitations on our ability to manage certain types of facts.

The antitrust rules governing predatory pricing provide a good example. The relevant statutes condemn predatory pricing when it threatens to monopolize a market or lessen competition substantially, but the statutes themselves do not define a cost test or a set of market conditions when predation is likely to be anticompetitive. The economic literature on predatory pricing is wide-ranging, and many models have been developed showing how prices can, as a "matter of fact," be anticompetitive at prices significantly above cost.[47] Nevertheless, the courts have developed a number of gateway requirements that the plaintiff must satisfy before a jury is entitled even to consider whether a price is predatory. One requirement is that the price must be below a certain measure of cost. This requirement is not dictated by any economic rule that only below-cost prices can be anticompetitive. Rather, the judicial rule is driven by the recognition that once we permit a jury to find predation on above-cost prices we have no good way to filter the information so that the jury can distinguish aggressive, procompetitive pricing, which is the most basic goal of the antitrust laws, from anticompetitive predatory pricing.

Regarded in a scientific sense, the question whether an above-cost price can be anticompetitive is one of economic theory, or fact. One determines its truthfulness not by reading a statute, but by constructing an economic model and then attempting to test it. This is precisely the stuff of empirical science, so the statement "prices above cost can injure competition" is just as much a matter of fact as the statement "the atmosphere limits the acceleration of free-falling bodies." Either statement might be always true, always false, or true only part of the time. But the point is that both are statements about how the world works. In the case of predatory pricing, however, a *policy* judgment about limitations on the fact-finding powers of the jury permits us to slide the question of above-cost predatory prices from the "fact" column into the "law" column.

To the extent that it rests on grounds of administrability, antitrust's reluctance to advocate a general use of post-Chicago economics is a contingent rather than immutable truth. There is nothing inherently wrong with much of post-Chicago antitrust analysis. The problem is that in many cases the analysis has not yet been transformed into rules that a court can apply with confidence that it is making markets work better.

In other cases, however, post-Chicago writers have been sensitive to questions of administrability, and our techniques of empirical analysis have improved greatly in the last generation. Here refined economic analysis has enabled us to identify anticompetitive outcomes with more predictive power than older methodologies allowed. In such cases, fashioning of new antitrust rules is not merely appropriate but essential. Several such theories will be discussed in later chapters.

Some Principles of Antitrust Administration

While this entire book is dedicated to exploring the limitations of antitrust and developing simple rules for administering it, a few basic principles can be stated here:

1. NOT EVERY ANTICOMPETITIVE PRACTICE CAN BE CONDEMNED

We must simply live with the fact that antitrust is too blunt an instrument to detect and remedy every anticompetitive act. Some practices will effectively be immune because our institutions are not up to the task of identifying them without producing an unacceptable number of false positives. The previously mentioned law of predatory pricing provides a strong example. As an opening proposition, predatory pricing is not only extremely hard to identify, but it is also relatively uncommon. An overly deterrent predatory pricing rule tends to discourage aggressive pricing by everyone, making consumers pay a large price. By contrast, an underdeterrent rule may permit a few instances of predation to slip by, but the social cost of such "false negatives" is very likely much less than the social cost of false positives. The antitrust case law is filled with examples of practices that may very well have been anticompetitive, but one can never be sure enough to risk the public cost of condemnation that might deter socially beneficial conduct.

2. INTENT EVIDENCE SHOULD BE USED SPARINGLY

Oliver Wendell Holmes, Jr., gave us the "external standard" for legal analysis, mainly of the common law. Holmes argued that society is not concerned about what is in peoples' hearts, which it cannot see or control, but rather with their conduct. He argued that while the common law had always spoken of bad conduct in terms of "intent," in fact it never condemned anything but the conduct itself.[48] In that case, wouldn't it be much better if we simply dropped this useless minor premise from the syllogism? The external standard seeks to define conduct "objectively," by reference to what a reasonable person would do in certain circumstances.

While Holmes was interested in common law rules for such things as torts, his argument applies even more strongly to antitrust for three reasons: *first*, the relevant actors in antitrust law are usually business firms. *Second*, antitrust is not concerned with the morality of conduct but rather with its competitive effect. *Third,* anticompetitive intent is very difficult to identify.

While biological persons are utility maximizers, business firms generally exist to make profits. This difference is crucial because measuring the utility curve of a person other than oneself is extraordinarily difficult. I might know that you like chocolate ice cream more than broccoli, but there is no way I can quantify how much more, or compare the strength of your preferences with the strength of mine or of any third person.

Profits are a different matter: they can be ranked cardinally as well as ordinally. For the business firm $2 is worth precisely twice as much as $1, and so on. As a result we can usually rely on objective evidence to predict a business firm's "preferences." It is more likely to enter markets that appear to be profitable. It will not cut price unless it predicts sufficiently increased sales. Indeed, the criteria for determining profit-maximization are sufficiently objective that inside and outside analysts often agree on the firm's proper course of action. This ability to analyze the "intent" of the business firm externally gives us a valuable although incomplete ability to describe a firm's conduct as competitive or anticompetitive under a given set of circumstances. For example, while a firm might cut its price to increase sales, it would not ordinarily cut its price below marginal cost, for then it would lose money in the short run—the more it sold the more it would lose. In that case there must be an alternative explanation for the price cut.

Another reason intent is relatively unimportant to antitrust analysis is that antitrust is not part of the tort or criminal law system that was the principal focus of Holmes's concern. Antitrust is not concerned with ethical or community standards of conduct, but only with whether the conduct is anticompetitive—that is, whether it tends toward reduced innovation or reduced output and higher prices in some market. These are fundamentally objective rather than subjective inquiries.

The third and most practical factor making intent evidence relatively unimportant in antitrust cases is that competitive and anticompetitive intent are so difficult to tell apart. Holmes himself recognized the problem in 1894, in a famous article entitled "Privilege, Malice and Intent,"[49] in which he observed that society generally abhors intentional harms directed at neighbors but creates a privilege, or legal exemption, for certain harms. One of these is the harm caused by competition. If I open a chocolate shop across the street from your chocolate shop, I probably know that your business will suffer. I may even "intend" that your business suffer or perhaps fail. But society places such a high value on competition that it does not care how evil my motive might be. In any situation where demand is limited, one seller increases its sales only at the expense of another seller. The state of mind that accompanies this act is irrelevant for antitrust purposes.

In competitively structured markets the intent to do harm to a rival is likely not even present. For example, if Farmer Brown plants ten additional acres of corn, his neighbor Farmer Green is unlikely to care. They both sell corn in a world market that takes no notice of Brown's increased production. But if General Motors begins to build a large new facility for making pickup trucks, rivals such as Ford, Chrysler, and Toyota are certain to care. Would GM do this "intending" to destroy Chrysler? Perhaps. But the more likely explanation is that GM sees a sales opportunity. To be sure, the sales opportunity may exist because Chrysler's model in that area is inferior, and the new plant will injure Chrysler severely. But that fact will never give rise to an antitrust claim unless we want to make seizure of business opportunities an antitrust offense.

The principle states that intent evidence should be used "sparingly," not that it should be ignored altogether. In a few cases intent evidence may help us characterize ambiguous conduct. In others, there may be unambiguous evidence of anticompetitive purpose. But intent evidence should never be a *substitute* for evidence of market structure or conduct making an anticompetitive outcome plausible.

3. WHETHER INTERVENTION IS JUSTIFIED MAY DEPEND ON THE REMEDY

Antitrust remedies are diverse, ranging from imprisonment, forced breakup, or treble damages at one extreme, to a simple injunction against repetition of unlawful conduct at the other. One has to be pretty sure that conduct is anticompetitive, with little or no redeeming value, before sending a CEO to prison, breaking a firm into small pieces, or assessing a damage award of $1,000,000,000 after trebling.

While courts must find anticompetitive conduct before any remedy is justified, confidence levels in antitrust cases are often unusually low. On balance a practice appears anticompetitive, but we cannot be sure. Often defendants will not be able to present a convincing justification for an apparently anticompetitive practice. In that case we are left with less than certain knowledge of anticompetitive effects, but a relatively strong belief that the practice is not beneficial either. An injunction against repetition is fairly easy to justify. Even if our finding of liability was a false positive, little is lost by prohibiting socially useless behavior. The case for a more aggressive remedy is weaker, however, depending on the strength of our conclusion about anticompetitive effects and our ability to measure them.

4. AN ANTITRUST RULE THAT CANNOT BE ADMINISTERED EFFECTIVELY IS WORSE THAN NO RULE AT ALL

Derek Bok, who was an antitrust scholar before he became president of Harvard University, once lamented that merger enforcement was so complex that "consideration of all relevant factors may actually detract from the accuracy" of the court's decision.[50] Although Bok stated his conclusion as a complaint, what he was observing is actually an important key to the neoclassical approach to empirical economics: stripped-down models that isolate essential variables often have greater predictive power than more complex explanations that attempt to take every quirk into account. This is particularly true when the complex model is more difficult to administer, leading to a greater likelihood of error. Indeed, if an antitrust rule is so complex that it cannot reliably produce correct results, then we are better off with no antitrust rule at all, which is the same thing as nonliability.

Complexity in antitrust analysis sometimes appears to confer predictive power, but this appearance is often false. Consider the Herfindahl-Hirschman Index (HHI), used by antitrust enforcers to measure industrial concentration, which provides a way of estimating a market's proclivity to noncompetitive behavior. The HHI equals the sum of the squares of the market shares of each firm in a market. A monopoly, which is a single firm whose market share is 100 percent, has an HHI of 100^2, or 10,000. A market of two equal firms has an HHI of $50^2 + 50^2$, or 5,000. A market of ten equal firms has an HHI of $10^2 \times 10$, or 1,000. The HHI requires a fair amount of information. One needs to know a market's boundaries accurately, as well as the market shares of every firm in the market. But having those numbers can enable a court to produce very precise-sounding descriptions of a merger's effect.

As Chapter 9 shows, however, the HHI incorporates difficult-to-verify assumptions about where market boundaries are located, particularly if products are differentiated. Furthermore, firm behavior often changes from one period to the next. Once we relax our assumptions about how firms behave, the HHI loses much of its predictive power. As a result a great deal of our effort in collecting the data to compute the HHI may be wasted. We would probably be better off with a much simpler rule—for example, that any time a well-defined market has as few as five or six significant firms a merger of two of them is likely to increase the risk of collusion. From that point we would want to make some adjustments to take easy entry or other factors into account. But the basic analysis need not be much more complicated than that.

5. ADMINISTRATIVE AND COMPLIANCE COSTS COUNT

As noted previously, antitrust is not concerned with the morality of conduct but only with whether it is competitive—that is, whether it makes the economic pie larger or smaller. Implicit in this concern with overall wealth is that the costs of running the enforcement and legal system are always important. In legal areas with a high moral content we may choose to spend dollars on enforcement that cannot be justified on the basis of economic value alone. For example, enforcing the laws against race or gender discrimination may be costly and may not increase the aggregate value of the economy by all that much. We enforce these laws because we believe that a world free from invidious race or sex discrimination is better than one that is not, in spite of possible costs.

But if antitrust is concerned only with the value of the economy, then administrative costs must be counted much more strictly. If enforcing the law against X increases economic value by $1,000, considering all short- and long-run effects, but enforcement costs are $1,500, then the economic world would be a better place if we did not enforce the law against X at all. We should tolerate anticompetitive practices any time the costs of identifying such practices with acceptable accuracy and implementing effective deterrents are greater than the cost of the practice itself. This principle also applies to compliance costs. Firms need rules that they can understand and apply with tolerable accuracy. Another cost of ambiguous or overly complicated antitrust rules is the money that firms invest in tailoring their operations—often inefficiently—in order to avoid crossing an ambiguous or complex legal rule.

The principal problem with these observations is not the theory, but the application. Enforcement costs vary widely among relatively similar antitrust actions, and the social gain to be had from any particular enforcement action is difficult or impossible to measure. We do not have even a crude calculus for linking enforcement costs to the gains from antitrust enforcement. To be sure, we can say a few things about the extreme positions. Enforcement of the law against naked price-fixing is relatively cheap and probably produces significant economic gains. At the other extreme, many instances of enforcement of the laws against monopolization, price discrimination, and vertical restraints are relatively costly and produce no social gains whatsoever because the underlying theories were misguided to begin with. These enforcement efforts should be abandoned. In the middle, things are much more ambiguous. So about the best we can do is develop a crude ordering of higher- and lower-priority antitrust enforcement efforts, ranging down to efforts that should be abandoned altogether. Further, we must search continuously for cost-justified ways of simplifying antitrust enforcement.

Some enforcement cost reductions are justifiable even if they reduce accuracy. Because our only interest is in the overall size of the pie, an enforcement cost reduction is socially worthwhile whenever the savings in administrative costs exceed the increased costs of errors that streamlined enforcement produces. For example, suppose that applying an administratively simple per se rule to price-fixing saves $1,000,000 in enforcement costs. However, the simplified rule is overdeterrent and condemns a few arrangements that are in fact socially valuable. Perhaps the lost social value is $300,000. In that case this simplified rule is cost-justified even though it is less "correct" as an abstract matter than a more complex rule would be. This is basically the justification for antitrust's per se rule, discussed in Chapters 5 and 6.

It may seem unfair to condemn socially beneficial arrangements simply in order to save administrative costs. That argument would have force if defendants did not have fair warning. But the law is clear that naked price-fixing agreements are per se unlawful, whether or not a particular instance is cost-justified. As a result firms are warned away from the conduct. Incidentally, the law does this all the time in other areas. For example, one could imagine a costly system of intellectual, motor, and psychological testing that would determine when teenagers are ready to drive, because in fact some fourteen-year-olds are more ready than some seventeen-year-olds. But the costs of more accurate metering of driving preparedness would very likely exceed the gains. Consequently, the system prevailing in most states declares that driving by children under the age of sixteen is unlawful "per se." Precocious teenagers pay the price of having to wait.

Streamlined procedures need not be perfect. They must merely be cost-justified, which means that the savings in administrative costs exceed any costs of incorrect outcomes. One might imagine a kind of sliding scale in which antitrust meters the cost of administration to the point that it just equals expected returns. Under such a scale an additional dollar's worth of inquiry would be proper if the incremental accuracy of the final decision leads to anticipated gains of a dollar or more. But since our calculus for determining the optimal amount of administration is very crude, we can do no better than rely on our experience to tell us whether certain inquiries are likely to be worthwhile. For example, determining whether the defendant or defendants have significant market power is often costly; nevertheless, it may be essential in cases where the challenged practice is likely to be efficient, or cost-reducing. It is probably not essential if experience shows that a particular practice is almost certain to have no redeeming social value. The sum total of these decisions accounts for the differences between the relatively elaborate antitrust inquiry that goes under the name "rule of reason," and also the variety of shortcuts that make up the "per se rule." This device, just as many others in antitrust, is a concession to the brevity of life and the costliness of fact finding.

3

The Promises and Hazards of Private Antitrust Enforcement

Ever since the seventeenth century the laws against monopolies have permitted private persons or firms to sue and, if they win, to obtain treble damages. The damages provision of the antitrust laws is contained in §4 of the Clayton Act:

> . . . any person who shall be injured in his business or property by reason of anything forbidden in the antitrust laws may sue therefor . . . and shall recover threefold the damages by him sustained, and the cost of suit, including a reasonable attorney's fee.[1]

The statutory right to bring a damages action against an antitrust violator is well established, although many applications are controversial. One common complaint is that lawsuits by competitors of the defendant are unjustified because competitors have the wrong incentives. They are injured not only by anticompetitive actions, but also by their rivals' lower costs or superior products or distribution.[2] Universal and automatic trebling of antitrust damages is also troublesome. Trebling is often excessive in principle, and encourages too many marginal or frivolous lawsuits. Additional problems arise when considering how clearly causation must be proven, whether embryonic firms that have never earned a profit may obtain damages for lost future profits, and whether private parties should have the right to obtain "divestiture," which is mandatory restructuring of a firm.[3]

An orderly system of private antitrust administration is essential because so much of our antitrust enforcement is private. To be sure, two federal agencies are charged with public enforcement of the antitrust laws. The Antitrust Division of the Department of Justice brings both criminal and civil cases in federal courts in all parts of the country. In addition, the Federal Trade Commission, or FTC, has authority to enforce the noncriminal provisions of the antitrust laws through administrative actions. The state attorneys general also bring federal antitrust actions, but when they do so they are considered to be private parties for most purposes. In any event, the number of lawsuits filed by these agencies collectively is dwarfed by the number of private cases. Over the years private complaints have accounted for roughly 95 percent of antitrust lawsuits.[4]

Most of the recommendations made in this chapter are significant deviations from existing law, and a few would require new legislation. Briefly,

- The current system of private treble damage and equity (injunction) suits is not easily defended, but abandoning it would require a major revision in the way we think about antitrust enforcement.
- In most cases the measure of damages should be actual, rather than treble. Treble damages should generally be reserved for cases involving naked price-fixing or other practices that are effective only so long as they are kept secret. The current system of damage incentives produces excessive litigation involving alleged exclusionary practices while cartel deterrence remains inadequate.
- Antitrust policy should abandon the indirect purchaser rule, which prohibits purchasers from recovering damages for overcharge injuries unless they have purchased directly from the defendant.
- As long as our existing system of private and public enforcement is preserved, competitor lawsuits should also be preserved, but with strict attention to requirements of competitive injury.
- Private parties should be able to obtain an injunction against unlawful practices, but they should not be permitted to obtain structural relief such as divestiture, or the breakup of firms.

The Delicate Case for Private Enforcement

Private plaintiffs do not sue under the antitrust laws in order to improve the general welfare. They sue in order to further their own interests. Of course, this fact does not distinguish antitrust from private enforcement in any other legal area. Private plaintiffs do not bring breach of contract suits in order to make the market system work better, or medical malpractice suits in order to make health care providers more responsive. For the most part, private plaintiffs sue in order to redress private grievances. Most plaintiffs are seeking compensation for themselves. To be sure, lawyers often describe their clients' cases in terms of the public interest. But in most cases not involving express public interests suits, the actual motives are private.

Is antitrust distinctive on this point? There are two reasons for thinking that private antitrust suits diverge from the public interest more frequently than private contract or other common law suits. One reason is purely statutory and Congress could remedy it if it wished—namely, the provision of automatic treble damages and attorneys' fees exaggerates private incentives to sue. As a result many marginal and even frivolous antitrust cases are filed every year, and antitrust litigation is often used as a bargaining chip to strengthen the hands of plaintiffs who really have other complaints.

The second problem is inherent in the antitrust enterprise itself: economic injuries have a way of rippling through markets, creating large numbers of victims. The victims are not only consumers, but also rivals, suppliers, and firms operating in complementary markets. Consequently, an antitrust violation can create many more victims than a typical contract breach or a traditional tort (although a few torts produce thousands of victims). This creates a broader range of potential plaintiffs, and accounts for many judicially developed rules that deny recovery to those who are too "remote" from the violation.

If we were writing on a clean slate we might wish to create a system of purely public antitrust enforcement in which the role of private parties is limited to the filing of complaints with government agencies, who then investigate and decide whether to sue and what kind of relief to request. In most foreign nations the role of direct private plaintiff enforcement is much less significant than it is in the United States, and in some there is no private enforcement at all.[5] But there is little reason for thinking that such arrangements work better than our current legal system, which creates a market for legal entitlements and, speaking idealistically, the correct set of private incentives to sue.

Dropping private lawsuits would come at a significant price. If we wanted to keep antitrust enforcement at current levels we would need much larger enforcement agencies than we currently have. This would require bigger budgets, and this in turn would require either massive appropriations or else permitting the relevant government agencies to finance their operations by fines or surrogate damage recoveries from defendants.

Public enforcement actions are not only fewer than private actions; their substance differs as well. The government enforcement agencies, particularly the Antitrust Division, tend to place most of their enforcement resources into prosecuting a relatively small range of violations. Today most public enforcement efforts go into evaluation and prosecution of horizontal mergers and various forms of horizontal collusion. The Justice Department does not enforce the price discrimination provisions of the Robinson-Patman Act at all, and the FTC does so only rarely. Neither government agency challenges very many vertical practices and, notwithstanding the highly publicized *Microsoft* case, monopolization challenges are infrequent.

In general, the government agencies enforce the antitrust "core"— or the central set of practices related most closely to horizontal price-fixing, where there is a strong consensus finding competitive danger. This means mainly the law governing collusion and mergers of competitors.

Significantly, this governmental conservatism in antitrust enforcement choices is a contingent rather than absolute truth. The government has not always stuck to the core. Indeed, most of the extreme and even harebrained theories that private plaintiffs rely on today were first developed during the 1970s and earlier in cases brought by one of the government agencies. These include the theory that horizontal mergers should be condemned because they reduce costs, thus giving the merging firms an unfair advantage over smaller rivals; the variety of silly theories under which vertical integration and vertical mergers were considered harmful; the long history of enforcing the per se rule against resale price maintenance; challenges to competitively harmless joint ventures; and some of the most anticompetitive holdings under the Robinson-Patman Act.[6]

Historically, public enforcement of the antitrust laws has expanded and contracted like an accordion, and since 1980 we have experienced a general period of contraction, heavily encouraged by a string of Republican presidencies and the presidency of one Democrat, Bill Clinton, who was relatively conservative on antitrust matters. A possible explanation for the dramatic rise of private antitrust suits since the 1970s is that the government largely abandoned older, more aggressive, theories. Private plaintiffs then stepped in to assert them. Further, the doctrine of *stare decisis* often forces lower courts to look backward rather than forward. So today private plaintiffs continue to reap the benefits of expansionist antitrust doctrines that were developed in government cases in the 1970s and earlier. Every year those benefits shrink a little, but they do remain. In any event, a decade or two from now the landscape could be entirely different, and we could see the government agencies once again leading the way with expansionist antitrust theories.

Another reason to limit the role of private antitrust enforcement is the prevalence of jury trials in private damage actions. Juries are never used in FTC actions, and generally not in civil actions brought by the Antitrust Division. (Criminal actions are an exception, because every felony defendant is entitled to a jury.) Jury trials are a truly unfortunate way to decide most of the contested issues in complex antitrust cases. In any civil case judges decide questions of law and juries decide issues of fact. The concept of a legal "fact" makes sense when we are speaking of conflicting observations about an event, or about witnesses who might be lying. But by and large the facts that a jury decides in a civil antitrust case have to do with two things: subjective intent and expert testimony.

For most antitrust violations the defendants' subjective intent is, or should be, irrelevant. Unfortunately, the courts have not entirely gotten that message. Even when intent evidence is formally irrelevant lawyers try to contaminate jurors' minds with evidence about evil intent. Jurors are often unskilled in business and have a difficult time distinguishing aggressive competitive intent from anticompetitive intent. In the minds of many jurors "intending" to knock out a rival sounds evil. The fact is that such intentions are the subject of hundreds of business seminars every day. In markets of every type sales personnel are urged to "destroy" or "kill" the competition or to sink new rivals before they have a chance. But this is nothing more than the rhetoric of competition, which antitrust seeks to preserve but jurors often misinterpret.

Making juries choose among contending experts is also a problem-plagued exercise, as the next chapter develops. Experts often dispute highly technical issues, such as whether two variables are so closely correlated with each other that one should be excluded from a regression analysis, or whether a methodology for defining a market is defective because it fails to include a certain group of consumer substitutions, or whether the commingling of two sets of computer code is the only efficient way to achieve a certain result.

To be sure, within both science and law these questions are ones of "fact." But they are not the types of facts that juries are competent to address, and often cross-examination of experts does not solve the problem. Historically, common law juries decided issues of both law and fact. The law-fact distinction in jury trials emerged in the late eighteenth and nineteenth centuries as a device for precluding juries from deciding technical issues that were believed to be beyond their competence.[7] But expert testimony presents the same problem, perhaps even magnifies it. A jury in an antitrust trial might listen to two different experts debate whether a certain data point in a regression analysis is an "outlier," or anomaly, that must be excluded. In any reasonably close case, asking a jury to decide this question makes even less sense than asking a jury to apply the technical legal rules of statutory interpretation. Indeed, often the question is given to the jury because the judge did not know how to answer it and therefore declined to rule at an earlier stage of the litigation.

When a jury does not understand what is going on it typically bases its decision on such things as rhetorical skills, personalities, or the expert's rate of pay. The evidence also suggests that laypersons can be taught over long experience to become better at understanding and perceiving defects in expert testimony—but for most jurors this is a once-in-a-lifetime situation. Only the judge is likely to see a variety of experts over several years. This gives the judge a significant comparative advantage in the evaluation of expert testimony.

The Supreme Court has developed legal doctrines that serve to transfer more decision-making authority from the jury to the judge. One of these is the *Daubert* decision discussed in the next chapter, which permits a judge to exclude expert testimony that is unlikely to be helpful to the jury in reaching a good decision. Another is an aggressive rule of "summary judgment," developed by the Supreme Court in its 1986 *Matsushita* decision, which essentially permits a judge to review the record to determine whether there are sufficient disputed facts to warrant sending the case to a jury. One consequence of *Matsushita* has been an increase in the number of cases that are resolved without a trial. For example, cases where market or economic evidence is very weak but there are statements of intent that can mislead a jury should be resolved by a judge. Judges typically have a better understanding of how the business world works and what kinds of rhetoric it uses. They are less likely to be deceived by "field of battle" statements about rivals.[8]

Do these jury-limiting rules do enough to assure us that juries are deciding antitrust cases correctly? Certainly not, although they do help. But juries remain a very weak link in a system where most of the relevant evidence is economic and technical. Today the United States is virtually the only jurisdiction where competition policy issues are decided by lay juries in this fashion.

Finally, although private plaintiffs are clearly entitled to an injunction against repetition of antitrust violations, they should ordinarily not be permitted to have "structural" relief, or judicially mandated breakup or divestiture of a firm. In 1990 the Supreme Court held to the contrary, permitting the state of California acting as a private plaintiff to seek breakup of a recently merged grocery chain even though the FTC had already approved the merger.[9] The Supreme Court noted that a state may have a special interest in protecting retail competition within its borders, and thus it might look more favorably on a divestiture request from a state attorney general than one from a private party. Nevertheless, it affirmed the general proposition that private plaintiffs as well as public agencies are entitled to seek divestiture or dissolution as an antitrust remedy.

The problem with granting such remedies to private plaintiffs is that they have too many spillovers. Divestiture decrees necessarily affect the structure of a market and, assuming the court is correct about the market definition, finding a violation indicates that the defendant is a significant player in that market. This effectively gives private plaintiffs the power to make industrial policy in a way that should be reserved to the government itself. This argument is strengthened by the fact that the judicial record in administering divestiture or dissolution is not very favorable.[10] Many, perhaps most, judicially mandated restructurings have been harmful to the economy. This is a power that should be exercised rarely, and only by a government agency whose interests reach beyond the purely private interests of a single antitrust plaintiff.

Tailoring the Offense to the Remedy

Antitrust tribunals often act under uncertainty, particularly in complex cases involving exclusionary practices, mergers, or joint ventures. Courts often condemn actions without absolute assurance that they are anticompetitive, or refuse to condemn actions without assurance that they are competitively harmless.

One way to counteract the effects of uncertainty is to define the offense narrowly or broadly depending on the remedy the plaintiff is seeking. The full range of antitrust remedies is very broad. Going roughly from most to least severe, they include: (1) criminal punishment for guilty managers; (2) divestiture or other "structural" breakup; (3) broad mandatory orders such as compulsory dealing; (4) treble damages; (5) fines; (6) narrowly tailored injunctions in the form of "cease and desist" orders. The ranking is very crude. Where fines or treble damages will fall depends entirely on how large they are, but historically treble damage awards provide larger penalties than fines. The effects of a compulsory dealing order can be significant or minor depending on the scope and terms of the duty to deal. In general, criminal punishment and structural breakups are considered to be harsh penalties imposing significant costs on the firm, while simple cease and desist orders require no more than that a party stop engaging in unlawful conduct. However, even a cease and desist order can be extremely costly. One example is when a defendant who has misused a patent is forbidden from enforcing it in the future or from charging royalties.

The antitrust statutes provide almost no basis for differentiating an antitrust offense according to the remedy that is being sought. The private treble damages provision permits recovery for "anything forbidden in the antitrust laws." The statute is mandatory: once a violation and the amount of damages are proven, trebling is automatic. As for injunctions, when the government sues it is entitled to a court order that will "prevent and restrain" antitrust violations—a concept that clearly includes divestiture. Private parties are entitled to obtain an injunction "against threatened loss or damage by a violation of the antitrust laws."[11] None of these provisions suggests anything like a sliding scale. Of course, some gradation is built in by proof requirements. Antitrust violations producing a small injury will produce a relatively small amount of provable damages. But nothing in the statutory structure suggests that treble damages are permissible only for blatant violations such as naked price-fixing, but not for much more questionable violations such as conglomerate mergers or resale price maintenance. Indeed, the statutes do not explicitly distinguish criminal from civil violations, although today the Antitrust Division limits criminal prosecutions to naked price-fixing and market division agreements.[12]

Varying the offense according to the remedy sought makes the most sense when the conduct appears to have little social value but competitive harm is difficult and costly to prove. Consider tacit collusion as an antitrust violation. Rivals can often "fix" prices tacitly, or without explicit communications of the kind that judges are willing to characterize as a "contract," "combination," or "conspiracy" in restraint of trade. This issue is considered in Chapter 6. One of the reasons that judges have been fairly strict in their requirement of an explicit agreement is that express price-fixing can be a criminal offense, and criminal offenses must be defined with clarity. Treble damages awards are also highly punitive, often running into the hundreds of millions of dollars.

The behavior generally described as "tacit" collusion includes such things as pricing or output signals sent by one firm to be observed by others, or direct verification of prices. Often this conduct has little value other than as an aid to price-fixing. At the same time, however, it may fail to meet the orthodox Sherman Act requirement of an "agreement" among the communicating firms. There are good economic justifications for relaxing proof of agreement requirements in such cases. However, as the behavior moves further and further from anything that can be characterized as an agreement, criminal prosecution is less appropriate, and injury and damages are more difficult to establish. The excessive strictness of court decisions in this area largely results from concerns for condemning ambiguous conduct when fairly draconian remedies are on the horizon.

However, the courts could be much more willing to condemn the conduct if the available remedy were restricted to an injunction or cease and desist order forbidding repetition of certain behaviors. This argument has considerable force when we consider the Federal Trade Commission. The FTC is an administrative body that employs its own experts, and is not burdened by the jury trial requirements or strict procedural rules of courts. Furthermore, the FTC enforces §5 of the Federal Trade Commission Act, which condemns "unfair methods of competition," a term that is said to include everything in the Sherman Act, plus an undefined list of practices that might not be reachable under that act.[13] In particular, §5 does not explicitly include the Sherman Act's "contract," "combination," or "conspiracy" requirements. Finally, the most typical remedy for a §5 violation is a simple cease and desist order, which is an injunction against repetition of the cited practice. This makes the FTC an ideal vehicle for considering cases where the coverage of the antitrust laws must be defined broadly, such as tacit collusion, and leaving to the Justice Department and private plaintiffs those cases where violation and proof of injury can be proven in more orthodox terms.

When the effects of business practices are ambiguous and judicial fact finding imperfect, harsh penalties can deter procompetitive conduct. For example, firms might attempt an efficient but possibly unlawful venture when reasonable minds could differ about legality and antitrust remedies were limited to an injunction dissolving the venture or changing one of its terms. The calculus is quite different, however, when the possibility of private enforcement and treble damages is thrown into the mix. The widespread availability of treble damages deters at least some efficient economic activity.

Tailoring the Remedy to the Offense—Treble Damages

As noted above, §4 of the Clayton Act provides treble (triple) damages for all antitrust violations. The statute requires that there be a violation, that the plaintiff show causation and an appropriate injury, and that the damages be provable with sufficient clarity.

A damages multiplier might make sense when the offense in question is something like naked price-fixing, which firms do in secret, often taking elaborate steps to ensure that they are not caught. In such cases the buyers' overcharge is equal to the cartel member's additional profits, so a single damage penalty equal to the overcharge offers inadequate deterrence.[14] It would be roughly equivalent to a criminal penalty for theft that requires the convicted criminal to give back the stolen property. If the thief believed there was a 100 percent chance of detection, he would break even on the goods but lose money on the costs of engaging in theft. However, if the detection rate is less than 100 percent, he would come out ahead. For that reason the optimal fine must be larger than the offense's value to the offender. The antitrust damages multiplier serves to offset the fact that not every antitrust violation is detected.

Whether multiplying by three is the right number is anyone's guess. Assuming conduct that clearly violates the antitrust laws, such as naked price-fixing, the impact of trebling is to deter cartels when the chances of getting caught are greater than one in three, and to encourage them when the chances of getting caught are less than one in three, for such cartels are profitable even under a treble damages rule. Assuming unquestionably unlawful activity with no redeeming social value, a higher damages multiplier would actually be better, for it would deter more harmful antitrust violations.

Treble damages make no sense at all when they are assessed for public acts and reasonable minds can differ about substantive illegality. One problem that plagues antitrust enforcement is that so many of the offenses are either poorly defined or are defined purely by reference to a specific set of facts. In monopolization cases in particular, while most opinions might make sense upon first reading, they often provide little guidance for determining how the next case should come out. We have nothing resembling the police officer's radar gun for detecting anticompetitive exclusionary practices. Joint ventures and mergers are less problematic, but even here illegality depends on such matters as market definition, efficiencies, and anticompetitive effects that honest experts can dispute.

Given that many challenged exclusionary practices, mergers, and joint ventures are actually efficient, the availability of treble damages serves to deter firms from pursuing efficient arrangements in moderately close cases. Indeed, a private plaintiff can obtain treble damages for a merger even after a government agency has reviewed the merger and found it lawful. Of course, the government can make mistakes, but so can private plaintiffs and subsequent court decisions.[15] Because events such as mergers and most joint ventures are public, no damages increment is necessary to offset a low probability of detection. And even the traditional conception of treble damages, which is punitive, would not award them to something that is not done maliciously but rather in pursuit of cost savings, although well-intended experts might differ about the net outcome. In such cases the best remedy if illegality is found is a simple injunction or order undoing the merger or joint venture.

To summarize, treble damages (or some other multiplier) make sense when an antitrust violation is clear and its success depends on its secrecy. Damages for public acts, or acts that are known to victims immediately when they occur, should be single. This would be the case for mergers, most joint ventures, many exclusionary practices, and nearly all vertical contract practices. For example, consider tying arrangements and exclusive dealing. While agreements such as franchise contracts that contain tying or exclusive dealing requirements are typically not public, the plaintiff is usually the purchaser under the contract. That purchaser knows immediately when tying or exclusive dealing is imposed, and thus should be limited to single damages. Not only is the "detection" rate 100 percent, but most tying and exclusive dealing are economically beneficial and lawful, and defining the boundary of legality is notoriously difficult.

The Relative Advantages of Consumer versus Competitor Suits

Damages actions by consumers who purchase from antitrust violators are the easiest to defend, for such injuries lie at the core of antitrust's concern. The injury that consumers most generally claim is an "overcharge," which follows from the high prices that result from the antitrust violation. The paradigm case is consumer actions challenging price-fixing. If a group of pharmaceutical manufacturers agree not to compete in each other's markets or fix drug prices, consumers pay more. For example, if the competitive price of a pharmaceutical would have been $5 per 100 tablets but a cartel succeeded in getting the price up to $7, consumers would be entitled to damages of $2 for each 100 tablets they purchased. This number would then be trebled to $6.

But consumer damage actions face two conceptual limitations. The first is that for many antitrust violations the higher price does not occur until after the antitrust violation has already done a great deal of damage. This makes consumers late rather than early detectors and argues in favor of preserving competitor lawsuits. The second is the problem of computing "passed on" damages when the consumers did not purchase from the violator directly but rather through one or more intermediaries, such as retailers.

Consumers, Competitors, and Early Warning

Price-fixing is an antitrust violation that produces an almost immediate consumer injury. A group of gasoline retailers or airlines might agree on Tuesday night to raise their prices by 10 percent, and by Wednesday morning the price increase is in place. Because consumer injury results almost immediately, a consumer challenge can be expected to provide an early penalty, assuming that the violation is detected.

But other antitrust violations are different. Consider predatory pricing, which occurs when a firm destroys rivals by setting its own prices below cost, hoping to recoup monopoly overcharges later. Competitors are likely to be familiar with the dominant firm's technology and costs, perhaps because their own technology and costs are similar. Further, competitors are the immediate victims of predatory pricing. Their losses will be large, perhaps to the extent of threatening their business's survival. Most important of all, their losses occur as soon as the predator cuts its price; they don't have to wait until some later period when the predator raises its price to monopoly levels. So the competitor is in a much better position to condemn the monopoly practice before it produces harmful results. Consumers have such poor knowledge of costs that they may never be aware of either the predation or the subsequent monopoly price. In all of these senses the competitor is in a much better position than the consumer to bring an antitrust suit.

Alternatively, suppose a dominant firm maintains its monopoly position by filing fraudulent patent infringement suits, brought even though the monopolist knows that the new firm's technology does not infringe the patent or that the patent itself is invalid. Defending intellectual property (IP) suits is costly, and the costs are not proportional to size. As a result dominant firms may have incentives to assert IP rights inappropriately in order to protect monopoly positions. Once again, the rivals being sued are in a far better position than consumers to evaluate such lawsuits. The rivals are more likely to be familiar with the technology, because their own technology is the claimed infringement. Second, they have a strong incentive to sue because their injury is significant. Third, they are first in line. Consumer harm shows up much later in created or prolonged monopoly. In sum, while filing a lawsuit on a fraudulently obtained patent is an anticompetitive act without any significant social value, the injury to consumers might not show up for many years and they may never detect it at all.

Many types of consumer antitrust actions suffer from two serious problems. First, the injury often occurs only during a very late stage of the violation, or after the unlawful acts have been committed. By contrast, competitor injuries occur almost immediately. Second, customers often lack sufficient information to bring suit. They typically do not have detailed knowledge of what has gone on in the upstream portions of the market in which they purchase. Often consumers are highly diffuse, with each suffering only a small portion of the injury. This latter problem can be partially remedied through the use of government agencies or private lawyers who are skilled at detecting violations.

But competitors are not always the best plaintiffs either. Indeed, they are simultaneously the best and the worst of private antitrust plaintiffs. On the one hand, often they are in the best position to detect and prosecute many antitrust violations early, before they cause significant consumer harm. On the other hand, they lack the correct incentives. While consumers are injured mainly by the higher prices that result from anticompetitive practices, rivals are harmed by both anticompetitive exclusionary practices and the lower prices, improved products, or other efficiencies that make it harder for them to compete.

The case against overly broad grants of lawsuits to competitors is implicit in the simple model of consumer harm developed in Chapter 1. Consumers are benefited by low prices and innovation; so an antitrust regime concerned with consumer welfare would try to facilitate market conditions and practices that lead to low prices and high innovation. Furthermore, in this simple picture competitors are *injured* by the very same things that tend to benefit consumers. One firm's low prices are likely to make life difficult for competitors, who must compete against the lower prices and may even be driven out of business if they have higher costs. The same thing applies to innovation. If Ford develops a highly fuel-efficient engine that attracts many consumers, the latter will be much better off. But GM, Chrysler, and other automobile manufacturers will have a more difficult time; they will have to cut prices or come up with competing innovations if they do not want to lose significant market share to Ford.

Such observations have fed the many arguments that consumers are the most valued enforcers of the antitrust laws while competitors are the worst. Historically, this argument was most persuasive during the 1960s and 1970s, when the federal courts routinely condemned practices that injured competitors, without seriously considering whether consumer harm was in prospect. Such decisions are much less frequent today, although there are still a few, such as the 2002 *Conwood* decision, which permitted a competitor to collect damages for practices that were mainly proconsumer, without making any serious attempt to distinguish harm caused to rivals by anticompetitive practices from those caused by healthy competition.[16] But the fact remains that, while anticompetitive decisions were once relatively common, they are much less frequent today.

The consumer welfare story is more complicated than the simple model portrays. The model usually looks at monopoly status as a completed act. Within that model monopolists tend to charge high prices and competitors low ones. Monopolists may also have less incentive to innovate than competitors. But in the markets that constitute the core of antitrust enforcement, monopoly is *de facto*. Although many firms may aspire to it, few achieve it. Those who do achieve it, however, often do so by practices that injure rivals. Some of these may be beneficial to consumers, such as cutting costs to the bone and lowering prices, or innovating aggressively so that consumers continuously prefer the innovator's product. But other practices that lead to monopoly are anticompetitive or at least competitively ambiguous and require further inquiry. These include properly defined predatory pricing, misuses of the innovation process or the intellectual property laws that protect it, or exclusive contracting.

These competing concerns suggest that eliminating competitor lawsuits altogether would be socially costly unless we can trust the government enforcement agencies to pick up the slack. For a wide range of violations competitors are in the best position to provide early detection and preemptive relief. But competitor lawsuits must be vigorously policed to ensure that the challenged practices are in fact anticompetitive. This analysis also suggests that treble damages should rarely be available to competitors. This would be the case if the suggestion made previously were followed and treble damages were available only for secret violations. Most, but not all, exclusionary practices are known quickly to rivals. This includes nearly all vertical practices. For example, rivals generally know very soon if anticompetitive tying or exclusive dealing precludes a dealer from purchasing the rival's product. Likewise, most victims of improper patent or other IP practices are aware of them almost immediately. One exception is predatory pricing, where rivals may not understand the predator's costs. Nevertheless, rivals clearly have the comparative advantage because they sell in the same market and typically employ the same technology and business methods. While they may not know everything about the dominant firm's costs, consumers are likely to know much less.

In sum, the solution to the problem of overly aggressive competitor lawsuits is not to eliminate them, but to limit the remedies and take a hard look at substantive claims. This entails not only that offenses be carefully defined, but also that fact findings by juries and speculation by experts be appropriately limited.

Consumer Suits by Indirect Purchasers

Both distribution and the organization of production in modern industry are complex. Every business firm purchases at least a few of its inputs, and most of them purchase a great deal. When Hewlett-Packard produces a computer, it might use disc drives it obtained from Toshiba, which in turn purchased electronic components from GE. Further, when Hewlett-Packard sells the computer, it will very likely not be to a consumer but rather to a distributor who sells to a retailer who sells to the final consumer.

Monopoly prices generally filter down through the entire distribution ladder, although in complex ways. If GE charges a monopoly or cartel price for an electronic component for disc drives, Toshiba may try to design around that component, find a lower-priced substitute, or simply pay the monopoly price. If it does the latter, it will try to "pass on" as much of the monopoly price as it can via higher prices to its own customers. Hewlett-Packard may respond by looking for drives elsewhere, using fewer drives in its computers, or simply paying the higher price. Once again, if it does the latter it will probably charge a higher price for the computer. In that case both the distributor and the retailer will charge higher resale prices. The ultimate consumer will pay more, and is often stuck with nearly the entire overcharge even though it originated several transactions upstream.

In the simplest cases of pass-on the selfsame good whose price is fixed is handled by two or more resellers. For example, Schlitz Brewing Corporation might sell beer to a distributor who in turn sells it to John's grocery, who then sells it to consumers. If we know the elasticities of supply and demand facing each firm, we can compute how much of the overcharge it "absorbs" and how much it passes on to the next person in line.[17] In most cases, however, computing this pass-on in litigation is very difficult.

In any event, as soon as other complicating factors are taken into account, the problems of computing passed-on damages become unmanageable. For example, the typical retail grocer has relatively generic shelf space that can be allocated among different products depending on demand. It will respond to a price hike in canned peas by giving less space to peas and more to beans or corn. As a result it will sell fewer monopolized peas, but it will probably sell more of the other vegetables as customers make substitutions. Since customers try to respond to high prices by buying a substitute, the grocer will be better off to the extent it can offer the range of substitutes that customers will likely buy.

Further, the grocer probably uses a standard markup across all its canned goods, say, 20 percent above the wholesale price. As a result it will not absorb any of the monopoly *markup* at all. If the grocer loses money, it is because it sells fewer peas at the higher price, offset by the additional beans or corn that it sells. In this case the grocer's injury is not measured by the "overcharge" at all, but rather by lost sales volume.[18] In sum, the prevailing rule today that measures middlemen's damages by the overcharge is economically incorrect.

The problem of tracing the overcharge becomes even more intractable when the middleman does not simply pass the good through its distribution system, but rather uses it in its own production process to make some other good. For example, in the *Illinois Brick* case (1977), the Supreme Court described the complaint this way:

> masonry contractors, who incorporated [the defendants' price-fixed concrete] block into walls and other masonry structures, passed on the alleged overcharge on the block to general contractors, who incorporated the masonry structures into entire buildings, and . . . the general contractors in turn passed on the overcharge to [the plaintiffs] in the bids submitted for those buildings.[19]

A contractor (or its customer) might respond to a price increase in concrete blocks in a variety of ways. First, it might simply pay more. Second, it might alter its architectural plans so as to use fewer concrete blocks and more poured concrete or other structural material. Third, it might drop concrete blocks as a construction material altogether and use something else. Fourth, it might not build at all. The contractor would be injured not because it paid a higher price for blocks: ordinarily in the bidding process the contractor would pass on the full overcharge. Rather, the contractor's injuries might flow from the fact that customers buy less at monopoly prices, so it would construct fewer projects. If the response to the concrete block overcharge is a project that uses fewer blocks and more poured concrete, the contractor may not be injured at all.

In *Illinois Brick,* the Supreme Court held that those who dealt only indirectly with a cartel or monopolist were not entitled to collect any damages; rather, the direct purchaser could collect the entire amount without reduction for any amount passed on. The main rationale that the Supreme Court stated was that tracing the "complex economic adjustments" that occur as a monopolized good is passed down would "greatly complicate and reduce the effectiveness" of antitrust damages actions. In addition, the Court reasoned that permitting pass-on "would transform treble-damages actions into massive efforts to apportion the recovery among all potential plaintiffs that could have absorbed part of the overcharge." The Supreme Court thus assumed, first, that the "overcharge" was the proper method of damages for each successive firm in the distribution chain; and, second, that measuring damages on down the line would require that the overcharge be traced and "apportioned" among different levels of claimants. In most cases both assumptions are false.

The critique supporting the *Illinois Brick* indirect purchaser rule generally rests on the great difficulty of computing "passed-on" damages.[20] Computing that portion of the overcharge absorbed by the intermediary and that part passed on to consumers is said to be impossible in litigation. While that is true, computing actual consumer injury need not, and ordinarily does not, involve any computation of pass-on. In the typical case overcharge damages are measured by either the "yardstick" method or the "before-and-after" method, and in the typical case neither requires computation of the pass-on.

The "yardstick" method estimates damages by comparing prices in the plaintiff's market with prices in some different but reasonably similar market where the violation is not occurring. The "before-and-after" method compares prices during the cartel period with prices in the same market prior to and subsequent to that period. To illustrate, suppose manufacturers of liquor fix its price in Texas, from a competitive level of $10 to a cartel level of $14. Suppose that such a bottle of liquor is sold to a retailer at the $14 price, and then the same bottle is sold to consumers for $16. Let us assume also that in a competitive market the retailer would have paid $10 and resold the liquor for $13. So in this simple example the retailer paid a $4 overcharge for the liquor bottle and passed $3 of that overcharge on to customers, absorbing the other dollar.

In estimating consumer overcharge damages under the yardstick method the economist would identify a "yardstick" market similar to the affected market but without the price-fixing. Suppose that market is Oklahoma, where no price-fixing is occurring, and that the same bottle of liquor in Oklahoma costs $13 at retail. In that case the consumer overcharge would be computed by comparing the $13 Oklahoma retail price with the $16 Texas retail price during the cartel period. The "pass-on" is not computed at all. The expert need only compare what the Oklahoma "yardstick" customer paid with what the customer in the price-fixed market paid.

The same thing is true of the before-and-after method. Under that methodology the expert examines prices before the cartel came into existence and after it fell apart. She would find that during the "before" and "after" periods the retail customer paid $13 (after necessary adjustments are made), while during the cartel period that customer paid $16. Once again, no calculation of "pass-on" is necessary.

And how about the retailer's injury? If we really wanted to compute the retailer's *overcharge* injury we could do so by comparing markups, or margins, which are usually readily identified by invoice and pricing data. For example, during the cartel period the Texas retailer's markup was $2, while the Oklahoma retailer's markup was $3. However, the markup does not capture the retailer's injury, because it is injured not only by the reduced profits on each bottle sold, but also by the reduction in the number of bottles sold. In fact, computing the overcharge *never* captures the losses resulting from lost volume. This is simply another way of observing that "overcharge" is not even theoretically the correct way of measuring the injury that accrues to a reseller who passes on some, but not all, of a cartel overcharge.

This analysis suggests two things. First, end users, or consumers, should have a damage action for any overcharge they paid, whether or not they purchased directly from the defendant. The overcharge will typically be measured by a methodology (the "yardstick" or "before-and-after" tests) that does not require any computation of passed-on damages. Second, for all intermediaries such as assemblers, distributors, or retailers, the "overcharge" is not the correct measure of damages. Their damages are an amalgamation of the losses caused by lost sales volume, plus any reduction in markup that they may have been forced to take, although in many cases this will be zero. This number might then have to be offset by increased profits on substitute products. The Supreme Court's concern with duplication of damages would vanish, for no element of the retailer's damages from lost sales duplicates the consumer's overcharge damages.

Ironically, the existing system *creates* duplication of damages when one considers the several state antitrust statutes that have indirect purchaser provisions. While state statutes may award treble damages to indirect purchasers, they cannot alter the federal rule that already awards full treble damages to the direct purchaser. This creates the possibility that a direct purchaser can recover the entire trebled overcharge under federal law, while consumers recover the entire overcharge that they paid under state law. In an extreme case where everything was passed on the result could be sixfold damages.[21]

Conclusion

While substantive antitrust law is much healthier than it was a quarter century ago, its remedies system still needs many repairs. Furthermore, fixing the remedies problems would very likely give us a better set of substantive rules as well. Often judges respond to an overly aggressive remedies system by defining substantive violations too narrowly, as in cases involving collusion and proof of agreement. The result often gives us the worst of both worlds, a substantive system that fails to prosecute anticompetitive practices that it is capable of prosecuting, and a remedies system that strikes haphazardly while leaving other, equally serious, practices undeterred.

4

Expert Testimony and the Predicament of Antitrust Fact Finding

Antitrust suits are often complex, frequently more complex than they need to be. Legally, the statutes are short and imprecise and give judges enormous decision-making power. As a result over the decades the courts have developed many technical rules for identifying such matters as the difference between competitive joint ventures and anticompetitive cartels, unlawful tying arrangements, or illegal resale price maintenance. This substantive intricacy is often compounded by procedural complexity. Antitrust suits often involve many parties. Many are conducted as class actions. Often similar cases are filed in many courts at the same time and must be coordinated or consolidated. Some have international elements that involve questions about our economic relationships with other sovereigns, collision with their antitrust policies, or our wish to extend our law-making power to conduct that occurs somewhere else.

Antitrust suits are also factually complicated. Simply figuring out what happened is often difficult enough, particularly when the defendant is a large firm or group of firms and the fact finding requires thousands of documents or the testimony of many corporate officials. Beyond that, facts have to be characterized. Was it anticompetitive for the members of a joint venture to agree on a price, or for the defendant intentionally to select a technology incompatible with a competitor's technology? Was there a reasonable business justification for the defendant's exclusivity agreements, pricing practices, or refusal to share its technology? Even more difficult are questions about causation and damages. Was the plaintiff really injured by its rival's retailing practices? If it suffered losses, what percentage of the losses were caused by the challenged practices and what percentage must be attributed to other causes? These questions are common in antitrust litigation, but answering them can be extraordinarily challenging and often the answers boil down to matters of expert opinion.

Conducting a complex antitrust case today without engaging an expert is unthinkable. The principal type of expert is the antitrust economist, but antitrust litigation also uses accountants and statisticians, as well as industry specialists. The Federal Rules of Evidence expressly recognize the value of experts. Rule 702 provides that expert testimony is admissible when the expert is properly qualified and his or her testimony is helpful to the trier of fact. Expert testimony is treated as presenting issues of fact, which means that the task of evaluating it often falls to a jury.

Just as other areas of the law, antitrust has had to confront serious problems of quality control. While the majority of testifying experts are undoubtedly both competent and principled, some are not. Many experts used in the federal court system today are "hired guns," engaged by one of the parties to litigation and paid (typically by the hour or the day) for their testimony. While it is illegal for an expert to charge a contingency fee, paid only if the expert wins the case for his side, there are nevertheless major rewards for winners. An expert who wins a high-profile antitrust suit will be in demand in subsequent years and be able to charge greater fees than an expert whose testimony is excluded or who ends up losing. So even the expert who is paid strictly by the hour has a strong incentive to win. Furthermore, parties seek out experts willing to speak most favorably to their side of a case, and if the case is weak this may entail the use of experts who are willing to "push the envelope," so to speak. Pushing the envelope often means little more than engaging in a species of academic fraud. Then the courthouse becomes the site for a type of "junk science" that would never pass muster in the laboratory or the university classroom.[1]

The Supreme Court's *Daubert* Decision

The Supreme Court has addressed the junk science problem, but only incompletely, by setting standards for expert testimony. Its decision in *Daubert v. Merrell Dow Pharmaceuticals* held that trial judges should have a fair amount of discretion to exclude expert testimony. The judge's evaluation of testimony requires "a preliminary assessment of whether the reasoning or methodology underlying the testimony is scientifically valid and of whether that reasoning or methodology properly can be applied to the facts in issue."[2]

The Court refused to give any "definitive checklist or test" for making this determination, but provided some important factors for courts to consider:

1. Whether the proffered scientific evidence "can be (and has been) tested." The Court noted that "[s]cientific methodology today is based on generating hypotheses and testing them to see if they can be falsified."[3]
2. "Whether the theory or technique has been subjected to peer review and publication. . . ."
3. "[I]n the case of a particular scientific technique, . . . the known or potential rate of error. . . ."
4. "[T]he existence and maintenance of standards controlling the technique's operation. . . ."
5. "General acceptance" in the relevant scientific community: a "reliability assessment does not require, although it does permit, explicit identification of a relevant scientific community and an express determination of a particular degree of acceptance within that community."

Daubert's technical demands have led some federal judges to protest that ruling on the admissibility of expert testimony requires the judge to be a better expert than the expert himself. Judge Alex Kozinski once complained:

Federal judges ruling on the admissibility of expert scientific testimony face a far more complex and daunting task in a post-*Daubert* world than before. . . . [T]hough we are largely untrained in science and certainly no match for any of the witnesses whose testimony we are reviewing, it is our responsibility to determine whether those experts' proposed testimony amounts to "scientific knowledge," constitutes "good science," and was "derived by the scientific method." . . . Our responsibility . . . is to resolve disputes among respected, well-credentialed scientists about matters squarely within their expertise, in areas where there is no scientific consensus as to what is and what is not "good science," and occasionally to reject such expert testimony because it was not "derived by the scientific method."[4]

Judge Kozinski's protests are well taken, but he left out one important point: the consequence of a judge's *not* ruling on the admissibility of an expert's testimony is that the testimony goes to a jury. No matter what we think are a federal judge's qualifications to determine whether an economist's or statistician's testimony is "good science," a typical jury of laypersons is far, far less qualified. A judge's difficulty in understanding whether an expert's testimony is scientifically or technically valid should never be the basis for transferring the decision to a jury. Not only will the jury be less technically competent; it will also be less skilled in listening to experts, and more likely to be persuaded by things that are irrelevant to the issue. Juries tend to discriminate in favor of experts who are the best explainers or rhetoricians, or who do not have unpleasant mannerisms. Many technically qualified experts are not skilled at communicating their thoughts to laypersons. So when the jury has to decide between conflicting experts in complex areas, rhetoric may have a significant impact on the decision.[5]

Nevertheless, Judge Kozinski's point still carries weight. Federal district judges are trained as lawyers and for the most part their dockets are generalized over the full range of federal claims. A judge might have to listen to a sexual harassment suit in the morning, sentence a drug dealer at 1 P.M., and listen to a motion to exclude a statistician's testimony in an antitrust case at midafternoon. With a few exceptions, judges are not qualified to second-guess the procedures and methodologies employed by experts in technically demanding areas such as economics, statistics, psychiatry, pathology, and so on.

But the problem should not be overstated. The *Daubert* criteria do not necessarily require the judge to outstatistize the statistician. Rather, they look for some signs that the expert's methodology has achieved recognition in the expert's own discipline. The fact that there is no literature in the field that recognizes a methodology, or that its validity has never been tested in professional papers written outside the litigation context, or that there is no information about rates of error, can speak volumes about a methodology's helpfulness.

Unfortunately, judges frequently look at expert methodologies in a superficial manner, often at too high a level of generality to make the determinations that *Daubert* had in mind. In too many cases the judge has observed that the expert relied on "statistics" or "regression analysis," and that statistical methodologies are generally accepted in the academic community, subjected to peer review, and have a known error rate. Of course, one could say the same thing about arithmetic or geometry. At a high enough level of generality virtually any methodology seems to pass muster under the *Daubert* criteria.

But statistical methodologies can be misused, and often are grossly misused. If the judge does not pass judgment on the methodology, then the job falls to the jury. Suppose, for example, that the plaintiff's expert uses statistics in a highly idiosyncratic way, perhaps making serious errors by failing to control for obvious outliers in the data, or drawing conclusions much stronger than the data permit. It is hardly useful for the judge to proclaim that "statistics" is a widely accepted and reliable methodology of scientific investigation. Even an astrologer might use a telescope properly to observe the motions of celestial bodies, but that would not serve to validate his testimony that the alignment of the planets explained why his client murdered the victim.[6]

For example, in the *Conwood* case, to be discussed later, the court admitted a linear regression analysis in spite of the fact that the plaintiff's expert had ignored a clear "outlier" in the data (see Figure 4.1). The regression was produced in order to indicate changes in market share across the states caused by the defendant's conduct. The dots indicated changes in individual states, and the horizontal line drawn across them was the least squares regression on those dots. The impact of including Washington, D.C., a significant outlier in the expert's simple linear regression, was to make the plaintiff's market share growth appear statistically correlated with the expert's theory of damages, when in fact it was not.[7] The expert should have "cleaned" the regression by removing the outlier or adjusting for it. A judge or law clerk with even an undergraduate background in statistics or econometrics would probably have recognized the error. Further, if corrected the result would have changed the damages estimate from $1 billion, the largest in antitrust history, to zero. The court's view was that arguments about the competence of the regression should be presented to the jury.

The expert's use of the regression analysis in *Conwood* may raise ethical as well as technical issues, but the fundamental problem is the same in both cases: in order to proceed rationally a court must know whether the expert testimony being presented is of sufficient quality to aid the jury in making a reasonable estimate. *Daubert's* criteria for evaluating expert testimony can provide federal judges with the ammunition they need to assess many, but certainly not all, expert claims. *First,* the party seeking to have testimony excluded needs to point out to the judge how the expert's particular use of a methodology is idiosyncratic and unacceptable. At that point the judge must consider whether the idiosyncrasies are sufficiently momentous to warrant exclusion. This itself requires careful judgment and perhaps some minimal knowledge of the expert's field. *No* expert's methodology is a perfect replication of something that went before, for the world rarely offers such perfect repetition of events. So the judge needs to do more than identify some assumption or technique that has not been made or employed before in the scientific literature. There has to be a significant departure from accepted scientific procedures.

Second, something that courts should and do consider is whether the expert has employed realistic assumptions that are properly connected

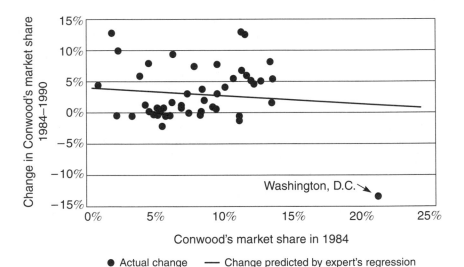

Figure 4.1. The *Conwood* expert's regression. *Source:* Daniel L. McFadden, in Brief Amicus Curiae in Support of Defendant United States Tobacco Co., United States Court of Appeals, Sixth Circuit, #00-6267 (Dec. 11, 2000), at 25.

to the facts of the case, and that do not ignore significant facts that are likely to affect the outcome. In antitrust cases in particular, untested methodologies are less likely to be the problem than assumptions that are unfaithful to the record. One of the most common concerns, particularly in antitrust cases, is assumptions about causation and damages that go far beyond the record. For example, the expert's analysis might attribute all of the plaintiff's business losses to an antitrust violation, even though it seems clear that other factors accounted for a significant portion.

In the *Brunswick* boat motor case, for example, the plaintiff's expert estimated damages by assuming that in a world without antitrust violations the plaintiff and the defendant would have had equal market shares. In the real world the defendant's market share was closer to 70 percent, and the expert's model attributed the entire difference in shares to anticompetitive practices.[8] Aside from completely ignoring that most concentrated markets exhibit unequal market shares, the model overlooked the fact that the rival had experienced significant business disasters that had nothing to do with antitrust violations. During the relevant period it had produced a defective motor that led to widespread problems and eventually a 100 percent recall. Numerous boat builders switched to the defendant's motor as a result. In that case, a model that attributed all of the rival's business losses to antitrust violations could overstate damages by a very wide margin. The court excluded the expert's testimony mainly for that reason.

To be sure, the difficulties with the expert's model in *Brunswick* confront an old problem in the sciences: every scientific model necessarily contains fewer variables than the full set of facts that the world presents. Indeed, we favor elegant models that have good predictive power while making relatively few assumptions. So the generalist judge may have to make a judgment call about whether the expert's failure to consider some market circumstance is fatal to the model's use as an estimator. In the case of multiple regression analysis, the Supreme Court has suggested a basic rule: a regression must take into account those variables that are likely to affect the result.[9] That provides a rough rule for most methodologies for proving causation and damages in antitrust cases. For example, it was obvious to the appeals court in *Brunswick* that the rival's complete engine recall was a significant factor explaining why Brunswick had a market share greater than 50 percent. If the expert cannot quantify that factor and isolate the impact of the antitrust violation with at least modest accuracy, then his model is worthless.

Daubert's Limitations: Questions of Fact and Neutral Experts

The federal judicial system treats expert testimony as creating questions of fact. Indeed, experts are not generally permitted to testify about questions of law, which is for the attorneys to argue and the judge to decide. Federal Rule of Evidence 702 makes expert testimony admissible if it "will assist the trier of fact. . . ."

The modern distinction between questions of fact (decided by a jury) and questions of law (decided by the judge) was institutionalized in the early nineteenth century. The principal cause was an increasingly professionalized bar that wanted more "scientific" trials than was possible under the kind of jury justice handed out when juries decided nearly everything. The principal basis of the fact-law distinction was that juries should decide issues that did not involve legal technicalities and that were unique to a particular case. "Was the sun in the defendant's eyes when he ran into the plaintiff?" is such a question. By contrast, issues were considered to present questions of law when expertise was required to answer them and consistency of result among different trials was important. "Should a child operating a motor vehicle be held to the same standard of care as an adult?" is a good example.[10]

The rationales for calling something a question of law apply to many of the technical disputes that arise from expert testimony. A jury is no more qualified to decide whether an anomalous data point should be excluded from a regression analysis than it would be in weighing the standard of care for a child's negligence. First of all, exclusion of outliers is a technical area of regression analysis that requires expertise. Second, the scientific standards for making such determinations should be applied consistently across all cases in which regression analysis is used. The traditional way judges respond to these technical disputes is to encourage the parties to engage in vigorous cross-examination of experts. But that method is not well calculated to get juries to understand complex issues. The jury is more likely to be confused, or swayed by the rhetorical skills of either the expert or the cross-examining attorney.

Treating technical disputes involving expert testimony as presenting questions of law does not fully address the problem either, although it would be a significant improvement over what we do today. Often judges are not qualified to evaluate the competence or relevance of expert testimony. The important point is that *Daubert* defines the beginning, but not necessarily the end, of the trial court's obligation to ensure that expert testimony is reliable. *Daubert's* criteria for evaluating expert testimony will not be sufficient in every case, and when they are not sufficient the court must do something else lest the jury and the judge be left at the mercy of experts whom they do not fully understand.

I do not want to sound too cynical here. If used properly, the *Daubert* criteria are often extremely helpful, and the judge can apply them accurately, even if he or she is not an expert in the relevant field. One recurring problem is that judges, perhaps because they lack confidence in their abilities, do not even perform their basic gate-keeping function of ensuring that the testimony meets the criteria that *Daubert* listed. *Daubert* does not require a judge to outexpert the expert; rather, it develops criteria that even a generalist judge can use to flag testimony that is irrelevant or scientifically inappropriate. If testimony flunks the *Daubert* test, it is excluded. If it clearly passes, it is admitted. In the middle will be a troublesome ambiguous group, and in those cases the judge should consider giving the experts' reports to a neutral, court-appointed expert.

The *Conwood* case illustrates a situation in which the *Daubert* criteria were sufficient for the task, but neither the trial court nor the appellate court applied them with sufficient care.[11] The plaintiff and defendant were two out of the four firms that produce "moist snuff," a tobacco product that comes in a small can and that people use by putting a small pinch between their cheek and gums. United States Tobacco (UST) was the largest of the four producers, and it was accused by Conwood, the second largest producer, of monopolizing the market. Briefly, UST designed a rack that would hold the brands of all four producers, and frequently replaced the existing racks in retail stores with this integrated rack. In some instances it did so at the request of retailers, and in others having sought their permission, and in still others without obtaining it. There was no way to tell from the record how many rack substitutions fell into each of these three categories. In addition, UST offered small discounts (less than 1 percent) to retailers who gave it sales information and preferred advertising space, and it also may have provided false information about how well rivals' products were selling so as to obtain more shelf space for itself.

The plaintiff's expert attempted to prove causation and damages by using two comparative regression analyses. He described these two comparisons as the "before-and-after" method and the "yardstick" method of assessing damages. These two methodologies, which are described briefly in the previous chapter, are well established in antitrust damages analysis. Experts use them all the time. Indeed, some courts hold that they are the exclusive methodologies for measuring damages.[12] Under the "before-and-after" method the expert identifies the time period of the violation and the time period just before or just after the violation. Then the expert compares the plaintiff's performance during the "before" or "after" period with the violation period. This usually requires the use of a multiple regression analysis that considers other factors that might explain the differences in the periods. The variable that is chosen for comparison could be profits, sales, market share, or share growth. For example, suppose that the expert's model showed that, after taking other differences into account, prior to the violation period the plaintiff was steadily selling 100 units per year, and resumed doing so after the violation period was over. During the violation period, however, it sold only 80 units per year. By knowing the amount of lost profits on each lost sale the expert could estimate the plaintiff's lost profits. While few cases are this simple, the example illustrates that the concept is not all that difficult in principle.

The "yardstick" method works the same way except that the expert compares the plaintiff's performance with its performance in some other market that was not affected by the violation. This could be either a different geographic market or a market for a different but reasonably similar product. For example, in one well-known case the plaintiff manufactured gravestones. Some cemeteries required purchasers of cemetery lots to purchase gravestones from the cemetery as well, and this requirement was found to be an unlawful tying arrangement. The plaintiff's expert was able to show that the plaintiff generally attained a 50 percent market share in cemeteries where there was no tying, but only a 4 percent market share in the cemeteries where the defendant imposed the unlawful tying arrangements. It would then be relatively simple to estimate lost profits by considering how many sales the plaintiff lost as a result of the unlawful ties.[13]

The plaintiff's expert in *Conwood* chose a "before and after" method that compared Conwood's performance in moist snuff during the damage period of 1990–1997 with its performance during the prior period,

1984–1990. He also used a "yardstick" method that compared Conwood's performance in moist snuff with its performance in the market for "looseleaf" snuff. Looseleaf is a dry tobacco product that is sold in a pouch rather than a can, but is distributed through the same retail stores and marketed in the same way as moist snuff. The defendant UST did not manufacture looseleaf; thus it would provide a suitable "yardstick" comparison in that it was free of the violation. The performance variable that the expert used was market share point growth.

Both of the damage methodologies, if they had been properly applied, would have resulted in a finding of zero damages. That is, Conwood actually did the same or a little better in market share growth during the 1990–1997 damages period than it did during the 1984–1990 comparison period. It also did better in moist snuff during the damages period than it did in looseleaf. This indicates that it was not injured by any practices during the 1990–1997 period.

But the expert came up with an entirely new, untested approach that ultimately generated the largest damage award to be sustained in the history of antitrust law, a little over a billion dollars. He did this by taking Conwood's market share growth state by state and running three sets of linear regressions. The first one, covering the "before" period, showed no correlation between Conwood's market share in each state at the beginning of the measurement period and its subsequent growth in that state. The second one, covering the "yardstick" looseleaf snuff market, showed the same thing—a random relationship between initial market share and subsequent growth. Finally, the third regression, which covered the damage period, purported to show a positive correlation: that is, if Conwood's market share in a state tended to be low at the beginning of the period, it tended to grow slowly in that state during the remainder of the period; if Conwood's share was high at the beginning, then it tended to grow more quickly. As noted previously, this regression was worthless because the expert neglected to exclude an extreme outlier, but that is a different issue.

The expert then testified that consistency of growth rates (i.e., growth remains slow in states that start slow) is unusual. Further, he said, this proved his hypothesis that the exclusionary practices had a greater impact in states where Conwood's share was low to begin with. He testified that but for the exclusionary practices Conwood would have grown at a constant rate of 8.1 percentage points in all of the states.[14]

Applying the *Daubert* criteria to this methodology should have been easy even for a judge without much knowledge in either statistics or in proof of causation and damages. In fact, the methodology flunked all of the criteria that the Supreme Court provided in *Daubert*. While the expert offered a hypothesis and purported to test it, what he was testing had absolutely nothing to do with the presence or absence of unlawful practices, or their effect on the plaintiff's sales. His test simply purported to show that the plaintiff's state-by-state growth rates were consistent. Before this test can be meaningful there must be some good reason for believing that consistency of growth rates is closely related to the presence of exclusionary practices. For example, the Hubble Telescope was launched on April 25, 1990, the same year the plaintiff's claimed injuries began. The expert could just as plausibly have testified that "the launching of the Hubble Telescope caused Conwood to have slow growth in states where its share was low to begin with." In fact, the expert's regression could have "confirmed" any hypothesis that the expert chose to assert, say, that Iraq's invasion of Kuwait (August 2, 1990) caused Conwood to grow more slowly where it had experienced slow growth previously.

Furthermore, even a cursory examination of the professional literature would have revealed plenty of accounts of methodologies that assessed causation and damages by comparing growth rates or profits or output during a "before and after" market or a "yardstick" market. As noted above, these generally accepted methodologies would have generated a damages number of zero. But that literature contains nothing suggesting that one can test for causation or damages simply by identifying consistency of growth rates. So the methodology flunked the criteria indicating the importance of peer review and publication, as well as the criteria for developing standards for application.

Most seriously, the court also failed to test whether the expert's methodology had a "known or potential rate of error," as *Daubert* requires. The errors that result from expert methodologies include "false positives" and "false negatives." A false positive is an indicator that the tested-for practice is present when it is really not. A false negative is an indicator that the tested-for practice is not present when it really is. In the present context the realistic danger is of false positives. There is no reason to be concerned about a plaintiff's own methodology that tends to understate damages.

In this case the false positives issue relates to the claim that market share stability proves anticompetitive practices. If the expert's test had been perfect, then there would be a very strong correlation between market share stability as he measured it and the presence of such practices. But if such stability occurs in some instances when no exclusionary practices are present and the methodology cannot distinguish those instances, then we have a problem of false positives. A very low percentage of false positives might not be enough to require rejection of a methodology, but a significant number would.

A quick look at the standard industrial organization literature would have shown that stability in market share growth is a very common phenomenon. The market in the *Conwood* case was a four-firm oligopoly. Under "strong" oligopoly theories, the market shares of the firms remain in lockstep, and there is a perfect correlation between beginning and ending market shares during the testing period. Under weaker theories about oligopoly behavior, market shares vary more. Nevertheless, many decades of empirical studies indicate that oligopoly markets have very stable market shares. In fact, well over half and perhaps as many as 90 percent of oligopoly markets have even more stability of market share than the *Conwood* expert found in his study.[15] In sum, the expert had identified a phenomenon so common that it occurs in well over half of concentrated markets, yet he maintained that its presence proved anticompetitive practices.

As the *Conwood* case illustrates, while the *Daubert* criteria are not perfectly reliable in evaluating expert testimony, they can be made to work quite well in many cases if they are just applied diligently. The trial judge in *Conwood* appears to have given up once he saw that the expert employed a regression analysis, something that the judge apparently knew nothing about. Regression analysis is certainly an acceptable methodology, and it is used every day to provide evidence of a variety of things, including causation and damages in antitrust cases. *Daubert* requires the judge to probe a little deeper, but it absolutely does not require the judge to be a better expert than the expert is.

In some cases, however, the *Daubert* methodology is insufficient and then the judge must seek help of another sort. Sometime both the plaintiff's and the defendant's experts will use methodologies in ways that seem quite competent to the layperson, and only another expert can sort out the inconsistencies. In those situations the best course of action is for the judge to appoint a neutral expert. Federal Rule of Evidence 706 authorizes a judge to make such an appointment. Unfortunately, judges do not do so very often, even though in *Daubert* itself the Supreme Court recognized court-appointed experts as one way that the court could screen party-selected experts.[16]

Judge Richard Posner breathed new life into the idea in his book, *Antitrust Law*, in 2001, and suggested it again in the *High Fructose Corn Syrup (HFCS)* antitrust case a year later.[17] The plaintiff's expert had testified to price-fixing by offering a regression analysis that he said showed higher prices during the claimed period of collusion than at other times. The defendant's expert disputed this regression analysis, saying that it did not include all of the variables it should have included. If they had been included, the inference of higher prices would disappear. The dispute was a highly technical one concerning "multicollinearity," which occurs when two variables have very similar effects—that is, they are not completely independent of each other. In that case each one may be extremely important but the presence of both means that when the two are considered together, each one individually seems to have only a small impact on the result.[18]

In such a case the *Daubert* criteria do not give the federal judge adequate guidance. While there is a large literature on multicollinearity in regression analysis, it is quite technical and in all probability no one but an expert could assess whether the additional variables should have been included in this particular regression. Judge Posner suggested that the trial judge ask each party to produce a list of acceptable experts on multiple regression analysis. The judge could then choose a name that was common to both lists. This procedure is widely used in arbitration cases for selecting a private arbitrator. The court-appointed expert could then examine the plaintiff expert's model and the defendant expert's objections and determine which of the two was more faithful to the data.

Whether a court should appoint a neutral expert, and the manner of defining this expert's task, depends on the situation. A few factors are important. *First,* the trial judge should have applied the *Daubert* criteria and found them to be inconclusive. At that point the more focused the dispute over the expert's methodologies, the more likely that a neutral expert will be helpful. In the *HFCS* case, for example, Judge Posner went straight to the problem of multicollinearity among variables, producing a reasonably well-defined question for the neutral expert to address. Not many federal judges have Judge Posner's knowledge of economics or statistics; but judges can always ask the parties to submit additional briefs and affidavits on claimed errors, and these can later be given to the neutral expert to guide his or her decision. And of course there will be cases like *Conwood*, where the errors in the expert's model are so broad and fundamental that the neutral expert is unlikely to require much guidance.

Second, the impact of the suspected error must be "substantial," in the sense of undermining or establishing causation, or having a significant impact on the amount of damages that could be recovered. *Third,* the parties jointly must be able to pay for the additional expert, given the costs in relation to the amount at stake, or else one party must express its willingness to pay the costs.[19]

Fourth, the court-appointed expert does not necessarily need to re-prove the case. The plaintiff has the burden of proof, and the real question for the neutral expert is whether the plaintiff's study is adequate for meeting that burden. Nor does the expert have to repeat the entire study. Typically, he needs only to evaluate problems that have already been pointed out by the challenging party. Evaluating an existing model in this fashion will usually be far less costly than creating a new one.

Will the use of the *Daubert* criteria plus occasional engagement of neutral experts solve all the many problems of expert testimony in anti-trust cases? No, although these two methodologies properly used together might produce defensible results in most cases and limit the jury's role to issues that are within its competence.

II

TRADITIONAL ANTITRUST RULES

Part II of this book considers the role of antitrust in traditional, well-established areas of the economy, including manufacturing, services, and distribution. Antitrust is most established and its role most clearly defined in these markets, although not as clear as it could be. Part III then deals more particularly with problems of regulation, innovation, and new economy markets such as computers and telecommunications. There the role of antitrust is less clearly defined, and more ambiguity exists about how antitrust policy should relate to other forms of government intervention in the market.

Antitrust's fundamental concern is the same, no matter what the market. Its purpose is to remedy, within its abilities, unreasonable exercises of market power by dominant firms or groups of firms. If antitrust takes its eye off this ball and becomes concerned with business torts, unfair competition, or wealth redistribution, it often ends up condemning procompetitive practices. Today most unreasonable business actions that harm rivals or consumers are unlawful under some body of law, but only a few are antitrust violations. Identifying anticompetitive practices with reasonable accuracy is critical because of the extraordinary penalties that antitrust imposes, including treble damages to private plaintiffs, criminalization, and occasionally the forced breakup of firms.

5

Unreasonable Exercises of Market Power

"Market power" refers to firms' ability to profit by reducing output and raising price above the competitive level. As Chapter 1 showed, when firms can do this some consumers pay more, while others forgo the monopolized product and substitute an inferior choice. The overall economy works less efficiently. The antitrust enterprise accepts the premises that (1) all things being equal, the exercise of market power is usually a bad thing; but (2) not all exercises of market power are equally bad, and some are actually socially beneficial; and (3) the empirical and legal machinery we use for measuring market power and dealing with it is both costly and too crude for making fine adjustments.

So we need to focus on the most flagrant abuses, accepting that the complete elimination of market power from the economy is neither attainable nor desirable. This idea that optimal deterrence is incomplete is hardly unique to antitrust. One can find it even in very simple areas of law such as speed limit enforcement. While they might not admit it, the police generally do not define their goal as ensuring that no driver exceeds the posted limit. Virtually all drivers know that they can get away with a speed five or ten miles over the limit. This is true because perfect enforcement is very costly in relation to the improvement in results. Measurement equipment is imperfect, for both officers and drivers, and if people going one mile an hour over the limit were routinely ticketed there would be many more challenges and costly litigation. In the case of market power, our measurement tools are probably not one-tenth as accurate as the police officer's radar gun.

Another reason perfect competition is not a suitable antitrust goal is that, if applied rigidly, it seriously limits innovation. The very concept of "innovation" denotes doing something that others are not doing, whether making a new product, using a new process, or creating a new way of distributing an existing product or service. A firm innovates in order to make money by earning some return above the cost of producing and distributing the product. At the same time, most innovation neither requires nor produces large amounts of market power. We can be reasonably confident that disciplining truly dominant firms or market-dominating cartels for anticompetitive practices will not hinder innovation unnecessarily.

The Antitrust Appraisal of Market Power

Antitrust is not a business tort statute. The Sherman Act was not intended to correct unethical or deceptive business behavior. Nor is antitrust good at identifying and condemning anticompetitive intent. Antitrust's purpose is to promote competition, which it does by encouraging competitive market structures, and intervening selectively when practices pose a genuine threat to competition.

This concern for competition means that nearly all practices are lawful, as far as antitrust is concerned, in competitively structured markets. If one Italian restaurant in Manhattan makes false claims about a competitor, the competitor may be injured. But Manhattan's Italian restaurant business is unlikely to stumble because there are many Italian restaurants and even the complete destruction of one would not noticeably affect competition. As far as antitrust is concerned, Italian restaurants in Manhattan can make false claims about rivals; they can cut prices to the bone, even selling at a loss; they can steal one another's talented head chefs; they can merge; they can refuse to help one another out in times of trouble or shortage. They can do almost anything except divide markets or agree with each other about prices. Antitrust aside, many of these competitive practices are unlawful under some other federal, state, or local statute. And the tort system has plenty of rules that are designed to protect some notion of business "fairness" or standards of ethical behavior.

Most antitrust claims require a showing either that the defendants have market power, or else that the market in which they operate is conducive to the exercise of market power. Market power is typically expressed as a relation between a firm's (or group of firms') profit-maximizing price (*P*) and its (or their) marginal cost (*MC*). A firm that maximizes its profits by selling at marginal cost is said to have no market power, or to be a perfect competitor. By contrast, a firm whose profit-maximizing price is 50 percent higher than its marginal costs is thought to have significant power. In the 1930s economist Abba Lerner (1903–1982) developed the following index for assessing market power:

$$\frac{P - MC}{P}$$

The Lerner Index reads zero under perfect competition (where price equals marginal cost) and approaches 1 as a firm's price-cost margins become infinitely high (or as its marginal cost approaches zero).[1]

The Lerner Index is not very useful in this form because relevant costs are so difficult to compute in litigation. However, the Index plus a little price theory generates several formulas that economists use for measuring market power in antitrust cases. Furthermore, both the quality of data and our empirical methodologies for measuring power have greatly improved in the last generation.[2]

Traditionally, antitrust has estimated power by defining a "relevant market" and computing the defendant's share of it.[3] Econometric methodologies can enable economists to assess market power directly, without the need for a market definition. But in the law old habits die particularly hard, and courts continue to insist on a market definition in most antitrust cases. So instead of measuring market power directly, testifying economists typically use the empirical methodologies as an aid in defining relevant markets.

A properly defined relevant market is a grouping of sales sufficiently isolated from other output that it is capable of being monopolized or cartelized for a prolonged period (typically, one year or more). For example, if all of the producers of taxicabs should get together and fix prices, their cartel would fail if (1) producers of other automobiles could readily outfit their cars as taxicabs and place them on the market; or (2) purchasers of taxicabs could readily switch to ordinary automobiles, which are available in large quantities, and make the necessary alterations themselves. Antitrust would express this conclusion by saying that the product market for "taxicabs" is too narrowly defined and must include other automobiles as well.

The merger of newer methodologies with traditional formulations has added considerable rigor to the market definition process. Today there are fewer decisions upholding findings of market power based on small, idiosyncratically drawn markets that could never be monopolized—such as "Dodge automobiles in Mount Lebanon, Pennsylvania," or "Bar-Mitzvah tours to Israel by Jewish travelers from Chicago."[4]

But other significant problems remain. One bleak spot in a generation of positive developments in market power analysis is the Supreme Court's 1992 *Kodak* decision holding that a nondominant firm could have antitrust market power with respect to its own "locked in" purchasers.[5] Kodak sold high-speed photocopiers. The largest firm in the market was Xerox, and Kodak's share of the copier market was only 23 percent. However, people who already owned a Kodak photocopier were said to be "locked in" to Kodak's replacement parts because these parts were unique in that many of them were not interchangeable with the replacement parts for Xerox or other machines. Clearly, not every firm is a monopolist merely because its aftermarket parts are unique. For example, a nondominant automobile manufacturer such as Chrysler cannot reap monopoly profits simply by charging $10,000 for replacement transmissions. The word would quickly get out and no one would buy Chryslers anymore.

But the Supreme Court found two possible exceptions to this basic rule. First, there might be a group of myopic, or uninformed, buyers who could be duped because they lack the information to engage in long-term, or life-cycle, cost calculations. These buyers would not discover that aftermarket prices were too high until after they had made their machine purchase. Second, Kodak might have increased its aftermarket parts price after it already had a large installed base of owners. For example, Chrysler might decide to abandon some portion of the automobile market and then raise the price of aftermarket parts in that portion significantly. It could then earn high profits from people who had already purchased these cars. It would sell fewer new cars, but this would not be a problem for a firm that was exiting the new-car market anyway. The Supreme Court permitted the case to go to trial, where the plaintiffs won a large judgment.[6]

While *Kodak* has some supporters among those rallying for a "post-Chicago" antitrust, most of the scholarly writing on *Kodak* has been negative. Many courts have distanced themselves from its holdings, and for good reason.[7] The "market power" conclusion blurs the distinction between economic market power and the wide range of practices that can lead to overcharges. If I lie to you about the health of a horse, you may end up paying more for it than its market value. Or if I perform a construction job for you and we encounter a difficulty halfway through, I may be in a position to take advantage of you. To call these situations abuses of market power, however, turns antitrust into a free-ranging engine for repair of any contract that either deceives or has not taken every possible contingency into account.

More problematically, Kodak was accused of refusing to sell aftermarket parts to rival repair organizations. Assuming Kodak did have market power in its aftermarket parts, it would "exercise" its market power by charging a high price for them, not by refusing to sell them at all. The logic of the *Kodak* case is that in an imperfectly competitive primary market (e.g., photocopiers) Kodak might be able to exploit its installed base by raising the price of aftermarket parts. It could do this either by charging its customers a high price for parts that its own service technicians installed, or else by charging high prices to independent service organizations (ISOs) wishing to install these parts. That is to say, the refusal to sell parts to ISOs has nothing to do with Kodak's ability to profit by charging monopoly prices for aftermarket parts. It could do this whether or not it sold to ISOs. Kodak's motive for refusing to sell parts must have been something *other* than any market power it may have had.

To be sure, the ISOs may have charged lower service prices than Kodak's own service technicians or they may have done a better job or they may have been free riding on Kodak's investment in technician training. If the ISOs charged lower prices for labor or did better work than Kodak's technicians, Kodak could profit even more by capturing these gains in the form of yet higher parts prices. ISO free riding on Kodak's investment in training might explain Kodak's reluctance to sell parts to them, but that explanation has nothing to do with market power. Kodak could be a victim of free riding even if it were an intense competitor.

The rival service organizations generally sold and repaired used and new office equipment, including photocopying machines produced by several manufacturers. For any given type of machine, their ability to repair depended on factors such as the length of the machine's warranty, the availability of aftermarket parts, or whether the manufacturer sold or leased the machines. A manufacturer would very likely insist on servicing machines that it leased out. The ISOs were claiming exclusion, or "foreclosure," but they were not being excluded from any grouping of sales that is meaningful in the antitrust sense of exclusion from a relevant market. For example, if I rent out an apartment building and paint the individual units myself, professional house painters are foreclosed from painting them. But no monopoly is threatened because there is no relevant market for "painting my apartment building."

Kodak ignored the eminently sensible principle that foreclosure must be measured against the array of opportunities from which a rival firm is foreclosed. For example, in an exclusive dealing case the buyer under a long-term requirements contract is "locked in" by the contract to purchase all of its needs from the seller, perhaps even at a monopoly price. But the courts uniformly require that foreclosure of competing sellers be measured against the entire market in which they do or can make sales.[8] In *Kodak* no one ever considered whether the ISOs serviced (or were capable of servicing) both Kodak and non-Kodak photocopiers, or even other types of office equipment. If they did, they were foreclosed from only a small portion of the market in which they did business.

These same factors explain why most courts have wisely declined to extend *Kodak* to so-called "relational" market power created by long-term business contracts, such as franchise arrangements.[9] In the typical situation a franchisee enters into an open-ended contract that involves licensing the franchisor's intellectual property and using the franchisor's business methods and name. For example, the franchisee might become a McDonald's restaurant or a Dairy Queen or a Domino's pizza store. The franchise agreement also requires the franchisee to use ingredients or other items that are sold by either the franchisor or its approved vendors, but says nothing about the price that the franchisor will charge. Domino's requires franchisees to purchase pizza dough from itself, while Dairy Queen requires franchisees to use only Oreo-brand cookies in various ice cream concoctions.[10] The antitrust dispute arises later when the franchisees claim that they are required to pay monopoly overcharges for these tied goods.

The franchisors are not monopolists in either the franchise market or the market for the tied items. For example, Domino's is a large pizza chain but does not occupy a dominant position even if the relevant market is limited to pizza restaurants. The pizza dough that constitutes the tied product is readily made from flour, oil, salt, water, and perhaps some other common ingredients. It could never be monopolized by any-one. The "market power" at issue exists only because of the contractual position in which the franchisees find themselves. That is, the Domino's franchisor has the contractual power to raise the price of its pizza dough and require its franchisees to purchase it. Alternatively, it has the power to force the franchisees to adhere to more onerous terms upon pain of losing their franchises.[11]

But calling such control "market power" is not merely legally incor-rect; it is also extremely dangerous as a policy matter. It makes anti-trust the vehicle for fixing contracts that we might think unfair or, worse yet, for protecting people from their own carelessly made bargains. The wrong, if there is one, lies in the franchisees' failure to study contracts carefully before they read them, or perhaps in the franchisor's improper use of form franchise agreements that take advantage of less experienced businesspersons.

The antitrust analogies always fall apart upon inspection. For exam-ple, suppose that I as a Standard Oil franchisee foolishly agree to pur-chase all of my gasoline from Standard at any price it wishes to charge me. When I enter this agreement Standard is charging market prices for gasoline, plus two cents per gallon as a franchise fee. But after I have built the station and formed a successful business, Standard raises its price to twenty-five cents above the market price. I am free to terminate the franchise agreement, but then I will lose my own investment in the franchise, which could be substantial. In this case the overcharge on gas-oline is the way that the franchisor obtains its franchise fee, or the roy-alty on its intellectual property. The franchisee has effectively signed an intellectual property licensing agreement in which the franchise fee was not specified, and the franchisor is free to charge any fee it wishes upon pain of termination.

This may be a serious problem of contracting, and it serves to caution prospective franchisees to negotiate their franchise contracts carefully.[12] But this story does not suggest an antitrust problem unless we believe that antitrust should police poorly negotiated or unfair long-term agree-ments. Indeed, the franchise lock-in cases do not even represent a seri-ous imbalance of information as between franchisors and franchisees, but only the franchisees' naiveté in accepting a contract that permits un-limited future escalation of fees.[13]

The indicia of antitrust harm, reduced output and higher prices in a properly defined relevant market, are uniformly absent in the franchise lock-in cases. Consumer prices do not rise unless the franchisor has market power in the primary market for the good it is selling. Nor is marketwide output reduced. If Domino's, with 5 percent of the pizza market, overcharges its franchisees for pizza dough, they will have higher marginal costs and will sell fewer pizzas. But in a competitively structured pizza market the shortfall will immediately be offset by the increased production of other pizza vendors. The Domino's franchisee, who is in competition with other pizza sellers, cannot raise pizza prices significantly above the competitive level.

Finally, there is the problem of remedy. In order to provide relief in *Kodak*-style refusal-to-deal situations, including the franchise lock-in cases, the court would have to determine the correct price and order the defendant to charge it. In the process we would be turning competitive firms with no significant market power into regulated public utilities.

Barriers to Entry

If we could confidently predict that new firms would enter a market whenever price exceeded the competitive level, antitrust would have little to do. Its administrative machinery is too crude and expensive to deal with monopoly that is unlikely to be durable. Thus the importance of entry barriers, which are factors that make entry unattractive even when the firms in the market are earning profits above the competitive level. When entry barriers are high, market power can be inferred simply from a large market share or high levels of industry concentration, coupled with evidence that the firms already in the market are not competing aggressively. Economists and antitrust decisions have identified economies of scale, high entry risk or capital requirements, intellectual property rights, branding and advertising, and government-imposed entry restrictions as entry barriers.

The definition of entry barriers, however, has been controversial. The Harvard School definition, championed by industrial organization economist Joe S. Bain, was that an entry barrier is some market factor that permits sellers to "persistently raise their prices above a competitive level without attracting new firms to enter the industry."[14] Significantly, this definition includes economies of scale, which may permit a very large firm to price above its costs while keeping smaller, higher-costs, rivals out. The Chicago School economist George J. Stigler proposed an influential alternative definition that excludes scale economies. He defined an entry barrier as "a cost of producing (at some or every rate of output) which must be borne by a firm which seeks to enter an industry but is not borne by firms already in the industry."[15]

One important difference between the Harvard and Chicago definitions lies in their treatment of risk. A firm already successfully producing in a market has overcome the risk of entry, while a prospective entrant has not. Although significant risk can deter new entry, the Chicago School would not count it as a barrier unless the risk faced by a new entrant is greater than that which was faced by established firms at the time that *they* entered.

The Stiglerian definition is based on strong concerns for efficiency. It is counterproductive to include economies of scale as an entry barrier, the argument goes, because the presence of entry barriers encourages more intervention and we do not want to punish firms for being efficient by attaining economies of scale. Largely the same thing applies to risk. The whole point of overcoming risk is to earn the higher returns that result on the back end, after the risk has been overcome. We do not want to punish firms for succeeding.

If government intervention in the market was based entirely on structural concerns, these arguments would have considerable weight. The Stigler approach would be essential, for example, if we broke up the firms in highly concentrated markets without requiring anticompetitive conduct. Indeed, Stigler's argument was developed during the heyday of Harvard School structuralism, when dismembering big firms was a popular idea.

But the arguments lose most of their force when our concern is with anticompetitive acts. For example, a large firm's filing of a fraudulent patent claim in order to exclude a rival violates §2 of the Sherman Act only if the firm is or threatens to be a monopolist. To say that the firm lacks monopoly power because its dominance depends on scale economies misses the point. When we apply §2 in this case we are not punishing the firm for attaining economies of scale but for engaging in anticompetitive conduct that threatens monopoly.[16]

While the presence or absence of entry barriers is always essential to estimating market power, their relevance in antitrust cases varies with the conduct at issue. Evaluation of entry barriers is most critical in cases that involve unilateral exclusionary practices. Yet monopolistic conduct is often ambiguous and difficult to assess. Conduct that excludes rivals can also be efficient and socially beneficial. Furthermore, unilateral creation of monopoly is costly, difficult, and usually time-consuming. As a result courts want to intervene under the antitrust laws only when there is a realistic threat of durable monopoly power.

At the opposite extreme, a naked cartel can be created in a single meeting and be socially harmful even if it is relatively short-lived. In some markets cartels are continuously created and re-created even though entry is easy. The per se rule against naked price-fixing dispenses with any entry barrier requirement. But proof of entry barriers is properly relaxed even in cases involving joint ventures. If such ventures create power, they typically do so quickly, usually by facilitating collusion. Once again, such an exercise of power can be profitable and socially harmful even if it is relatively short-lived. So as the antitrust concerns fade from single-firm monopolization to collusion, the importance of showing high entry barriers diminishes.

Identifying Unreasonable Restraints: Variations on the Rule of Reason

In antitrust "unreasonable" is a term of art and is simply another way of saying that a practice is unlawful. In order to be condemned under the antitrust laws a practice

- must create, increase, or prolong market power, or seriously threaten to do so; and
- cause injury to at least one group of market participants that is
- not offset by any justifications claimed for it; and
- be correctable through the antitrust enforcement system.

Each of these elements is present in every decision that properly condemns a practice under the antitrust laws. That does not mean, however, that we always require full proof of each one. The antitrust process is expensive, cumbersome, and not particularly accurate. We compensate for high administrative costs and uncertainties by adopting a variety of presumptions, or shortcuts.

In this respect antitrust resembles other bodies of law. Indeed, the entire legal system is filled with administrative shortcuts. For example, the state may require 1,000 hours of apprenticeship before someone can be licensed as an electrician. Some individuals may learn very quickly and not need anything like 1,000 hours to acquire the necessary skills, while 1,000 hours may not be enough for others. But the cost of making individual determinations is very high, so the process generalizes about prospective electricians as a class. Likewise, drunk-driving rules might specify .08 blood alcohol as a standard for DWI, even though some individuals may have most of their faculties intact at that level while others are barely conscious. Making individual assessments of ability to operate a motor vehicle safely at a given alcohol level is simply too costly. So the law makes a "class" judgment about what is reasonable under the circumstances. The variations in analysis that antitrust employs are essentially "class" judgments about the competitive dangers posed by various types of practice.

Courts analyze most claimed antitrust offenses under the "rule of reason," first introduced by the Supreme Court in the 1911 *Standard Oil* decision.[17] *Standard Oil* limited earlier decisions concluding that certain practices should automatically be held unlawful without regard to competitive effects.[18] The rule of reason was famously articulated by Justice Brandeis in 1918, in perhaps the most quoted passage in antitrust case law:

> The true test of legality is whether the restraint imposed is such as merely regulates and perhaps thereby promotes competition or whether it is such as may suppress or even destroy competition. To determine that question the court must ordinarily consider the facts peculiar to the business to which the restraint is applied; its condition before and after the restraint was imposed; the nature of the restraint and its effect, actual or probable.[19]

Justice Brandeis's version of the rule of reason created one of the most costly procedures in antitrust practice. Under it courts have engaged in unfocused, wide-ranging expeditions into practically everything about the business of large firms in order to determine whether a challenged practice was unlawful. Justice Brandeis's celebrated statement never defines what it is that courts are supposed to look for. His distinction between a restraint that "merely regulates" or "promotes" competition and those that "may suppress or even destroy" it can expand and contract like a blowfish, meaning almost anything at all.

If the rule of reason is to be administered rationally through the costly antitrust enterprise, it should never be an unfocused inquiry into all aspects of a defendant's business. Rather, it must determine whether a particular practice reduces marketwide output (measured by quantity or quality) and thus leads to higher prices or inferior products. Such a query rarely demands a broad history of the business that Justice Brandeis suggested. It is the plaintiff's job first to allege and explain how a particular practice harms competition. For example, a complaint might claim that a dentist association's restrictions on advertising hinder members' ability to communicate information about price and quality to prospective customers, leading to higher prices or reduced quality of service.[20] In order to do this, the plaintiff will ordinarily also have to identify a market, such as dental services, in which reduced output or higher prices occur, and show that the defendants have sufficient power to make their restraint work.

At that point the defendants' response should identify most of the issues that are worth disputing. The defendants might deny that the alleged agreement or other practice is occurring at all. They might admit that a practice exists, but explain how it tends toward higher rather than lower output, perhaps because the restraint operates only to suppress false and misleading information. Or the defendants might deny that they have any market power, perhaps because only 5 percent of the state's dentists actually belong to the association, or the association confers so few advantages that dentists drop out and reenter all the time. Any one of these claims, if true, would serve to make the restraint "reasonable" for antitrust purposes and thus lawful.

The sequence of questions and proof proceeds through a series of steps, something like the following:

Step 1: Does the challenged practice arguably threaten either to reduce output or raise price? If not, it should generally be declared legal. If yes, proceed to the next step. In determining whether an agreement arguably threatens to reduce marketwide output, at least a cursory examination of market power may be necessary.

Step 2: Is the challenged practice naked, or is it ancillary to some other joint venture or agreement that is itself plausibly efficient or otherwise beneficial to consumers? An agreement is "naked" if it is formed with the objectively intended purpose or likely effect of increasing price or decreasing output in the short run. As a result a naked agreement is rational only if the participants have market power. By contrast, an ancillary agreement reduces cost or improves the product and can be profitable whether or not the firms have any market power. If the agreement is naked, it is illegal. If the arrangement is ancillary, continue on.

Step 3: Examine the market power held by the parties to the challenged restraint. How numerous are they? How concentrated is the market? Is there a substantial competitive market outside the arrangement? Are entry barriers high or low? Is the venture nonexclusive—that is, are participants to the venture free to offer the covered product or service outside the restraints imposed upon the venture? If so, a marketwide output reduction is far less likely. If this quick analysis suggests that the exercise of market power is not plausible, the challenged practice is legal. If the exercise of market power *is* plausible, go to Step 4.

Step 4: Is there strong evidence that the challenged practice creates substantial efficiencies by reducing participants' costs or improving product or service quality? If not, the practice is illegal. If yes, go to Step 5.

Step 5: Can the efficiencies identified in Step 4 be achieved by reasonably available alternatives that have less potential to harm competition? If yes, the practice in its present form is illegal, although the injunctive remedy should be limited to condemning the current form or ordering the alternative. If no less restrictive alternative is available, go to Step 6.

Step 6: The analysis arrives at balancing. Hopefully, few cases will require real balancing; but if a challenged restraint simultaneously produces opportunities for anticompetitive practices and substantial efficiencies, a court must have a guide one way or the other. If the threat to competition is real, and if the defendants cannot restructure their venture so that this threat is substantially dissipated, the court's only conclusion must be to condemn the arrangement. At this point intent may become relevant, particularly when the defendants' professional judgment is required for their market to function properly (e.g., only licensed anesthesiologists may be qualified to set competency standards in their field). Nevertheless, any court faced with the prospect of balancing must go back to Step 5 and look hard for less restrictive workable alternatives.

While the given sequence of inquiries is logical and typical, alternative sequences may sometimes be more effective.[21] Once a question is answered in a particular way, the answer may either stop the litigation or involve a new set of questions. As a result the staged inquiry is particularly conducive to summary judgment or other early termination of the dispute. For example, if the complaint alleges that surgeons in a town have fixed prices, and the answer replies that price-fixing is necessary in this market in order to maintain the quality of surgery, then the plaintiff is entitled to a judgment of unlawfulness. The defendants have admitted that their restraint is naked, and no further inquiry is necessary. By contrast, the litigation must be terminated in the defendants' favor any time it becomes clear that an essential element of the plaintiff's case will fail.

For its part the court must try to assess conflicting claims without "balancing." Meaningful balancing, which involves placing cardinal values on both sides of a scale and determining which is heavier, is virtually never possible. A court will rarely be in a position to compute a number that measures the social cost of any market power being exercised, and then another number that measures claimed benefits, and net them out. Rather, the approach is a version of the "razor" invented by William of Occam in the fourteenth century. Applying Occam's razor to a restraint means stripping away those explanations that are implausible or unproven until we have a "core" left that characterizes the practice as pro- or anticompetitive. We say a practice is unlawful "per se" if there is relatively little to be stripped away before we can condemn the practice with reasonable assurance that we are making the economic world a better place. By contrast, we apply a more full-blown "rule of reason" when competitive effects are less immediately obvious. In such cases we need first to find out whether there is market power capable of being exercised. If so, we must know whether this particular exercise is harmful, and that being so, whether it is essential to any benefits claimed for it.

Unilateral versus Multilateral Conduct

Antitrust is more hospitable to unilateral conduct than to conduct that results from an agreement between two or more firms. Not every unilateral act is lawful, and it is hardly the case that every multilateral act is unlawful. Nevertheless, the difference in attitude is both clear and justified.

Unilateral conduct is ubiquitous. Firms act unilaterally most of the time: they determine their own output and set prices, and decide how much to innovate, whether to add or remove a product from their line, and whether to distribute on their own or through independent dealers. None of this behavior is even presumptively suspicious, and the costs of monitoring every unilateral act, even by dominant firms, would be extraordinarily high, for both government observation and the chill it would place on innovation and competition.

Furthermore, substantial market power is not something that a firm acting alone can easily create. Many firms very likely aspire to be monopolists. Some firms inherit monopoly positions simply by being lucky or getting there first. But try as they might, the vast majority of firms never come close to attaining a monopoly of anything. Creating a monopoly by *destroying* rivals is bound to produce resistance, retaliation, and attention from antitrust enforcers. Moreover, we are not particularly good at locating the line between anticompetitive and innovative practices. An overly aggressive antitrust rule would chill innovative conduct, so we frequently give the firm acting unilaterally the benefit of the doubt.

Multilateral activity is very different. Creating a monopoly by *cooperating* with rivals is much easier than destroying them. If a smaller firm is given the choice between ruinous competitive warfare or joining a highly profitable cartel, it will have every incentive to choose the second. Further, multilateral activity is somewhat exceptional and more readily observed. Secret cartels are worth examining for obvious reasons. But even significant joint ventures or other consortia are easy to watch. For example, when General Motors decides to build a new production plant, no antitrust authority is likely to take notice. But if GM and Toyota announce that they will build and operate a plant jointly, there is immediately something worth looking at. In the actual case the GM-Toyota joint venture to build automobiles in Fremont, California, was procompetitive, but that does not mean that it was not worth at least a brief examination.[22]

Multilateral conduct deserves closer scrutiny because in the proper setting it can create market power very quickly. A market with ten robust automobile manufacturers is not likely to produce a monopolist. If it did happen, it would take years of either anticompetitive practices such as predatory pricing or else extraordinary success in innovation against other firms that would be innovating in return. But if the CEOs of the ten firms met secretly to fix prices, they could create a "monopoly" almost immediately. This is true even of efficient joint ventures. For example, the NCAA joint venture is probably essential to the production of collegiate sports, which cannot exist without agreements among teams to create leagues, schedule games, and make rules. But the instant this efficient joint venture with rule-making authority is formed, it also acquires the ability to fix coaches' salaries or place anticompetitive limitations on television advertising—both practices that courts have properly condemned under the antitrust laws.[23]

Finally, and never to be underestimated, is the problem of producing a suitable antitrust remedy. Antitrust is a justifiable enterprise only if it can make the economy work better, and identifying wrongs without producing suitable remedies seldom accomplishes that goal. Antitrust remedies against unilateral conduct have proven to be notoriously difficult to devise and monitor. Regulating a firm's price and output decisions requires not only continuous monitoring, but also detailed and complex analysis of costs. Or ordering a monopolist to share something with its rivals requires a court to identify what must be shared, and to supervise the terms of sharing, including the price.

Remedies against multilateral conduct are typically much easier to devise and impose. If a collective of firms is fixing prices or dividing markets, it can be ordered not to, and competition will once again determine output and price. To be sure, the firms may not comply with the injunction, but that is the same problem that confronts any court supervising a private actor's activities. Once the decree is issued, individual members of the association typically have an incentive to bring price or output back to the competitive level. For example, once the Supreme Court in the *NCAA* case condemned the collective limitation on televised games, individual teams had the right to make their own decisions. The number of nationally televised games increased dramatically. The court order was all that was necessary. An injunction ordering a single actor to increase its output of television advertising would immediately make the court a regulatory agency, producing standards for how much advertising is necessary, and listening to objections from others claiming that the standards were either too high or too low.

The same is true of anticompetitive refusals to deal. The great majority of concerted refusals, or boycotts, can be effectively remedied by an injunction condemning the agreement not to deal. In the *Wilk* case, for example, the court enjoined the American Medical Association from enforcing accreditation and licensing rules whose purpose was to exclude chiropractors from the health care market.[24] Once the injunction issued, individual hospitals and care providers could decide for themselves whether to make x-ray and related facilities available to chiropractors, and most did so. In contrast, if a refusal to deal is unilateral, as when a large electric utility refuses to wholesale electric power to smaller utilities,[25] then the antitrust court can intervene only by becoming a public utility regulator. It would have to determine when power wholesaling is necessary, whether every small utility or just a few are entitled to be served, and what the price must be for various types of service. Furthermore, because markets change over time ongoing supervision would be necessary.

So antitrust begins with a fairly benign attitude toward a firm's unilateral conduct, and a more suspicious attitude toward multilateral conduct, with the degree of suspicion varying with the conduct itself. This is plain from the budgets and agendas of the government enforcement agencies, which put far more resources into evaluating various forms of multilateral conduct (cartels, joint ventures, and mergers) than the actions of single firms. This differential treatment of multilateral and unilateral conduct is the principal subject of the next two chapters.

Self-Limiting versus Exclusionary Conduct

As Chapter 1 illustrated, a firm or association of firms "monopolizes" by reducing total market output. Price will then rise to meet the increased demand that results. In order to achieve a marketwide output reduction the firm or association must accomplish two things. First, it must limit its *own* output to something less than obtains under competition. Second, it must prevent others from entering the market or expanding their output, which they will be motivated to do when sales in the affected market become more profitable. As a result both monopolists and cartels may engage in "exclusionary" practices in addition to increasing their own prices.

Antitrust law treats self-limitations on output differently depending on whether the actor is a firm or a group of firms acting together. If the conduct in question is multilateral, the output reduction standing alone is sufficient to warrant antitrust intervention. We tolerate collaborative activity such as joint ventures of competitors because they can produce economic gains, but prefer competition when those gains are not apparent. So, for example, if a cartel reduces market output and raises price, we condemn it. To be sure, not all of the cases are easy. In many, pro- and anticompetitive potential both need to be examined. But if we are convinced that the principal effect of a joint venture is to reduce marketwide output, we do not hesitate to intervene.

By contrast, we do not condemn monopolists for the simple act of reducing output and raising price. Rather, we insist on a showing of unreasonable "exclusionary" conduct. This difference in attitude is easily justified. As noted before, single-firm conduct is ubiquitous and unavoidable, and a firm necessarily charges a price that reflects its market position. Furthermore, condemning the cartel requires nothing more than an injunction, while condemning a unilateral output and pricing decision requires the antitrust authorities to identify the "proper" output level and price, and engage in ongoing supervision when costs or other market conditions change.

"Naked" Restraints and the Per Se Rule

We often speak of horizontal agreements such as cartels as "naked" because they merely fix prices, without offering any offsetting benefits such as integration of production, innovation, or distribution. A serviceable definition of a naked restraint is one whose profitability depends on the exercise of market power.[26] For example, price-fixing is profitable only if the participants collectively occupy enough of the market to make their price increase stick. If two Italian restaurants in Manhattan agree to fix prices at higher levels than equivalent rivals are charging, they will fail because Manhattan contains many Italian restaurants.

Defining a restraint as naked if it depends on market power for its profitability is useful because some naked restraints are accompanied by significant integration of production or distribution. As a result we can avoid the error of classifying restraints as ancillary simply because they are included in otherwise efficient joint ventures. For example, the National Collegiate Athletic Association (NCAA) contains roughly 1,200 colleges and universities that administer intercollegiate sports. Doing this requires a great deal of rule making, and many of the rules can be characterized as output-reducing. For example, the NCAA may decide that a collegiate football season consists of ten games rather than fifty; that only thirty players may be on a squad; or that a game will be one hour on the clock rather than six, which would permit more advertising.

In the *NCAA* case the Supreme Court condemned a rule limiting the number of nationally televised games a team could have, after characterizing that particular limitation as "naked."[27] The profitability of the limit on televised games depended on increased advertising revenues. The Supreme Court correctly rejected the argument that the limit was necessary in order to increase game attendance—more people would be forced to go to footballs games if fewer of them were televised. But *every* cartel increases demand for substitute products. For example, price-fixing in coffee will increase the demand for tea, or monopolization of air travel will increase the demand for rail or road travel. The important consideration is that by looking for the source of profit from a particular agreement within the very large NCAA joint venture, the Supreme Court was able to identify agreements whose profitability depended on the exercise of market power. This enables a court to fashion a kind of relief that preserves the portions of the joint venture that are efficient and worth keeping, while suppressing those that are anticompetitive and unnecessary to the venture's effective operation.

Consider a different joint venture, Pediatric Associates, which is a loose association of six pediatricians. Each member could be engaged in solo practice. Instead, they agree to rent a building and operate it together; to hire and share a receptionist and nursing and laboratory staff; to purchase jointly and operate expensive durable equipment; and to fill in for each other and be "on call" when others are off or on vacation. When someone with a sick child calls in for an appointment, that parent can have the next slot available from any of six physicians, rather than having to wait for a particular one. In order to make this scheme work, however, it may be necessary for Pediatric Associates to agree on a price schedule for both physician services and laboratory services; to agree on hours of operation and "on call" policies; and perhaps even agree on the types of services they will perform in their office. Indeed, they may even "divide" the market by adopting specialties for certain types of illnesses or injuries.

In analyzing an association such as Pediatric Associates it is useful to ask whether Pediatric Associates with all its policies could be profitable in a large market such as New York City. The answer seems to be yes.

The profitability of Pediatric Associates does not depend on the six pediatricians' collective power to reduce output and raise prices, but on their ability to cut costs by sharing expensive staff and equipment, or to offer a more desirable product jointly than each could offer separately. To the extent that each of Pediatric Associates' various agreements satisfied that test, they should be considered ancillary rather than naked restraints.

Properly defined, the per se rule is limited to naked restraints. Unfortunately, the courts have not yet arrived at that position, and continue to apply the rule to some clearly ancillary vertical practices (tying and resale price maintenance) and some ancillary market division agreements. Nevertheless, once we know that the profitability of a restraint depends on the exercise of market power, we can confidently condemn that restraint without concern that we are destroying socially beneficial arrangements.

To say that a naked practice such as price-fixing is "unlawful per se" means that once we know that a group of firms has fixed prices we are ready to condemn them without asking whether price-fixing was likely to be profitable in that particular market, whether it was really successful and harmed consumers, or even if there was some justification for it under the circumstances. The per se rule largely eliminates these inquiries. The principal savings in administrative costs brought about by the per se rule are that market power need not be proven and the range of permissible defenses is severely limited.

The per se rule is said to result from repeated judicial experience, which describes a fairly crude but nevertheless serviceable empirical methodology. Scientists test hypotheses by trying to disprove them. If an hypothesis repeatedly survives testing it is said to be robust, which means that it becomes a kind of working rule for scientific endeavor until someone finally disproves it or develops an alternative hypothesis that is simpler or more successful. We never say that a scientific hypothesis is "true" in any final sense, but only that it has survived all efforts to disprove it to date.

So it is with the per se rule. In its much-idealized formulation a practice is presented to a court for the first time and the court does a full analysis of competitive effects, concluding that the practice is anticompetitive. This outcome happens each time the defendants present a new variation or defense: the court repeatedly finds the practice to be anticompetitive. Finally, the court confidently declares the practice so likely to be anticompetitive, and the offered defenses so unlikely to save it, that asserting them is not worth the great expense of case-by-case analysis. At that point a court declares the practice unlawful "per se," which means that it will no longer require a detailed workup of anticompetitive effects, and the defenses will be disallowed.

One difficulty in applying the per se rule is defining the domain of activities that fit into the per se classification. For example, while we generally say that price-fixing is unlawful per se, the term "price-fixing" is not self-defining and could include not only the naked cartel but also (1) the group of physicians in the preceding illustration who organize a practice and charge the same fees; (2) two contractors who pool their equipment and bid jointly on a construction project; or (3) owners of copyrights to recordings who agree in advance on royalties so that users can perform their works without prior negotiation.[28] Not only are these practices *not* per se unlawful; they are ancillary restraints and generally procompetitive. The per se rule is properly limited to naked price-fixing.

At What Stage Must Per Se Conduct Be Identified?

So conduct must be characterized before it can be made subject to the per se rule. Furthermore, the characterization process must be less costly than a full rule of reason analysis. Otherwise the per se rule would be pointless. If determining that something ought to be governed by the per se rule is just as costly as applying the rule of reason, then we haven't saved anything.

This point may seem too obvious to mention, but the fact is that the cost savings that the per se rule promises are often lost because of the judicial decision-making sequence. The story that often unfolds is something like this: the plaintiff alleges that a certain agreement is unlawful per se and develops its case on that premise. The defendant objects that the full rule of reason should be applied. After discovery is completed, the judge agrees with the defendant that the rule of reason should be applied and then dismisses the complaint because the record does not contain evidence of a relevant market or some other element that is essential to a rule of reason decision.

If this scenario is a significant possibility at the beginning of the litigation, then the plaintiff has no choice but to pursue its case under the full rule of reason, even though it believes that the per se rule is appropriate. If discovery and expert testimony must be developed on the assumption that the rule of reason will be applied, then most of the value of the per se rule has been lost. The cost savings that the per se rule promises are not the reduced cost of writing a judicial opinion, which is modest, but the reduced cost of all the evidence production, including expert testimony, that leads up to trial. In particular, inquiries into market power, which are unnecessary in a per se case, often cost hundreds of thousands of dollars and add greatly to the complexity of antitrust litigation.

A plaintiff who believes that it has a good per se case should be able to identify the facts it needs for per se condemnation and obtain judicial approval to proceed to discovery of those facts. If the facts support the plaintiff's claim, or if some fact (such as proof of agreement) that is essential to any antitrust claim is lacking, then the case can be disposed of without the additional costly rule of reason inquiries. However, if the per se record is inconclusive, then further discovery under the rule of reason will be necessary.

Stare Decisis *and the Per Se Rule*

Today the per se rule is in disrepute, though not because of any fundamental flaw in the rule itself. Rather, we are experiencing a reaction to the flagrant overuse of the rule in the past. The Supreme Court insisted that the lower courts apply the per se rule to a number of practices, including resale price maintenance, tying arrangements, and ancillary horizontal market division agreements, which are procompetitive most of the time. Despite our knowing much more about the competitive effects of these practices than we did at the time their per se rules were formulated, the lower courts decline to apply a rule of reason because the Supreme Court has sternly warned that the lower courts are not to "anticipate" that the Court will overrule one of its own decisions.[29] When one combines this warning with a Supreme Court that grants review of only a few antitrust cases, the result is outmoded rules that cling simply from the force of institutional lethargy.

In its *California Dental Association (CDA)* decision the Supreme Court observed that there is no bright line between per se and rule of reason analysis, but rather a continuum. Quoting the late Philip E. Areeda, the Court noted:

> "There is always something of a sliding scale in appraising reasonableness, but the sliding scale formula deceptively suggests greater precision than we can hope for. . . . Nevertheless, the quality of proof

required should vary with the circumstances." At the same time, Professor Areeda also emphasized the necessity, particularly great in the quasi-common law realm of antitrust, that courts explain the logic of their conclusions. "By exposing their reasoning, judges . . . are subjected to others' critical analyses, which in turn can lead to better understanding for the future."[30]

When there are "no categorical lines" between restraints producing an "intuitively obvious inference of anticompetitive effect" and those requiring "more detailed treatment," the Court said, the inquiry must be tailored so as to be "meet for the case, looking to the circumstances, details, and logic of a restraint." The purpose is

> to see whether the experience of the market has been so clear, or necessarily will be, that a confident conclusion about the principal tendency of a restriction will follow from a quick (or at least quicker) look, in place of a more sedulous one. And of course what we see may vary over time, if rule-of-reason analyses in case after case reach identical conclusions.

The Court thus acknowledged that over time judicial experience with markets will change and may require a change in the presumptive rule to be employed. Clearly the Court was speaking not merely about the amount of variation within rule of reason queries. Even the per se rule is subject to revision when appropriate shifts in perspective occur.

Courts generally believe that *stare decisis* limits their ability to switch from per se to rule of reason analysis of a particular practice. But the *CDA* decision makes clear that the difference between rule of reason and per se inquiries depends on judicial experience rather than *stare decisis*. Rules of *stare decisis* require adherence to older decisions notwithstanding otherwise persuasive arguments to the contrary, merely because the courts developed the rule a long time ago, repeated it numerous times, and others have relied on it. Furthermore, at least in the legislative arena the negative impact of *stare decisis* is mitigated by the fact that unappealing judicial rules can be changed by Congress.

But the per se rule was never legislatively created in the first place. It was defined and developed exclusively by the federal judiciary. Moreover, it is explicitly driven by policies informed by judicial experience, the high cost of antitrust litigation, and our relative knowledge or ignorance of a particular practice. As these factors change, a judicial conclusion about a certain practice or set of practices may be subject to modification as well.

The federal courts ordinarily do not apply the per se rule to a practice the first time they encounter it. That judgment can be made only after "considerable judicial experience" showing that anticompetitive effects dominate any alternative explanation.[31] Thus courts faced with a novel practice may initially require full trials under the rule of reason, perhaps in several cases and over many years. Eventually, however, a consistent string of decisions condemning a practice makes the per se rule a logical way to manage costly and cumbersome judicial resources. When the Court finally decides that it has seen enough to apply a per se rule, *stare decisis* is not a factor.

Irrationally, however, if a court wishes to go in the other direction and apply the rule of reason to a practice that previously had been illegal per se, *stare decisis* becomes a major obstruction, often compelling the incorrect outcome. In the relatively few antitrust decisions where the Supreme Court has been asked to reject earlier decisions applying the per se rule, it has always found concerns of *stare decisis* to have considerable weight. For example, in *Jefferson Parish* five Justices relied on *stare decisis* to adhere to the completely senseless per se rule against tying arrangements.[32] The *Khan* and *GTE Sylvania* decisions discussed below both overruled per se rules, but only after quite defensive discussions of *stare decisis* concerns.

The antitrust rule governing vertical nonprice restraints illustrates both sides of this observation. In its *Schwinn* decision the Supreme Court adopted a per se rule against vertical nonprice restrictions with no *stare decisis* concern expressed about its own previous *White Motor* decision four years earlier, which had applied the rule of reason. The rationale was that at the time the courts had insufficient experience with vertical nonprice restraints to understand how they should be classified. But by the time of *Schwinn* judicial experience was thought to be adequate, and the court moved without mentioning *stare decisis*. A decade later when the Supreme Court overruled *Schwinn* and returned to the rule of reason for vertical nonprice restraints, concerns of *stare decisis* were thought to be significant.[33]

Stare decisis has effectively created a ratchet for the per se rule, permitting courts to move in one direction but not the other. But knowledge about the competitive effects of business practices must be regarded as a two-way street. Just as increased judicial experience with a practice can lead judges to conclude that it is virtually always anti-competitive and can be disapproved after a truncated inquiry, judicial experience can also reveal the opposite. Earlier decisions to apply the per se rule may have been made too hastily. Both the per se rule against tying arrangements, which dates to the 1940s,[34] and the per se rule against vertical nonprice restraints, which dates to the mid-1960s *Schwinn* decision, came out of a period when courts were hostile toward vertical integration. For example, vertical mergers were condemned under an aggressive standard that struck down many mergers that would never be challenged today. Both our theory and most of our law of vertical integration have changed very considerably since that time.[35]

Judges continue to accumulate experience even *after* they decide to apply the per se rule, and further accumulations may lead them to have second thoughts. The *Khan* decision, which overruled the old per se rule against maximum resale price maintenance, urged "utmost caution" in overruling a prior decision that had adopted a per se rule. It regarded *stare decisis* as the "preferred course," for it "promotes the evenhanded, predictable, and consistent development of legal principles, fosters reliance on judicial decisions, and contributes to the actual and perceived integrity of the judicial process." Nevertheless, *Khan* found *stare decisis* inadequate to support the widely criticized per se rule in this case:

> In the area of antitrust law, there is a competing interest, well-represented in this Court's decisions, in recognizing and adapting to changed circumstances and the lessons of accumulated experience. Thus, the general presumption that legislative changes should be left to Congress has less force with respect to the Sherman Act in light of the accepted view that Congress "expected the courts to give shape to the statute's broad mandate by drawing on common-law tradition." As we have explained, the term "restraint of trade," as used in § 1, also "invokes the common law itself, and not merely the static content that the common law had assigned to the term in 1890." Accordingly, this Court has reconsidered its decisions construing the Sherman Act when the theoretical underpinnings of those decisions are called into serious question.[36]

One could say that while per se rules are clearly subject to *stare decisis*, the "common law" nature of antitrust adjudication requires that *stare decisis* be applied in a flexible manner. But there is more going on here. The doctrine of *stare decisis* applies a given rule even when the court has determined that the rule is incorrect. Competing concerns for stability and integrity trump the concern for technical correctness. For example, strong concern for *stare decisis* is the only way to explain Justice Marshall's statement for the Court in *Topco,* which applied the per se rule to a clearly ancillary market division agreement. Marshall said that "[w]hether or not we would decide this case the same way under the rule of reason . . . is irrelevant."[37] Manifestly, however, the rule of reason and the per se rule are not calculated *ex ante* to yield different outcomes. We apply the per se rule only after we have a high degree of confidence developed through experience that the rule of reason would result in the same outcome, provided that all the facts were known.

By contrast, the "judicial experience" rationale for per se rules permits the judge to make his or her best judgment at the time, rejecting a rule when it is no longer the correct one. To be sure, one must not bounce back and forth too hastily, and the *Khan* Court permitted a change only when the "theoretical underpinnings of earlier decisions were called into serious question."[38] But nothing in *Khan* required enforcement of a competition rule conceded to be incorrect *merely* to preserve the stability of the antitrust system, to protect business reliance, or to maintain the integrity of the courts. In any event, the theoretical underpinnings of the per se rules against vertical practices such as tying and resale price maintenance have been thoroughly undermined as well.

The Per Se Rule as Analytic Rather Than Categorical

The best solution to the per se dilemma is to formulate antitrust rules of *stare decisis* analytically rather than by category. The proper rule to which *stare decisis* attaches should never have been that maximum resale price maintenance is unlawful per se. Rather, it should have been much more general—namely, that a "naked" agreement, with its significant potential to reduce marketwide output and with no integration or other ancillarity in its defense, is unlawful per se. Maximum resale price maintenance agreements rarely reduce output in any market. Nor do resale price maintenance or tying.

Such a rule of *stare decisis* operates to stabilize a *method of analyzing* antitrust restraints. It does not force categorical application of the per se rule to a particular "type" of restraint, for restraints often come in so many varieties that the judiciary can never say it has experienced enough of them to know what it needs to know. Even the sturdiest of per se rules—the one against horizontal price-fixing—contains exceptions for joint ventures where price-setting is necessary to make the venture work properly.

The per se rules against practices such as tying and resale price maintenance were developed without real inquiry into the effects of the challenged practice on marketwide output. Rather, they were concerned with such values as maximizing the freedom of independent dealers, which is often limited by practices that enlarge rather than reduce output. The form of per se analysis that the courts apply to horizontal agreements such as joint ventures is much more appropriate than the rules applied to vertical practices such as tying and resale price maintenance.

An unfortunate result of the history of *stare decisis* in antitrust rule making is a completely indefensible set of antitrust rules that are lenient toward cartel-facilitating restraints created by competitors, such as those in the *California Dental Association (CDA)* case to be further discussed in the next chapter, but hostile toward vertical practices such as tying and resale price maintenance that are procompetitive most of the time. In *CDA* the Supreme Court was unwilling to condemn a horizontal agreement limiting price advertising without an inquiry into the effect of the arrangement on output. In very sharp contrast, once a practice has been characterized as "tying" or "resale price maintenance," such inquiries become irrelevant and the per se rule is applied. This difference in treatment is perverse.

The time for jettisoning some of antitrust's outmoded per se rules is long overdue. The following in particular merit reconsideration:

JOINT-VENTURE ANCILLARY MARKET DIVISION AGREEMENTS. In its *Topco* decision the Supreme Court applied the per se rule to condemn a horizontal territorial division agreement in a production and distribution joint venture. The restraints were clearly ancillary, designed to limit free riding among the individual Topco grocers. The members' market shares, which averaged about 6 percent in their respective territories, were far too small to support any inference of cartelization. Justice Marshall's majority opinion derisively spoke of the rule of reason as "leav[ing] courts free to ramble through the wilds of economic theory in order to maintain a flexible approach."

In a brief concurring opinion Justice Blackmun noted rather unhappily that condemnation of the agreements in question would tend to "stultify" Topco's attempts to compete with the larger chain stores—in sum, that the Court's decision was anticompetitive.[39] Nevertheless, he thought it too late in the day to revisit the per se rule, which seemed "firmly established" in the Court's jurisprudence. He then suggested legislation as the only possible solution. He believed the per se rule was strongly mandated by *stare decisis,* even though this was the first time that the Supreme Court had encountered a territorial division scheme in the context of a production and distribution joint venture that clearly lacked market power. If *stare decisis* had been applied to a methodology of antitrust analysis, rather than simply to the category of "market division," the outcome would have been different. Chief Justice Burger's dissent would have applied a full rule of reason. He correctly identified the restraints at issue as ancillary rather than naked and opined that the development of a Topco line of products and the absence of any market power made these restraints procompetitive.

California Dental (CDA) appears to be a complete repudiation of the majority's approach in *Topco,* and a complete espousal of Chief Justice Burger's dissent. The literature on *Topco* drew this conclusion a quarter century ago, and a few lower court decisions have indicated the same.[40] Problematically, however, the Supreme Court has cited *Topco* as good authority as recently as 1990.[41] But any close reading of *Topco* indicates that what the Supreme Court majority did in that decision is inconsistent with the mode of analysis it adopted in *CDA.* In fact, our litigation experience with ancillary market division agreements indicates that such arrangements are procompetitive or at least not harmful in a wide variety of circumstances.

TYING ARRANGEMENTS. Many tying arrangements, discussed in Chapter 8, are undertaken in the context of joint productive activity, although the relevant agreements are vertical rather than horizontal. In its 1984 *Jefferson Parish* decision a bare five-Justice majority cited *stare decisis* concerns for refusing to reject the per se rule, although they exonerated the defendant for other reasons.

But *California Dental's* discussion of antitrust rules indicates that it is never too late for a court to revise its views about a certain class of situations. Inertia alone is not sufficient to warrant intervention when there is a reasonable basis for thinking that more complete analysis will produce a different result. The per se rule against tying was predicated on the judicial experience such as it existed in the 1940s that "tying agreements serve hardly any purpose beyond the suppression of competition."[42] Subsequent experience has been significantly to the contrary. Most tying arrangements are efficient mechanisms for organizing distribution of one's good or service in order to increase consumer satisfaction, prevent free riding, or meter the use of intellectual property rights. The rule of reason is the only way to distinguish the small minority of arrangements that are legitimately anticompetitive.

In this case, the per se rule has forced the courts to go through expensive and bizarre contortions in order to restrict the domain of per se unlawful ties—applying rule of reason-like criteria while nominally expressing a per se rule. A rule of reason inquiry in tying cases would simply consider (1) whether the firm imposing the tie had sufficient power to force an anticompetitive arrangement, (2) whether the tie foreclosed a sufficiently large part of the tied market to force competitor exit or significantly increased costs, and (3) whether the arrangement was unnecessarily harmful to rivals in light of any proffered justifications. This modification in antitrust doctrine would save many millions of dollars annually in legal fees and administrative costs.

MINIMUM RESALE PRICE MAINTENANCE (RPM). Most of the observations just made about tying arrangements also apply to resale price maintenance. While it is nominally illegal per se, the courts have construed RPM narrowly by distinguishing unilateral from collaborative conduct,[43] and by defining "price" very strictly.[44] Once again, academic thinking has been almost uniformly hostile to the per se rule, with the majority favoring a rule of reason approach to RPM and a minority suggesting per se legality.[45] Most instances of resale price maintenance are beneficial to consumers and cannot be reasonably construed as efforts to restrain trade or monopolize any product or service. The analytic methodology outlined above allows no place for a per se rule against RPM. Once again, it would be perverse to apply a per se rule to a purely vertical practice affecting only the producer's own brand, while insisting on proof of actual output effects in challenges to competitor collaborations that pose a much more serious threat of competitive harm.

Conclusion

The following chapters consider the rules that should be applied to various types of antitrust violations. For each the relevant question is: Given what we know about this kind of practice, what is the best way to treat it in a world where knowledge is incomplete, fact finding costly, rule making highly imperfect, and judicial institutions cumbersome? At all times we must remember that if we believe that markets generally work well when left alone, then intervention is justified only in the relatively few cases where the judiciary can fix the problem more reliably, more cheaply, or more quickly than the market can fix itself.

6

Combinations of Competitors

Agreements among competitors are the most suspect class of antitrust conduct. Firms deal with customers and suppliers daily. By contrast, agreements among competitors are both more suspicious and less frequent, making them easier to observe. In addition, for a single firm to obtain significant market power is difficult and costly, and most fail in the attempt. As a result persistent monopoly is rare and exists only under narrowly defined structural conditions. However, a cartel of competitors can create market power quickly and cheaply. This means that collusion can be profitable even if it is imperfect or lasts a short time. Many markets that are not prone to structural monopoly may be the targets of collusion.

This hardly means that all or even most agreements among rivals should be unlawful. Many agreements are reasonably "ancillary" to other activities, such as coordinated research or production, and are profitable because they reduce firms' costs or improve their products. Ever since Judge William H. Taft's famous 1898 decision in the *Addyston Pipe* case, antitrust has divided the world of horizontal agreements into "naked" and "ancillary" restraints.[1] A naked agreement is not accompanied by any significant integration of production and its profitability depends on power over price.

Consider two different agreements between Farmer Brown and Farmer Green. If they simply agreed to charge twenty-five cents more for a bushel of corn, they would fail because even two very large farmers produce a trivial output in relation to the entire market. They would sell no corn at the higher price. This agreement is "naked" because its profitability depends on the exercise of market power, which they lack. But suppose they agreed to build an irrigation well serving both their properties, or to share an expensive piece of equipment such as a large tractor. These agreements *could* be profitable, because their success does not depend on the farmers' power over price, but only on their ability to reduce their costs by sharing a costly input.

Today the law of horizontal restraints is muddled by two quite different problems. The first is proof of agreement in cases involving naked restraints. The second is the proper use of the rule of reason for ancillary restraints.

Proving Naked Agreements

Section 1 of the Sherman Act condemns every "contract," "combination," or "conspiracy" that restrains trade. While those terms had distinctive common law usages, today they all mean about the same thing; namely, there must be a proven "agreement" among firms to fix prices, divide markets, boycott outsiders, or engage in some other anticompetitive activity. Over the last two decades conspiracy doctrine has been frustrated by overly expansive readings of the Supreme Court's *Matsushita* decision, which required strong evidence of a conspiracy before plaintiffs could take their cartel claims to a jury.[2]

One reason the courts have had difficulty writing conspiracy rules is that lawyers and economists understand the concept so differently. For lawyers, collusion consists mainly of communicated words. To be sure, there are plenty of common law contract decisions in which acceptances are communicated by conduct. I may offer you $1,000 to paint my house. You say nothing, but the next day you show up with a paintbrush and demand payment when you are finished. Courts are generally willing to infer an agreement from an express offer plus a silent acceptance, but that is about as far as the common law is willing to stretch nonverbal behavior. It almost never inferred *both* an offer and an acceptance from completely nonverbal conduct.

In contrast, when industrial organization economists think of collusion, their minds typically do not call up "contracts." Rather, they think of "games" or "strategies," and these are typically much less verbal than a lawyer's idea of agreement will permit. The lawyer's understanding of collusion is fundamentally subjective, while the economist's is fundamentally objective. The lawyer looks for words, or sometimes actions, that can be said to constitute "assent" or "offer and acceptance." However, the economist tends to look at the structure of the market, the position of the firms in it, and then ask what the maximizing strategy would be for each firm. Economic theories of oligopoly pricing, such as the one developed by Augustin Cournot in the nineteenth century and widely used, do not depend at all on either verbal communication or any knowledge about someone else's subjective state of mind. The Cournot firm, which wishes to maximize its own profits, first observes the output of rival firms and then selects its own profit-maximizing rate of output. Words are unnecessary. Indeed, the theory can predict the firms' joint price and output quite apart from any communications they might have with rivals. The theory rests instead on economic knowledge about the conditions facing the firm, a consideration of alternative strategies, and finally a selection of the strategy that is likely to produce the greatest profit.

In concentrated markets with fungible products and observable prices firms may reach a tacit understanding about output, and thus price, without ever engaging in verbal communication with one another. In other cases the courts observe communications among competitors but the communications themselves are incomplete in that they do not include all the elements of a traditional contract.[3] When agreements are unlawful, firms communicate no more than necessary to reach an understanding. Furthermore, the structure of the market may enable firms to reach an understanding on the basis of far less communication than they would need in a more competitively structured market.

The following principles provide some guidance for determining when antitrust intervention is warranted on the basis of interdependent pricing but only incomplete evidence of a traditional agreement:

First, in markets that are highly prone to oligopoly behavior, agreement cannot be inferred from *mere* matching of publicly known prices.

Second, when a market is conducive toward oligopolistic or cartel behavior, but only imperfectly, the firms in it may develop "facilitating practices," which are communications (often nonverbal) that make the cartel work better; the facilitators themselves can be evidence of agreement.

Third, when information and decision making are imperfect, a price-fixing agreement is more readily found when collusion is rational under the circumstances and the conduct has little or no offsetting social value.

Fourth, failing to find an agreement on the basis of a certain type of cartel-facilitating conduct gives firms an incentive to engage in that conduct.

"Simple" and More Complex Price-Matching

On the first point, implicit in condemnation of any practice under the antitrust laws is that the defendant was obliged to behave in some other way than it did. When natural market conditions come very close to those that obtain in a pure Cournot oligopoly, then firms may have little choice but to set their prices in a certain way. Consider four gasoline stations on the four corners of a busy intersection. Price is communicated by large signs, rendering them immediately known to both drivers and rivals. The signs are probably necessary because motorists like to see gas prices before they enter a station. Any firm that fails to match a price cut initiated by one of the other firms, or that increases its own price, will immediately lose many sales. As a result any firm that is thinking about cutting its price below that of the others can confidently predict that the cut will be immediately matched. The cut will not generate very much new business but will maintain market shares at a lower price. Furthermore, gasoline is a fungible product, subject to some differences in branding but not in performance, basic technology, or costs of production. Most motorists know this. In such a setting it would be counterproductive to find that the firms acted unlawfully just because they matched prices. They may have little choice except to match.

But strict oligopoly behavior is probably "inherent" in only a few markets. Judge Richard Posner began arguing in the 1960s that the Cournot oligopoly theory that had dominated Harvard School antitrust analysis had to yield to a more finessed understanding of concentrated markets that considered strategic alternatives. Posner was influenced by Nobel laureate economist George J. Stigler, who argued that markets differ in numerous ways that classic Cournot theory did not capture, mainly in the means and speed by which information is communicated. Orthodox oligopoly theory may be an adequate explanatory model when each firm in a concentrated market has instant and reliable information about the output or pricing decisions of rivals. But once these assumptions are relaxed, maintaining the oligopoly equilibrium becomes more difficult. For example, if firms are able to make secret price cuts or provide other consumer benefits that are not immediately detected, they will have a greater incentive to cut. Price will fall and output will rise toward the competitive level. What Posner added to this is that firms in a "poorly functioning" Cournot oligopoly will have strong incentives to make the oligopoly function better, by manipulating the way in which information is communicated. While antitrust cannot do much about the structure itself, which is generally dictated by production efficiencies, it can pursue these efforts to regiment the industry.[4]

Thus anticompetitive behavior is not necessarily inherent in any market structure. Even in concentrated markets firms will naturally try to find ways of competing. *Avoidance* of competition is what requires the special effort. Furthermore, in many cases these avoidance efforts can with only modest tweaking be characterized as Sherman Act "agreements." Judge Posner notes that even the common law has found some nonverbal behavior sufficient to form a contract. He writes:

> [1] If someone advertises in a newspaper that he will pay $10 to the person who finds and returns his dog, anyone who meets the condition has an enforceable claim against him to the promised reward.

He then proposes this variation:

> [2] If seller A restricts his output in the expectation that B will do likewise, and B restricts his output in a like expectation there is a literal meeting of the minds—a mutual understanding—even if there is no overt communication.[5]

The common law routinely found contracts based on a silent act in response to a sufficiently explicit offer.[6] The Supreme Court found a "conspiracy" on analogous facts in the famous *Interstate Circuit* case, in which an express offer communicated simultaneously to eight firms plus their silent but factually clear acceptance was held to constitute a Sherman Act conspiracy among the firms.[7]

Nevertheless, there is considerable distance between Posner's examples [1] and [2]. In the second case *both* the "offer" and the "acceptance" are implied. The common law, with its focus on buyer-seller agreements, almost never went that far. In Judge Posner's second example the "offer" almost certainly lacks sufficient specificity to lead to a binding contract. Firm A restricts its output. By how much? Is this an offer to B to restrict output by the same absolute amount? the same percentage of its sales? To reduce output to the Cournot level? to the cartel level? or something else?[8]

But such strictness may be requiring too much when the "agreement" at issue is between rivals and we have a pretty good idea of how rational actors would act in a given situation. While a court should not condemn firms after observing nothing more than an output reduction followed by competitor matching, a small amount of additional evidence should be sufficient.

Today our understanding of Sherman Act agreements is driven excessively by the lawyers' conception of a common law contract. But the law of contracts was never developed with reference to arrangements involving competitors. Most common law contracts are commercial ones between vertically related firms—that is, between buyers and sellers. Theories about competitor behavior, such as Cournot's theory of oligopoly, apply only to relationships among rivals. This difference is important because all contracts are "incomplete" in the sense that they do not take every conceivable contingency into account. Depending on what happens that gives rise to a dispute, courts often have to "fill in the gaps," or reconstruct portions of the agreement.

Filling in contractual gaps is largely a matter of objective reconstruction from the circumstances. Relatively determinate blanks are filled in while more ambiguous ones are not. For example, the Uniform Commercial Code permits a court to fill in a missing price term with a "reasonable" price, but not a missing quantity term.[9] That pair of rules makes perfect sense because price can often be reconstructed from objective market factors, but quantity typically cannot. For example, if the price of corn on a given day in late 2005 is $2.30 per bushel, we can expect that most sales will occur close to that price. Quantity is a different matter. One buyer may take 500 bushels, another 5,000, and another 50,000. In the case of price the court fills the gap, not by looking for the intent of the parties (it could do that for both price and quantity), but rather by asking what a reasonable (i.e., profit-maximizing) buyer and seller would likely have agreed about when bargaining for a good with an objectively identifiable price.

Cartel contracts are highly likely to be incomplete for the simple reason that they are illegal. While firms go to great lengths to preserve evidence of their lawful agreements, they go to equally great lengths to avoid an evidentiary trail of unlawful ones. Furthermore, when we move from buyer-seller relationships to relationships among competitors, *both* price and quantity can become relatively determinate numbers, particularly if the market contains few sellers. To be sure, the terms are not always as definite as the price term in a contract for the sale of corn on a given day, but they are much more determinate than the missing quantity term in that same agreement. The criteria that courts use to fill the gaps in incomplete buyer-seller contracts could be tailored to apply to competitor agreements, and the result would be increased willingness to infer Sherman Act conspiracies from purely objective evidence.

There is one other important difference between cartel and buy-sell agreements. In the latter case the purpose of filling in gaps is to enforce the contract, which the court cannot do without reconstructing the terms with a fair degree of confidence. By contrast, in the cartel case the court is seeking to identify an agreement only for the purposes of condemning it. The amount of information one needs to enforce an agreement is considerably greater than the amount one needs to strike it down. The former requires a basis for establishing the precise terms, while the latter requires only a sufficient basis for concluding that an agreement exists (proof of damages may require more, but that is a different issue).

So an agreement can be inferred from additional actions that firms take in order to make an oligopoly market more stable or to raise prices from the oligopoly level to the cartel, or monopoly, level. Nevertheless, the fact remains that the Sherman Act requires an *agreement,* and an agreement cannot be inferred simply from pricing interdependence or prices higher than cost in concentrated markets. Economists commonly say that in such markets an equilibrium exists at an above-cost price level, and a firm that is charging that equilibrium price is simply acting in its individual best interest, given the situation that it is facing.

Facilitators in Cartel-Prone Markets

Courts are more willing to fill gaps in incomplete contracts when they can approximate from market circumstances what the parties would have bargained for had they been more explicit. In commercial buyer-seller agreements the price of commodities can often be inferred from market data; quantity cannot be. This basic doctrine can be tailored for proof of cartel agreements: the more rational an agreement is under the circumstances and the more certainty we have about what the terms of such an agreement would be, the more readily we can infer its existence from incomplete evidence.

A "facilitator" is a condition or practice designed to make a concentrated market operate more like a well-functioning oligopoly or cartel. Oligopolies work best when the following conditions obtain:

a. The market has a small number of significant players, small enough that one firm's change in output has a measurable effect on the profits of the other firms. Presumptively, a maximum of five or six seems about right, although more explicit cartels can work with larger numbers.

b. Fellow oligopolists can readily observe their rivals' true prices. By "true prices" I mean the price that is actually charged and not the nominal price prior to any individually negotiated discounts, secret rebates, and the like. The latter tend to undermine collusion. Few things make a price cut in an oligopoly market less appealing than an intending cutter's knowledge that the cut will be immediately recognized and matched by rivals. As a result courts should be suspicious of arrangements in concentrated markets that serve to bring prices out into the open when they would not otherwise be. The qualifier is important, however. Many markets, such as consumer air travel and retail gasoline, can function in their present form only if everyone is able to observe prices, and this means competitors as well as consumers. In addition, customers may want public information about prices. For example, published advance price lists may aid wholesale purchasers in their own business planning.

c. The product is fungible or the differences pertain mainly to branding or cosmetic factors. As an example of the latter, ready-to-eat breakfast cereals may seem very different from one another, perhaps more so to a three-year-old than to an adult. In fact, they use different proportions of common ingredients such as sugar, wheat, corn, or oats; different food colorings; different extruders in the mixing machine to produce different shapes; and, of course, lots of different packaging and advertising. They are generally produced with the same technology. These differences are unlikely to undermine collusion attempts significantly, although price-fixing may be more difficult than it is in the market for a perfectly fungible product such as cement. By contrast, products like television programming, computer software, or aircraft may differ greatly, not merely in features but also in complexity and cost of development.

Judge Posner proposes a longer list of factors, which is probably more accurate as an abstract proposition, but also more difficult for courts to manage. He would have courts consider the absence of a competitive fringe capable of increasing output, entry that takes a long time, unconcentrated buyers, a standardized and nondurable product, a high ratio of fixed to variable costs, similar cost structures and production processes, static or falling demand, prices that can be changed quickly, the use of sealed bids, local markets, the existence of lawful cooperative practices, and a record of antitrust problems.[10] Requiring all of these seems unnecessary, given that collusive groups can be readily and cheaply formed, but the more factors that are present the more willing a court should be to infer collusion from nonverbal evidence.

Reaching facilitators created by explicit agreement is relatively easy because then the agreement requirement is met for the facilitator itself. Examples are agreements to post prices; to post prices and adhere to them for a specified time; agreed methodologies for computing freight charges or credit terms; and product standardization agreements that are unnecessary for purposes of quality control. The courts routinely condemn such agreements.[11]

The more ambiguous situations involve practices that may be facilitators, but appear to be imposed unilaterally. Other market characteristics may suggest that collusion is occurring. Judge Posner would permit the following conditions and practices to be presented as evidence of price-fixing, even in the absence of explicit evidence of an agreement: (a) fixed relative market shares; (b) marketwide price discrimination; (c) exchanges of price information; (d) regional price variations; (e) identical bids; (f) price, output, and capacity changes at the formation of the cartel; (g) industrywide resale price maintenance; (h) declining market shares of leaders; (i) responsiveness and amplitude of price changes;

(j) demand that is elastic at the market price; (k) level and pattern of profits; (l) market price that is inversely correlated with the number of firms or elasticity of demand; (m) basing-point pricing; and (n) the existence of exclusionary practices.[12]

Determining the presence or significance of some of these factors, such as marketwide price discrimination or the relationship between elasticity of market demand and the price, can pose formidable administrative difficulties. In addition, inferences of price-fixing would be stronger or weaker depending on the number of these practices that are found and other market conditions. For example, systematic price discrimination is suspicious in a market for a fungible product, but not in markets for differentiated products.

Rationality and Inference of Collusion

The third point in the above list of policy factors is that a court can more readily infer a Sherman Act "agreement" from nonverbal conduct when price-fixing seems rational under the circumstances and the conduct has little redeeming social value. The entire antitrust enterprise is dedicated to the proposition that business firms behave rationally. Indeed, if they did not do so as a general matter our market economy would crash. Furthermore, in all aspects of our experience we require less evidence to create an inference that something entirely rational has happened than that something very unusual has occurred. Antitrust is no exception.

The issue in the Supreme Court's *Matsushita* case was the amount and quality of evidence necessary to permit a jury to decide that collusion occurred. Some courts have read *Matsushita* as requiring a certain quantum of evidence of *verbal agreement* before summary judgment is required. *Matsushita*, however, never insisted on any particular kind of evidence of collusion, but only that the evidence be sufficient to make collusion a likely explanation of the activity before the court. Circumstantial evidence is sufficient.[13] *Matsushita* spoke in the context of an alleged expensive and improbable twenty-year-long predatory pricing conspiracy—something that no rational firm would be likely to undertake. The Court responded by requiring high-quality evidence before such a case could be given to a jury. The flip side, of course, is that when the conspiracy claim is rather plausible, less evidence is required.[14]

Failure to account for the distinction between rational and irrational conspiracies has led several courts to dismiss conspiracy claims incorrectly. For example, the *Blomkest* case involved the market for potash, a generic ingredient in fertilizer. The demand for potash is relatively inelastic at the competitive price, which means that demand would not fall very much in response to a price increase above that level. However, the firms had competed aggressively and profits in the industry were low. There was plenty of evidence that the firms had the motive and an opportunity to conspire. There were also memoranda suggesting that joint action had been contemplated by individual firms. Then a sudden change in pricing patterns occurred, with the market quickly adopting higher prices and becoming more profitable. In addition, there was a great deal of evidence that one firm freely solicited price-fixing, and one rival frequently complained to another rival about the latter's failure to adhere to its published price lists. The CEO of one firm even went to officers at another firm, carrying charts showing that the CEO's firm was losing market share to rivals and asking what they would do about it. In one case a firm apologized to another firm for making a low bid and stealing the second firm's customer. The court faulted reliance on this evidence because it "assumes a conspiracy first, and then sets out to 'prove' it."[15] The court would not permit a conspiracy to be inferred from the structural and behavioral evidence as augmented by the evidence of explicit communications. Rather, it wanted communications that established the conspiracy first.

Given a market structure highly conducive to collusion, and the fact that none of this conduct appears to have any positive social value, a jury should have been permitted to consider the evidence. The majority misread the evidence as "based on a theory of conscious parallelism." But conscious parallelism is what occurs when firms reach a price consensus *without* explicitly communicating about anything. Cajoling competitors into adhering to their posted price lists, or reprimanding them when they steal sales, is not conscious parallelism; it is collusion. The combination of market structure and history and these communications was more than enough to create an inference of agreement.

Too few courts have paid attention to the important distinction between rational and irrational conspiracy claims. Contrast Judge Posner's decision in the *High Fructose* case. Under his approach, if the market structure indicates that the alleged conduct is improbable because the costs and risks are high in relation to the payoff, then he would follow

Matsushita and insist on strong evidence that the conduct occurred. However, *Matsushita* itself said very little about proof requirements when structural evidence indicates that the offense is quite plausible and would be profitable for the defendants.[16]

Courts should also be less reluctant to condemn a business practice that has no obvious social (as opposed to purely private) benefits. This is the main reason proof standards for unlawful exclusionary practices by dominant firms are so high. Most of the practices challenged as monopolistic are socially ambiguous on first look. For example, while properly defined predatory pricing is anticompetitive, the great majority of aggressive price cuts benefit consumers. While a few patent practices are anticompetitive, most are consistent with the Patent Act's policy of encouraging invention. A court that condemns such behavior too quickly may be chilling or preventing socially desirable conduct.

By contrast, for rivals to coax each other not to undercut their published prices, as in the *Blomkest* case, is socially useless behavior. About the best thing to be said for it is that in a competitive market it would not be effective; but if it has any effects at all, they are bad. Faced with such facts a court need not hesitate to find an unlawful agreement. There is little danger that a false positive is going to discourage socially useful conduct.

Creating Bad Incentives

When a court approves certain activities, such as those that occurred in *Blomkest,* it effectively gives future, similarly situated, firms a license to do the same thing. For example, that case held that complaints to competitors that they were undercutting prices were insufficient to establish collusion, apparently because they were not accompanied by statements of assent. Such decisions make it extremely easy for colluders to avoid liability simply by ensuring that they suppress the most obvious evidence of offer and assent.

Joint Ventures, Trade Associations, and the Rule of Reason

A joint venture is a form of organization in which two or more firms produce some input jointly that they would otherwise have produced individually, acquired on the market, or perhaps done without. A joint venture can involve any aspect of a firm's business, including production, distribution, or research. For example, computer manufacturers might establish a jointly owned plant to manufacture processor chips. Physicians might share a laboratory for analyzing tissue samples. Or two bicycle manufacturers might jointly establish a dealership for both their brands. Information is also an "input" into production, and many joint ventures involve the creation, provision, or exchange of information.

Economically, trade and professional associations are joint ventures. Their members typically are firms producing a product or service. In general, trade associations exchange information so that their members can make more informed market decisions, but they also engage in rule making and standard setting for their industries. Professional associations, such as the American Medical Association or the American Bar Association, may also regulate conduct, including advertising, and some are involved in licensing. Most lobby all levels of government for favorable legislation. As with other joint ventures, the great majority of trade associations' activities are procompetitive, but there are a few exceptions.

Antitrust analysis of restraints in joint venture agreements is very different from the problem of proving collusion. In the naked cartel cases the agreements at issue are unreasonable if they exist, and the main question is whether they exist. In most of the joint venture cases the existence of *an* agreement is not disputed, although it may not be the particular agreement that is being challenged.

While joint ventures of competitors are sometimes analogized to horizontal mergers, most are more complex and correspondingly difficult to evaluate. A merger is typically a complete union of two firms.[17] We know in advance that firms participating in the merger will "fix" price and output once the merger is completed. After a merger there is only a single firm and its individual units lack pricing discretion. We generally evaluate mergers by studying the market's postmerger structure. In general, a merger that reduces the number of significant players in a market to three or four or fewer is likely to cause trouble if entry into the market is difficult and other factors suggest that collusion is likely.

Antitrust analysis of joint ventures is also likely to consider market structure and the relative size of the venture. But we must similarly look at its purpose, the types of rules it makes for its members, and the incentives that it creates. Because joint ventures can be almost as varied as people's imaginations permit, evaluating them is not as formulaic as the analysis of mergers has become. For example, while a merger of any two significant firms in a five-firm market might be unlawful, a joint venture of these two firms or even all of them need not be of concern, depending on the venture's activities. For example, all five firms could probably engage in a research joint venture that left each firm free to make individual choices about how to use the innovations produced by the venture. In contrast, a venture among two of them that created a common sales agency and forbade the members from making extra-venture sales might be regarded as little more than a cartel.

The following list of litigated cases illustrates the great variety of ancillary horizontal agreements:

- The NCAA's member colleges agree to permit its teams to televise only two games a year, or to limit the salaries paid to coaches.[18]
- General Motors and Toyota agree to produce 30,000 cars annually at a jointly run plant, but without any restriction on their production in separately owned plants.[19]
- Developers of a common brand agree to market it in exclusive territories.[20]
- A trade or professional association (a) sets qualifications for membership or standards for products;[21] or (b) supplies the group with information about the price and output of individual members, or with information about problems with particular suppliers or customers;[22] or (c) restrains its members' price and quality advertising, citing a concern for preventing misleading advertising.[23]
- A joint venture of banks issues a general purpose credit card, and its members agree that none of them will issue a competing card.[24]
- A joint purchasing venture expels a member without explanation.[25]
- A joint venture of physicians offers an employer-paid health plan, agreeing in advance on the maximum fees its member physicians will charge.[26]
- Several thousand owners of performance rights in recorded music, acting through a common agent, issue "blanket" licenses permitting radio stations to play any song they own without prior notification.[27]
- A commodity exchange run by a group of brokers agrees that,

while its members may engage in after-hours trading, they may do so only at the last closing price of the regular market session.[28]

The very ubiquity and variety of joint ventures may have led Justice Brandeis to conclude in the *Chicago Board* case discussed in the last chapter that rule of reason analysis requires knowledge about the entire history of the industry. But what one really wants to know is the impact of a particular restraint on output, with output measured by the number of units, their quality, or occasionally their price. This requires us to examine two things—the venture's power, and the effects of its rules on market output.

The very first cartel case the Supreme Court considered really involved a complex joint venture, and the Supreme Court acted too quickly in granting the government's request to dissolve it. The *Trans-Missouri* case was a challenge to an eighteen-railroad joint operating arrangement, such as was quite common in the second half of the nineteenth century.[29] Before the age of significant government regulation these "traffic associations" coordinated runs so as to facilitate the transfer of cargo, developed freight classifications, and promulgated equipment standards for such things as the width, or gauge, of track. As the lower court observed in its decision that refused to condemn the restraints:

> The fact that the business of railway companies is irretrievably interwoven, that they interchange cars and traffic, that they act as agents for each other in the delivery and receipt of freight and in paying and collecting freight charges, and that commodities received for transportation generally pass through the hands of several carriers, renders it of vital importance to the public that uniform rules and regulations governing railway traffic should be framed by those who have a practical acquaintance with the subject.[30]

These attributes of railroading made cooperation necessary if small railroads were to piece their operations together into a workable regional system. Whether price-fixing was an essential part of the venture remains unclear. If a package had to be shipped to a location requiring the participation of several railroads, the freight agent had to be able to calculate the freight quickly—and with pencil and paper, not a computer. But even if price-fixing was not essential to the joint venture's operations, the appropriate remedy would have been not to dissolve the venture, as the government requested, but rather to issue an injunction against the price-fixing. This would permit the parties to coordinate other aspects of their business, such as scheduling and cargo transfers, but forbid them from setting prices.

The *Trans-Missouri* case illustrates both the promise and the threat of joint ventures. On the one hand, a venture enables a group of firms to do something jointly more efficiently, or to produce a more desirable product, than each firm could do acting alone. In an era of largely single-state railroads, shipping a package from Detroit to Omaha could require the participation of four or five different railroads. A well-functioning venture could greatly improve service by coordinating schedules, transfers, and the like. But that same venture would have an incentive, and perhaps even the need, to fix prices on interstate shipments. Furthermore, most of the region's railroads were in the venture, and railroad transportation had a significant advantage over alternatives, mainly barges and horse-drawn vehicles. So the venture's collective membership almost certainly had enough market power to make cartel pricing work. Antitrust's obligation is to sort out the practices that threaten competition and determine whether these can be stopped without undermining the venture's beneficial practices; and if not, determine whether the venture is worth preserving anyway.

Assessing the Threat of Joint Venture Collusion

The antitrust threat of joint ventures is that they will facilitate monopoly pricing among their members. This requires the venture to reduce marketwide output. To do so, a joint venture's members have to be able to do two things simultaneously. First, they must reduce their own collective output. Second, they must keep the output of others out of the market. Figure 6.1 illustrates.

Point *A* represents the competitive price and output, while point *B* represents the monopoly price and output. The bracket along the bottom of the figure marked *C* represents the output that the venture must keep out of the market if it is to sustain a monopoly price. Remember, the venture need not do this perfectly in order to be both profitable and anticompetitive. A venture policy that succeeded in keeping two-thirds of the *C*-bracket output off the market could be both highly profitable and impose significant costs on society. Nevertheless, output increases into the *C*-bracket area tend to move price back to the competitive level, regardless of where the additional output comes from. The venture will be injured by its own members' output increases into the *C*-bracket area, but also by output increases that occur when outside firms enter the market or competing nonparticipants increase their output.

The figure suggests that when analyzing a joint venture we need to

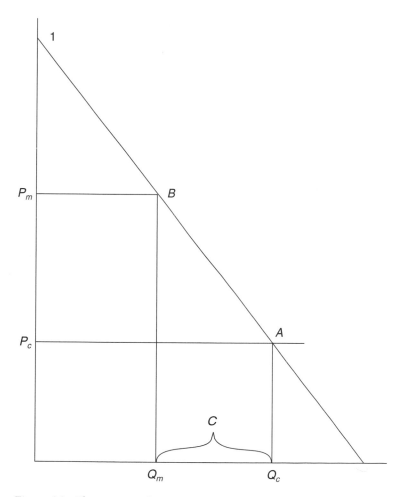

Figure 6.1. The antitrust threat posed by joint ventures

look at both the venture's structure and its rules, focusing on three "power" questions: (1) what is the members' aggregate power to reduce market output?; (2) to what extent does the venture limit the output of its own members?; and (3) to what extent does the venture operate to keep rivals (nonmembers of the venture) out of the market?

The first question is structural, examining the market in which the venture is contained and the relative position of the venture within that market. Before a venture will have the power to reduce marketwide output it must control a fair share of the relevant market—in most cases, 60 percent or more. In addition, the market must be reasonably protected from new entry and the venture reasonably capable of restraining the output of nonmembers. This structural inquiry is similar to the one we make in monopolization cases, although the power and entry barrier thresholds are not as high, given that the venture poses more immediate dangers to competition.

The second question looks at the venture's output rules for its own members. Some ventures give their members unlimited power to make "nonventure" sales, while others severely restrict or even prohibit them. As examples of the first, consider the *Broadcast Music, Inc. (BMI)* and *Maricopa* cases. *BMI* involved an association of more than 20,000 performance right holders who collectively licensed their copyrights through an agent to radio stations that wanted immediate access to a large repertory. Before they could share the revenue from a blanket license, however, the members had to agree on prices. *Maricopa* involved an arrangement among 1,750 physicians to offer a health plan in which each physician agreed in advance on the maximum fee he or she would charge. The Supreme Court approved the *BMI* arrangement but condemned the *Maricopa* arrangement, concerned that the avowed maximum price-fixing plan might also involve disguised minimums.[31]

The Court got *BMI* right but probably erred in *Maricopa*. Both of the arrangements were nonexclusive in the sense that any member of the venture was freely permitted to make unlimited nonventure sales. The threat of a marketwide output reduction largely disappears if members are free to make all the nonventure sales they want at any price they choose. The cartel price, point *B* in Figure 6.1, is well above costs and highly profitable for the members. Unless restrained, they will begin making additional sales into the *C*-bracket area and continue to expand all the way to point *A*, where price and output are restored to the competitive level. Of course, we must be sure that joint venture members really are free and able to make unlimited nonventure sales. In both *BMI* and *Maricopa* that seems assured by the fact that these ventures had a very large membership and publicly announced nonexclusivity policies. We might be more suspicious of a smaller venture that is nominally nonexclusive but in fact is able to put pressure on members to do business only inside the venture.

Naked and Ancillary Joint Venture Exclusions

As noted, the C-bracket output in Figure 6.1 can come from two different sources, the output of members or that of nonmembers. In order to keep price above the competitive level the venture must restrain its own members' output, but it must also prevent the output of nonmembers from getting into the market.

Depending on its purpose, a joint venture's efforts to keep others out of the market can range from nothing at all to complete market exclusion. For example, two farmers involved in a tractor-sharing joint venture literally do not care if a neighbor starts growing corn in competition with them. No single farmer's production decision has any measurable effect on their profits. At the other extreme, a market-dominating trade association whose members are fixing prices may use membership rules as a means to exclude price cutters or new firms. Many antitrust cases involving cartels have been challenges to boycotts. For example, a cartel of lumber retailers might attempt to prevent lumber producers from entering the market. Or a group of car dealers might persuade their supplier not to sell to other dealers who cut prices.[32]

Exclusivity, however, is not always a bad thing. It may be necessary to create competitive incentives or assure quality control. As a result antitrust condones many "ancillary" concerted refusals. The most clearly justified exclusion occurs with fixed membership joint ventures. A lawyers' or pediatricians' partnership has the right to choose its members and need not take everyone who claims to be qualified. Even professional sports leagues, which do occasionally take on new teams, cannot be obliged to admit every team that wants to join.[33] A universal admissions rule would tend to create large, single joint ventures, but competition in most markets would be furthered if several joint ventures competed against each other. Furthermore, a broad admission-granting rule would create perverse incentives. Firms would refuse to join ventures during the early period when money must be poured in and the risk of failure is high. After all, the antitrust laws would provide them with a right to join later, when success has been assured.

More fundamentally, determining the correct size of any organization is not antitrust's mission, and is way outside the scope of its competence. If six patent lawyers want to form an intellectual property practice and believe six partners are large enough, would anyone think that a court could make a better decision, perhaps determining that the firm should have seven or eight members instead?

"Open membership" joint ventures present a different problem, because they often end up dominating markets and sometimes use membership rules to suppress competition. An open membership venture does not have a predefined number of members; rather, it sets membership criteria and qualified members can join. The AMA, the National Restaurant Association, and the American Plastics Council are all examples.

Local real estate boards are one example of open membership ventures that have provoked antitrust problems. Such boards typically accept all licensed real estate brokers or agents as members. The board may also provide valuable network services that are virtually impossible to duplicate outside the venture. For example, the real estate multiple listing service (MLS) is a continuously updated database showing all of the listed real properties for sale in the board's service area. A broker without access to the MLS is at such a competitive disadvantage that he may be unable to survive. But suppose that the board makes the MLS available only to its members, and then surreptitiously bases membership on the broker's willingness to charge a certain commission on sales. In that case the real estate board has employed board membership, which everyone agrees is socially beneficial, as a cartel device. The solution is not to dissolve the board, but to make clear through injunction or damages actions that board membership cannot be conditioned on a member's agreement to keep commissions high.[34]

The *Visa* case raised similar issues, although restraints on innovation, not price-fixing, were the greater danger. Visa and MasterCard are joint ventures of financial institutions that issue general purpose credit cards, which most adults carry. Any bank qualified to carry national deposit insurance may issue a Visa, MasterCard, or both. Virtually every significant bank in the United States has done so, some 20,000 of them. Both ventures forbade their member banks from issuing any competitor's credit card, but excepted the other venture's card. That is, the Visa rule permitted a Visa member bank to issue a MasterCard, but not any other card, and the MasterCard rule worked vice versa. The result was that no other general purpose credit card could be issued by virtually the entire United States banking system, and banks have many advantages in credit card issuance. Existing general purpose cards, such as American Express and Discover, had to operate their own separate financial networks for dealing with merchants, and it was much more difficult for any new card issuer to come into the market, since a financial network would have to be built from scratch. Discover was the only new entrant into the market in nearly half a century, and large firms such as AT&T and Citibank did entry studies but decided that the investment, thought to exceed $1 billion, would be unlikely to pay off.[35]

What can be said in defense of a private rule that excludes so many rivals and potential rivals from the market? One possibility is free riding. For example, banks might use information gleaned from their affiliation with Visa to service a new card. However, the exception for MasterCard illustrates either that free riding is not a problem or else that it can be managed effectively; that is, if Visa can protect its information investment from MasterCard, it can do so equally well from others. In any event, Visa was unable to produce evidence of significant free riding that its exclusivity rule would prevent.

While member banks compete on prices (interest rates and other service fees and terms), the effective inability of new general card products to enter the market had been a major restraint on innovation. The government offered evidence that various types of encrypted, or "smart," cards were technologically available but the industry had been slow to adopt them. Whether such technologies would actually be adopted is uncertain, although foreign countries that did not have the exclusion rules enjoyed significantly greater card competition. In any event, once a significant restraint without an adequate explanation is found, it is not up to antitrust to provide the details of how innovation will work its way out in some future unrestrained market. Antitrust's task is finished when it opens up the market so that competition can chart its course.

Plausibility and the Burden of Proof

One of the most perplexing issues in the antitrust law of joint ventures has been assignment of the burden of proof. In general, of course, we say that plaintiffs must prove all elements of their claim. But courts in fact assign burdens of proof in different ways depending on such factors as control of the evidence or the motives for producing it.

If evidence were always both perfect and completely available, assignment of the burden of proof would make little difference. The evidence would be there, it would be available to either side, and whoever had the burden would bring it forward. Assignment of the burden becomes an issue when there is some chance that the evidence is imperfect—that is, it may not be sufficient to establish a fact issue one way or the other. The greater the likelihood of an evidentiary failure, the more important assignment of the proof burden becomes. In the extreme case, assignment of the proof burden decides the issue. Whoever has the burden of proof will lose.

As a result an important factor in deciding how proof burdens should be assigned is plausibility. The burden of proof should generally be given to the party with the claim that is hardest to believe. If the plaintiff's claim is implausible, make him prove it. If a defense seems far-fetched, make the defendant come forward with the evidence supporting it. If market structure makes anticompetitive results seem highly unlikely, then require that the plaintiff prove the contrary; or, alternatively, if structural evidence makes the practice look suspicious, force the defendant to show why it should be exonerated.

Suppose there is a 20 percent chance that a certain body of questionable evidence, once produced, will show that a restraint is competitive. There is an 80 percent chance that the evidence will not prove anything at all. Our other information about the restraint makes it highly suspicious, and leads us to think there is an 80–20 chance that it is anticompetitive. Giving the plaintiff the burden on this issue produces the wrong answer 80 percent of the time that the evidence fails, or 64 percent of the time (80 × 80). By contrast, assigning the burden to the defendant means that we will get the wrong answer 20 percent of the time the evidence fails, or 16 percent of the time (20 × 80). In sum, assuming equal access to the evidence, we are four times as likely to get the right answer in this case because our basic presumption about the legality of this restraint indicated to us that it is four times as likely to be anticompetitive as it is to be harmless.[36]

In litigation we will never have numbers like this. But judges can have informed intuitions about the restraint, depending on what is known about the market and the incentives facing the defendants. The greater the doubts that the evidence will be sufficient to resolve the issue, the more important it is that the burden of proof be assigned to the person whose position runs counter to these intuitions.

In its *California Dental Association (CDA)* decision the Supreme Court acted too quickly in giving the plaintiff the burden to show that the defendant's restraints on advertising were anticompetitive.[37] The defendant's professional association claimed a dominant share of California dentists as its members and provided significant membership advantages. However, its rules effectively forbade most price and quality claims as misleading, without individual inquiries into whether advertisements were misleading in fact. The CDA even prohibited dentists from advertising guarantees, condemning statements such as "we guarantee all dental work for 1 year."

A closely divided (5–4) Court approved these restraints. The majority noted the possibility that the rules were anticompetitive, but they might also be procompetitive or competitively harmless. To the extent they did little more than restrain misleading advertising they might actually increase consumer confidence in dentistry. But the Court jumped too quickly from the premise that restrictions on false and misleading advertising are a good thing, to the conclusion that these very broad restrictions, made and enforced by the dentists themselves, were an appropriate way to get the job done. The result was to assign the plaintiff the burden of showing anticompetitive restraints, and such a task would be virtually impossible.

The Supreme Court found support for this position in evidence that most information in the dental care market is controlled by producers rather than consumers. But that is hardly an argument for giving producers control of advertising. In fact, it cuts very strongly in the opposite direction, showing a market where customers are vulnerable and suppliers can be trusted mainly to act in their own best interest.

The Court's requirement that the plaintiff prove everything is a throwback to the unstructured rule of reason of the early twentieth century. As a matter of pure logic, the Court was certainly right when it said that competitor-created restraints on advertising could increase, decrease, or have no impact at all on the output of dental services. As a matter of evidence and history, however, that position is myopic. As a matter of logic, a fox going into a hen house at night might be intending to kill chickens, to take a harmless nap, or to gather eggs and clean cages. But the farmer, knowing the history of foxes in hen houses, need not wait until the fox's intentions are clear.

A long history of collusion shows that price-affecting restraints enforced by market-dominating groups are highly suspicious unless they are reasonably ancillary to joint production. In this case, what should have aroused the Court's suspicion even more was the rather poor fit between the restraints themselves and proven fraudulent advertising. The rules and the way they were administered were not narrowly tailored to correct fraud; rather, they were designed to prevent dentists from advertising price and quality. Furthermore, there was no showing that state and federal authorities were not up to the task of protecting consumers from false and misleading advertising.

Presumptions in rule of reason cases are designed to enable judges to draw on past experience to create shortcuts favoring the party with the most plausible claim. By contrast, the unstructured rule of reason tends to require the plaintiff to prove everything. A more appropriate opening presumption in *CDA* would have been that given the market dominance enjoyed by the defendant sellers, the burden should have been on them to show a significant danger of misleading advertising that was not effectively remedied by government enforcers, and that producer-controlled restraints were the least threatening way to solve the problem without injuring competition.

"Balancing"

Once a court is required to "balance," at least in a close case, it has entered territory where the error rate is unacceptably high. By "balancing," I mean any kind of analysis in which the court must identify and measure gains, identify and measure competitive losses, and net them out against each other. Of course, we can make this sound very simple, saying something like "This venture produces $3 million in efficiency gains and a 40 percent risk of competitive harm that would cost $7 million if it materializes. As a result the anticipated value ($3 million) is greater than the anticipated harm ($2.8 million)."

While a court, if constrained, might produce a fact finding such as the above, its confidence level would be extremely low. Notably, what we "learn" in antitrust litigation has very little to do with what we are capable of asking a jury. Judges can ask jurors anything they want, including questions about the dollar values of expected gains and losses, and then lock them up until they produce an answer. But in most cases the best experts in the world could not give more than ballpark estimates of the above numbers. While juries dutifully answer the questions they are asked, there is little reason to think that their answers to such questions are anything but rank speculation. "Balancing," which is a kind of cost-benefit analysis, seems to fit quite well into Justice Brandeis's gestalt conception of the rule of reason in *Chicago Board:* one dumps every scrap of information available about an industry onto a large table and then tries to sort out the positives and negatives. But our limited ability to analyze requires a much more focused approach.

So instead, antitrust applies the rule of reason by going through a series of questions, with each one eliminating the need to balance for a significant subset of ventures. *First,* is the challenged practice reasonably ancillary to joint productive activity, which is activity that is profitable without regard to power? If the answer is no, condemn the venture. If yes, we go to the next question. *Second,* do the venturers collectively have sufficient power to reduce output in a properly defined market? If yes, go to the next question. If no, dismiss the complaint. *Third,* does the challenged rule or the venture's other practices effectively limit the venture's output or the ability of individual venturers to compete outside the venture? If no, dismiss the complaint. *Fourth,* assuming the venturers can limit their own output, is the output of outsiders also limited? If outsiders can freely enter or expand production (whether within the venture or in competition with it), dismiss the complaint. *Fifth,* assuming the benefits and dangers that we have now uncovered, can the venture obtain roughly the same benefits with some alternative practice that is not so threatening to competition? If the answer is yes, condemn the challenged practice, and the venture will presumably adopt the alternative.

Only if we get to this fifth question and must answer it with a "no" are we in territory where balancing is necessary. Balancing need not always be hard. There will be some cases where competitive dangers seem great and benefits slight, or vice versa. But when cases are close we need to remember the most basic presumption of all. In our economic system we presume that free contracting produces beneficial results. The only purpose of the antitrust laws is to make our private economy work better. If a court cannot conclude with confidence that condemning a practice will improve welfare, it is obliged to let it alone.

7

Dominant Firms and Exclusionary Practices

"Monopolization," which is condemned by §2 of the Sherman Act, is the most poorly defined antitrust offense. The statute tells us nothing about what it means to "monopolize," and the common law history is not helpful. Unlike the proscription of contracts "in restraint of trade" condemned by §1 of the Sherman Act, the monopolization offense cannot claim any important common law roots. Although British law historically had a concept of "monopoly," it was much different than the one antitrust laws recognize today. "Monopoly" at common law referred to an exclusive privilege granted by the government. For example, the famous Case of Monopolies (1603) condemned Queen Elizabeth's grant to a private citizen of the exclusive right to import playing cards into the kingdom.[1] Medieval statutes condemning "engrossing," "forestalling," and "regrating" have also been compared to the monopolization offense. But the analogies are very poor. These medieval offenses were driven by hostility toward "middlemen," or people who bought up agricultural products in order to resell them at a profit. The statutes expressed a preference for producers who sold directly to consumers.[2]

Today, applying the Sherman Act to state-created monopolies is exceptional, although not unheard of. The development of independent distribution markets in the nineteenth century has made the engrossing, forestalling, and regrating offenses obsolete. Indeed, those offenses were directed at resellers, and today we believe that the resources needed for resale are so generic and easy to duplicate that monopolization of distribution markets is rare. To be sure, "mere" resellers may be very large firms, such as Wal-Mart. But Wal-Mart operates in a robustly competitive market.

150

The lack of history is but one impediment in defining the monopolization offense. The very ubiquity and diversity of unilateral conduct render classification of offenses extremely difficult. Almost any conduct by a dominant firm that makes life more difficult for rivals could be characterized as "monopolization." While agreements among competitors are relatively uncommon, somewhat suspicious, and easy to observe, unilateral conduct is omnipresent. Further, most of the things a firm does unilaterally, such as buying and selling, building new plants, and innovating and protecting intellectual property rights, are neither offensive nor unusual.

An additional problem with the monopolization offense is that it forces antitrust courts to confront the fact that they are not regulatory agencies. A government agency regulating a public utility, such as an electric power company, might supervise the firm's prices or its decisions to enter into new markets or develop new technologies. But antitrust views firms as "regulated" mainly by the market. Failure to preserve the distinction between regulation and competition has explained many of the failures of §2 policy. Markets can be unpredictable, even wild, and they reward people for taking risks, trying new things, and behaving aggressively. But new things often seem suspicious to juries and to judges who lack familiarity with the business world.

Most of the monopolists in recent American antitrust history have been innovators. Even monopolists that acquired their dominant position by legislation, such as AT&T before its 1982 breakup, innovated a great deal. While Microsoft borrowed many innovations from other firms, it did and continues to innovate in its own right. Innovation is always opening up new frontiers, making way for practices that may have few historical analogies. This lends monopolization law a kind of "nonrepetitive" quality that explains why the offense is difficult to define and increases the danger of overreaching.

Although monopoly conduct consequently must be defined with extreme care, single-firm monopolization remains the least clearly defined antitrust offense. Stating its formal requirements is easy. The offense of monopolization requires proof of a dominant firm with substantial market power and at least one qualifying "exclusionary" practice. The law of attempt to monopolize requires proof of specific intent to create a monopoly by improper means, conduct manifesting that intent, and a "dangerous probability" that the conduct, if permitted to run its course, will succeed in creating a monopoly.

The requirement of substantial market power, discussed in Chapter 5, has recently become less troublesome as our techniques for assessing power have improved. There are far fewer cases today that find monopoly power on the basis of tiny, idiosyncratically drawn markets. The Supreme Court's 1992 *Kodak* decision discussed in Chapter 5 remains an obstacle to a responsible doctrine of monopoly power, but other than *Kodak* itself, few monopolization cases have based their market power findings on *Kodak*-style lock-in.

A serviceable working definition of the monopolization offense is that, first, the firm must have monopoly power. Second, it must commit at least one exclusionary act, which we define as something that

1. is reasonably capable of creating, enlarging, or prolonging monopoly power by limiting the opportunities of rivals; and
2. either does not benefit consumers at all, or is unnecessary for the particular consumer benefits produced, or produces harms seriously disproportionate to the resulting benefits.[3]

Although this definition is very general, I believe it is preferable to several narrower ones that have been offered. For example, in recent cases the government has advocated the "sacrifice" test for monopolization—namely, that conduct monopolizes when the defendant sacrifices immediate profits as part of a strategy whose profitability depends on the exclusion of rivals.[4] That test is both too broad and too narrow. It is too broad because it would condemn competitive activity. For example, a firm might invest heavily in designing a better mousetrap that, once marketed, will ruin rivals or significantly limit their sales. This is a "sacrifice" that creates a monopoly, but antitrust should not condemn innovation even when monopoly results. The sacrifice test is also too narrow, because some exclusionary practices don't involve sacrifice at all. For example, tying and exclusive dealing contracts, such as Microsoft's insistence that Windows users also take Internet Explorer, may be profitable the instant they are in place yet also anticompetitive. Such practices do not involve any sacrifice at all. Nevertheless, the sacrifice inquiry can be helpful even though it is not dispositive. In some cases a firm does something that clearly seems costly and even irrational, but is profitable only because it creates or enlarges monopoly. As we will see later, the sacrifice test is decisive in predatory pricing cases and quite helpful in cases involving unilateral refusals to deal.

Another set of definitions identify monopolization with practices that raise rivals' costs or impair their efficiency.[5] These formulations are also helpful but incomplete. For example, any significant output expansion by a monopolist could impair the efficiency of a rival who becomes unable to attain economies of scale. But antitrust correctly refuses to condemn output expansions unless they drive the price below the monopolist's costs. On the other side, an anticompetitive predatory pricing campaign operates by depriving a rival of revenue, but it does not necessarily increase the rival's costs or reduce its efficiency.[6]

A more useful definition is Judge Richard Posner's suggestion that a monopolistic practice is one that is "likely in the circumstances to exclude from the defendant's market an equally or more efficient competitor."[7] That definition works well much of the time and occasionally provides the best analytic tool for determining whether a practice is anticompetitive.

But Judge Posner's definition can be too narrow as well. Many markets prone to monopolization also exhibit significant economies of scale or scope, or else bottlenecks that can exclude equally efficient firms. In such cases a dominant firm with, say, 70 percent or more of the market, will almost always have cost advantages over a new rival. If so, socially useless practices that would not exclude an equally efficient firm may in fact exclude the only actual rivals that the dominant firm is ever likely to face. While one might accept Judge Posner's definition as a presumption, an exception should be made for cases where the dominant firm is able to keep the output of rivals inefficiently low by engaging in practices that confer no significant social benefits.

To illustrate, a large firm is a more efficient bearer of litigation costs than a small firm. An infringement suit based on a fraudulent patent claim is costly for both plaintiff and the defendant, but considered as a percentage of output or profits it is more costly to the rival, whose output is much smaller. If both firms were equally efficient bearers of litigation costs, then the fraudulent suit would not be a particularly useful exclusion strategy. But actual or threatened litigation is an effective exclusion device when the rival has not yet begun to produce, or is producing at such a low level that the costs and risks of litigation overwhelm it. Of course, even the monopolist has a right to enforce valid intellectual property (IP) claims. But its invalid claim should not be excused simply because the litigation would not have been effective against an equally efficient rival.

Costs that decline continuously as output increases are a common characteristic of IP rights, and allow the dominant firm a cost advantage over lesser firms. Indeed, most of Microsoft's exclusionary practices would not have been effective against an equally efficient rival—say, in a market that Microsoft and a rival split evenly. The practices succeeded only because the combination of radical scale economies and network effects gave Microsoft a considerable cost advantage over any rival. In many network situations the only firm that is equally efficient is one that claims an equally large network—but such a firm is not the likeliest rival to appear on the scene.

A better question is not whether the conduct is capable of excluding a hypothetical "equally efficient" rival, but whether the conduct produces insubstantial social benefits and is apt to exclude rivals who can realistically be expected to emerge under the circumstances. Often this range of rivals will be less efficient, at least at the entry stage. Indeed, that is what makes many exclusionary practices plausible—they succeed precisely because incipient rivals are less efficient than established firms.

So monopolistic conduct is something done by a monopolist; that injures a rival by excluding it from a market, preventing its entry or limiting its growth; and that does this without significant benefit to consumers. The final requirement is essential. Many efficient acts, such as cost cutting or innovation, impair the opportunities of rivals. However, antitrust does not condemn them because they also leave consumers better off. At the same time, nearly every act might be thought to produce a consumer benefit if one speculates hard enough. So the law does not require consumer benefits of zero, but only that the amount of harm be significantly disproportionate to the benefits.

"Intent" is not part of the definition of monopolizing conduct. Claims of unlawful monopolization are to be analyzed by looking at market structure and conduct, not by assessing the defendant's state of mind. Indeed, the best way to deal with the intent problem is to assume the worst: every firm realistically capable of acquiring a monopoly intends to do so, and every monopolist intends to hang on to its monopoly position as long as possible. This is simply profit-maximizing behavior. The observation that intent should not count is more than a half century old.[8] While courts have repeated it frequently, they have also frequently dishonored it. A good example is the *Conwood* decision discussed below, where the court seemed overwhelmed by evidence of seemingly bad intent and ignored the fact that most of the conduct it was describing was either procompetitive or competitively harmless.

The case law has identified these practices among others as monopolistic:

- acquisitions and agreements of various kinds
- abuses of intellectual property rights
- predatory pricing and related practices
- practices relating to vertical integration, including vertical integration by new entry, tying, and exclusive dealing
- unilateral refusals to deal, including "essential facility" violations
- business torts

It should be apparent from this list that the law of monopolization duplicates the other antitrust laws in many areas. Acquisitions are treated in Chapter 9 on mergers, and any agreement that violates §1 might also violate §2 when the party compelling the agreement is a monopolist. Some types of vertical integration are treated under the law of vertical mergers, and others under the law of tying or exclusive dealing, which is discussed in Chapter 8. Tying as a §2 violation is also discussed in Chapter 12 regarding the *Microsoft* case. Other IP abuses are taken up in Chapter 11. Finally, the subjects of unilateral refusals to deal and antitrust's controversial "essential facility" doctrine are discussed in Chapter 10.

This chapter first explains why antitrust does not condemn durable but "innocent" monopolists, and why the questions of power and conduct cannot be viewed in isolation. Then it discusses two troublesome areas of §2 liability: (1) strategic pricing, including "predatory" pricing and discounting practices, and (2) business torts or unfair competition challenged as antitrust violations. Along the way we also discuss the "disaggregation" requirement—namely, that before a court can award damages to a private plaintiff it must be able to distinguish the harms that result from anticompetitive acts and those that result from aggressive but competitive behavior.

Exclusionary Conduct and "No-Fault" Monopolization

For nearly a century the Supreme Court and others have debated various proposals to condemn "mere monopoly," or significant, durable market power held by a firm that has not committed any provable anticompetitive practices. Already in the *Standard Oil* decision of 1911 the Supreme Court spoke of the "dread of enhancement of prices" as antitrust's principal motivator.[9] If the goal of antitrust enforcement is to control monopoly, why shouldn't antitrust simply correct any situation where a firm is charging monopoly prices? In the 1940s Judge Learned Hand suggested that the "mere existence" of the power to charge high prices should suffice, although the defendant could avoid a penalty by showing that the monopoly was a result of its own superior skill, efficiency, or natural advantage.[10] And as recently as the late 1970s Professors Areeda and Turner endorsed a proposal that would permit the government, but not private parties, to break up "innocent" monopolies.[11]

Proposals to correct monopoly without proof of "fault" underestimate the extent to which efficient practices can produce and maintain monopoly. They also overestimate the ability of courts to identify harmful monopoly merely on the basis of its structure, as well as courts' ability to improve the situation by mandatory breakup. Monopolies are created by means both fair and foul, but the first group represents a very large number. First movers into markets, the developers of market-shifting patents or copyrights, and talented managers almost certainly create more monopolies than do anticompetitive exclusionary practices. A common monopoly story is that of a firm that acquires a monopoly by efficient practices, mainly innovation, but later on uses anticompetitive practices to protect itself from new competitors. To one degree or another that is the story of Standard Oil, DuPont, Alcoa, and Microsoft.

Even if we could identify monopolies that seem excessively harmful, perhaps because they have survived for decades, coming up with a solution has eluded antitrust enforcers. First of all, monopolies created by merger are not without fault, and the case for correcting them is fairly strong. So we are dealing only with monopolies that are the result of internal growth. While fairly recent mergers create fault lines that can make enforced breakup fairly easy, firms that have never merged are a different matter. To say that courts are not good at creating economically beneficial ways of restructuring firms is a gross understatement. Issuing an order breaking up a large firm is relatively easy. But if scale economies are at all significant, the component firms would have higher costs. Further, with few exceptions markets with significant scale economies are the only ones that are conducive to monopoly to begin with.[12] If small firms are able to function just as efficiently as large ones, durable monopoly is unlikely to emerge because the market will produce a continual supply of new rivals.

Another reason for limiting intervention to monopolists who have committed identifiable anticompetitive practices is that the goal of legal policy is general deterrence, and this is particularly true in economic areas. For example, a strong policy against the filing of fraudulent patent infringement suits discourages firms from doing so. The more clearly anticompetitive practices are defined and the more effective the penalties, the better we can ensure that monopoly will not be created by foul means. By contrast, a law of no-fault monopolization does not discriminate between monopolists created or maintained by efficiency and those created by socially harmful acts. In any event, when we are confronted with a monopoly "without fault" we cannot justify a breakup as punishment or deterrence. The *only* rationale for intervention is that we believe we can produce higher output and lower prices. History gives us little reason to have faith in the judicial system's ability to achieve such goals through mandatory restructuring.

Relating Conduct to Power

A responsible monopolization offense condemns business conduct that is likely to create, increase, or prolong monopoly power without giving significant benefits to society. The final qualifier is essential because many procompetitive practices, such as innovation and aggressive pricing, can create monopoly power. But they do so by creating significant social benefits as well.

We generally say that the monopolization offense requires proof of a power component and a conduct component, as if these were completely distinct elements. In fact, there is a close link between the two. Some acts can be unreasonably exclusionary at much lower market shares than others. Thus monopolization law's two requirements are related to each other, even though the calculus is imprecise. Consider the personnel manager making hiring decisions based on the applicant's education and experience. An applicant with less education might be acceptable provided that she had relatively more experience, or vice versa. What the wise personnel manager would not do, however, is look at education in isolation, permitting the applicant to convince him that she had the bare minimum others had; and then look at experience in isolation, making the same argument. The result would be the hiring of someone who lacked either sufficient education or experience.

Some courts have myopically viewed power and conduct in isolation. A severe example of such myopia is the 1997 *Kodak* case in the

Ninth Circuit, the same case that the Supreme Court had permitted to go to trial five years earlier by accepting the "lock-in" theory discussed in Chapter 5. The Ninth Circuit later permitted the plaintiffs not only to take advantage of the lock-in theory, but also to define an "all parts" market on the theory that someone repairing a Kodak photocopier needed access to "all parts."[13] The court confused complements and substitutes. A relevant market consists of things that are *substitutes* for each other, such as two gasoline stations on opposite sides of the street or two brands of toothpaste. The two producers are forced to compete with each other precisely because the purchaser does *not* need to go to both. He needs only one and will select the one providing the best value. Not only do complements not compete with each other; they frequently are made with entirely different technologies and under totally different competitive conditions. For example, bread and toasters are complementary products in the making of toast; one needs both. But toasters could perhaps be monopolized (maybe because of an important patent) while bread is made by thousands of small bakers. Finding a single market for "bread/toasters" would be nonsense.

As a result of the court's confusing these elements, no one ever found out how many parts Kodak was even capable of monopolizing. Very likely there were a few, such as the patented image loop that captures the marks on a document being photocopied. But most parts were much more generic, actually produced or capable of being produced by numerous firms. The court's truncated "all parts" analysis effectively prevented it from ever identifying those parts in which monopolization was even possible. But then the court compounded the error by failing to realize in its analysis of conduct that it was dealing with a firm whose monopoly power had not been proven. It condemned a simple refusal to deal as a §2 violation and even created an absurd doctrine of compulsory patent licensing that required an inquiry into the defendant's state of mind.[14] Today there is very little disagreement about the proposition that condemnation for unilateral refusals to deal should be reserved for situations in which firms have extraordinary amounts of very durable market power.

The Problem of Strategic Pricing

Strategic pricing comes in many varieties and has provoked a great deal of debate. Consider these practices:

- A dominant firm sets its price below its costs, anticipating that it has more staying power than rivals and thus can drive them out of business, or perhaps force them to maintain their prices at higher levels; alternatively, one member of an oligopoly disciplines a price-cutting "cheater" with a drastic price cut.
- A dominant firm that enjoys significant economies of scale sets a price that is profitable, but just low enough to keep smaller, higher-cost rivals out of the market.
- A dominant firm gives a discount to wholesale buyers who agree (a) to purchase exclusively from that firm; (b) to purchase a minimum number of units per year; (c) to purchase a minimum share of their purchases of that particular product; or (d) to provide the dominant firm with sales data or other information, or perhaps with superior display space or advertising.
- A firm pays a retailer for preferred or exclusive access to shelf or display space ("slotting" fees).

For analytic purposes one can roughly divide these practices into two types. "Pure predation" refers to situations where the thing being challenged is the unconditioned price itself, on the theory that rivals cannot effectively compete against that price. The other set of practices is best characterized as "purchases of exclusionary rights."

The Antitrust Law of Predatory Pricing

Predatory pricing claims force courts to confront the limits of their fact-finding power. The reason is easily stated: low prices are a principal goal of the antitrust laws. But in a predatory pricing suit the plaintiff claims that a price is anticompetitive because it is too low. Furthermore, the plaintiff is typically a competitor and thus has all the wrong incentives. Rivals are injured by any low price, whether competitive or predatory, and they will take advantage of any legal rule that permits them to complain. Finally, our tools for measuring costs and prices in litigation, or even for determining which costs or prices are relevant, are crude at best.

Economics provides an abundance of predatory pricing theories. Problematically, however, for many of them not even a trained economist can "play the tape backwards." That is, while it might be easy to model a particular anticompetitive predatory pricing strategy, it is very difficult to look at a particular set of pricing practices or outcomes and rule out procompetitive or competitively harmless explanations. For example, a common strategy involves a dominant firm in an industry with significant economies of scale. That is, larger firms tend to produce more cheaply than smaller ones. The dominant firm then constructs a much bigger plant than it needs and operates with substantial excess capacity. Seeing this situation, rivals are reluctant to build their own plants even though current prices are well above the competitive level. The potential rivals know that the established firm can increase its output and dump its price dramatically any time it wants. The rival will end up making a costly, irreversible investment in a years-long construction project only to see the dominant firm double its output a few months before the new plant is functional. At that point the remaining market will be too small to generate profits and the entrant's investment will be lost.

Telling this little story makes the strategy sound quite plausible, even fairly simple, under the right set of industry conditions. But showing plausibility is a far cry from looking at a particular instance where a firm built an unusually large plant and proclaiming that act to be anticompetitive. Firms build large plants for many reasons. Most likely, they are aggressive and planning for growth, and sometimes these expectations do not pan out. They may simultaneously hope for growth but realize that if the growth does not materialize the excess capacity will deter rivals. The one thing antitrust does *not* want to do is send a message that firms build large plants at their peril, for larger plants are generally conducive to higher output, which everyone agrees is procompetitive.[15]

Predatory pricing rules are technical and difficult for courts to administer. The error rate is high, and competitors, who are injured by both competitive and predatory price cuts, frequently bring nonmeritorious claims. A high error rate gives reason to believe that predatory pricing law does more harm than good. Suppose that 15 percent of predation claims are meritorious but that the court's error rate is a random 20 percent, which is probably a conservative number. Out of 100 claims, 15 would be meritorious. But the court would erroneously find approximately 17 meritorious claims out of the 85 nonmeritorious claims, and three nonmeritorious ones out of the 15 meritorious claims. Nearly two-thirds (17/29) of the decisions finding predatory pricing would be incorrect. Even excluding litigation costs and the costs of competitive disincentives to aggressive pricing, the world would very likely be better off with no law of predatory pricing at all. When these costs are included, a law of predatory pricing seems like a large waste of social resources.

Nevertheless, we do not adopt that conclusion. First, the numbers given above are hypothetical. In fact, we do not know the rate of predation or the court's error rate in detecting it. Second, while an overly aggressive predatory pricing law deters some legitimate conduct, complete nonenforcement encourages anticompetitive conduct.

Most important, depending on the predation definition we select, the errors need not be randomly distributed. An intentionally *under-*deterrent predatory pricing rule may do much good by reaching many instances of predation while permitting all instances of bona fide competition. For example, suppose that under a given legal rule the court's error rate is 20 percent of false negatives, or instances where actual predation is exonerated, but zero percent of false positives, or instances when nonpredation is condemned. Then the numbers given in the previous example look quite different. Of 100 claims, 15 are in fact meritorious. The court ends up condemning 12 out of 15, or 80 percent of the instances of actual predation, while condemning no cases of nonpredatory behavior.

Given the enormous stake that antitrust has in low prices, and our extraordinary difficulties assessing predation claims, the best course is to develop predation rules that are both simple and somewhat underdeterrent. The goal should be to identify most cases of actual predation, while exonerating all those who have engaged in only competitive behavior or where the predation claims are doubtful. Note that an underdeterrent rule may be the best option even if we all agree that there are some instances of predatory behavior that our definition does not capture.

One legal rule that seriously limits the range of predatory pricing claims is the current one that only "below cost" pricing counts as predatory. The source of this rule is *not* a robust belief that above-cost prices can never be competitively harmful; many economists believe they can be, and many above-cost anticompetitive pricing strategies have been modeled.[16] One problem is that if we admit claims of predatory pricing on above-cost prices there will be hundreds of claimants, and the courts are simply not up to the task of separating out good from bad claims.

An antitrust rule that permits branding above-cost pricing as "predatory" also creates serious problems in designing a remedy. Consider "limit" pricing, which can occur when a firm has lower costs than potential rivals. The firm sets a price lower than the price that would maximize its immediate profits. It does this because the monopoly price will invite new entry, but the lower price will deter new entrants, perhaps indefinitely. The strategy is profitable because the indefinite stream of somewhat lower profits is more valuable than a shorter run of very high profits. Suppose we could show that this firm's monopoly price is $1.40, and that rivals have costs of $1.20, so any price below that level will keep them out. The dominant firm has costs of $1.00, but charges $1.19, earning 19 percent monopoly profits while deterring rivals. Should a court then order this firm to increase its price to $1.40 so that new entrants can come into the market? The court would have to have extraordinary self-confidence to believe that such a remedy would improve consumer welfare. Alternatively, perhaps the court could order the firm to charge $1.00, the competitive price, which would maximize consumer welfare immediately. This would hardly be what a competitor-plaintiff would want: rivals would be even worse off if the firm charged the competitive price. It would also put the court in the position of a regulatory agency, constantly monitoring the dominant firm's prices to ensure that they stayed near the competitive level.

So the first way to deal with the problem of false positives is to define the concept of a predatory *price* very narrowly, even in a way that is intentionally underdeterrent. At the very least a predatory price for antitrust purposes must be below cost. Such a definition largely takes courts out of the metering business—that is, of deciding *how much* a price can be above cost.[17]

No court has ever developed a workable test for determining when an above-cost price is anticompetitive. But what about a price below a firm's reasonably anticipated marginal cost? Marginal cost is the cost a firm will encounter in increasing its output by one unit. Suppose a firm believes that a contemplated increase in widget production will cost $5.00 per widget, with cost calculated to include a competitive rate of return. If the anticipated market price is $5.00 or more, increasing output by that amount will produce at least the competitive rate of profit. But what if the anticipated market price is $4.95? A rational firm would not ordinarily expand output, for it would lose five cents on each additional unit it sells.

In sum, a rational, profit-maximizing firm would not set a price below marginal cost. Thus prices below marginal cost require an explanation. To be sure, predation is not the only one. Firms can and do make errors, particularly when product decisions must be made today in anticipation of tomorrow's demand. Farmer Brown, anticipating a September price of $3.00 for corn, may plant an extra field where marginal costs are $2.90. If she has mispredicted and the price is $2.80 she will lose money, but predatory pricing is not the explanation.

The influential Areeda-Turner test for predatory pricing began with the premise that courts could confidently conclude that prices below reasonably anticipated marginal cost were predatory. However, they then added an element that made the Areeda-Turner test more useful but also more controversial. True marginal cost, or the incremental cost that a firm incurs in expanding output by one unit, is extremely difficult to measure in litigation. As a result Areeda and Turner proposed a surrogate: average variable cost, or AVC. In theory at least, AVC is much easier to measure than marginal cost: one simply adds up all the costs that vary with output (labor, ingredients, energy, but not land, plant depreciation, or taxes unrelated to profits or sales) and divides by the number of units. For example, a wholesale baker might incur $1,000 in costs for bread, salt, yeast, labor, and electricity for its ovens. It also incurs a mortgage payment on its plant and real property taxes, but these costs do not vary with the number of units the baker produces. If the baker produced 10,000 loaves of bread over the time period in which it incurred these costs, then AVC would be ten cents per loaf. Intuitively, this number seems about right, although underdeterrent: no reasonable firm would sell bread at less than the cost of the basic ingredients, energy, and labor that went into it. The firm would be better off if it simply shut down. Areeda and Turner proposed that a price be regarded as predatory if it is less than AVC.

Although there has been some variation in details, the Areeda-Turner test has been adopted by most of the federal courts that have considered it.[18] Nevertheless, it has been the subject of several fairly severe criticisms. The first critique is a technical one that while AVC is a suitable surrogate for marginal cost when a plant is producing in its optimal range, AVC falls below marginal cost when output is high. As Figure 7.1 shows, marginal cost (MC) is a more aggressive curve than AVC because the latter is a running average that tends to neutralize highs and lows. As MC rises, it intersects the AVC curve at the latter's lowest point. To the right of that intersection—that is, in higher output ranges—*MC* and *AVC* diverge, and *MC* is always higher.[19] Because predatory pricing is a high output strategy (the defendant increases output and dumps price), an AVC test gives the defendant extra breathing room to set a price that is in fact lower than marginal cost but above AVC. For that reason the Areeda-Turner test has been described as a defendant's "paradise" by some critics.[20] Nevertheless, the test seems to satisfy our concern that predatory pricing rules be moderately underdeterrent.

A second critique, which ultimately has more bite, is that the AVC test works very poorly in industries that have high fixed costs and relatively low marginal costs, such as airlines and public utilities, and perhaps some markets that have a large intellectual property component in their value. Fuel, labor, and food service represent only a small percentage of the cost of running an airline. Much greater is the cost of the aircraft themselves and gate space, both of which seem to be fixed rather than variable costs. Thus in the airline industry the AVC test amounts to a virtual license to engage in predatory pricing. Further, predatory pricing is likely to succeed in only a few industries, and most of these have a significant fixed-cost component.

Part of the problem is that AVC must be defined properly. Many costs

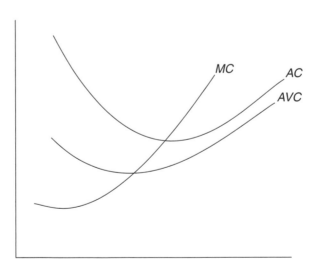

Figure 7.1. The AVC test for predatory pricing

that appear at first glance to be fixed actually become variable when one considers the purposes of the law against predatory pricing. For example, in *AMR* the defendant American Airlines was the dominant carrier, with about 70 percent of the traffic at the Dallas/Fort Worth (DFW) hub airport. When faced with new competition on its routes by smaller carriers, American cut its own prices to match the new entrant's prices and increased the number of its own flights on the same routes. When the new carrier abandoned its routes or went out of business, American raised its prices and reduced its scheduled flights back to pre-entry levels. While American had higher operating costs than its upstart rivals, it also had a significant advantage in that it was able to offer connecting service to numerous other destinations or from other points of origin. The small carriers typically offered only limited flights and few connecting flights.

In rejecting the government's predation claim, the court made an error that noneconomists often make: it ignored opportunity costs. An opportunity cost is simply the cost associated with not making some alternative choice. Consider this example: a firm has an old building it is not using. Because the building is fully depreciated, its cost as carried on the ledger book is zero, except for maintenance and utilities. The firm then begins using the building for storage, producing value of $1,000 per month. If one looks only at the accounting costs, using the building for storage seems to be profitable, given that these costs are near zero. But suppose that the building were worth $1,600 per month if rented to someone else. The firm doesn't have an infinite number of old buildings. In a world of scarce resources the "cost" of not using the building, or of using it for any purpose, also includes the forgone revenue of not using it for some other purpose. In this particular case, using the building for storage is costly and irrational.

An opportunity cost is thus the value of the "best forgone alternative." In *AMR* the defendant pulled aircraft out of more profitable routes in order to place them in routes where they faced competition from smaller firms, earning less on these routes during the "predatory" period. The government correctly treated American's "forgone or 'sacrificed' profits as costs," but the court rejected that claim.[21]

The court concluded that taking opportunity costs into account would condemn the defendant for "failure to maximize" its profits, rather than for pricing at below cost. But that is incorrect. To be sure, every instance of below-cost pricing is a failure to maximize. But the vice of failure to maximize tests is that they condemn a price above all relevant costs because it is lower than the profit-maximizing price. For example, a monopolist with costs of $1.00 and a profit-maximizing price of $1.30 might charge a price of $1.15. By contrast, a cost-based test condemns only below-cost prices. When such a test fails to include opportunity costs it is deficient, for no rational firm would embark on a strategy of transferring production from a more profitable to a less profitable product, unless there is more to the story.

A sounder argument against weighing the opportunity cost of forgone revenues is that such a cost is not one that the rival must incur. What we really want to know when we analyze predation is not what the predator's costs are, but what the costs of an equally efficient rival would be.[22] A rival can be equally efficient even though it does not forgo revenue on alternative routes.

But this puts the cart before the horse and illustrates the point made at the beginning of this chapter: ability to exclude an equally efficient rival should not be the only test for an exclusionary practice. The fact that the defendant is pricing at less than its opportunity costs serves to explain why the price is irrational but for its impact on a rival, and socially harmful in that it prevents a more competitive market structure from emerging. What matters is not whether a hypothetical equally efficient rival would be excluded, but whether any of the rivals who are likely to appear on the scene will be excluded. A hub-dominant carrier nearly always has scale and scope advantages over new entrants. Under the Tenth Circuit's *AMR* ruling the antitrust laws would simply be impotent against predatory pricing by hub-dominant carriers.

To be sure, too wide a conception of opportunity costs could send courts on ill-defined fishing expeditions in search of hypothetical, more profitable, investments that a firm might have made. But those were not the facts of the American Airlines case. American shifted flights from *actual* higher-profit routes into routes where there had been recent entry or expansion by a small carrier, flooded the route with its own flights, and then transferred these aircraft back out of the predated route after the small rival had cut back or exited from the market.

Is the AVC test useless for assessing predation in an industry such as airlines? A traditional answer has been yes, because variable costs in that industry, as for common carriers or utilities generally, are very low. In-

deed, on a per-seat basis the cost is very close to zero, or only a few dollars, because the cost of filling an extra seat on an already scheduled
airline is little more than the cost of processing the transaction and providing a small amount of in-flight service.

But that is not the correct way to view the problem. American Airlines
was not simply filling seats on existing flights. It was transferring entire
aircraft into new routes in competition with upstart rivals. In this instance the entire cost of supplying the airline was "incremental" in the
sense that it was an added cost that American encountered only in order
to supply these additional flights. Even the gate space was incremental
in this sense—American either had to make arrangements for additional gates to support the additional flights, or else it had to use vacant
gates that it controlled and could have sublet to someone else (another
forgone opportunity cost). In either case, the cost of leasing additional
gates or the forgone revenue from leasing them out was a direct cost of
putting the additional flights into the competitive routes.

Once these costs, including relevant opportunity costs, are all calculated into the base, American's resulting prices might be below its
costs—or they might not. If the prices are still higher than costs, then
American's decision to transfer was profitable in its own right and cannot be condemned by the antitrust laws, even if it injured a rival and
served to maintain American's dominant position in the market.

Recoupment

In order to prove unlawful predatory pricing a plaintiff must show not
only a below-cost price, but also a market structure that makes "recoupment" of the predatory investment likely. Because the prevailing test
for unlawful predation requires below-cost prices, the recoupment requirement plays out like this: Predation is an "investment" in monopoly.
Before a rational predator will invest, say, $1 million in predatory pric-
ing, it must reasonably believe that the postpredation stream of monopoly profits will exceed the predatory investment, after discounting
for the time value of the investment and the risk of failure. Recoupment
is unlikely if, for example, new rivals can enter or existing rivals can
quickly expand their output once the predation period is over and prices
are increased to monopoly levels. Because predatory prices are so difficult to measure and error rates so high, the recoupment requirement is

conclusive under the Supreme Court's *Brooke Group* decision: if the evidence indicates that predation would not be followed by a recoupment period sufficient to make the investment in predation profitable, then we presume that predatory pricing did not occur.[23]

The recoupment requirement for predatory pricing is one instance in which antitrust embraces the "sacrifice" test for monopolization described at the beginning of this chapter. By charging below-cost prices the defendant sacrifices immediate profits in anticipation of future monopoly returns that will materialize only if rivals are destroyed or disciplined.

Some have argued that the recoupment requirement disappears under rules permitting above-cost prices to be condemned as predatory.[24] But that is not true, although recoupment does take a different form when the predatory prices are above cost. Firms invest only if they anticipate a profitable payoff. Furthermore, above-cost predatory pricing is costly in the sense that short-run prices are lower than they would be if the firm simply charged its monopoly price.

To illustrate, suppose the firm calculates that if it charges its full monopoly price it will have annual profits of $10 million and entry will occur in three years. If it charges a lower "limit" price, its annual profits drop to $5 million, but entry will be deterred indefinitely. Ignoring the time value of money, under this "limit" strategy the firm will need six years to earn the same $30 million it would have earned by simply charging its monopoly price. The period is in fact longer because dollars earned in the future are not as valuable as dollars earned today. The strategy will not become profitable until at least the seventh year. So the "recoupment" question in this case is whether the firm can reasonably anticipate that the limit strategy will delay entry for six years or more. If it does not—for example, if entry occurs within five years—then the limit strategy will be unprofitable. For this reason a *Brooke Group*-style recoupment analysis would be important even if the courts were willing to condemn above-costs prices as predatory. Indeed, it is all the more important because there are so many alternative explanations for an above-cost price.

Predatory Pricing and Oligopoly

Pricing strategies designed to support an oligopoly are inherently more plausible than "monopolistic" pricing strategies, which are intended to destroy rivals. Oligopoly in many industries is relatively but imperfectly stable. Occasional discipline may be necessary to encourage maverick firms to refrain from increasing their output or cutting price. Drastic price cuts by the oligopoly leadership are one form of discipline, particularly if the cuts can be confined to a particular market niche where they will inflict the largest amount of harm on the price cutter.[25] The ever-present threat of such cuts serves to make the oligopoly more stable. Cheaters know that their own price cut will be matched in their "home market," so to speak, by severe price cuts by one or more rivals.

Those were essentially the facts of the *Brooke Group* case, in which the Supreme Court was too sanguine about the social cost of oligopoly and the effectiveness of price as a disciplinary tool. The case involved cigarettes, a half-century-old textbook example of rigid oligopoly. When a maverick firm introduced generic cigarettes and began to market them at a low price, the oligopoly leader introduced its own generic alternative and marketed it at a price that was conceded to be lower than average variable cost.[26]

Predatory pricing is a more viable strategy in these circumstances because of the alternatives available to targets. In traditional monopoly situations the predator is intent on destroying its rivals, and such firms are likely to be tenacious opponents. The predator seeking to stabilize an oligopoly presents its target with a more attractive alternative: cut price and we will impose immediate losses on you, or return to the fold and earn oligopoly profits with the rest of us. In that case predatory pricing is likely to be of much shorter duration and to face a much greater chance of success than the traditional variety.

In *Brooke Group* the Supreme Court believed that oligopolies were inherently frail, and that a firm would be unlikely to invest resources in predation in the hope of winning its investment back through rivals' adherence to the oligopoly equilibrium. That attitude reflects a non-economic, lawyerly judgment that explicit anticompetitive "agreements" are inherently stable and threatening, even if they are not legally enforceable, while less explicit understandings are unstable.[27]

But in many cases involving concentrated industries precisely the opposite is true: whether the parties have "agreed" about something is not nearly as important as what the profit-maximizing equilibrium strategy may be. Some oligopolies are stable, but not because the parties have reached a verbal "agreement," which would be unenforceable in any event. Rather, oligopolies become stable because adherence to a certain output and price level is consistent with each firm's economic interest. Failure to understand this led the Court in *Brooke Group* to impose too high a standard for recoupment, given that prices were conceded to be below AVC.

That hardly means that every price cut in an oligopoly market should be regarded as suspicious. Many are simply evidence that the oligopoly is falling apart and the price moving toward the competitive level, so antitrust policy should encourage oligopolists to cut their prices. But price cuts that are nonremunerative in the short run are more suspicious, particularly when future events or other circumstances suggest that they were being used for disciplinary reasons. While recoupment still matters, the amount of time needed for recoupment is much less because typically the cost of the predation is less. *Brooke Group* itself was an unusual case involving a fairly protracted period of predation against an unusually tenacious rival that had introduced a new product variation (the generic cigarettes). The typical oligopoly predation story is more prosaic, with "disciplinary" price cuts that last perhaps a few weeks until the price cutter rescinds its cuts.

Quantity, Market Share, and "Package" Discounts

Discounting is a pervasive feature of the American economy. Firms offer discounts if the buyer takes three instead of one, agrees to purchase all of its needs from the seller, or takes both the stereo receiver and the speakers together. Discounts make buyers feel good, they help sellers sell more, and they serve the far more jejune purpose of reducing transaction costs. For example, package discounts often reflect the lower costs of selling two things together.

Some discounts are so clearly procompetitive that they should never be the basis of an antitrust claim. In *Conwood* the Sixth Circuit condemned a defendant's very small (less than 1 percent) discounts in exchange for provision of market information and preferred shelf space and advertising. The court also noted that the defendant had extremely high margins, which means that the discounted price was way above cost, so any equally efficient firm could have matched them. Indeed, the court never even required a showing that existing rivals (whether equally efficient or not) were unable to match the discounts. The court believed that the discounts were part of a broader anticompetitive scheme that involved replacement of rivals' display racks but, as we note later, courts should never mix pro- and anticompetitive behavior together in looking for §2 violations. Doing so deters procompetitive conduct because if even a small percentage of a firm's conduct is anticompetitive, the firm will be punished for everything, and unlawful exclusionary conduct under §2 is very poorly defined. *Conwood* assessed a very high damages award for conduct that was mainly procompetitive even by the court's own description. To the extent that decision is followed, consumers will end up paying billions of dollars in higher prices.[28]

One poorly understood discount that is sometimes challenged under the antitrust laws is "slotting" fees, or upfront fixed fees by which manufacturers purchase scarce shelf space. For example, in addition to any price cuts or discounts that a manufacturer might offer to a retailer, the manufacturer might also offer $1,000 per month for access to three linear feet of desirable display space. It is difficult to make a cogent argument why slotting fees are anticompetitive, with the possible exception of those resulting in a below-cost price.

The main function of slotting fees is to transfer risk from the retailer to the manufacturer. Economically, a slotting fee is a discount whose size varies inversely with sales volume. Retailers such as grocers have a serious problem of shelf-space scarcity. This places a premium on products that move well. Suppose the wholesale price of a product is $2 and the product retails for $3. The product needs three feet of shelf space, for which the manufacturer offers to make an upfront fixed payment of $100 per month. Because the size of this rebate is fixed, it operates as a per unit discount that varies inversely with the number of units sold. If the grocer sells 100 units of the product per month, the $100 slotting fee operates as a prohibitively high $1, or 50 percent, discount from the wholesale price. But if the grocer sells 1,000 units the discount drops to ten cents, and if it sells 5,000 units the discount drops to two cents per package. Thus the slotting fee shows the merchant that the manufacturer's promise of good sales is more than empty words. The manufacturer who pays a $100 slotting fee is betting that sales of its product in that store will be sufficiently high that the net discount that results from the fee will be affordably small. Significantly, any equally efficient and confident firm could match the fee. A firm that claims it cannot afford such a fee is in fact telegraphing that it lacks confidence that sales of its product will be high enough to merit the grocer's investment.

Quantity and market share discounts are virtually always competitive unless they amount to outright exclusive dealing, which is discussed in Chapter 8. But even exclusive dealing is competitively harmless in most circumstances. If the discount is on a single product, an equally efficient firm can match it. In *Concord Boat* Brunswick, which made boat motors, gave boat builders a progressive discount as they took an increasing percentage of their motors from Brunswick. In order to get the maximum discount a boat builder had to purchase 70 or 80 percent of its motors from Brunswick. But the court correctly noted that boat builders were free to walk away from Brunswick at any time, and another firm could steal Brunswick's sales simply by matching its discounted price. Furthermore, the prices were acknowledged by the plaintiff to be far above cost, so this should not have been difficult for a rival to pull off.[29]

"Bundled" discounts may be different, particularly if the defendant offers several products while rivals offer only one. In *LePage's* the Third Circuit condemned the defendant 3M for offering large buyers (e.g., Wal-Mart and Office Depot) individually crafted discount packages that aggregated the discount across multiple products, including office tape. 3M sold "Scotch" brand tape, which was the market leader, while LePage's sold tape packaged under the name of the retailer.

To illustrate the anticompetitive problem of bundled discounts, suppose that 3M supplied a large retailer with Scotch tape, Post-it notes, and staples. The retailer ordinarily uses $100,000 of each of these products per year, and 3M offers an aggregated discount of 10 percent provided that the buyer takes $300,000 in any combination of all three products. An equally efficient tape manufacturer could match the tape discount. But by purchasing its tape from LePage's the retailer would also lose the discount on the Post-it notes and the staples. Indeed, in an extreme case LePage's could steal the sale only by offering a 30 percent discount on its tape, sufficient to match 3M's discounted tape price as well as the lost discount on the Post-its and the staples. A divided court found that the practice violated §2, although the majority did not explain why the bundling was anticompetitive on the particular facts of that case. The voluminous recent literature on the issue is largely inconclusive as well.[30]

While bundled discounts of this fashion can be anticompetitive, the practice should not be analogized to predatory pricing unless prices are below cost. Bundled discounts are really a form of tying. In tying arrangements, which are discussed in the next chapter, a buyer is contractually obligated to take two products together. The gravamen of the offense is "foreclosure," or forcing the buyer to take the defendant's tied product rather than the competing product of someone else. The bundled discount simply gives the buyer a price incentive to take both products from the same seller. Such a discount works in only a limited number of circumstances, and requires a seller who offers a larger range of products than rivals do.

One might say that bundled discounts could not exclude an equally efficient firm, if we defined such a firm as one that was an efficient producer of every product that went into the bundled discount. But to do so could exonerate an anticompetitive practice for no good reason. Bundled discounts exclude precisely because a dominant multiproduct firm is likely to face upstart single-product rivals—or at least, rivals who produce a smaller range of products than the dominant firm does. If this is the set of rivals that are likely to appear on the horizon to challenge a monopoly, antitrust policy should take that fact into account.

The more serious problem with monopolization challenges to bundled discounts is administrative. The great majority of discounts, bundled and otherwise, are procompetitive. The anticompetitive bundled discount is the small subset that is "excessive" because the discounts would be irrational but for their ability to exclude an equally efficient rival. Making such determinations presumes that the court has much greater cost-measuring capacity than it has in fact. Even though the theory of the bundled discount is properly analogized to tying or exclusive dealing rather than predatory pricing, an administratively prudent rule might insist on a showing that the discounted package is priced below average variable cost. While one can always debate whether this or that above-cost discount is unreasonable on a variety of grounds, a price lower than average variable cost is presumptively irrational and requires an explanation. Such a rule might be somewhat underdeterrent, but it would eliminate most of the false positives that are likely to occur if the courts permit challenges to above-cost discount packages.

The final discounting practice worth mentioning involves "package" pricing that occurs when a seller competes by throwing in some extra component or service at less than the incremental cost of supplying it. For example, suppose a car dealer is having trouble closing a deal on a car at a price of $20,000. She then offers to include an optional stereo system for an additional $100, even though the cost of the system is $350. A seller of independently installed car stereos claims predatory pricing, pointing out that the dealer sold a $350 system for $100. But suppose the facts further reveal that at a price of $20,000 the dealer was making $1,000 in profits on the car. By throwing in the stereo for $100 the dealer was reducing her profits by $250, but the overall sale was still very profitable.

A few courts have erroneously found predatory pricing by looking at the relationship between the price and cost of the stereo alone rather than the entire package of stereo-plus-car.[31] As an administrative matter, doing so could involve courts in dissecting packages of all kinds to ensure that the price of each individual component exceeded its costs. More important, one characteristic of oligopoly markets is that sellers are reluctant to compete on price, which is often transparent to rivals. Rather, they compete on quality, by doing such things as including car stereos in order to win a deal. By condemning such arrangements as "predatory" the court is unwittingly shoring up the oligopoly. In general, no price should be deemed predatory unless the cost of the transferred package of goods and services as a whole exceeds the price. There is no useful way of disaggregating components and assigning a lawful minimum price to each one separately.

Business Torts as Antitrust Violations

Most business torts come in two varieties. First are practices that deceive customers when a firm misrepresents either its own goods or those sold by its rivals. These include fraud and misrepresentation, false advertising, passing off, and product disparagement. The other variety of business torts involves more direct interferences with the normal workings of the market. These include inducement of breach of contract or interference with contract, theft of employees, misappropriation of economic rights, sabotage, and industrial espionage.[32]

Antitrust is not a business tort statute. Its purpose is not to correct unethical or even deceptive business behavior. Nor is it good at identifying and condemning harmful intent, which is often relevant in tort cases. Antitrust's purpose is to promote competition, which it does by encouraging competitive market structures and intervening selectively when practices pose a genuine threat to competition.

To be sure, some of the conduct that antitrust condemns also falls into the realm of business torts. But antitrust policy imposes far more stringent structural conditions and requires more than harm to a rival. A business tort becomes an antitrust violation only if there is a significant injury to competition. The typical defendant in a business tort case is not a dominant firm threatening a monopoly. More typically, it is a small fly-by-night operation that is trying to free ride off a larger firm's business by stealing its intellectual property or employees, scaring its customers, or making its own product confusingly similar to a more established firm's product.[33]

One impact of antitrust's concern for competition is that most of the activities it condemns can be perfectly lawful in competitively structured markets. As far as antitrust is concerned, firms in a competitive market can steal each other's employees and intellectual property or make false claims about each other all they want. Even in markets that are susceptible to monopolization, torts rarely accomplish more than the injury of a rival. They become antitrust violations only when they are so pervasive and injurious that they make a significant and durable contribution to the defendant's market power. Moreover, the antitrust court must tread lightly lest the types of aggressive competition that tort law frequently condemns be branded an antitrust violation as well. For example, a misrepresentation to buyers is tortious but would not become an antitrust violation unless its effects were so pervasive that they forced rivals out of business or significantly undermined their ability to compete effectively. That would not occur unless a plaintiff could show that misrepresentations were clearly false and material to the buyer's decision, that the buyers were ignorant and depended on the provision of such information, and that rival firms could not easily correct the falsity.

In the Sixth Circuit's *Conwood* decision the defendant United States Tobacco (UST) was the industry leader in a four-firm market for moist snuff, a form of chewing tobacco. UST was an innovative firm, although not as innovative as its two smallest rivals. The plaintiff was less aggressive, and had not participated in many product or distributional innovations. During the relevant period the defendant's market share was declining while those of its rivals, including the plaintiff, were growing. Historically, moist snuff was sold from wire racks in retail stores and each firm supplied its own racks. By law, all tobacco products had to be placed out of customer reach behind the checker's counter, where space is even scarcer than it is in the store in general.

UST developed a single integrated rack that was designed to hold the products of all four firms in several rows, or "facings." The principal antitrust claim, which ultimately generated more than a billion dollars in damages, was that UST was too aggressive about deploying these racks, and that its sales personnel loaded the racks in such a way as to give UST's products more facings than rivals' products received. Of course, the racks themselves were fully in the control of retailers, who could change the number of UST's or rivals' facings any time they pleased, and they apparently refused UST's persistent requests to have a proportion of facings equal to its market share. Nevertheless, the plaintiff's theory was that retailers were largely indifferent because moist snuff was such a small part of their overall sales. As a result the retailers let the moist-snuff sellers display their goods as they saw fit. One point went unappreciated by the court: both the plaintiff and the defendant enjoyed extraordinarily high margins, and the plaintiff did not cut its price in response to any competitive pressure it received. Every firm in the market was highly profitable throughout the complaint period.

UST's placement of its multibrand racks fell into three categories. Sometimes UST's racks were placed at a retailer's specific request. For example, this was true of Wal-Mart, the single largest seller of moist snuff, which held a design competition for new racks that UST won. In a second set of stores UST obtained permission to replace a rack, although some of these requests were made to lower-level employees who may not have had authority to grant them. Finally, some racks were replaced without permission, and rivals' racks unceremoniously dumped. UST's employees were instructed to get rid of the independent racks used by other firms whenever they could. In addition to rack replacements, UST also gave the kinds of modest discounts, as described in the previous section, in exchange for sales data and preferred shelf space. An expert, although not the retailers themselves, also testified that UST supplied the retailers with false information about retailers' sales.

How should a court respond to this mélange of practices, which seem to be largely procompetitive, perhaps too aggressive, and sometimes tortious? First of all, the definitional problem is not too serious if we want to reward only injunctive relief. For example, a court might order UST not to deploy its new racks without permission from retailers, and perhaps to notify retailers when changing the product mix on the racks. This would be an example of tailoring the offense to the remedy, as Chapter 3 suggests.

But damages are a different matter. We certainly do not want to make it unlawful to innovate a new space-efficient rack, and once the rack is invented to deploy it at a retailer's request or with a retailer's permission. Tortious destruction of racks might be different, although in a monopolization case we would want proof that this made a significant contribution to the maintenance of UST's large market share. The court abandoned any possibility of proving an antitrust violation rather than a tort by concluding that it was "impractical" for the plaintiff to look at the 300,000 stores in which Conwood and UST sold their product and determine which rack replacements were procompetitive and which were tortious.[34] The court cited a few other facts that satisfied it that the impact of the conduct was substantial, although none of them related tortious rack removals to market share or injury to competition. The court noted that Conwood replaced approximately 20,000 removed racks per month and that such replacements cost it $100,000 per month. But spread over the 300,000 stores in which the products were sold, this indicates that one wire rack per fifteen stores was replaced each month, and that replacement costs were roughly thirty-three cents per store per month. Far from showing a significant contribution to market power, these numbers indicate that the competitive impact of rack replacements was *de minimis*. Of the other practices that the court condemned, the very modest discounts in exchange for information were clearly procompetitive. The court agreed with the expert and condemned the provision of false information without considering well-established requirements that the supplied information be material to a buyer's decision and that rivals be unable to respond by supplying their own information.[35]

Errors like those in the *Conwood* decision are fairly uncommon today, although many courts committed them in the 1960s and 1970s. Mainly, the court confused intent with conduct. The evidence indicated that UST's sales personnel were instructed to get their racks into retailers' stores by any means they could. If the retailer wanted UST's racks and asked for them, great, but if it did not, then the UST salesperson should get them in by some other means. But this is probably the story of nearly every innovation that is marketed. The firm that has something different to offer pushes it hard. In the process it may step over a line between fair and unfair competition. But hard pushing of one's own product, service, or enhancement does not become unlawful monopolization simply because the defendant intended to monopolize.

When dealing with subjective intent and §2, courts should simply assume the worst. Every firm intends to get all the business it can, and it will use means fair or foul, particularly when there is no bright line separating the two. Intent evidence is never an excuse for skipping proof of anticompetitive *conduct*. The Supreme Court made this clear in the *Brooke Group* predatory pricing case, when it declared that even an act of "pure malice" does not become an antitrust violation unless the evidence of market structure, clearly defined anticompetitive conduct, and competitive harm is there to back it up.[36] While intent evidence can sometimes be useful in assessing ambiguous conduct, there were no ambiguities in the moist-snuff wars that intent evidence could illuminate. The intent to injure rivals does not turn the development of an integrated rack and installing it at a retailer's invitation into an anticompetitive act, any more than inventing the electronic calculator becomes an antitrust violation if the inventor intended to destroy slide rule manufacturers. In the corpus of bad antitrust decisions few have gone so far as to make it unlawful for a firm to innovate a new product and then provide it to someone who actually requested it.

The Disaggregation Requirement and Section 2

Once private plaintiffs have succeeded in showing an antitrust violation, they would naturally like to collect damages for every one of the defendant's acts that injured them. But antitrust awards damages only for those acts that are found to be violations. As a result a plaintiff's evidence of damages must be able to "disaggregate" injuries caused by anticompetitive behavior from those caused by the kind of aggressive competition that antitrust tolerates and even encourages. This requirement is explicit in the antitrust damages provision, §4 of the Clayton Act, which awards damages only for injuries caused "by reason of" an antitrust violation.[37]

Some types of conduct can readily be branded as "anticompetitive" and the plaintiffs compensated for all of it. A good example is price-fixing. Once we know that the defendants have formed a cartel and fixed the price of widgets at, say, $7, we assume that every sale under the cartel is unlawful. A defendant might be able to show that some sales would have been made at the $7 price anyway, but that is not a defense. Price-fixing is an antitrust violation whether or not the defendants are successful in raising the price. Of course, damages are measured by the trebled "overcharge," and the overcharge will be smaller when the price increase is less.

But monopolization is entirely different. The list of things condemned as unlawful monopolization is very poorly defined. Typically firms do not set out to violate §2 in defined ways; a better way of characterizing their behavior is that they compete aggressively, sometimes even maliciously, and some of this conduct steps over the line and becomes an antitrust violation.

We could say that once a firm steps over the line, all of its conduct that injures a rival should become the basis for antitrust damages. But such a rule would yield gross overdeterrence and would require firms to pull their competitive punches for risk of going too far. We need to recognize that aggressive competition *requires* injury to rivals, particularly in concentrated markets. For example, a firm cuts price in order to obtain more business, and we want to encourage it to do so. If the price occasionally dips below cost, we do not want to condemn all of the firm's price-cutting behavior.

The disaggregation requirement is well established in antitrust case law, and easily stated: the damages expert must quantify the amount by which anticompetitive conduct is responsible for the plaintiff's harm. The principle is hardly unique to antitrust law: in medical malpractice cases we do not award damages for the plaintiff's pre-existing conditions, and the victim of a fender bender cannot collect from the insurance company for the dent that already existed before the accident occurred.

In the *Conwood* case just discussed, the court concluded that it would be "impractical" to force the defendant to examine what happened at each of 300,000 stores in order to determine whether substitutions of display racks at a particular store were pro- or anticompetitive. It then permitted the plaintiff to offer a methodology that purported to measure damages by comparing the plaintiff's overall growth rate in states where the harmful conduct was thought to be effective with those in which it was not. The methodology, which is described in more detail in Chapter 4, could not separate out injuries caused by tortious conduct (such as unapproved removals of display racks) from those caused by competition and even innovation, such as winning a rack design competition requested by a retailer. The message that sends to dominant firms is that if they compete aggressively they had better make sure that none of their conduct steps over some poorly defined line, or else they will be answerable in treble damages even for their competitive behavior that benefits consumers.

Sometimes the presence of at least some anticompetitive behavior seems clear but the court is unable to distinguish between harms that resulted from that behavior and that which may have resulted from other behavior that is procompetitive or competitively harmless. The best solution in such cases is to grant the plaintiff an injunction but not damages. Once the *Conwood* court was satisfied that anticompetitive conduct had occurred, but not having any basis in the expert's study for assessing its extent, an injunction against replacing racks without permission would have solved the problem without penalizing procompetitive rack replacements and other efficient conduct.

The *Conwood* decision is deeply troublesome and offensive to antitrust policy, and will be used as ammunition by those who believe that competitor lawsuits should be abolished.[38] The argument is that federal courts are simply not capable of separating competitive from anticompetitive conduct, that they focus so excessively on intent that they do not seriously consider whether conduct truly harmed competition, and that such suits chill aggressive competition unnecessarily because plaintiffs are almost always complaining about increased rather than decreased competition.

I do not believe that such despair is in order. *Conwood* was an outlier. The solution lies not in abolition of competitor lawsuits, but in better supervision of circuit panels. Circuit courts decide major questions of law and evidence through three-judge panels that probably get it right 95 percent of the time, but the supervisory power over poor decisions has become much weaker than it used to be. Too few panel decisions are reviewed by the entire court "en banc." In addition, the Supreme Court has drastically cut back on the number of antitrust cases it reviews. As a result the divisions among circuits are much more widespread and undisciplined than they used to be.

Unfortunately, the self-correction process takes years. The most serious impact of anticompetitive antitrust decisions is not the large damage awards paid by particular defendants. Rather, it is the billions of dollars in higher prices and loss of innovation that consumers will pay because prudent antitrust lawyers will warn their clients away from aggressive competition.

8

Antitrust and Distribution

The American system for distributing goods and services is a wonder to behold for its variety and its remarkable efficiency.[1] It could not have been created without a legal tradition that values contract rights. Firms want to maximize profits, which means that they are constantly searching for the lowest cost or most effective way of doing things. The Nobel Prize economist Ronald H. Coase provided the insight that the size and scope of a firm are determined by the economics of doing things for oneself as opposed to purchasing them on the market. As Coase observed, while building one's own distribution networks or retail stores is costly, using the market is also costly. If Ford sells directly to the consumer through a company-owned dealership, the only transaction in a finished car is the consumer sale itself. By contrast, if Ford sells to an independent distributor who then sells to an independent dealer, we have multiplied the number of transactions to three. If distribution is relatively cheaper when the firm does so for itself, then the firm tends to become vertically integrated and relatively larger. If distribution is relatively cheaper when the firm contracts it to other firms, then the firm tends to be relatively smaller and leaves distribution up to others.[2]

Both self-distribution and contract distribution are ubiquitous in our economy. Furthermore, the difference is not driven by absolute firm size. Tiny pizza restaurants usually deliver their own pizzas rather than hire taxicab companies or UPS. By contrast, very large manufacturers such as Maytag, Colgate-Palmolive, or General Electric do little of their own consumer selling. Rather, they sell to distributors, dealers, or large retailers. The basic economics of distribution explains both sets of decisions. For the pizza restaurant, delivery by employees is cheaper, quicker, or more reliable. Perhaps the delivery agent does double duty as kitchen crew, and is available to make a delivery on a moment's notice. By contrast, selling washing machines, toothpaste, or lightbulbs is most efficiently accomplished by multiproduct stores that sell many brands. One can imagine a world in which Colgate-Palmolive owned many little kiosks that sold nothing but Colgate-brand toothpaste. But distribution would be far more costly than it would be through Wal-Mart, Osco Drugs, A&P Grocery, or an array of other retailers. Each of these retailers takes advantage of the fact that it is cheaper to organize many products in one place, using the same facility and employees to stock and maintain all of them. For their part, consumers ordinarily prefer not to go to one store for their toothpaste, another for their milk, and still another for their fresh salad greens. Of course, Colgate-Palmolive does not produce these other things, so it "wholesales" its products. The independent retail market for groceries and related items works most efficiently when it aggregates the products of many manufacturers into one place.

In other situations manufacturers use independent dealers because doing so increases dealer incentives or permits the firms to share business risks. Franchising is a particularly good example. Carvel, which sells high-quality ice cream, could open its own little stores all over the country. For the most part, however, Carvel sells through independently owned franchisees whose stores bear Carvel trademarks recognized by consumers. These franchisees are, typically, locally owned family businesses. This arrangement works for Carvel because the franchisee usually puts up a sizable share of the capital to get into the business. Furthermore, local business owners often have greater incentives to work hard than do employees; their fortunes are intimately tied to the success of the business in which they have made a significant investment.

From its high point in the 1960s and 1970s, antitrust regulation of distribution has undergone a well-justified decline. One issue worth considering, however, is whether we have gone too far, and now tolerate some practices that have a significant potential for competitive harm. In general, manufacturers and other suppliers have every incentive to make their distribution systems operate as efficiently as possible. If manufacturer incentives were the only matter we had to worry about, the role of the antitrust laws would be small, limited to a few cases of manufacturer collusion, anticompetitive tying, or exclusive dealing. But *dealers* have different incentives: they can profit by high markups and lessened competition in the distribution market. The principal focus of antitrust should be protection of the distribution market from the occasional situation where excessive dealer power rather than manufacturer policy explains a distribution restraint.

Antitrust concerns about distribution have historically been so great that every substantive antitrust provision has been applied to distribution practices. First, §2 of the Sherman Act, which condemns monopolization and attempt to monopolize, prohibits at least some vertical practices by firms that have significant market power, something that is rare in distribution markets. Second, §1 of the Sherman Act condemns "unreasonable" trade restraints, and has been applied to manufacturer fixing of dealer's prices (resale price maintenance) and manufacturer specification of the territories within which resellers can operate, or other "nonprice" restrictions on dealer behavior. Third, the Robinson-Patman Act limits a manufacturer's power to charge competing dealers different prices. Fourth, §7 of the Clayton Act (treated in the next chapter) and occasionally §1 of the Sherman Act address vertical acquisitions, which include a firm's acquisitions of its distributors or dealers. Finally, "interbrand" restraints, mainly tying and exclusive dealing, are governed by both §1 of the Sherman Act and §3 of the Clayton Act. Tying occurs when a manufacturer insists that a dealer take certain "tied" products as a condition of getting the manufacturer's "tying" product, which is the one that the dealer really wants. Tying is common in franchise arrangements, but today most of it is lawful even though tying is said to be illegal per se. Exclusive dealing occurs when a manufacturer insists that a dealer sell that manufacturer's brand of a product exclusively. For example, a Carvel ice cream franchise is very likely prohibited from selling a competitor's ice cream, or a General Motors car dealership may be forbidden to sell non-GM automobiles.

Resale price maintenance (RPM), vertical nonprice restraints, and the Robinson-Patman Act all deal with what we generally call "intrabrand" restraints—that is, restraints that affect the way a manufacturer's own brand is distributed. By contrast, tying arrangements and exclusive dealing are called "interbrand" restraints because they govern the relationship between one manufacturer's brand and the brands of others. Tying would occur if Colgate-Palmolive insisted that no druggist could purchase its toothpaste unless it took an equal amount of shampoo. The possible impact would be that the store would have less shelf space to dedicate to a rival's shampoos, which it might otherwise prefer. Exclusive dealing in this setting would be more aggressive: it would occur if Colgate-Palmolive insisted that the druggist sell only Colgate toothpaste and no one else's brand. In that case rival toothpaste manufacturers would be completely foreclosed from access to that store's shelf space. As the illustration suggests, exclusive dealing often has more exclusionary power than tying does. Irrationally, however, the courts have been significantly more hostile toward tying.

Each of these areas has experienced major shifts in antitrust enforcement since the late 1970s.

The Logic of Intrabrand Restraints

Manufacturers profit when their distribution systems work as efficiently as possible. While dealers collectively profit when a manufacturer's product is highly successful, individual dealers often profit even more when they can earn high markups by limiting competition with other dealers in the same brand. The interests of manufacturers and dealers are thus sometimes at odds, and this tension explains most vertical intrabrand restraints.

The procompetitive rationales for vertical restraints are numerous and varied. The most commonly cited one is the "free rider" problem. Manufacturers need dealers to perform certain point-of-sale functions, such as displaying the product and educating consumers about it via trained sales staff. A price-cutting dealer might take advantage of the fact that one cannot charge separately for these services. This dealer will charge a very low markup and refuse to provide the services, knowing that the customer will go to the "full service" dealer to be educated, and then switch to the discounting dealer to make her purchase. But dealers cannot survive by supplying uncompensated services that benefit other dealers. The manufacturer can minimize free riding by using territorial restraints to keep its dealers far apart. Alternatively, it can use resale price maintenance to prevent discounting, thus forcing each dealer to compete by providing every cost-justified point-of-sale service.[3]

Vertical restraints might also give dealers a greater incentive to promote the manufacturer's brand rather than someone else's. Resale price maintenance in particular may provide higher margins that encourage a retailer to give the manufacturer preferred rather than inferior shelf space. Alternatively, RPM may compensate dealers for handling unprofitable products. The recorded music and book markets are good examples. A high percentage of CDs and books are commercial flops, but we only know that after the fact, and retailers need to carry a full line at least for a certain period after they are released. Supplier-imposed RPM induces the stores to carry a full line by assuring high markups on both the popular and unpopular titles. Otherwise stores would compete by reducing their markup and carrying only the most popular titles.[4]

The two distinguishing features of *intra*brand restraints are that they explicitly control only a particular manufacturer's own brand, and powerful dealers have an incentive to impose them, sometimes for anticompetitive purposes. So one can draw this pair of generalizations: intrabrand restraints initiated by manufacturers acting without coercion from their dealers are almost certain to be competitive. By contrast, restraints imposed on manufacturers by powerful dealers or dealers' groups are more likely to be anticompetitive.

Both of these rules have exceptions. Manufacturers might impose a vertical restraint in order to make collusion easier to enforce. For example, manufacturers might carry out a market division agreement by imposing territorial limits on their dealers. However, there is little empirical evidence that manufacturer collusion explains a significant number of vertical restraints.[5] On the other side, dealers are injured by free riding just as much as manufacturers are. As a result they may request that a rival dealer be terminated, limited, or disciplined, and the discipline may take the form of a price or nonprice restraint. For this reason the courts have held that it is not per se unlawful for a manufacturer to terminate one dealer at the request of a competing dealer.[6]

Because intrabrand restraints are presumptively procompetitive, with relatively few exceptions, they are perfect grist for the rule of reason, where power and anticompetitive effects have to be proven. Historically, however, the courts have not understood vertical restraints very well. Both the law and policy have been all over the place. Highly regarded academic commentators have proposed both per se legality and per se illegality,[7] and the case law has been incoherent. So-called minimum resale price maintenance, where a manufacturer stipulates the minimum price at which its product can be sold, has technically been unlawful per se since 1911. By contrast, maximum resale price maintenance was declared per se unlawful in 1968, but brought under the rule of reason in 1997. No cases have subsequently condemned it. After a decade-long period of per se illegality, vertical nonprice restraints were brought under the rule of reason in 1977, and few nonprice restraints have been condemned since that date.

Resale Price Maintenance

The most unfortunate development in the law of resale price maintenance was the Supreme Court's *Dr. Miles* decision, which was interpreted to hold that RPM is unlawful per se.[8] On the facts of that particular case, condemnation was appropriate. Retail druggists were fixing prices and using manufacturers as their "enforcer." Manufacturers such as Dr. Miles entered into resale price maintenance agreements with individual druggists and enforced them by inspecting the stores and collecting violation reports.[9] Although the Supreme Court never said it in so many words, its examination of the record may have led it to believe that facilitating cartels was the principal function of RPM. Nevertheless, the Court never distinguished between condemnation of the horizontal price-fixing conspiracy and RPM itself.

The *Dr. Miles* per se rule was unfortunate in a double sense. First, it was the wrong rule, given that much RPM is competitively benign in the great majority of situations when it is not being used to facilitate collusion. But, second, the rule hindered the development of an economic understanding of the rationales and effects of RPM. The per se rule makes proof of actual anticompetitive effects immaterial. As a result litigants do not spend much effort looking for economic rationales. All that is relevant is whether the manufacturer and the dealer agreed on a minimum resale price. Had RPM been assessed under the rule of reason, the courts would have required answers to such questions as: When does RPM result in lower manufacturer output or higher prices? When are these higher prices marketwide, thus placing them within the concern of the antitrust laws? Or how often is a cartel lurking in the background, as it was in the *Dr. Miles* case? One of the costs of per se rules is that once they are created the courts lose much of their incentive to engage in an economic analysis of the challenged restraint; they need to know only whether it fits the definition under the rule. This makes it critical that per se rules be cautiously developed and carefully defined.

In 1984 and again in 1988 the Supreme Court began to respond to widespread criticism of the per se rule for RPM, but not by abolishing the rule itself. First, it put new teeth into the requirement that RPM is unlawful only if there is an "agreement" between the manufacturer and the dealer.[10] Second, it adopted a very strict definition of "price" that applies the per se rule only to an agreement under which the retailer must charge a specific retail price.[11] The result of these two limitations is that unlawful RPM is difficult to prove even though it is nominally unlawful per se.

While any rule that reduces the number of times RPM is condemned might be regarded as an improvement, these hypertechnical "agreement" and "price" requirements are not the correct way to address the problem. RPM should be analyzed under the rule of reason. Whether a particular instance of RPM is pro- or anticompetitive depends much less on whether there was an agreement about a specific price than on the origin of the impetus to agree and the economic rationale. For example, one court applying these two decisions refused to find a price agreement when a large distributor threatened the manufacturer in these terms: "make [the plaintiff] raise its prices to our . . . level or drop [it] as a distributor." The court held that this language failed to show that the "defendants agreed to set the prices" at which the complaining distributor would sell the manufacturer's products.[12] But what the court really needed to know was whether the large distributor was using its economic position to force the manufacturer to accede to higher retail markups and thus reduced distribution of its product, or whether the large distributor had legitimate free rider concerns. The per se approach made these inquiries irrelevant.

In another case a large retailer with 200 stores complained to clothing manufacturer Jantzen about the price cutting of a single store operation. The court found no qualifying "agreement," but admitted that "Jantzen, weighting the advantage of selling to 200 Belk [complaining dealer] stores against selling to the Garment District [the price-cutting plaintiff], opted to drop the Garment District."[13] To be sure, the Garment District may have been taking a free ride on a full-service dealer. Free riding, however, harms manufacturers as much as it harms full-service dealers. In that case Jantzen would not have waited until it was threatened by a powerful dealer. But the quoted statement indicated that Belk was coercing Jantzen into terminating a retailer against its best interest.

If so, the termination foisted higher distribution costs on Jantzen and higher prices on consumers.

How many instances of RPM are efficient and imposed by manufacturers, and how many are anticompetitive and imposed by powerful dealers, is difficult to say. But the latter may represent a significant minority of cases.[14] In the *Toys"R"Us* decision the defendant, a large retailer of toys, cajoled toy suppliers into discriminating against low-price dealers such as warehouse clubs by selling to the latter only less desirable toys or by packaging toys in large, unattractive bundles.[15] One can also not ignore the possibility of dealer cartels that collectively pressure a supplier to police the cartel through vertical restraints that punish dealers unwilling to go along with the cartel—effectively, the facts of the *Dr. Miles* case.[16]

The courts need to jettison the per se rule for RPM and adopt a form of analysis that is more concerned about powerful dealers or dealer collusion, and less concerned about whether the challenged restraint requires a dealer to set a specific price. Restraints at the behest of a powerful dealer or dealer groups can be anticompetitive whether or not they require a specific price, and many cartels operate on the basis of general understandings rather than agreements about specific prices. The Supreme Court's insistence on a narrowly defined "price" restraint reflected the differential treatment of minimum price restraints, which are unlawful per se, and nonprice restraints, which are addressed under the rule of reason. Once both types of restraints are placed under the rule of reason, however, the price/nonprice distinction becomes relatively unimportant. Courts will be able to get on with the job they should have started nearly a century ago, which is to understand when RPM and related vertical practices serve anticompetitive ends.

Maximum RPM, or manufacturer stipulation of the maximum price at which a product is sold, is probably the least controversial of the vertical restraints. Maximum RPM was declared unlawful per se in a very poorly reasoned Supreme Court decision in 1968, and so it remained until the Supreme Court changed its mind in 1997.[17] No case has condemned maximum RPM since then, and there are not likely to be any. Manufacturers wish their products to be distributed as efficiently as possible, which means forcing dealers to charge only a competitive markup. In some cases interdealer competition solves that problem, but when it fails, a manufacturer may resort to other means. For example, if an isolated gasoline station is able to charge a fifteen-cent markup when the competitive markup is nine cents, the manufacturer may seek to control that dealer's maximum price. Condemning maximum RPM injures consumers, manufacturers, and dealers generally, benefiting only the particular dealer who is then free to set as high a price as it pleases. Maximum RPM thus presents the strongest case for per se legality.

Vertical Nonprice Restraints

The law of vertical nonprice restraints was also subject to a great deal of indirection until the Supreme Court's *GTE Sylvania* decision in 1977. There were relatively few challenges prior to the *White Motor* case in 1963, when the Supreme Court concluded it was premature to declare them unlawful per se. However, the Court changed its mind four years later in *Schwinn*. Then followed a confusing decade in which the lower courts tried to administer a per se rule against nonprice restraints that on the whole seemed socially beneficial and competitively harmless. Since *Sylvania* overruled *Schwinn* and applied a rule of reason, very few purely vertical nonprice restraints have been condemned.[18]

Nonprice restraints share most of the same explanations underlying RPM. Which one works better under the circumstance depends on the nature of the product and of the distribution mechanism. In general, restraints specifying retailer locations are unnecessary for small-ticket items such as electric shavers or can openers, but tend to encourage more aggressive dealer promotion for items such as large appliances or automobiles. Territorial restraints are also used when the seller is a distributor or traveling sales representative, who is assigned a specific "territory" in which he or she is authorized to make sales.

It is critical to keep in mind that territorial restrictions operate as the manufacturer's alternative to self-distribution through its own employees. If Maytag sold washing machines through wholly owned stores, it would be unlikely to build three stores four blocks apart in the same city. Customers are willing to drive a little further for more expensive goods, and dealerships need to make enough sales to cover their overhead and promote the product properly. While the ownership structure differs when a manufacturer sells to independent distributors or retailers, these basic economic attributes remain the same. Independent, multibrand dealerships push the products that are most profitable, and they are more likely to do this when they can promote over a wider geographic range with some assurance that the payoff will accrue to them rather than a rival dealer. For example, Sylvania's foundering sales received a significant boost when it adopted the spatial restrictions on dealerships that the Supreme Court approved in 1977.[19]

Not all nonprice restraints are locational. Manufacturers might control dealers through such devices as limiting mail order sales,[20] or limiting the product lines that a dealer can sell.[21] These are virtually never shown to have anticompetitive effects. Other restraints do not plausibly limit competition at all. For example, a gasoline station franchisor may require that rest rooms be cleaned every four hours, or a fast-food franchisor may require that french fries be held under hot lamps for no more than thirty minutes. It is difficult to come up with a credible anticompetitive story about such restraints.

Dealer power or dealer collusion may explain some nonprice restraints. One possibility is horizontal market division by dealers, which manufacturers could enforce if they were willing. The manufacturer does business with the dealers on a daily basis, while dealers consulting each other might arouse suspicion. In any event, the empirical case for nonprice restraints as exercises of dealer power is far weaker than it is for price restraints.[22] On the other side, the full range of nonprice restraints creates much more obvious benefits than price restraints. By and large, the manufacturer has a much more direct interest in the dealer's provision of the appropriate amount of promotion and service than in maintaining the price that the dealer charges. The manufacturer can be expected to control distribution practices directly where possible, rather than indirectly through resale price maintenance.

The Benefits of a Single Antitrust Rule

While the effects of vertical price and nonprice restraints are not absolutely identical, there is a common core of concern and considerable overlap in those effects. The same fundamental logic applies to both: even if a manufacturer has market power in its brand, there are few obvious ways of exercising power by limiting the distribution of one's own products. While the monopolist "exercises" monopoly power by reducing output and raising price, in the manufacturer's case this means raising its *own* wholesale price. It cannot profit by making its distribution system less efficient and giving monopoly prices to its dealers. So all vertical restraints are presumptively procompetitive. While restraints that reflect dealer power or collusion are an exception, they appear to account for only a few situations.

One of the considerable costs of administering antitrust policy governing vertical restraints is the cost of applying two different antitrust rules to practices that have largely similar economic effects. Lawyer and judicial resources are wasted in disputes about whether a particular restraint falls into the "price" or "nonprice" category.[23] But this dispute has taken center stage in vertical restraints cases because price restraints are unlawful per se, while virtually all nonprice restraints are legal.

While price restraints have a statistically greater propensity to be anticompetitive, a well-formulated rule of reason would be able to identify specific anticompetitive restraints, in particular those compelled by powerful dealers or distributors. Furthermore, application of the rule of reason to both classes of vertical restraints would still permit some per se challenges where the true restraint was *horizontal* rather than vertical. A few cases, including *Dr. Miles* itself, have involved cartels of dealers effected through supplier-imposed restraints. When these dealer agreements are naked, they are unlawful per se. A complicating factor, however, is that not all horizontal dealer agreements are naked. Groups of dealers may have legitimate complaints about free riding by other dealers, or concerns that certain dealer services can be provided effectively only if every dealer is required to provide them. In such cases it is quite legitimate for the dealers acting as a group to report their concerns to the manufacturer.[24]

Applying the rule of reason to both classes of restraints would largely eliminate the overly fastidious concerns about whether the restraint was sufficiently about "price" and turn the attention of courts to uncovering the relatively small subset of anticompetitively imposed restraints.

Wholesale Pricing and the Robinson-Patman Act

Other than per se illegality for RPM, the most anticompetitive antitrust rules governing intrabrand distribution are those imposed by the Robinson-Patman Act. That statute requires manufacturers to charge competing dealers the same price for similar goods. For example, suppose Ford has two independently owned auto dealerships in Lincoln, Nebraska.

One of them is aggressive and moves many cars. The other is more content to rest on its laurels. Ford responds by giving the aggressive dealer rebates or discounts that reward its growing sales. As a result the aggressive dealer ends up paying less per car than the less ambitious dealer. This is the grist for a Robinson-Patman case.[25]

Most antitrust books treat the Robinson-Patman Act separately from everything else, as if it were a kind of bastard child of the antitrust laws. The statute is sometimes described as the "Wrong Way Corrigan" of antitrust. On July 18, 1938, pilot Douglas "Wrong Way" Corrigan took off from New York City intending to fly to Los Angeles, but landed twenty hours later in Dublin, Ireland. The characterization is appropriate, because the Robinson-Patman Act often operates to harm consumers for the benefit of weaker or less efficient dealers. It moves antitrust policy in precisely the wrong direction.

Nevertheless, treating the Robinson-Patman Act separately as a "meta" antitrust provision obscures its origins and intended purpose, which was to limit the way that producers distribute their goods. The statute was born out of the Great Depression and New Deal, a period of hostility toward vertical integration, and one in which the fortunes of many small family-owned businesses were destroyed. The intended beneficiaries of the statute were small retail grocers who were having a difficult time warding off large chain stores like A&P. The Robinson-Patman Act served to limit the discretion of suppliers in pricing their goods to competing dealers, or in supporting advertising or other services. Whatever deal Borden Dairies might give A&P it also had to give to Mom & Pop's Corner Grocery. While these concerns for protection of the independent small business were expressed in a unique way in the Robinson-Patman Act, the same fundamental concerns guided antitrust's aggressive rules against vertical restraints and vertical mergers.

The Robinson-Patman Act makes it unlawful for a supplier to "discriminate" in price between two of its dealers where the requisite injury to "competition" is shown. "Discrimination" under the statute means nothing more than a difference in price, and the injury to competition refers to the dealer who pays more and thus is placed at a competitive disadvantage to another dealer. The subject matter of the Robinson-Patman Act is the wholesale price that the manufacturer charges to the dealer, not the retail price that the dealer must charge its customers. As a result the per se rule for RPM does not apply. Were it not for the Robinson-Patman Act, a manufacturer's pricing to its various dealers would be treated in the same way as vertical nonprice restraints generally. Harm to competition would be highly exceptional, but might occasionally result from package discounts or similar practices.[26]

What was said previously about other distributional restraints applies equally to the Robinson-Patman Act: a manufacturer cannot profit by weakening its own distribution system or reducing its competitiveness. A producer earns the most when its network is operating as efficiently as possible. In trying to achieve this goal a manufacturer might reward the more successful, aggressive, or innovative dealers. *Ex ante,* its goal is certainly not to damage its dealership network, but only to give dealers an inducement to sell more and thus compete more effectively with competing brands. A dealer inducement operates no differently than a bonus or reward given to a productive employee.

As is true for intrabrand restraints generally, a powerful *dealer* has different incentives. It would prefer to get the best wholesale price possible for itself, but it also benefits when rival dealers in the same brand are forced to pay more so that it can undersell them. These incentives are not very complicated. While the competitive process has very little to fear from differential wholesale prices that are initiated by uncoerced manufacturers, competition may be harmed when wholesale price differences are forced on a manufacturer by a well-placed dealer.

Unfortunately, the distinction between price differences imposed by manufacturers (procompetitive) and those imposed by powerful dealer-purchasers (sometimes anticompetitive) is largely irrelevant to antitrust policy under the Robinson-Patman Act. Indeed, the Supreme Court has made Robinson-Patman Act claims against powerful buyers almost impossible to prove. Consider the manufacturer of automobiles who gives price concessions to a successful dealer. Less successful dealers do not receive the same price concessions because they have not been as aggressive against other manufacturers' brands. While this is the basis for a Robinson-Patman complaint, it is not even superficially reasonable to say that the manufacturer has injured competition between the two dealers. On the contrary, the manufacturer has facilitated competition by providing an incentive to dealers to become more aggressive in promoting the seller's brand. Whenever anyone takes a longer view than the shortest one possible, incentive discounts further rather than injure competition. Indeed, this is the only view other than coercion by a powerful dealer that makes the manufacturer's scheme a rational act.

To be sure, different treatment in pricing or provision of collateral services injures disfavored resellers. In extreme cases it might even reduce rivalry by forcing some dealers to abandon the manufacturer's product or quit the business. But the general proposition is not controversial: a manufacturer does not make more money, and certainly cannot "monopolize" anything, by making its own distribution system more costly, by restricting the volume of product it is capable of handling, or by reducing its effectiveness. In the absence of buyer coercion, the various price discriminations resulting from a supplier's unilateral pricing decisions must enjoy a very strong presumption that they are economically beneficial.

A manufacturer that owns its own distribution network is likely to "discriminate" by rewarding its more successful branches or employees. The manufacturer may establish incentives programs to encourage sales personnel to push the manufacturer's product aggressively. These incentives might include higher wages for good performance, or other rewards ranging from stock options, annual vacation trips, or other perks. Such a manufacturer is also likely to invest more promotional funds in the more successful distributorships or stores, while reducing its investment in those whose growth is stagnant, or even shutting them down. The manufacturer selling its products through independent dealers is in much the same position. The best way to encourage dealers to sell more is to give them financial rewards, and to promote the product more aggressively in the more successful outlets.[27] But since in these cases the dealers buy and resell the product, financial rewards often take the form of a price discount or rebate that the Robinson-Patman Act condemns without any proof of injury to competition.

One ironic result of Robinson-Patman Act enforcement is that manufacturers who depend on incentive mechanisms to sell their product are likely to replace independent dealerships with wholly owned subsidiaries. Internal firm transfers are not covered by the statute. A manufacturer required by law to give a small, lagging, dealer the same treatment as a larger, more successful, dealer is highly motivated to terminate the smaller dealer, just as a vertically integrated retailer is likely to close its less successful stores. The result subverts the very set of interests that the Robinson-Patman Act was intended to protect—namely, small businesses engaged mainly in resale.[28]

The idiosyncratic and harmful idea that injury to "competition" under the Robinson-Patman Act is nothing more than financial injury to a dysfunctional dealer has been ratified by the Supreme Court, as well as numerous lower court decisions. As one court put it:

> [C]ompetitive injury in a secondary-line Robinson-Patman case may be inferred from evidence of injury to an individual competitor. More specifically, [the Supreme Court] permits a fact finder to infer injury to competition from evidence of a substantial price difference over time, because such a price difference may harm the competitive opportunities of individual merchants, *and thus create a "reasonable possibility" that competition itself may be harmed.*[29]

But the concluding italicized inference is nonsense unless we believe that manufacturers intentionally shoot themselves in the feet. Why would General Motors, Maytag, Texaco, or anyone else engage in a protracted period of rewarding some dealers and not others if they believed the result would be a less competitive distribution system? Nevertheless, this is precisely what the lobbyists for the Robinson-Patman Act argued to Congress. Congress concluded that discrimination in wholesale prices would not only injure individual dealers, but would in the long run damage the vitality of the American distribution system.[30] Congress was in fact witnessing a major revolution in distribution as American retailing passed from the control of small family-owned stores to larger, lower-cost retailers that are often bigger than the manufacturers who supply them. Thanks to highly successful lobbying by the well-organized small grocers, Congress saw this development as economically harmful.

Few statutes have survived such long-lived and unrelenting criticism as has been directed against the Robinson-Patman Act.[31] It is practically a commonplace that the statute's legislative history is anticompetitive and excessively concerned with the protection of small business at the expense of more efficient rivals. What is not always appreciated, however, is that the legislative histories of other antitrust provisions are also filled with these concerns. The legislative histories of the Sherman Act, the Clayton Act, and particularly of the 1950 Amendments to §7 of the Clayton Act were fairly dominated by a fear of big business that we would today regard as exaggerated, and by a strong desire to protect small business from excessive competition. In justifying application of the Robinson-Patman Act in situations where competitive injury is impossible, courts sometimes make it sound as if other antitrust provisions were strictly concerned with injuries to consumer welfare. For example, two appellate courts have suggested that

> [i]n contrast to the Sherman Act and the Clayton Act, which were intended to proscribe only conduct that threatens consumer welfare, the Robinson-Patman Act's framers "intended to punish perceived economic evils not necessarily threatening to consumer welfare per se."[32]

But the legislative history of the 1950 amendments to §7 was hardly dominated by consumer welfare concerns, and was heavily concerned with mergers creating larger firms that could undersell smaller ones—that is, with a set of interests that are largely contrary to the goals of merger policy today.[33]

A great deal of revisionism has gone into our interpretations of the Sherman Act and §7 of the Clayton Act. Predatory pricing is analyzed today under standards that are significantly more restrictive on plaintiffs than the framers of either the Sherman Act or original §2 of the Clayton Act revealed. Mergers are tolerated today that would never have been accepted by the framers of the 1950 amendments to the merger statute. But the courts often seem reluctant to treat the Robinson-Patman Act the same way, as if its legislative history deserves a degree of deference and durability not given to the legislative history of these other antitrust statutes.

In any event, the statute that Congress intended did not condemn injuries to small dealers for their own sake, but rather injury to a competitor's ability to compete with a rival when such injury can reasonably be viewed as a prerequisite to a "larger, general injury" to competition.[34] That larger injury does not obtain when retailer buying power is absent.

Congress's and the FTC's own prior investigations leading up to the Robinson-Patman Act had not focused on the price discrimination of competitive manufacturers seeking to improve their distribution systems. Rather, they were concerned with the practices of very large buyers. As one of the principal non-congressional drafters of the legislation explained at the hearings, "The bill is based entirely upon the fact that large buyers, by the coercive use of their buying power, extract from the seller differentials greater than the cost differences between the two buyers warrant. That is the evil at which the bill is aimed."[35] The House Report explicitly disavowed any notion that the bill was designed to undermine any "physical economies" that might come about from "mass buying and distribution," even by the chain stores.[36]

The one situation where a manufacturer's price discrimination to re-sellers can be anticompetitive occurs when the low price is coerced by a powerful dealer. For example, A&P may have hundreds of stores while its rivals have only one each. A&P may then be in a position to force manufacturers to charge other dealers higher prices, in the same way that a dealer might force manufacturers to impose resale price mainte-nance or nonprice restraints on rival dealers.

In that case a reasonable interpretation of the Robinson-Patman Act is to identify and discipline such situations, but leave manufacturers gen-erally free to use rebates or other price concessions as a device to reward dealer effectiveness. Consistent with that proposition, a prerequisite to secondary-line recovery should be a showing that the supplied market is not performing competitively, and that dealer buying power rather than manufacturer reward explains the price discrimination under consider-ation.[37]

While the courts have read parts of the Robinson-Patman Act's legisla-tive history as woodenly as possible, they have largely ignored its perva-sive concern with the power of large retailers such as A&P to extract price concessions from suppliers. Nor has the Supreme Court been help-ful. In the *Vanco Beverage* decision it rejected the defendant's argument that competitive injury should be inferred only in cases where price dis-crimination was compelled by large powerful buyers.[38]

Concerns about large-chain buying power were more pressing in 1936 than they are today. The constituents of the Robinson-Patman Act had witnessed the rise of the great chain stores and a serious economic de-pression that gave United States producers significant excess capacity. During a period of rapid expansion of efficient multistore retailer opera-tions and numerous distressed sellers who needed to keep their plants running, these large buyers may have wielded considerable power. By contrast, large chain stores today have become a fact of life, and in most markets competition among them is robust. That is to say, even though large retailers have lower costs and purchase in great quantities, they generally face intense competition from equally large retailers operating in the same markets. Indeed, American retailing operates on some of the lowest margins in the business world.

This author, as many others, would prefer to see the Robinson-Patman Act repealed. Any social benefit it confers certainly does not match the compliance and enforcement costs associated with it. Fur-thermore, any legitimately anticompetitive price concessions compelled by powerful buyers could be dealt with under §1 or occasionally §2 of the Sherman Act. But academics like myself have been calling for repeal for a half century, and Congress has never come close to responding. Instead, the courts could go a long way toward correcting the problem without legislative repeal, merely by reading the legislative history of this statute in the same way they have read the history of the other antitrust provisions. Under that approach a Robinson-Patman Act violation would require proof of an injury to "competition" in the antitrust sense, and this would rarely occur except when price concessions were forced on manufacturers by powerful retailers.

Distribution and Interbrand Restraints

An interbrand restraint is typically imposed by a seller and limits a dealer's ability to sell the goods of a rival seller. The most explicit interbrand restraint is exclusive dealing, where the dealer agrees not to handle a competitor's goods. For example, a prospective Ford truck dealer may not be able to obtain a dealership unless he agrees not to sell new trucks made by other manufacturers, or a prospective Carvel ice cream franchisee may have to agree that she will sell Carvel's line of ice cream exclusively.

The other principal interbrand restraint is tying, which occurs when a seller insists that the buyer take a second, or "tied," product as a condition of obtaining the seller's "tying" product. Tying may or may not limit a dealer's sales of rival products, depending on the circumstances. For example, a manufacturer of motorcycles and snowmobiles may insist that anyone wishing to be its bike dealer sell its snowmobiles as well. That would be a tying arrangement in which motorcycles are the "tying" product and snowmobiles are the "tied" product. If no exclusive dealing agreement were imposed, however, this dealer would be free to handle the motorcycles or snowmobiles of other manufacturers.

Exclusive dealing is addressed under the rule of reason and is usually lawful. Over the last generation courts have become more tolerant of exclusive dealing, and usually do not condemn the practice unless it significantly impairs the opportunities of rivals to enter or expand in a relevant market. This requires proof of a significant position in two different markets, the "primary" market, which constitutes the defendant's base, and a "secondary" market in which exclusion is thought to occur. For example, suppose a hospital accounted for 80 percent of an area's admissions for surgery, and that surgical anesthesiology can be practiced only in a hospital. Now the hospital enters into a contract promising to use only a particular anesthesiological firm. Foreclosure is possible because (1) the hospital controls a significant proportion of surgical admissions, *and* (2) a significant portion of the anesthesiological market is foreclosed from rival anesthesiologists. The two-level analysis is necessary because not every exclusive contract by a dominant firm represents significant foreclosure. For example, this same hospital might enter into an exclusive contract with a firm to supply its bandages. Although the hospital controls 80 percent of surgical admissions, bandages are purchased by clinics, physicians' offices, nursing homes, pharmacists, and even general purpose discount stores. The bandage contract very likely forecloses only a small percentage of the local bandage market.

A high foreclosure percentage is a necessary but not a sufficient condition for competitive harm. While a dominant hospital's exclusive contract with an anesthesiologist might deprive rival anesthesiologists of a chance to practice, it is not apparent why prices would be higher. Even a monopoly hospital has no interest in using overpriced anesthesiologists, and the anesthesiologist has no interest in working in an overcharging hospital. While either might be a monopolist, it could charge its full monopoly price with or without an exclusive agreement with the other.

Foreclosure becomes anticompetitive only when it imposes higher costs on rivals or denies them the access they need to make the market more competitive. For example, in *American Can* the defendant entered exclusive contracts requiring most of the existing makers of can-making machinery to supply the defendant and no one else.[39] As a result rival can makers were relegated to inferior methods of making cans. When rivals' cans were either lower quality or more expensive, American Can could charge more for its cans. Eventually the market would likely become more competitive anyway, but the exclusive dealing agreements might enable American Can's monopoly to last longer.

Unlike exclusive dealing, tying is said to be illegal per se when the defendant ties two separate products and has market power in the tying product.[40] This idiosyncratic per se rule, which has been around since the 1940s, suggests that ties are more likely to be anticompetitive than exclusive dealing is. In fact, the reverse is typically true. Exclusive dealing can exclude a rival entirely from an outlet, while tying is likely to exclude only from a particular product. The motorcycle/snowmobile example illustrates the difference. If Yamaha engages in tying, the dealer must sell both Yamaha bikes and Yamaha snowmobiles, but it is free to sell bikes made by Honda or Harley, or snowmobiles made by Polaris. However, if Yamaha requires exclusive dealing of either motorcycles or snowmobiles, then the dealer will not be able to sell rival machines at all. Under tying, but not exclusive dealing, customers would be able to compare prices and models of different manufacturers' motorcycles in the same store.

Many of the franchise agreements treated by the courts as tying arrangements really involve exclusive dealing. For example, in the famous *Siegel v. Chicken Delight* case the franchisor conditioned the grant of a franchise on the franchisee's use of the franchisor's paper products bearing the Chicken Delight logo, as well as its herbs and spices. Notably, the franchisee was not merely required to use these things; it was required to use them *exclusively*. Any injury to competition that might result would come from the exclusive dealing.[41] Such cases are characterized as "tying" because the plaintiffs were trying to take advantage of tying's irrational "per se" rule, so they claimed that the entire business, or the franchise itself, was the tying product. Many exclusive dealing agreements can be turned into tying by this sleight of hand. For example, the Yamaha motorcycle dealer who would also like to sell Honda bikes is likely to challenge exclusive dealing by claiming an unlawful tie. In this case the "right to be a Yamaha dealer," or some equivalent formulation, becomes the tying product, while the Yamaha motorbikes are the tied product.

In this sense the relationship between tying and exclusive dealing is much like the relationship between vertical price and nonprice restraints discussed earlier. Economically, tying and exclusive dealing are very similar, and often the difference is no more than the name given to the practice. After a half century of economic analysis we know that both practices are efficient and procompetitive most of the time, but there are a few exceptional cases where competitive harm is possible. This makes both practices perfect candidates for the rule of reason. If that rule were adopted for both, the legal distinctions between the two practices would virtually evaporate. By contrast, under the existing regime plaintiffs try to claim tying in order to avail themselves of the per se rule. As a result many litigation resources go into determining whether a particular practice is one or the other. In the Supreme Court's *Jefferson Parish* decision five Justices concluded that a hospital's exclusive contract with an anesthesiologist should be treated as tying, while four concluded that it was exclusive dealing.[42]

In nearly a century courts and advocates have developed a number of rationales why tying is anticompetitive. The "leverage" theory articulated by Justice Brandeis in the 1930s and described in Chapter 2 feared that the owner of a monopoly in one product could enlarge the monopoly by tying a second product, and thus monopolize both together.[43] Economically, the leverage theory has been discredited: a firm that is already charging its monopoly price for one product cannot earn more in monopoly profits by tying a second, currently competitive, product and hiking price on that as well. When someone purchases two products together the only thing she cares about is the price of the package. So the size of the monopoly price on the first product depends on the price of the second product. The monopolist can charge more for a tied product only by taking a corresponding reduction in the tying product.

While the orthodox version of the leverage theory lacks economic traction, it continues to have legal vitality. But the per se rule for ties can be explained *only* as a relic of the leverage theory. It results from a mode of thinking that ties were "extensions" of a monopoly, initially of a patented good, but later expanded to cover unpatented goods as well.

The principal concern of tying law is anticompetitive foreclosure. But foreclosure can only be assessed by examining effects in the relevant market in which the foreclosure occurs. As a result foreclosure concerns can be assessed meaningfully only via the rule of reason. In fact, anticompetitive foreclosure from tying or exclusive dealing is uncommon, and procompetitive explanations overwhelm the legitimate anticompetitive explanations. Before anticompetitive foreclosure can occur there must be a reason for thinking that tying or exclusion has kept one or more significant rivals out of a market, destroyed them, or significantly limited their power to expand output. In the *Microsoft* case discussed in Chapter 12, Microsoft's tying of its Windows operating system to its Internet Explorer web browser served to make it almost impossible for rival browser Netscape to maintain its market position. But *Microsoft* is the exception that proves the rule; foreclosure occurred because the defendant had a dominating position in the computer platform market, with a market share exceeding 90 percent.

Much of our antitrust law of tying and exclusive dealing comes out of disputes between franchisees and franchisors, where the case for condemnation is much weaker than it was in *Microsoft*. Foreclosure is virtually never threatened by franchise tie-ins. The tied products have been everyday items such as paper napkins, cookies, pizza dough, herbs and spices, or automobile lubricants. All of these are commodities sold in large, competitive markets.[44] None of these cases was about injury to competition.

Franchisors tie goods or services for several reasons, all of which are procompetitive. Perhaps the principal one is the manufacturer's wish to distribute its own product. Franchisors contract with franchised outlets, which are merely a contract substitute for wholly owned outlets, so that they will sell the franchisor's products. For example, Shell Oil Company is in business to sell gasoline, which it could do by opening its own stations or else by entering franchise agreements with independent station owners who would then hold themselves out as Shell stations. That purpose would be frustrated if the stations were then free to sell anyone's gas they pleased.

Another reason for product exclusivity in franchise agreements is to prevent "interbrand" free riding. As noted earlier, one type of free riding occurs when price-cutting dealers take a free ride on the promotional efforts of other, full-service, dealers. Resale price maintenance or sometimes vertical nonprice restraints can address that problem. In contrast, interbrand free riding occurs when a single dealer is able to shift resources invested by one manufacturer into a product sold by a different manufacturer. For example, Standard Oil Company as franchisor might hire an architectural firm to design attractive, efficient service stations for franchisees, it might educate franchisees in a training school, and it might provide them with amenities that can be passed on to customers. The result of all this investment is that Standard might acquire a national reputation for quality that is attractive to motorists, particularly if they are in an unfamiliar location. But suppose that the Standard franchisee were free to sell a second brand of "no name" gasoline, which it can offer at a lower price because the manufacturer of this gasoline made none of the service investments that Standard did. Motorists might attribute many of the investments that Standard made to the cheaper gasoline as well. Standard might be able to charge separately for a few amenities, such as road maps given to customers. But some, such as the quality assurance communicated by the "Standard" sign, could never be segregated. Standard may be able to capitalize on its significant investment in franchisee development only by requiring the stations to sell Standard's gasoline exclusively.

A third reason franchisors use ties is to meter sales in order to determine the franchise fee. The franchisor develops and obtains intellectual property rights for its name, logo, and method of doing business. It then licenses the right to use these features for a fee that varies with the franchisee's sales. Successful franchises pay a higher fee than unsuccessful ones, just as a patent licensee who makes many patented units typically pays more than one who makes fewer. One way the franchisor can measure the franchisee's sales is by requiring the franchisee to purchase certain ingredients at higher-than-market prices. For example, since every pizza needs a crust, Domino's might require its franchisees to purchase its dough at a price fifty cents per pizza higher than the market price. The fifty cents in this case represents part of the franchise fee that Domino's earns.

Franchise fees are negotiated on the open market; it is not antitrust's duty to regulate their amount. Even if regulating licensee fees was an antitrust prerogative, there would be little reason to do it in highly competitive markets such as those for pizzas, automobile lubrication, or ice cream.

To be sure, the use of tying to collect franchise fees creates some opportunities for abuse. The main one is that the franchise contract may permit the franchisor to add additional items to the tied list, and generally permits it to charge any price it wants for tied products. The result may effectively be a franchise fee that the franchisor can increase unilaterally after the franchise has been established. That is a little like signing a five-year lease providing that the rent will be $500 the first month, and whatever the landlord wants to charge in subsequent months.

But improvident contracts are not antitrust problems simply because they were carelessly or naively made. The tenant who stupidly signs a lease permitting the landlord to vary the rent has not turned the landlord into a monopolist. To accept the contrary proposition turns antitrust into an engine for resolving contract disputes. Indeed, in the franchise cases the *only* reason the franchisees are in court is because the contract is enforceable. If franchisees are free to evade onerous terms, they cannot be subjected to extreme ties at all.

In all events, antitrust is an extremely poor tool for resolving these disputes. The *size* of a reasonable franchise fee is not even an issue in an antitrust tying challenge. If power and tying of separate products are found, then all of the tying is unlawful. Under tying law a franchisee could sign a franchise agreement at a time when tied product overcharges were 5 percent of revenue and go into court the very next day and have the tying arrangement declared unlawful. Antitrust has no mechanism for saying something like tying of products up to 5 percent of revenue is a reasonable license fee, while tying that creates a greater fee is not. If antitrust applies at all, it invalidates all tying, period. The alternative position would turn franchises into public utilities, and antitrust courts into price regulators.

Furthermore, the abuse problem would not go away if tying were universally prohibited. Suppose a franchise agreement has a six-month termination provision, and the initial franchise agreement stipulates a franchise fee of 5 percent of revenues. After the franchise is established, the franchisor announces that in six months the fee will be raised to 10 percent, and any unhappy franchisee is free to terminate its agreement. This is precisely the facts of the franchise tie cases except that no tying is involved because the fee is assessed directly on revenues rather than by overcharges on a tied product. Franchisors can increase the fee by tying more items only because once a franchisee has made a significant investment in its franchise, terminating the relationship is costly. But this fact has nothing to do with either tying or monopoly; it is simply a consequence of long-term contracting that often serves to commit parties to onerous positions. If the legal system should be invoked to correct this problem, the solution should come from contract law or perhaps from special statutes regulating the franchise relationship.

Finally, franchisors tie goods or services in order to control quality or to achieve uniformity across their franchise networks. Domino's as franchisor may develop a pizza dough that is distinctive but also more costly than generic doughs. The franchise as a whole profits if Domino's can guarantee its customers that, no matter where they buy their Domino's pizza, they will get dough of the same quality and consistency. By contrast, individual franchisees may have other motives. They might profit by skimping on the dough, trusting that Domino's overall reputation will outweigh one unsatisfactory experience that a customer has. Or a particular franchise with a highly transient customer base and little repeat business might use inferior dough simply because it knows that the customer will not be returning anyway, and her lower opinion of Domino's pizza resulting from one bad experience will be taken out on the franchise as a whole. So tying is simply a way that the franchisor tells the franchisees, "these things are distinctive, and if you want to be my franchisee you have to purchase them from me."

To be sure, we might disagree with what the franchisor puts on the list of quality-determining ingredients. Does Dairy Queen really need to use genuine Oreo cookies in its Blizzards, or would most customers not know the difference if franchisees used a cheaper substitute? Is Chicken Delight's pack of herbs and spices really that much better than a substitute set that the franchisee could buy from the local warehouse? Perhaps not. But these are market decisions, having nothing to do with the antitrust laws. For antitrust to prevent Dairy Queen from insisting on genuine Oreos is no more rational than it would be for antitrust to insist that Manhattan chef Tony Bourdain use margarine rather than butter in his sauces. After all, they would then be cheaper, and his restaurant could charge lower prices.

Closely related to quality control is achievement of inter-franchise uniformity. This is especially true if the franchise is national and serves transient populations—such as the McDonald's or Subway located on the Interstate or in an airport. If the franchisor supplies an ingredient, it will be the same across all stores, and customers will know what they are getting. Relatedly, franchisors may also tie such things as accounting services or point-of-sale computing systems so that the franchisor can collect similar information from all stores and make comparative judgments about how they are doing.[45]

One phenomenon that seems common to the franchise tying cases is that consumers are not injured. While Domino's might charge its franchisees a high price for pizza dough, Domino's customers are free to purchase pizzas wherever they please. If the local Domino's franchisee overprices its pizzas, the customers can and will go somewhere else. Perhaps one should consider the possibility that Domino's is using the tie to monopsonize the market for distribution services—that is, it is undercompensating the franchisees by overcharging them for ingredients. That proposition could be tested if we wanted to. We could compare the income of Domino's franchisees with that of other pizza franchisees, or we could see if franchisees were opting away from Domino's franchises by refusing to accept them or switching to a different franchisor. But even if we could show that Domino's was using its ties to drive franchise income below the competitive level, it would not follow that we would be looking at an antitrust problem. At most, it would be a problem in contracting. Hundreds of businesses earn less than the competitive return because they are locked in to high rents paid to their landlord or monthly payments for equipment that has become obsolete or is not as productive as they anticipated. Some of these may even have been deceived by landlords or creditors to enter unfair contracts. None of this is a monopoly concern, however. If it were, then every long-term contractual relationship that is unfavorable to one party becomes the justification for a claim of monopoly.

Today the antitrust law of exclusive dealing seems to be on the right track. Exclusive dealing is a rule of reason offense, requiring a plaintiff to show that the defendant has significant market power, that the exclusivity agreement serves to deny market access to one or more significant rivals, and that market output to consumers is lower (or prices higher) as a result. Perhaps within the next decade the Supreme Court will see fit to put tying law on the same course.

9

The National Policy on Business Mergers

A merger occurs when one firm acquires all or a significant portion of the production capability of another firm. Mergers are said to be "horizontal" if the merging firms were previously competitors in at least one affected market—for example, if GM should acquire Ford, or if a restaurateur purchases a competing restaurant. Horizontal mergers are unlawful when they are likely to permit the postmerger firm to increase its price unilaterally, or to facilitate tacit or express collusion with other firms in the market. Historically, antitrust law also condemned many vertical mergers, involving firms that stand in a buyer-seller relationship, such as an automobile manufacturer's acquisition of a dealership. The law of vertical mergers retains very little of the vitality it enjoyed in the 1970s and earlier, and today there are few relevant decisions. Finally, a set of largely defunct rules governs "conglomerate" mergers, which are mergers that are neither horizontal nor vertical but that involve firms making complementary products, or in some cases firms that have no significant economic relationship at all.[1]

The general policy of the antitrust laws is to permit mergers. Most mergers enable firms to reduce their costs or compete more effectively. The cost savings come mainly through increased economies of scale, which occur when a firm does a larger volume of business. Mergers can also create economies of scope, which occur when it is cheaper to do two different things together rather than separately. For example, a light-truck maker and an automobile maker might merge and then sell pickup trucks and cars more economically through the same dealerships. Mergers can also reduce research and development costs, as well

207

as costs of raising capital, of procuring employee benefits such as health care, or of purchasing inputs. Mergers are not per se lawful, however, because a few mergers in concentrated markets can facilitate collusion, oligopoly pricing, or even monopoly.

After great turbulence in the 1960s and 1970s, merger law today is fairly stable. Several issues continue to be controversial, but most of this debate has stayed out of the case law. Indeed, the Supreme Court's last merger decision on the merits appeared more than thirty years ago.[2] While the Court has strongly warned lower courts that they should not anticipatorily "overrule" Supreme Court decisions, even if they believe that the Court would do so itself,[3] this has largely happened in the law of mergers. Not to do so would be intolerable, for merger law is the largest area of public antitrust enforcement activity, and an area where the law as the Supreme Court last left it is indefensible. While antitrust casebooks continue to print 1960s-vintage merger decisions that have never been overruled, no one, not even federal judges and certainly not the government enforcement agencies, pay much attention to them.

Actually, the last sentence understates the extent to which 1960s precedent is ignored. It is not merely that Supreme Court decisions are not followed on technical grounds—the fundamental ideology of mergers has shifted dramatically over the last three decades and now embodies values that are inconsistent at the most fundamental level with those that the Supreme Court last articulated.

During the Warren Court era the Supreme Court decided approximately one merger case per year, more than were decided during any other Chief Justice's term. By contrast, the Burger Court decided fewer than one merger case every two years, and even this number overstates that Court's involvement: only two decisions during Chief Justice Burger's seventeen-year-term involved the substantive legal standards for horizontal mergers.[4] Most Burger-era merger decisions were concerned with cutting back on the reach of the antitrust laws to conglomerate mergers. At this writing the Rehnquist Court is entering its twentieth year and has not decided a single merger case on the merits.[5]

The basic ideology of the Warren Court merger decisions held that merger policy should ensure the maintenance of markets with large numbers of small players. The Supreme Court condemned mergers at market concentration levels that would be considered hilarious by today's standards. In the *Von's Grocery* case the market contained approximately 3,800 single-store grocers, and 150 "chains," which were defined as firms owning two or more stores. The four largest firms controlled less than one quarter of the market, and the combined market share of the merging firms was 7.5 percent.[6] Furthermore, new entry was easy. Under such conditions a price-fixing agreement would have been impossible to enforce. Today such a merger would not earn a second glance from the Antitrust Division or Federal Trade Commission.

The Supreme Court could not possibly have been concerned with monopoly pricing or collusion in the Los Angeles grocery business. Rather, the concern was that large chain stores could undersell smaller stores, forcing the latter to go out of business or to merge themselves. In that case, not only was there *not* an efficiency defense to a horizontal merger, but efficiencies were an affirmative reason for condemning it. Consider this passage from the district court's decision in the *Brown Shoe* case, which the Supreme Court affirmed:

> [I]ndependent retailers of shoes are having a harder and harder time in competing with company-owned and company-controlled retail outlets. National advertising by large concerns has increased their brand name acceptability and retail stores handling the brand named shoes have a definite advertising advantage. Company-owned and company-controlled retail stores have definite advantages in buying and credit; they have further advantages in advertising, insurance, inventory control . . . and price control. *These advantages result in lower prices or in higher quality for the same price and the independent retailer can no longer compete.*[7]

In one of the more bizarre twists in the history of legal policy, some firms felt compelled to argue that their mergers were lawful precisely because they did *not* create any efficiencies that might harm rivals. For example, Procter and Gamble defended its merger with Clorox by arguing that there was "no proof of any savings in any aspect of manufacturing. . . . [T]here is no showing here that the sales cost of Clorox would be any less whether it was merchandised by a one-product company or by Procter."[8]

In *The Antitrust Paradox* Robert H. Bork blamed the Supreme Court rather than Congress for this economically destructive merger policy. While the original 1914 merger provision had been amended by Congress in 1950, Bork believed that the amendment was merely technical, intended to close a loophole.[9] Under the original statute the law applied to stock acquisitions but not asset acquisitions, and the 1950 amendments repaired that shortcoming.

But Bork's explanation misstates Congress's concern in 1950. Just prior to that time, in its 1948 *Columbia Steel* decision, the Supreme Court applied a merger standard much like the one that Bork advocated, which considered the merger's impact on economic competition in a properly defined market. Because of the asset acquisition loophole, the Court applied §1 of the Sherman Act rather than §7 of the Clayton Act. *Columbia Steel* refused to condemn a merger challenged by the government after concluding that the relevant market was larger than the government alleged, and that the merging parties did not compete as much as the government believed.[10] *Columbia Steel*'s reliance on these strictly economic criteria for evaluating a merger upset Congress and inspired the 1950 amendments. What Congress wanted was not merely to close a loophole that limited the merger provision to stock acquisitions; it also wanted a substantive merger statute that used much more aggressive and protectionist criteria for evaluating mergers.

In *Brown Shoe* the Supreme Court looked carefully at this legislative history and reported what it read more or less accurately. While the merger law reached mergers where the effect "may be substantially to lessen competition," Congress—just as the Supreme Court—understood "competition" to refer to a situation where large numbers of small firms vied for business. Within that framework a larger, more efficient firm was not a benefit but an affirmative evil. Its lower costs and prices would force smaller firms either to exit from the market or merge themselves. As a result the district judge in *Brown Shoe* could say without flinching that the goal of the merger law was to prevent "lower prices or . . . higher quality for the same price."

Congress, again, just as the Supreme Court, has largely remained quiet since 1950, not returning to the question of the law's goals or standards of legality. The great revision that has occurred in the last four decades is largely the work of the Department of Justice's Antitrust Division and, more recently, the Federal Trade Commission. Merger guidelines issued by the Antitrust Division in 1968, when Donald F. Turner was the Division's head, made clear that the principal concern of merger law was with exercises of market power by firms acting unilaterally or in conjunction with other firms. Furthermore, those Guidelines recognized the theoretical relevance of an efficiency *defense,* thus repudiating any notion that economies were a rationale for condemning mergers. Later Guidelines issued by the Antitrust Division and eventually the FTC made these concerns more explicit and quantified them more rigorously.[11]

Today the basic ideology of mergers is well developed and can be briefly stated. *First,* mergers are fundamentally a good thing because they enable firms to take advantage of production or distribution efficiencies, or assign productive assets to more efficient managers. Our primary and most fundamental expectation from a business merger is better economic performance. Of course, firms sometimes miscalculate and not every merger works out as planned, but those failures are not antitrust problems.

Second, a merger can be anticompetitive when it creates a monopoly or increases a market's propensity toward collusion or oligopoly performance. But these outcomes are not typical. Rather, they occur only when the market has few significant players to begin with, substantial entry barriers, and other properties indicating a collusive threat. The fundamental role of antitrust is to recognize these situations and deal with them accordingly, perhaps by condemning the merger outright, or perhaps by limiting or restructuring it so as to reduce the threat to competition.

Third, mergers create efficiencies whether or not they pose a competitive threat, and sometimes the efficiency gains will more than outweigh any losses from reduced competition. As a result there should be at least some room for an "efficiency defense" to a presumptively unlawful merger.

The Competitive Threats of Horizontal Mergers

Collusion-Facilitating Mergers

Most challenged mergers are thought to threaten competition by making collusion or oligopoly more likely than it was before the merger. The 1992 Guidelines use the term "coordinated interaction" to refer to both explicit price-fixing, or collusion, and also oligopoly performance that may not require an explicit agreement among the parties. The distinction has been discussed in Chapter 6. A market's propensity toward coordinated interaction varies inversely with the number of firms. However, it is also affected by other factors, such as product differentiation, flow of information, ease of entry, size differences among firms, cost differences, and the amount of excess capacity the firms hold. Collusion and oligopoly work best when a market contains a small number of firms that make the identical product, have similar costs, and are producing without substantial excess capacity (which may induce a firm to produce more than its allotment under a cartel agreement), and when it is difficult for other firms to enter the market. Also relevant are the extent and quality of information that both sellers and buyers have about market prices, and the size and sophistication of buyers. For example, collusion works best if all prices are publicly posted and any deviation is immediately detected by rivals. Collusion tends to work less well as buyers are better informed about the market and in a better position to force sellers to bid against each other.

As Chapter 6 demonstrates, §1 of the Sherman Act has not been very effective at reaching oligopoly coordination absent evidence of a traditional "agreement." This shortcoming makes an effective merger policy especially important, and may justify somewhat overdeterrent merger rules in concentrated markets. We cannot have confidence that any tacit collusion that occurs after a merger will be reachable under the antitrust laws; thus it is better to condemn marginal mergers in order to prevent high concentration levels from occurring in the first place, particularly if the merger has not been shown to produce significant efficiency gains.

Basic market concentration is measured today by the Herfindahl-Hirschman Index, or HHI, which is the sum of the squares of the market shares of every firm in the market. Thus a market with ten equal-size firms has an HHI of $10^2 \times 10$, or 1,000. A market with five firms of share $A = 30$, $B = 30$, $C = 20$, $D = 10$, and $E = 10$, would have an HHI of $900 + 900 + 400 + 100 + 100$, or 2,400. The Merger Guidelines then divide markets into three classifications. If the market HHI after the merger is 1,000 or less, the merger is generally lawful. In the middle classification where the postmerger HHI is between 1,000 and 1,800, the market is considered moderately concentrated. According to the Guidelines, significant mergers in this area will be challenged, but not smaller mergers. Finally, markets with a postmerger HHI exceeding 1,800 are considered "highly concentrated," and here, according to the Guidelines, all but the smallest mergers will be challenged.

Six equal-size firms have an HHI of roughly 1,667; five equal-size firms have an HHI of 2,000. So the HHI thresholds reflect an intuition that in markets in the range of six to seven major players concerns about competition begin to be significant. Government enforcement policy today is actually much more tolerant, and most challenged mergers are in markets with fewer than five significant competitors prior to the merger. As a result the Merger Guidelines have become less trustworthy predictors of government action. FTC enforcement data covering the period 1999–2003 tell a much different story than the Guidelines' enforcement thresholds suggest. Except in the petroleum industry, the FTC rarely challenges a merger when the postmerger HHI falls below 2,000, unless it involves the largest firms in the market, and has not challenged that many where the HHI falls below 2,400, unless the merger increased the HHI by 300 points or more.[12]

Use of the HHI has added an appearance of great rigor to merger analysis. The HHI gives superficially precise "readouts" of market concentration, and also of the amount by which the HHI is increased as a result of a merger. But this ostensible rigor belies the extent to which our merger analysis relies on assumption, conjecture, and even speculation. The HHI is based on a strict Cournot oligopoly theory, which is extremely sensitive to the number of firms in the market and to their size disparities. Under the set of purely structural assumptions that go into the HHI, all firms behave the same way, so one can predict performance strictly from structure. For example, suppose a market has five firms with the following shares: $A = 40$, $B = 20$, $C = 20$, $D = 10$, $E = 10$. The premerger HHI of this market is 2,600. If B and D should merge, yielding a firm BD with a market share of 30, the HHI would increase to 3,000. That is a very significant increase of 400 points, and the Merger Guidelines indicate that this merger would be challenged.

But is this merger necessarily anticompetitive? Yes, if the firms are involved in a strict Cournot oligopoly where each is choosing an output level that maximizes its profits given the output level of other firms. But if the firms are doing something different, the story could differ as well. For example, if B is trying to compete by growing, its merger with D could yield a larger firm more able to confront A. Where A was formerly twice as big as the second biggest firm in the market, it is now only one-third bigger, and the competition between A and BD might be much more intense than it had been before. Furthermore, lower prices resulting from this competition might force the prices of other firms down as well.

The point of this story is not that this will always happen, but rather that the HHI gives us such a one-dimensional picture of a market that it is bound to be wrong much of the time. The HHI also offers an overly static vision of firms and their market shares. For example, its mathematics assumes that whenever two firms merge, the new firm's market share is the sum of that of the two merging partners, and other firms' shares remain the same. That may happen, but it may not. If mergers produce cost savings, the share of the postmerger firm is likely to grow. If the postmerger firm attempts to reduce output, other firms may either do the same or else make offsetting output increases. In the latter case the share of the postmerger firm will decline.

In sum, use of the HHI creates a vision of incredible accuracy, enabling judges to say things such as "[t]he proposed merger would increase the index to 5285, an increase of 510 points."[13] But the inferences we can reliably draw about impact on competition are far more ambiguous. The basic HHI numbers are no more accurate than the underlying market definition, and squaring the numbers tends to exaggerate errors if the market definition is too broad or narrow. Even measuring market share is an exercise in judgment. For example, in the *Heinz* case, from which the quotation is taken, there were both "premium" and "regular" baby foods, which sold at different prices. In that case market shares differ depending on whether one uses units of product or dollar amounts of sales. If the products are less than perfect substitutes, then simply summing the output of the two firms tends to overstate the extent to which the merger eliminates competition.

We would do about as well in most cases if we simply queried how many significant firms a market contained. Once the number drops below four or five, our concerns should be sufficient to warrant a hard look. We would then want to know a little about the relative significance of the merging firms themselves. For example, a merger of the two smallest among four firms might lead us to inquire whether the postmerger firm promises to be a more aggressive competitor. We should always consider whether new entry is easy or difficult. And we should pay particular attention to the degree of price coordination that already exists in a market.

Theoretically, product differentiation is also worth examining. As a practical matter, the evidence is often inconclusive, pointing in different directions. On the one hand, strong product differentiation can frustrate collusion. But the degree of difficulty depends on the extent of differentiation, and the impact is readily exaggerated. If product differentiation extends mainly to packaging or cosmetic differences, such as in ready-to-eat breakfast cereal, collusion may be almost as easy as it is for a fungible product. But if significant quality and performance differences exist, as among automobiles or stereos, then the impact is greater. Even in these cases, however, agreements setting output or dividing markets are possible.

The other side of the coin is that product differentiation can enhance market power, and mergers among relatively "adjacent" firms in the product market spectrum can result in price increases or collusion in that sector. For example, if a dozen manufacturers make automobiles but only BMW, Mercedes, Toyota (Lexus), and GM (Cadillac) make luxury cars, a merger between BMW and Lexus could result in higher prices for luxury cars that would not be effectively disciplined by the makers of nonluxury cars.

In most cases the best way to deal with the product differentiation problem is, first, to define markets carefully. Often significantly differentiated products will not even lie within the same market. For example, luxury cars may be sufficiently isolated from lower-priced cars to be in their own market. Many pharmaceutical drugs are so unique that they are probably a relevant market unto themselves. Second, differentiations within the same market should presumptively be ignored unless they very clearly point in one direction or the other.

In general, the tools that we use to analyze mergers are sophisticated. But they are also complex, and they are based on difficult-to-verify assumptions about how a market will behave after a merger. That is why Derek Bok once lamented that "consideration of all relevant factors may actually detract from the accuracy" of merger decisions.[14] Given our uncertainty about the criteria we use, their complexity, and the likelihood that many of them will point in different directions, we would probably be better off with a much simpler set of antimerger rules. They would predict about as well and be much easier to apply. In such a world the number of significant firms in a market and the height of entry barriers would be the most important factors. Provable, extraordinary efficiencies should also be relevant because most of the time a firm responds to lower costs by lowering its prices. This issue is taken up in the final section of this chapter. Other factors, including product differentiation, buyer sophistication, and the nature of transactions, are best ignored unless the structural case lies right on the boundary and these nonstructural indicators point clearly in a certain direction.

Mergers with Harmful Unilateral Effects

Some mergers are thought to be anticompetitive, not because they facilitate collusion, but because they permit the postmerger firm unilaterally to increase its prices. The most obvious of these is the merger to monopoly, which creates a single dominant firm. Such mergers have been unlawful since the beginning of the twentieth century.[15]

Since the late 1980s the government has also challenged some mergers in product-differentiated markets on the theory that the merger permits the postmerger firm to increase its price unilaterally. For example, even though the market for retail gasoline may be citywide, a station that is relatively isolated, with no competitors around it for a mile or so, can charge higher prices than other stations that are closer together. The same thing is true in product space: the product that finds a more unique niche can claim a higher price than product variations that resemble one another closely. This is why firms in product-differentiated markets are always trying to come up with variations that distinguish themselves from the competition. For example, expanding one's motor vehicle line by building the first SUV is more profitable than coming in with the fifteenth ordinary minivan.

Mergers in such markets can facilitate unilateral price increases when the output of the two merging firms resembles each other closely, but differs from the output of others. The effect of the merger is to create the product separation that permits a higher price. For example, consider a product-differentiated market of six firms, *A, B, C, D, E,* and *F.* Suppose *C* and *D* make closely similar products, while *A* and *B* make a lower-quality product, and *E* and *F* make a distinctly higher-quality product. In response to a unilateral 10 percent price increase, firm *C* would lose 20 percent of its sales, making the price increase unprofitable. However, suppose that three-fourths of these lost sales go from firm *C* to firm *D.* The other one-fourth are divided among *A, B, E,* and *F.* In this case a merger between *C* and *D* would very likely permit postmerger *CD* to profit from this price increase.

For example, in response to a 10 percent price increase firm C might lose eighty units of sales. But if sixty of these sales go to D, the impact of the CD merger would be that the postmerger firm would lose only twenty sales. That could make the price increase profitable. Since we assume that firms charge their profit-maximizing price, we can predict that a price increase of this magnitude is likely to result from the merger.[16]

Predicting the extent to which buyers substitute from C to D rather than to a different firm can be relatively easy, depending on the availability of data about transactions. For example, if a retailer sells three brands of baby food and the price of Heinz rises by 10 percent, scanner data might tell us how many people switched to Beech-Nut, how many to Gerber, and how many switched out of the jarred baby-food market altogether. That could tell us something about the price effects of a Heinz/Beech-Nut merger. An economist's predictions of unilateral price effects in product-differentiated markets can be just as robust as predictions about the price consequences of a merger thought to facilitate oligopoly pricing. As noted previously, while concentration measures such as the HHI have become quite conventional in antitrust merger analysis, their ease of use belies the many assumptions that go into our predictions. A great amount of guesswork underlies our theory about the impact of a concentration-increasing merger on the oligopoly game that the firms will play.[17]

Nevertheless, a merger theory based on unilateral effects faces some significant difficulties. One problem in estimating unilateral effects is that retail pricing data used alone can exaggerate the anticompetitive effects of mergers by focusing exclusively on the demand side of the market. Suppose Beech-Nut and Gerber both make "premium" baby food and decide to merge. Scanner data indicate that these firms are close substitutes for each other but that Heinz, which makes a lower-price brand, is more removed. As a result the data suggest that a price increase will result from the Beech-Nut and Gerber merger.

But the scanner data tell us only what customers' immediate responses are to price variations among the three brands. The data say nothing about whether Heinz would be in a position to modify its product so as to compete in the premium market niche itself. Nor do they say anything about grocers' ability to respond to a price increase in premium baby food by reallocating more shelf space to lower-priced brands. Excessive reliance on short-run consumer behavior gives us an exaggerated picture to the extent that such behavior is only one of many avenues along which substitution among products occurs. In large part, this emphasis results from the fact that the retail scanner has placed an enormous amount of data in the statistician's hands. Both the quality and the quantity of the data are beguiling. But one should not forget that these data create only an incomplete picture of the degree of substitutability among differentiated products.[18]

Before consumer data tell us reliably that a merger among two makers of similar products is anticompetitive, we also need to collect information about other factors. These mainly include manufacturers' ability to reconfigure their products in response to higher profits in one segment. Making higher-quality baby food may require little more than selecting different ingredients, and perhaps some advertising announcing the quality change. On the other hand, for Ford to enter the market niche occupied by BMW and Mercedes may require years of planning and design. We also need to know something about the ability of retailers to redesign their sales efforts. The multibrand retailer has its own profit incentives to push those products that sell the best and can be expected to disfavor product variations selling at monopoly prices.

A second problem with a unilateral effects theory is more conceptual. The theory postulates a single relevant market that under the Merger Guidelines must be well defined. This means that the goods in it must be reasonably good substitutes for each other. The unilateral effects theory then postulates that the output of the two merging firms is particularly close, while the output of nonmerging firms is sufficiently distinct that they cannot discipline a higher price charged by the merging firms. Returning to the previous example of a market containing firms A through F and a merger between C and D, why is it that firms A, B, E, and F are unable to respond to the CD price increase? If they cannot make such a response, then it seems reasonable to conclude that they were improperly included in this market to begin with. But if the market were really limited to firms C and D, then we have a simple merger to monopoly, which does not require any "unilateral effects" theory to analyze.[19]

The Efficiency Defense in Merger Cases

Most mergers produce efficiencies. The economies range from plant consolidation or specialization savings to lower costs from combining employee health plans. Merging firms might be able to streamline management, so that one person can supervise a greater number of or more specialized employees. A firm might make better deals by purchasing inputs in larger quantities. The very ubiquity of merger-created efficiencies is why we evaluate mergers under a fairly benign set of rules.

These observations are important because they explain both the justifications and the limitations of an "efficiency defense" in merger cases. The fact that most mergers produce efficiencies justifies a lenient policy toward mergers. But it also entails that once significant competitive threats are shown under these lenient criteria, these "ordinary" efficiencies have already been taken into account.

In 1968 Oliver Williamson produced an analysis showing that relatively modest efficiency gains can offset a fairly significant increase in market power.[20] But Williamson's story was incomplete in several respects. *First,* if a merger facilitates collusion, the output reduction will be marketwide, while the efficiency gains will accrue only to the merging firms. For example, if two firms merge into a single firm with 25 percent of the market and in doing so create a marketwide cartel, the cartel's overall output reduction would be four times as large as the output reduction produced by the postmerger firm. But the efficiencies from merging would accrue only to the merging firms.

Second, while mergers may result in efficiencies, often the efficiencies can be attained by better routes than a merger. Furthermore, the alternatives may be superior from a policy perspective. For example, acquiring a rival may enable a firm to attain economies in production because it can now specialize its plants more efficiently. But the firm might also specialize by building a new plant. Moreover, the new plant increases the amount of productive capacity in the market, while a simple switch in ownership of an existing plant does not. Of course, the market may not be able to absorb an additional plant (although this is likely to occur only at high concentration levels), or acquisition may be less costly or risky. These are empirical questions.

In most cases the courts lack the capacity to quantify and "balance" the social cost of loss of competition against any cost savings that the merger produces. This does not mean that a court can never evaluate efficiencies. Sometimes the relative threat to competition is slight while efficiencies to be gained are enormous, and sometimes the opposite is true. But in cases that are not obvious, quantifying and balancing gains and losses are simply not in the cards.

Antitrust could take a number of approaches to the efficiencies problem. *First,* it could acknowledge the presence of efficiencies generally in the formulation of basic merger rules, but ignore them in particular cases. The argument here is that if mergers did not produce any efficiencies, then very harsh treatment or even per se illegality would be appropriate. There is no point in condoning a practice that produces no gains but does entail competitive harm in a significant subset of cases. Legal policy does this all the time. For example, drunk driving is illegal whether or not the driver has an accident, because it is hard to think of any social benefits that accrue from drunk driving so we might as well condemn every instance. By condemning only a small minority of mergers in which threats to competition seem highly probable, we have already taken efficiencies into account. This makes case-by-case assessment of efficiencies unnecessary.[21]

Second, antitrust could look at efficiency gains in every case and try to assess their magnitude in light of the structural threat posed by the merger. As indicated previously, this could impose an enormous administrative burden on agencies and courts, and one that they lack the capacity to carry out except in fairly obvious cases. One could expect many false positives and false negatives.

Third, the structural indicators of anticompetitive harm could form the presumptive basis for determining a merger's legality. Presumably, application of these criteria takes into account all the efficiency gains that typically flow from a merger. However, a firm that believed its particular merger produced unusual, measurable, and extraordinary efficiency gains could try to convince the tribunal to approve its merger.

The third position is associated with the Harvard School, and I believe it is the correct one, although under it very few mergers would qualify for the defense.[22] Because most mergers are evaluated today before they occur, there is no actual performance data to analyze. The decision maker must make predictions of competitive performance entirely from data about the market's structure and knowledge about the merging firms. The government evaluates efficiency claims by examining such factors as the availability of further economies of scale or scope, the possibility for streamlining distribution systems, or cost savings associated with managerial gains or the redeployment of certain resources. As a contemplated merger moves down into the lower end of the range of presumptive illegality, our prediction about anticompetitive consequences becomes less robust. As a result other factors should be considered more heavily, and there is no good reason to ignore clear efficiency gains. By contrast, in highly concentrated markets where the competitive threat is high, efficiency claims should be ignored unless the gains are unambiguous and truly extraordinary.

What kinds of efficiency gains should count? Theoretically, all of them. A dollar in distribution cost savings is just as socially valuable as a dollar in production cost savings. Speaking practically, however, some kinds of efficiency gains are more readily provable than others, and some are more likely to be attainable only via merger. Simple production economies of scale are *not* the most common efficiency gain for the simple reason that mergers do not make plants larger. If two firms each own obsolete, inefficiently small plants, a merger will not produce a large efficient one. The postmerger firm will simply have two undersized inefficient plants. Nevertheless, the merger might give the postmerger firm a sufficient sales base to justify the construction of a single efficient plant. Alternatively, a merger might permit specialization because output can be reallocated among plants. For example, suppose two publishers each make books with expensive sewn bindings as well as cheaper glued bindings. The technologies differ, but each publisher produces both types of books in a single plant at inefficiently low rates of output. A merger might enable the firms to reallocate all sewn books to one plant and glued books to the other.[23]

One of the strongest cases for an efficiency defense occurs when makers of complementary products merge and are able to produce a new product or product variation that they had not produced before. The controversial *GE-Honeywell* merger, which was approved by the United States but subsequently blocked by the European Commission (EC), was of this sort. GE produced aircraft engines and Honeywell produced aircraft avionics. As a result of the merger the firm would have been able to offer a complete engine/avionics package to aircraft manufacturers. Indeed, the EC rejected the merger largely because it gave the firm an ability to offer aircraft manufacturers attractive packages that rivals could not match. The EC's decision is thus a throwback to 1960s-era cases in which United States courts condemned mergers because they enabled the postmerger firm to produce a superior product.[24]

Economies in distribution are harder to prove and less defensible in principle. To be sure, economies of scale in distribution are significant, particularly for such matters as transportation and storage of goods as well as retailing. But in most cases the economies can be fully attained through our highly competitive distribution market. Indeed, very large firms rely heavily on distribution services from independent firms. Both the local Wal-Mart and Mom'N'Pop's General Store are filled with products produced by the likes of General Foods, Campbell's, Borden's, and Mead. Despite the latter firms' size, they typically sell directly to very large retailers, or else through a network of independent distributors to smaller retailers.

One objection to this approach to the efficiencies defense is that while the defense will rarely succeed, it will be asserted in many cases. As a result the cost of litigating efficiencies will be unacceptably high in relation to any economic improvement they might yield. This objection carries considerable weight, but I do not believe it is decisive. First of all, the attainment of efficiencies is most likely to show up, not in litigation, but in government decisions about when to challenge a merger. Operating under the "substantially lessen competition" standard, the government agencies initially decide on the basis of market share criteria whether the merger crosses the line into prima facie illegality. Then they weigh a large number of other factors. Considering efficiencies at that point is inherently no more difficult than considering the impact of product differentiation, powerful buyers, or other factors. As a result the very low number of reported decisions recognizing an efficiency defense understates the role of efficiencies in merger analysis. It shows up mainly in governmental decisions not to challenge.

Furthermore, the measurement problem is ameliorated if the defendant has the burden of proving its claim of extraordinary efficiencies. In cases where such proof failed, the efficiency defense would be unavailable. For example, in the baby-food merger case the firms argued that a merger between Heinz and Beech-Nut would produce significant economies because Beech-Nut was currently producing out of an ancient plant with very high operating costs.[25] By contrast, Heinz had a modern efficient plant that was underutilized. As a result of the merger Beech-Nut's production would be switched to the Heinz plant.

This is a viable efficiencies claim in principle, although in this particular case the court concluded that cost savings of sufficient magnitude were not proven. While the merger led to lower production costs, it was impossible to determine how much of the relevant costs were costs of production and how much were costs that could not be reduced. To illustrate, suppose that the production of strained peas for babies requires two inputs, peas and processing. The peas themselves cost $200 a ton and processing them at the outmoded Beech-Nut plant costs $10 per ton. A more efficient plant reduces the cost of processing, but it cannot do anything about the market price of peas. In that case a 40 percent reduction in processing costs, to $6 per ton, would amount to about a 2 percent reduction in overall costs. Premerger costs would be $210 per ton, and postmerger costs would be $206 per ton. By contrast, the collusion risk would apply to the entire finished product, processed baby food, and to all firms making that product. In the actual case the merger reduced the number of significant firms from three to two, and the two merging parties had been particularly strong rivals for second place to Gerber, the market leader. Their merger very likely would have led to a significant price increase.

The Merger Guidelines' position on efficiencies is that the enforcement agencies will consider only substantial efficiencies that they are able to verify independently—that is, from market evidence rather than the parties' statements. Also, the claimed efficiencies must be "merger specific," which means that they could not reasonably be attained except by the merger. Further, the efficiencies must be of sufficient magnitude that the predicted price decrease resulting from them is enough to offset any predicted price increase that might result from increased market concentration. That is, the merger must not result in a price increase. Making this calculation with anything approaching precision is impossible, but it is important to remember that not all cases are close. Where anticompetitive effects are in the low end of the range and provable efficiencies are very high, one can conclude with some confidence that the merger will not result in a price increase.[26] When the defendants cannot meet this burden of proof, the merger will be condemned. This seems to be about the right balance.

III

REGULATION, INNOVATION, AND CONNECTIVITY

Part III of *The Antitrust Enterprise* examines the role of antitrust in markets that are thought to deviate from traditional economic norms for competition. The following three chapters deal in part with "new economy" industries, mainly computer technology and telecommunications, which are characterized by high rates of innovation, by costs that decline with output and over time, and often by a high degree of interconnection among market participants.

The term "new economy," however, does not accurately capture the set of markets and issues addressed here. While certain markets call for a different antitrust approach, "new economy" versus "old economy" is often not the proper place to draw the line. Government regulation is very old, long antedating the antitrust laws.[1] Many of the structural issues that arise in new economy markets also have a long history. For example, disputes that required antitrust to confront the intellectual property laws go back to the second decade of the twentieth century.[2] Because of the significant presence of intellectual property rights, new economy markets are characterized by declining average costs—that is, per unit costs that decline as volume rises. However, this phenomenon is hardly unique to the new economy. It also describes older, very low-tech markets such as franchising. Finally, networks, which are a prominent feature of new economy industries, are also very old. Indeed, the Supreme Court's first substantive antitrust decision involved an interconnection agreement in a network industry, the railroads.[3]

Chapter 10 deals with the relationship between antitrust and industry regulation, including the impact of deregulation. Chapter 11 addresses the historically troubled relationship between antitrust and the intellectual property laws. Finally, Chapter 12 is concerned with the role of the antitrust laws in network industries—everything from railroads to bank charge cards, and from sports leagues to the Microsoft computer platform monopoly.

10

Antitrust under Regulation
and Deregulation

Since before the Middle Ages economic policy in Western society has gone through cycles of greater and lesser confidence in markets. When confidence is low, governments intervene with everything from price regulations and output limitations to licensing restrictions on new firms.[1] Because economists often are not very sensitive to this long and cyclical history, they write as if today we finally have the right answers.[2] But just as certainly as the strongly pro-market period of classical political economy was followed by Progressivism in the 1920s and the New Deal in the 1930s, so too the strong free market ideologies currently in favor will someday yield to renewed interest in regulation.

This cyclical history inclines people to view antitrust and regulation as competing models for determining the appropriate scope of state intervention in the microeconomy.[3] At the margin they certainly are competing, because we are never certain about where the boundary lies. But a better way to view the two enterprises is as complementary products. We live in a world in which the great majority of markets operate at something close to efficient levels of output. But a few markets have serious imperfections—chiefly, imbalances of information, free rider problems, and scale economies—that prevent them from clearing at efficient levels, at least within the time frame that our government thinks is appropriate. To the extent government regulates, antitrust stands aside.

At some level even hard-core neoclassicists concede that a few markets require government intervention. For example, while extreme free marketers might rail at the excesses of regulation or antitrust, they tend to accept the system of intellectual property (IP) rights as it if were handed down from a mountaintop. In fact, however, the IP system is a very elaborate government effort to correct market failure, in this case free riding that occurs when innovations are too easily copied, and the corresponding decrease in the incentive to innovate. Anyone who does not believe that the IP laws are a form of regulation has not read the federal intellectual property statutes and the technical rules promulgated under them.

Most economic justifications for regulation in the modern era have rested on various theories of "market failure," a term used to describe physical or technological conditions that prevent a market from performing efficiently. The classic market failure is the natural monopoly, or industry in which the cost of service declines as volume increases, all the way up to the market's saturation point. For example, a hard network such as the retail electric power grid can serve additional customers more cheaply by adding capacity to the existing grid than by producing a second grid. Or a nineteenth-century railroad track between two towns can accommodate second, third, and fourth trains much more cheaply than would be the case were other railroad companies to lay their own tracks. In many of these markets the political, or "regulatory," solution we have adopted is to permit a single firm to have a monopoly over a certain portion of the market, but to regulate that firm's prices.

To describe these regulatory decisions as "political" is appropriate, for cost-of-service-regulated monopoly is a policy choice. Alternative policies may work just as well, or alternative technologies may permit more traditional competitive solutions. For example, while it is very likely cheaper to have a single power grid serving a town, or a single line of tracks stretched between two towns, that does not necessarily mean that a single power company or a single railroad has to own and operate those facilities. The grid or the tracks could be owned by the state, as the public highway system is. Competing carriers could use the system subject to some "traffic" rules that prevent collisions or other conflicts. Alternatively, competing service providers could own and operate the network jointly, agreeing on their own traffic regulations to prevent conflict, but competing on price, quality, and other terms of service. Realization of these possibilities accounts for much of deregulation in the last few decades and also defines a role for antitrust policy. Disentangling networks from monopoly has been one of the great accomplishments of the deregulation movement. It also explains why the outcome of the

Microsoft antitrust case is such a disappointing policy failure as we enter the twenty-first century. The leading operating system for the market-dominating computer technology remains the largest unregulated network monopoly in our economy, and its costs are severe. These issues are taken up in Chapter 12.

Another set of market failures thought to justify regulation are information asymmetries, which are a special subset of market failures. These include markets for complicated products or services, markets for financial instruments and risk (such as securities and insurance), or markets where buyers and sellers cannot efficiently meet each other to negotiate a price.

Over the years economists and policy makers have had widely different opinions about the extent to which information failure justifies regulation. At one extreme is the New Deal position that consumers are extremely vulnerable to any kind of complexity, particularly where products or services are differentiated from one seller to another. As a result broad government regulation is needed of everything from product quality to advertising to terms of service and perhaps even price. This has always been the nominal justification for extensive government regulation of financial and insurance markets, including corporate securities, banking, and some professional services. At the other extreme is what might be termed the Chicago School position that information, like any other product, is itself subject to competition, which forces firms to produce it at the optimal amount and quality. Firms that fail to inform, or that misrepresent, will be disciplined because customers will not return to them. Thus extensive regulation is not necessary, and the common law of contract and fraud is sufficient to correct most problems.[4]

In any event, the "gap" between regulatory theory and regulatory practice is large.[5] We undoubtedly regulate many more markets than require regulation, and we regulate many things that need not be regulated, assuming that the goal of regulation is economic efficiency. The last point, however, is important. The neoclassical economic critiques of regulation all rest on the premise that efficient allocation of resources is the only goal of regulatory policy. But policy making in a democratic society has always incorporated varied and sometimes even inconsistent goals. For example, supplying "universal service" in electricity or telecommunications may require serving some people at a price below short-run marginal cost, and this may require a rate structure that forces other consumers to pay more. Or the government itself may subsidize services to the elderly or the poor. In sum, regulatory policy has to one degree or another incorporated ideas about wealth distribution along with its concerns for efficiency.

The Place of Antitrust in Regulated Markets

One consequence of regulation is a reduced role for the antitrust laws. If the government makes rules about price or output, market forces no longer govern those decisions, and antitrust is shoved aside. A corollary is that as an industry undergoes "deregulation," or removal from the regulatory process, antitrust reenters as the residual regulator. The most important criterion for determining antitrust immunity in regulated industries is the extent of unsupervised private discretion. As deregulation turns more decision making back to the regulated firms, antitrust takes a more important part.

Regulation is one of those topics about which economists have disagreed over a very wide range. The differences vary according to ideology, and even according to the type of training that economists have. Economic attitudes toward regulation have also cycled over time. During the Middle Ages and up to the age of the great classical political economists such as Adam Smith and John Stuart Mill, price regulation even of ordinary commodities was relatively common. In sharp contrast, the classical period, which includes most of the nineteenth century, was dominated by concerns for liberty of contract and "free" markets, and a corresponding abhorrence of many forms of regulation.[6] Then, beginning during the Progressive Era and escalating during the New Deal, economic policy makers lost much of their confidence in open markets and at one time or another attempted to regulate virtually anything that could be regulated, creating giant bureaucratic agencies in the process. The high point of this regulation was in the 1970s, and since then we have experienced a free market revolution that may be starting to subside. Without speculating about where we are going next, I observe only that this ideological pendulum is likely to swing back and forth indefinitely. The solutions we achieve for regulatory problems are political as well as technical. To the extent they are political, a democracy is unlikely to produce final answers.[7]

A critical premise for understanding the relationship between antitrust and regulation is that it is not antitrust's purpose to throw itself into this centuries-old policy battle. On the question of which markets should be regulated, and by what means, legislatures have the final say, subject only to the limits imposed by the Constitution. It is not the role of federal judges or antitrust juries to decide whether price or entry regulation in the provision of electricity or taxi service is appropriate. Antitrust law takes as given a market's existing regulatory structure, warts and all, and tries to prevent injuries to competition that the regulatory process leaves untended.

A Single, Fairly Simple Antitrust Concern

Government regulation of business is pervasive in any complex capitalist economy. In the United States regulation comes from three different levels. Federal, state, and local governments all regulate. Sometimes all three regulate the very same markets (such as telephone service, land use, and housing discrimination). Even though antitrust law is predominantly federal, it does not run roughshod over state and local regulation with a broad preemption sweep. Many of the constraints imposed by state regulation of electricity, locally regulated zoning or taxicab fares, licensing requirements for sale of alcoholic beverages, or state insurance regulation would be antitrust violations if imposed by private parties.[8] But antitrust leaves them alone. If a state or local regulation is valid, federal antitrust is the residual regulator as to that provision, just as it is to federal regulation.

The antitrust laws have exhibited an unhelpful tendency to use different doctrinal formulations depending on the level of sovereign imposing the regulation. To be sure, the issues are not precisely the same. When the relevant regulatory regime is federal, such as for sales of corporate securities, much of telecommunications, or interstate energy regulation, then the courts try to harmonize two potentially conflicting federal regulatory regimes. For example, Congress probably did not design federal regulation of securities by the Securities and Exchange Commission so as to conflict with federal antitrust regulation.[9] Where inconsistent regulatory requirements do arise, the results are chaotic and inefficient, and thus we would not presume that Congress intended them.

State and local government regulation emanates from an inferior level of government. Under the Supremacy Clause of the Constitution federal antitrust *could* preempt conflicting state regulation, just as the federal law of labor relations or corporate securities preempts inconsistent state law. But that is not what has happened. A basic tenet of federalism is that states are entitled to regulate their own internal economies, and also to decide how much regulatory authority to cede to their municipalities, counties, or other units of local government.[10] As a result federal courts addressing potential conflicts between state or local regulation and the antitrust laws ask a series of questions that are somewhat similar to the ones they ask when the regulation is federal.

I say "somewhat similar" because largely by historical happenstance we use different verbal formulations for dealing with different types of regulatory conflict. Antitrust would be tidier and could produce a more satisfactory accommodation with regulation if these rules were simplified and unified. The relation between federal antitrust and various regulatory regimes is covered by three sets of antitrust rules: the doctrine of federal regulatory immunity, the "state action" exemption, and the *Noerr-Pennington* immunity for petitions to any level of government.

FEDERAL REGULATORY IMMUNITY. Federal regulatory immunity comes in two kinds, express and implied. When the antitrust immunity is express, then the role of the court is mainly to ensure that the statute's requirements have been satisfied. For example, a labor strike would be an unlawful price-fixing agreement among employees but for an express antitrust immunity created by federal legislation.[11]

Implied federal immunity is a more difficult concept. It exists when the statute in question does not expressly confer an antitrust immunity, but immunity seems necessary if we are to avoid conflicts between regulatory and antitrust requirements. In general, courts try to ensure that application of the antitrust laws does not interfere with an agency's ability to do its proper job. In addition, they are more likely to find an immunity if the agency itself considered competitive concerns in making its decision. This is not always the case. For example, a government regulation may be concerned entirely with safety or the financial solvency of regulated firms, and agency supervision may largely ignore competitive impact. By contrast, where the regulatory regime controls such things as pricing, entry by new firms, joint market behavior, mergers, or possible exclusionary practices, then antitrust immunity may be essential if regulatory goals are not to be frustrated.

The courts typically find implied immunity if they believe that an antitrust suit would interfere with an agency's operations, or if the agency has had a matter under study, even though it may not have reached a resolution. For example, in the *Options Trading* case the court granted antitrust immunity to an agreement among the major stock exchanges forbidding a particular stock option from being listed on more than a single exchange.[12] The Securities and Exchange Commission had been studying the problem of options listings for many years, approving them during some periods and disapproving them during other periods after concluding that multiple listing led to excessive chaos in securities sales. The court concluded that immunity was proper even though the SEC had been indecisive. If a group of experts studying an issue for many years could not come to a clear understanding, then it would be imprudent to permit the issue to be decided by a lay jury trial in an antitrust case. Doing so would render agency regulation moot on that point. To be sure, reasonable people might believe that Congress should never have given the issue to the SEC to begin with, but *that* complaint is not for antitrust to answer.

"STATE ACTION" IMMUNITY.   Regulation by state and local government is not only pervasive; it is probably more susceptible to political influences than is federal regulation. States and local governments regulate residential rents, liquor pricing, and intrastate trucking rates, insurance, and taxi fares. They grant exclusive rights for municipal waste disposal, cable television, billboards, and ambulance service.[13] Most of these regulations would not constitute antitrust violations even if there were no immunity, but some would.

The antitrust state action exemption can be reduced to two requirements, generally called authorization and supervision. Under the first requirement, the state must have "clearly articulated" and "affirmatively expressed" its wish to displace ordinary competitive processes with some form of regulation covering the challenged conduct. Second, if the conduct of private parties is at issue, and not merely that of the government itself, then the conduct must be "actively supervised" by a state agency or official. For example, the state could not simply pass a statute authorizing building contractors to fix prices and then leave them free to do so entirely on their own.[14]

The state action immunity is a creature of federalism. Its purpose is not to protect federal regulatory or competition goals, but to give appropriate recognition to state sovereignty. So when a court applies the state action doctrine it must try to avoid making substantive judgments about whether the state regulation at issue is a good idea. Suppose a state with a powerful potato growers' lobby wants to regulate the price of potatoes even though every economist in the country states that regulating potato prices is a terrible idea. If the state passes a statute that unambiguously regulates them anyway, and an agency created for this purpose actively administers the rate-making process, then the antitrust court has no choice but to find the regulation immune from the antitrust laws. Congress could of course intervene if it wants, but the state action immunity doctrine presumes that it has chosen not to do so.

Anticompetitive special interest regulations have often been immunized from antitrust challenge by the state action doctrine.[15] While this is disconcerting as a matter of policy, the more important principle is that correcting flaws in political processes is not an antitrust task. We would not interpret the Sherman Act to give district court juries a wide-ranging mandate to ensure that government regulation produces only efficient, or competitive, results—certainly not without a very clear indication that Congress had this in mind. There is no evidence in the legislative history of the antitrust laws that Congress was concerned with anything other than privately created restraints. Furthermore, juries of laypersons are ill-suited to determine the proper boundaries of regulatory intervention. At best, they could sort out the worst abuses, such as those that result from bribery or other corruption of the political process. But we already have plenty of laws that reach these practices.

NOERR-PENNINGTON PETITIONING IMMUNITY.   The *Noerr-Pennington* petitioning immunity is undergirded by the First Amendment guarantee that Congress will "make no law . . . abridging . . . the right of the people . . . to petition the Government." The basic antitrust immunity was defined in two Supreme Court decisions holding that citizens have a right to ask the government for regulation, even if the regulation that they want is anticompetitive. The *Noerr* case held that the railroad industry had a right to seek state legislation that would impose high costs and other obstacles on truckers. *Pennington* held that a labor union and mechanized coal mines had a right to petition the government for a higher minimum wage for companies seeking to sell coal to the government. This rule made it difficult for more labor-intensive unmechanized mines to compete.[16]

Noerr-Pennington immunity relates to government regulation in two general ways. First, regulation is often the result of interest group pressures, and *Noerr-Pennington* protects the right of these interest groups to request virtually any kind of regulation they wish. The Supreme Court has immunized requests from industry participants to permit them to cartelize their markets, and requests from one manufacturer to make its rival's product unlawful or to place costly regulatory burdens on it.[17] The second way that the *Noerr-Pennington* doctrine relates to regulation is through the litigation and administrative process. The doctrine permits people or firms to use courts or regulatory agencies against their rivals, even though their motives are anticompetitive.[18]

The petitioning immunity is extremely broad, but it does come with one strong exception. There is no right to petition if the petition itself is a "sham"—that is, if the petition is intended not to obtain from the government a response favorable to the petitioner, but rather to harass or suppress a rival. The classic example is the baseless lawsuit. For example, a dominant firm might file patent infringement suits against every new entrant into its market, even though it knows the suits are invalid. The dominant firm intends to "win," not with a courtroom victory, but by imposing high litigation costs on a smaller rival who is not able to bear them.[19]

A Unified Rule for Antitrust Regulatory Immunity

Concerns for federalism certainly compel us to allow ample room for state and local regulation, yet the Supremacy Clause may force broader deference to federal than to state regulation. As a result the scope of power to regulate and the proper domain of regulation will always be somewhat different for the states than for the federal government.

But these differences do not necessarily call for different antitrust treatment. The antitrust immunity doctrines come into play only after the tribunal has decided, or at least assumed, that the regulation in question is valid under both federal and state law. Once we know that a regulation is valid, then insofar as antitrust is concerned it should not matter very much whether the market interference in question emanates from the federal government or the states. Furthermore, just as correcting defects in the federal political process is not antitrust's task, nor is antitrust the proper tool for oversight of state or local political processes.

While the technical rules for these various immunity doctrines sound quite different from one another, all of them can be reduced to a single set of principles. First, antitrust is concerned about the private, discretionary exercise of market power, *not* with government decision making. What we really want to know is whether a private actor is causing harm without adequate government oversight of what it is doing. When the harm to the plaintiff is being caused by the government itself, there is no antitrust claim. Nor is there an antitrust violation when the harm is caused by a private party, but only after that party's conduct has been reviewed and approved by a disinterested government agency, or the agency is active and has the power to review the conduct. The last clause is essential, for the immunity must exist both before and after the agency has acted. Otherwise people would simply go to antitrust courts and bypass the agency. The relevant question is whether a regulatory regime is in place that either has reviewed and controlled the challenged conduct, or is likely to. No immunity is granted if the regulatory agency lacks jurisdiction over the practice, has jurisdiction but is not authorized to take competitive concerns into account, or if it simply rubber-stamps what private firms want.

Note, however, that this same set of queries defines the scope of the "state action" immunity. In that case, what we really want to know is whether the *state* authorized the challenged conduct by passing a statute that mandated it, contemplated that it would occur, or specifically permitted it. If the conduct is of the state or a government subdivision, that is the end of the inquiry. However, if the conduct is by a private party, then we also need to know whether a government agency or official "actively supervised" the conduct.

Finally, the *Noerr-Pennington* inquiry immunizes petitions to the government where the ultimate harm is caused by the government action itself. If I petition the city council for an ordinance approving my waste-disposal facility and disapproving yours, and the council passes this ordinance, then you have no antitrust claim against me. By contrast, if I know that my petition to the government is frivolous but I file it only because I know that you lack the resources to defend against it, then your harm is not caused by the government's decision but by my filing. In that case the injury to competition results from private conduct that has not been effectively supervised.

A single rule for antitrust immunity, no matter what its source, requires two things. First, the regulatory regime must be lawful and have jurisdiction over the conduct that is the subject of the antitrust complaint. "Jurisdiction" means the authority to evaluate conduct, including its competitive consequences, and approve or disapprove it. Second, if challenged private conduct is discretionary—that is, if a private firm could have done something in a different way that causes less competitive harm—that conduct must either have been reviewed and approved by the agency, must be under ongoing study, or the agency must have manifested its ability and will to evaluate the conduct if asked.

In its *Trinko* decision, discussed in more detail later, the Supreme Court took a first step in this direction. The Court held that the value of applying the antitrust laws to a regulated market must be determined by asking two questions. First, how well is the regulatory enterprise itself doing its job of identifying and controlling competitive harms? The better it is doing, the less incremental value antitrust will provide. Second, how much confidence do we have that application of the antitrust laws will improve competition in the situation at hand? If antitrust will be particularly difficult to apply and prone to error, then it would likely do more harm than good in a well-regulated regime. The Court here had little difficulty concluding that state and federal regulators had been doing an adequate job of supervising interconnection disputes between dominant and competitive telephone companies. Furthermore, the antitrust "essential facility" doctrine that the plaintiffs were invoking would be particularly prone to error. As a result antitrust was not likely to be worth its costs.

In getting to this result the Court did not rely on any of the established immunity doctrines. Significantly, local telecommunications is regulated by both federal and state regulatory agencies. In speaking of the effectiveness of regulation, the Court spoke of the two interchangeably, and there was no reason for it not to. Its concern was not with the source of the regulation for its own sake, but rather whether valid government regulation from any source was doing an adequate job of addressing the competitive concerns at hand.

Antitrust and Deregulation

The 1960s and 1970s were the high point of federal regulation, whether measured by the number of industries that were regulated, the extent of the regulation, or by our policy makers' overall confidence that government regulation allocated resources better than ordinary market forces did. But beginning in the late 1970s and extending to the present day, the government has undergone comprehensive deregulation to varying degrees in nearly every regulated market.[20]

Federal deregulation of specific markets began during the Carter administration with statutes that deregulated various parts of the trucking and railroad industries. Congress also abolished the Civil Aeronautics Board (CAB), which once controlled both new entry of passenger airlines and ticket prices. In 1996 it abolished the Interstate Commerce Commission, which mainly regulated trucking and the railroads. In telecommunications, competition now largely controls the long-distance portion of the market, although there is still a great deal of regulation of local service. The long-run goal of the Telecommunications Act of 1996, of which more is said later, is a fully competitive system covering both long-distance and local service.

Much of deregulation has been a consequence of technological change. All things being equal, both private choice and government policy rightfully prefer technologies that are readily capable of being sold in competitive markets. The single biggest change has occurred in telecommunications as a result of gradual displacement of portions of the hardwired telephone network with microwave, satellite, and other wireless technologies. While the hardwired network that continues to dominate local phone service was thought to be a natural monopoly, wireless telecommunication was not. Sophisticated computers and switching equipment in both the telephone industry and the electric power industry have permitted rapid transfer of services from one provider to another, facilitating the integration of long-distance, local, and cellular telecommunications in one industry, and of the "wholesaling" of electric power in the other.[21]

But changes in technology tell only part of the story. Beginning in the 1960s the economic rationales for deregulation were developed in two distinctive bodies of literature. The first severely criticized regulatory agencies for being too expensive, for often being "captured" by the very firms they were supposed to be regulating, and for developing solutions that were highly imperfect and inconsistent with efficient allocation of resources. The second body of literature argued that the traditional economic conception of "competition" was too narrowly drawn, particularly when applied to industries thought to be natural monopolies.

Regulation and Public Choice

Regulatory thinking from the New Deal through the 1950s generally assumed that regulation served the "public interest" by protecting consumers from price gouging or other abuses. However, it often turned out that the principal beneficiaries of industry regulation were the regulated firms themselves, who were shielded from competition and guaranteed profit margins.[22] Regulation also distorted the mix of capital and other resources and the incentives for cost reduction and innovation.[23] The first significant political critique of the regulatory process from an influential government insider came in 1960, in a report by James M. Landis to then-President-elect John F. Kennedy. A generation earlier Landis had presented his own, sharply contrasting, conclusions in *The Administrative Process*, which praised the virtues of government regulation for protecting consumers, and for supervising business activities much more efficiently than the courts could. But his 1960 report expressed considerable disillusionment over the modern regulatory enterprise, and dismay at the extent of "industry orientation" shown by regulatory agencies. Landis's report concluded that most federal regulatory agencies had taken sides with the regulated firms at the expense of the public interest. Furthermore, the cost of operating the regulatory machinery was significantly larger than anticipated.[24]

In addition, economists and political scientists such as James Buchanan, Gordon Tullock, and Mancur Olson began to write about the theory of interest groups, explaining that small, well-organized, homogenous interest groups could reach legislative decision makers much more effectively than could larger, heterogeneous, and more poorly organized interest groups. For example, taxicab owners are relatively few yet have common interests about which they feel strongly. Thus they find it quite easy to organize a taxicab owners lobby. By contrast, taxicab passengers are extremely numerous but the cost of taxi rides is a relatively small part of the financial concern of each individual passenger. Moreover, taxicab passengers do not have an organization in which to meet regularly to discuss their problems. Their very numerosity plus the small size of the perceived interest inclines each individual taxicab passenger to shrink from heavy political involvement in the taxicab pricing structure, preferring to rely on someone else. The result is that when the regulatory agency collects information and opinion upon which to base regulatory decisions, the taxicab owners speak with a single, well-organized, and well-informed voice. By contrast, the taxicab passengers either fail to speak, or else their spokespersons are less well informed, idiosyncratic, or inconsistent with one another. It comes as no surprise that the legislation ends up favoring cab owners over passengers, even though the interests of cab passengers in the aggregate are far larger.[25]

While public choice analysis is often used to support arguments against regulation, public choice is really an argument about why government sometimes makes decisions that favor one particular interest group rather than the interests of society as a whole. The theory explains both socially harmful decisions to regulate and socially harmful decisions *not* to regulate. For example, public choice theory may explain why a small, well-organized group of trucking firms can succeed in protecting interstate trucking from competition at the expense of consumers. But it also serves to explain why a small, well-organized group of cigarette or gun manufacturers can prevent Congress from enacting legislation restricting the distribution of smoking materials to minors or holding gun manufacturers accountable for the social cost of widespread access to weapons. In sum, public choice theory can account for bad regulation or bad failures to regulate, but the theory itself tells us little about whether any particular instance of regulation or failure to regulate is socially harmful or beneficial.[26]

Another weakness of public choice theory is its lack of empirical robustness. In a world in which public choice fully explains government design of regulatory policy, we would expect more regulation in markets that satisfy the Buchanan/Tullock requirements for well-organized special interests. Whether freedom from price competition or entry restrictions prevailed would have little to do with whether regulation in a market is justified by traditional neoclassical factors. But in the world we live in we find a fairly (although by no means perfect) "neoclassical" correlation. That is, regulation of retail electricity, natural gas, and taxicab service is well-nigh universal, even when the choice is left entirely up to the fifty states. By contrast, we do not find such regulation in the markets for office supplies, personal computers, or children's clothing.[27] One is hard-pressed to believe that retail electricity is price-regulated because power companies have the most effective lobbyists or low organization costs, while the grocery industry is competitive because its lobbying is less effective and its sellers cannot organize effectively. Rather, the traditional neoclassical doctrine of natural monopoly probably accounts for the regulatory differences between these markets.

Traditional Economics and Deregulation

Public choice theory explains how the *political* process can produce bad regulation, but traditional economics provides substantive reasons for regulation's numerous weaknesses and failures. One fundamental critique of regulation is that the process costs too much in proportion to any benefits it produces, and that bad results are magnified by chronically inadequate commitment of resources. Regulation is typically very expensive. Furthermore, the sizable budgets of the various regulatory agencies account for only a small percentage of the costs. Far larger is the cost of regulatory compliance by firms required to file a tariff describing every proposed change in price or product, and perhaps dispute or even litigate the proposal with the agency or various private opponents. One consequence of high administrative costs coupled with disappointing results is that legislatures chronically budget too little for regulatory decision making. As a result the agencies do an even poorer job, often leaving large portions of the market open to *de facto* private discretion. In extreme cases so-called "regulation" becomes nothing more than legalized private collusion.[28]

An equally damaging critique is that, while regulation seeks to approximate "competitive" behavior, the various formulas it applies distort incentives and reward inefficiency.[29] The traditional approach to cost-of-service rate making, as in electric power, is a prime example. Under competition, prices are forced to marginal cost, and each firm must operate as efficiently as possible so that it will not lose market share to rivals. Rate-of-return regulation distorts these incentives. Prices cannot be set at short-run marginal cost because that figure is too low to provide a reasonable return on the firm's very large capital investment. As an alternative, the regulatory agency generally permits the regulated firm to recover a "fair rate of return" on its capital investment, and then permits it to pass through its variable costs, such as labor and fuel. To the extent the firm receives its fair rate of return on both efficient and inefficient investments, it has no incentive to distinguish the two. An ordinary competitive firm grows only to the point that incremental gains match incremental costs, but the classically price-regulated firm never reaches that point because it is promised a "fair rate of return" on *all* its investment. There is always a positive return to expansion.[30] Finally, rate-of-return regulation undermines the incentive to innovate. For example, if an older switch costs $10,000 while a replacement could be innovated that does the job for $8,000, the competitive firm develops the switch and profits by pocketing the cost difference. By contrast, the regulated firm experiences only a decline in its rate base. Previously it earned its "fair rate of return" on the $10,000 switch, while under the new technology it earns that return on the lower-cost replacement.

Carefully designed regulatory policy partially controls these distortions, and close scrutiny by the regulatory agency prohibits at least some of the overinvestment. But the compensation is never complete, and careful agency oversight is expensive. As a result comprehensive price and service rate making offers, at best, a very rough approximation of the competitive price, deters innovation, perhaps significantly, and costs much to administer. These arguments are generally thought to be quite robust, and to counsel against regulation unless it is very clear that competition simply cannot work in a certain market.

Shifts in Competition Theory

Another economic argument against overbroad regulation is the result of a shift in economic thinking about the nature of competition. The neoclassical competition model developed during the late nineteenth and early twentieth centuries hypothesized "competitive" markets consisting of numerous relatively small firms, no single one having power to reduce marketwide output and thus increase the price.[31] Within this model, competition is thought to be threatened by significant decreases in the number of firms in the market. As a result significant economies of scale—the lower costs that attend higher output—are seen both as benefiting consumers by permitting lower production costs, but as injuring them by turning markets into oligopolies. The extreme case of scale economies is "natural monopoly," in which one firm occupying the entire market has lower costs than any possible combination of two or more firms. In that case *no* amount of competition is consistent with maximum productive efficiency, and only price regulation was thought to approximate competitive behavior.

But even natural monopoly markets might perform competitively if entry and exit are not unduly costly. "Contestability" theory posits that competition *for* a market can be as effective as competition *in* a market: if the incumbent firm charges too much, a second firm will quickly enter, and there will be a brief price war until one is forced to exit. The ongoing threat of such entry forces the incumbent firm to charge competitive prices. Similarly, a publicly awarded "franchise" monopoly, such as one for cable television, can be awarded to the firm offering to charge the competitive price. Every few years the franchise would again be put up for such bidding. Even though the market has room for a single provider at any given time, price will be competitive if a competitive bidding process is used to select and, if necessary, replace the franchisee.[32]

Practical application of contestability theory has encountered some difficulties. The main problems are "sunk" costs and bottlenecks. A sunk cost is an investment that cannot be recovered by an exiting firm. For example, the first cable television company to enter the market must build a cable network. When its franchise expires, the network has a significant useful life remaining. If a newcomer must build a new network, then the incumbent will have an overwhelming advantage in the second round of franchise bidding. The incumbent cannot be expected to transfer the network voluntarily to a new bidder; legislation might require it to do so, but it would also have to determine the price. Alternatively, the network could be publicly owned and merely operated by the private firm—but that solution results in the very public ownership that our regulatory enterprise seeks to avoid. To date, there have not been practical solutions to this problem. As a result franchise bidding rarely occurs in markets that contain costly, durable, and nontransferable networks, such as cable television or local electric power grids.[33]

Bottlenecks are the other problem impeding contestability, with the airline industry providing a good example. Sunk costs on any given route are low because, unlike a cable television network, an aircraft can be cheaply moved from one route to another. The route from Omaha to Sheboygan has room for but a single flight per day; however, if the incumbent carrier started charging monopoly prices, a competing carrier should be able to swoop in and take its business at a lower price. Fearing this, the incumbent would have to price at the competitive level.

But airplanes no longer land in cow pastures. They require airports and gate space, and in most cases the latter is hard to come by. Today hub-dominant carriers control a majority of the gate space at many

United States airports. As long as that remains the case, contestability will not produce the promised results even in the passenger airline market, which was initially believed to be the darling market for the theory.[34]

While contestability theory has never produced the results it once promised, it has served to refocus antitrust thinking on the importance of competitive entry in disciplining monopoly. Even a firm that is alone in its market may not have significant power if new entry is quick and cheap. Such a market is not a good candidate for either price regulation or aggressive antitrust enforcement.

Deregulation, Telecommunications, and Antitrust's Essential Facility Doctrine

The natural effect of deregulation is to enlarge the domain of antitrust by removing or narrowing antitrust immunities. For example, trucking and airline deregulation has very largely placed those industries under antitrust control. Many of the "collisions" of antitrust and regulatory law have faded as regulatory supervision has been narrowed or eliminated.

At the same time, antitrust sometimes has a different look and feel in formerly regulated industries, and the transition has not always been smooth. Antitrust has reentered most easily in markets that never should have been regulated to begin with, such as trucking, or where technological change has permitted competition among multiple firms, such as long-distance communications.[35] The road has been much bumpier in deregulated markets that continue to manifest many of the characteristics of natural monopoly, or where technologically complex networks make the transition to competition unusually difficult.

Perhaps the bumpiest transition of all has been deregulation of local telephone service under the 1996 Telecommunications Act. The telecommunications system is an elaborate network that links virtually every person in the United States as well as the world. Furthermore, while the system is a single network, it is also competitively supplied by hundreds of sellers of basic local and long-distance service, high-speed data transmission and Internet service, wireless service, and of course hundreds of types of "attachments," ranging from simple telephones to fax machines to high-speed computers.

This level of provider competition is a relatively recent development. As passed in 1934, the Federal Communications Act contemplated that a single firm, AT&T, would own and operate nearly the entire telecommunications system in the United States.[36] The monopoly extended even to instruments, and AT&T protected it aggressively. For example, the "Hush-A-Phone" was a mechanical gadget shaped like a tiny inverted megaphone that clipped over the mouthpiece of a telephone. It enabled a caller to whisper into the phone and be heard by the person on the other end of the line, but not by eavesdroppers in the same room as the caller. AT&T complained and got the FCC to agree that the Hush-A-Phone was an unauthorized "foreign attachment." However, the Commission was reversed by the court of appeals. That small victory turned out to be the camel's nose under the tent. A few years later Tom Carter, who had invented the Hush-A-Phone, won an even bigger victory with a decision permitting various communications devices to be connected to the AT&T system, provided that connection was through a coupler that protected the network from harm. Then MCI entered the telecommunications market with a set of booster antennas initially designed to enable truckers' CB radios to interconnect with the phone system. From that point, and in spite of opposition from both AT&T and initially the FCC, MCI expanded its service to encompass wireless alternatives to long distance, which it could do only by interconnecting its equipment with the AT&T system.[37]

The AT&T breakup, which occurred in 1982, was intended to assign the competitive and natural monopoly portions of the telecommunications network to distinct firms.[38] This division, plus the need for local and long-distance companies to interconnect, led to many disputes. Prior to 1996 these were decided by the late Judge Harold Greene, who had presided over the breakup. Thereafter the 1996 Telecommunications Act imposed broad interconnection obligations on the Bells and placed the process under the joint regulation of the FCC and state regulatory agencies. Under that statute the ILECs, or "incumbent local exchange carriers" (the Bells), are obligated not only to interconnect with CLECs, or "competitive local exchange carriers," but also to lease to them almost any input capable of being leased. In many but not all cases the CLECs have made only minimal investments in facilities themselves.

The 1996 Act was intended to foster the growth of competition, but the type of "competition" it produces is odd. Imagine that the local Kroger store is a town's only seller of bananas. Seeking to promote banana competition, the town passes a banana competition ordinance requiring Kroger to sell bananas at a steeply discounted wholesale price to individual entrepreneurs who push banana carts around the store, perhaps underselling Kroger itself by a few cents. Kroger supplies the store facility, storage, heat, light, and even the bananas themselves, with the small sellers supplying little more than their labor.

The banana competition ordinance simply confuses "competition" with large numbers of retailers. True banana competition would require individual stores having their own facilities, purchasing bananas on the wholesale market, and retailing them to consumers. Nevertheless, the Kroger's scenario largely describes what the 1996 Telecommunications Act does. Small CLECs can lease almost all of their inputs from the Bells at regulated wholesale prices, and then resell the services in competition with them.

Such sharing requirements may in the long run promote competition by encouraging small resellers to invest in their own facilities. The small banana retailers might eventually trade in their carts for their own stores and even start acquiring their own bananas. But more effective competition would likely have resulted if the Act had limited the number of CLECs and placed more stringent requirements on them—for example, requiring them to provide inputs that are reasonably capable of being produced under competitive conditions. Under such a policy, which is more similar to what the FCC does in cellular phone markets,[39] there would be fewer CLECs but their quality would be higher. Indeed, one of the ironies of the 1996 Telecom Act is that it may actually be retarding the development of a competitive infrastructure for local telephony because it permits CLECs simply to lease everything they want at steeply discounted prices, rather than forcing them to build for themselves when they could reasonably do so.[40]

The 1996 Telecommunications Act contemplates that compulsory interconnection agreements will produce conflicts, and there have been many. Disputes are to be resolved by the FCC or in some cases state regulatory agencies. In the *Trinko* case such a dispute ended up in an FCC-administered decree in which Verizon paid a penalty, mainly for delays in filling orders under an interconnection agreement.[41] The plaintiffs were consumers claiming that the breach of the interconnection agreement was also an antitrust violation.

The *Trinko* case illustrates why some antitrust immunity is essential even in a partially deregulated industry. Here a government agency was intended by Congress to resolve interconnection disputes and was actually doing that job far more expeditiously than any court could do it through jury trials.[42] In contrast, the *Trinko* antitrust claim was asserted mainly under the "essential facility" doctrine, a theory that has always pushed antitrust to its conceptual limit.

Under the essential facility doctrine a dominant firm violates §2 of the Sherman Act if it refuses to share certain "essential" inputs with rivals. What makes a facility "essential" has never been defined very clearly, but at the very least it must be an input that rivals need in order to survive in the market *and* one that they cannot make for themselves or obtain from other sources. Competition is always better served when firms supply their own inputs competitively rather than share them with a monopolist.[43] How many facilities are "essential" in this double sense? Certainly not many, but there may be a few, such as the hardwired loop that constitutes the backbone of the local telecommunications network. Perhaps a few gas pipelines or railroad tracks are essential, although competition is feasible in most of these markets. Another possibility is facilities such as athletic stadiums that are subsidized by the government, so a rival that had to finance its own facility would find it impossible to compete.[44]

Even after developing a workable definition of essential facilities, an antitrust rule imposing sharing obligations is virtually impossible to devise. *First,* there is the problem of price setting. A monopolist ordered to share will sell at the monopoly price, and in that case consumers are no better off. Instead of a single firm, we simply have a little cartel of firms jointly selling at monopoly levels. Of course, the court could order the defendant to charge less, perhaps even the competitive price. But that reconstitutes the antitrust court as a regulatory agency, employing the extraordinarily cumbersome vehicle of an antitrust trial to regulate a firm's prices. The "antitrust solution" to the problem of monopoly is not to force monopolists to share with rivals at judicially determined prices, but to have each firm obtain its own inputs and set its own prices. For this reason alone antitrust would do well to jettison the essential facility doctrine.[45]

Second, the court must determine the list of things that must be shared as well as the price to be charged. In *Trinko* the plaintiffs wanted Verizon not only to share its existing system, but also to add capacity by building new trunk lines or installing new switching equipment at the plaintiff's request. This means that the court must decide when a firm should increase its capacity by adding new plants or equipment. Unless we want to use the antitrust laws to turn a firm completely into a public utility, the essential facility doctrine must be limited to sharing out of a firm's existing capacity.

In *Trinko* the Supreme Court neither approved nor repudiated the essential facility doctrine. But it did impose severe limitations on the use of such claims. First, the Court limited the antitrust law of unilateral refusals to deal to refusals that are profitable only because they tend to create or maintain a monopoly. In the *Trinko* case the defendant was earning higher returns from serving customers directly than it could earn from sharing its facilities with a rival, who would then serve the same customers. No rational firm would give up more profitable business to consumers in order to make less profitable sales to competitors. It has a perfectly good profit motive for keeping such sales to itself. The Court also sharply distinguished its previous *Aspen* holding, which condemned a defendant for entering a joint marketing venture with a competitor and later abandoning it, severely injuring the competitor's business. Using the courts to impose a judicially created joint venture on competitors is a far more drastic interference in the market than simply recognizing the competitive value of a joint venture that already exists.[46]

The Court also refused to apply the essential facility doctrine to a good or service that the defendant was not already selling to others. In its *Otter Tail* decision, for example, the Supreme Court had held that a defendant who was already wholesaling electric power to others must also wholesale it to rivals, presumably at equivalent terms.[47] In *Trinko*, by contrast, Verizon was not in the general business of wholesaling access to its loop and other facilities. It did so only because such sharing was required by the 1996 Telecommunications Act. Concerns for administration fully explain that reasoning. Only a regulatory agency could break up a firm's output into intermediate goods and manage their forced sale to rivals. It would be like ordering Ford to sell partly finished automobile bodies or drivetrain assemblies to rivals, who could then finish them out into completed automobiles.

While not stating it in so many words, *Trinko* may effectively have brought the era of antitrust essential facility claims to an end, certainly in regulated industries where an agency is actively supervising the conduct that forms the basis of an antitrust claim. If so, that would be an important step in our recognition that competition is not regulation, and federal courts are not regulatory agencies.

11

The Conflict between Antitrust and Intellectual Property Rights

Antitrust is "public regarding" legislation whose purpose is to promote economic competition. The antitrust laws have not always been faithful to this goal. As Chapter 2 observes, the Congress that framed them was more concerned to protect politically well-organized small business from larger, more efficient firms and less concerned to promote high output, innovation, and low prices. From the New Deal through the 1960s both Congress and the courts used antitrust to further an agenda favoring small business, often at the expense of consumers. Some powerful vestiges of that period remain to this day, in particular the Robinson-Patman Act.

The intellectual property (IP) laws—mainly patent, copyright, and trademark—should also be regarded as enacted in the public interest. Under the United States Constitution, the purpose of the IP laws is: "To promote the Progress of Science and useful Arts, by securing for limited Times to Authors and Inventors the exclusive Right to their respective Writings and Discoveries."[1] A public-regarding set of IP laws would create exclusive rights that are just sufficient to encourage the optimal amount of innovation. With no protection at all, inventors and other innovators would probably not have a sufficient incentive to innovate because others could too easily copy their work without compensation. But too much protection can produce costly monopolies or exclusive rights that others must either license or innovate around. The social costs of these exclusive rights can become greater than the value of any innovations they produce. In addition, excessive protection can retard innovation by making it more difficult for people to build on the work of their predecessors, which all innovation does.

While both antitrust and IP law have cycled from public-regarding to special interest interpretations, they have not always been in the same place on the cycle. For example, during the 1930s and 1940s the Supreme Court was hostile toward patents, construing them as narrowly as possible, often invalidating them, and exaggerating their potential for competitive harm.[2] Today, after three decades of expansion we have probably reached the opposite extreme. IP protection has gradually been ratcheted up, with broader coverage and longer terms. While the idea that the IP laws overprotect and reflect significant interest-group capture originated with the IP "left," today it has become mainstream and even counts some members of the Chicago School among its adherents.[3]

A good example of legislative capture is the Sonny Bono Copyright Term Extension Act, upheld by the Supreme Court in 2003, which not only increased the length of the copyright term to seventy years following the author's death, but also made the extension retroactive so as to apply to copyrights that had already expired or were about to expire.[4] A principal protagonist of the legislation was Walt Disney Enterprises, whose copyrighted Mickey Mouse was about to enter the public domain. It is hard to come up with any serious argument that retroactive extensions of old copyrights serve the constitutional purpose of promoting the progress of the useful arts. Those inventions and ideas have already been created. The Copyright Term Extension Act shows us Congress at its worst, passing legislation at the behest of powerful interest groups at society's expense. As one observer described the extent of Congress's capture by entertainment and related interests:

> Copyright interest groups hold fund raisers for members of Congress, write campaign songs, invite members of Congress (and their staff) to private movie screenings or sold-out concerts, and draft legislation they expect Congress to pass without any changes. In the 104th Congress, they are drafting the committee reports and haggling among themselves about what needs to be in the report. In my experience, some copyright lawyers and lobbyists actually resent members of Congress and staff interfering with what they view as their legislation and their committee report. With the 104th Congress we have, I believe, reached a point where legislative history must be ignored because not even the hands of congressional staff have touched committee reports.[5]

The political market in which IP rights are created seems particularly susceptible to legislative capture. Those who favor broader protection and longer duration are typically large firms that engage in a great deal of research or production of entertainment. They are few in number, very well informed, and have an organized and carefully strategized agenda. By contrast, the beneficiaries of the more rapid invention that would probably result from shorter terms and narrower scope are numerous, with a diverse and poorly articulated agenda. The former group has an impressive lead over the latter in obtaining legislation.[6]

Another reason IP law is particularly susceptible to interest-group capture is that the optimal amount of protection for innovation is unknown. At least some IP protection is necessary to encourage innovation. Up to a point the trade-off is positive—that is, as protection increases, the marginal social gains from innovation are greater than the marginal losses from enforcement of exclusionary rights and the transaction costs of negotiating licenses. The problem is that no one knows what the optimal length of time is, or how broad the protection should be. Furthermore, it seems clear that the correct duration for patents and copyrights varies considerably depending on the technology or the market. The term should probably be much shorter in fast-moving industries like software design, and longer in slower-moving industries for durable goods where technology tends to stay in place for long periods.[7]

If the history of regulation is any guide, the more uncertainty there is about the best rule, the more room there is for interest group politics to interfere. Someone reading the public choice literature might get the impression that legislative deference to special interests is widespread and largely random, depending on how well interest groups are organized. But if that were true we could expect a random mix of, say, price regulation as between grocery stores and electric utilities, or as much regulation of shoe retailing as there is of insurance or banking. But that is not true, and the differences are not explained by more effective electric utility or insurance industry lobbying. An important factor in determining the extent to which special interest legislation takes hold in a particular market is knowledge or lack of knowledge about how that market works. Ambiguity begets obfuscation, and in such an environment interest groups tend to be far more influential than in markets where the way things work is relatively well known.

Since no one knows the optimal duration of a patent or copyright, it is much more difficult for critics to proclaim a term extension as private interest rather than public-regarding legislation. But occasionally Congress steps over the line and does something that is clearly contrary to the public interest. Retroactivity in the Copyright Term Extension Act is such an example. However long the optimal copyright period is, it is far-fetched to think that a *retroactive* term extension increases the incentive to innovate. To be sure, proponents felt obliged to look for incentives, and they found a few. For example, retroactive term extension may give the owners of old black and white movies an incentive to colorize them. Factually, that is hardly clear—release into the public domain might make it even more likely that they would be colorized, because many more firms would be in a position to do so and the colorized result could probably itself be copyrighted.[8] But the bigger point is that Congress extended copyrights retroactively for everything; if its concern was with colorizing old movies, it could have made a special provision.

Two other characteristics of IP markets suggest that they do not work particularly well: extreme product differentiation and lack of good information about ownership. Perfect competition requires numerous producers selling indistinguishable products. By their nature, IP rights are unique, although one does not want to push the point too far. While the patenting process requires that an invention be "new" and "non-obvious," often alternative patented technologies achieve the same result. Copyright protects expressions, not ideas, and many different expressions can compete with each other. For example, a copyrighted Italian cookbook may simply compete with hundreds of other cookbooks. Nevertheless, IP rights often are unique in the sense that for a particular user only one (or a small number) will do what that user needs to get done. In a world of optimal IP scope and coverage this uniqueness is not a problem. The higher prices that result from product differentiation are simply part of the return to invention that the IP laws promise. But in a world in which we protect too much, the result is needless transactions and unnecessarily high prices.

In addition, in most markets for traditional goods the bargaining parties are clear at the outset about who owns what. When I walk into an A&P grocery to purchase a banana, I presume that prior to the transaction the banana is not "public domain." A&P is the owner, so if I want the banana I must purchase it from A&P. By contrast, IP rights are often made ambiguous by uncertainties regarding validity, scope, misuse, and infringement. In the world of IP rights, simply determining who owns what or whether anything is owned at all is costly and the results often uncertain.

Jared Diamond has observed that historically most scientific progress has resulted from copying and producing variations on what already exists, and not from purely isolated acts of genius. The things we think of as great inventions were actually cumulations of inventiveness that finally reached a level sufficient to meet a market demand. James Watt's 1768 steam engine was actually an improvement over Thomas Newcome's engine, which in turn was an improvement over Thomas Savery's, who had been working on an unbuilt engine from a design by Denis Papin. An optimal IP system must balance inventors' rights to their rewards against the critical need each innovator has to build on the work of predecessors.

To that extent, the licensing thicket we have today in many areas is almost certainly counterproductive.[9] Broad IP coverage for modest improvements creates the anticommons problem that almost any innovation drawing on earlier ideas—and all innovations do—generates conflicting ownership claims. The result is too much costly searching, licensing, innovating around in order to avoid licensing, or even choices not to develop a certain technology in order to elude an infringement dispute.[10]

The Role of Antitrust in IP Markets

When antitrust litigation implicates intellectual property rights, how much should courts consider the extent to which an IP provision represents the wishes of a special interest rather than the public? One possibility is to take legislative capture into account. For example, we could say that the public-regarding character of the antitrust laws justifies a broad construction that trumps any IP right that smacks of special interest influence. A commonly cited canon of statutory interpretation is that "special interest" statutes should be narrowly construed. Our political process contains many defects, and occasionally special interests get their wish with Congress at the expense of everyone else, as in the Copyright Term Extension Act. However, these statutes are to be regarded as contracts giving the favored few precisely what they bargained for and nothing else. By contrast, public-regarding statutes can be interpreted broadly so as to give effect to their general thrust and intent as well as their precise language.

But I do not believe that is the right approach to antitrust analysis.

Legislative capture might justify a narrow construction of the patent or copyright acts themselves, but not the use of antitrust as a club. As the previous chapter observes, correcting defects in the political process is not antitrust's role. Rather, antitrust policy takes legislation as it finds it, even if the legislation serves the public interest poorly. Of course, the breadth of IP rights may have an impact on the number and kind of conflicts that arise between IP rights and the antitrust laws. But the antitrust laws are properly concerned with economic, not political, competition.

True and False Conflicts between IP and Antitrust

Over the years the courts have claimed to find many conflicts between the competition-furthering policies of the antitrust laws and the protection of exclusive rights that the IP laws afford. They have spoken of the "monopoly" created by IP rights as fundamentally inconsistent with the procompetitive policies of the Sherman Act. As one court said, speaking of patents: "The conflict between the antitrust and patent laws arises in the methods they embrace that were designed to achieve reciprocal goals. While the antitrust laws proscribe unreasonable restraints of competition, the patent laws reward the inventor with a temporary monopoly that insulates him from competitive exploitation of his patented art."[11]

But many of these conflicts were imagined, mainly because the courts committed one of two errors. In some cases they condemned an IP practice, citing antitrust principles, without asking whether the practice threatened competition in any important way. In such cases there should be no conflict because an antitrust violation requires an injury to competition. In other cases the courts exonerated an anticompetitive practice without a clear indication that the practice was necessary in order to protect a legitimate IP right.

At a high enough level of abstraction one can always find a conflict between antitrust and the IP laws. They balance economic growth in two different ways: through competition and innovation. Competition is efficient because it squeezes monopoly out of the economy. In the short run, competition maximizes the volume of trade and the aggregate value of resources. In the long run, however, perfect competition reduces the incentive to innovate. Prices are driven to cost, and knowledge flows freely. This means that innovations are readily copied by those who have not invested in creating them. Prices are competed down to a level that may prevent the innovator from getting a positive return on its investment.

That is where the IP laws step in. Their purpose is to prevent excessive free riding on innovations by giving inventors and artists a period of exclusive protection from copying. The amount of protection is principally a function of two factors, duration and scope.[12] The longer that patent or copyright protection lasts, the greater the returns to innovation. Returns also increase as more is covered by an IP right. For example, as courts interpret patents liberally and find more infringement, patents become more valuable. Conversely, the broader the "fair use" right to use copyrighted material without a license, the less valuable copyright protection becomes for the copyright's owner.

So the antitrust laws and the IP laws are in conflict in the very general sense that when the two bodies of law behave myopically, antitrust always wants more competition and IP law wants more protection for the right to exclude. But this conflict is largely illusory because when legal policy is not behaving myopically, then everyone should want the same thing, namely, the optimal balance between competition and protection for innovation.

This implies that there is still balancing to be done. Different opinions about where the balance should be struck can produce conflicts. But questions about the duration and scope of the IP laws belong to Congress and to judicial interpretation of the relevant IP statute, *not* to the antitrust laws. Questions about duration are always legislative and none of antitrust's business, even if an unusually long duration is clearly not in the public interest. Getting Congress to clean up its Act is not antitrust's job.

Questions about scope are more complex. Practices that reach beyond the scope of protection given by an IP right can violate the antitrust laws. Such issues arise, for example, when a patent license calls for price-fixing or some kind of exclusion that the relevant IP provision does not authorize, or when a dominant firm files an infringement suit based on a claim that is broader than its patent actually creates. Practices such as these can be both anticompetitive and antitrust violations. But they are so only when the IP right holder exceeds the scope of its IP right, and making that determination depends on the relevant IP provision, not on antitrust. Notably, there is no *antitrust* law that defines the scope of patent claims, or the breadth of copyright "fair use," or whether a competing product infringes a trademark.

The balance of this chapter examines a variety of IP/antitrust disputes that have claimed to find conflicts between the two essential policies of protecting competition and furthering innovation. Upon closer examination, most of the conflicts either disappear or become quite manageable.

Price-Fixing and Other Horizontal Restraints

During the first two generations of Sherman and Clayton Act enforcement (1890–1930) the courts did a relatively good job of accommodating the protections offered by the patent and copyright laws along with the antitrust concern for protecting competition. However, the Supreme Court's very first patent/antitrust decision produced a highly problematic resolution to a conflict between IP rights and competition policy.

The *National Harrow* decision of 1902 originated in patent conflicts that dated back to the 1860s, when several firms patented various horse-drawn devices for aerating ground prior to planting. After nearly three decades of litigation, these companies settled their disputes by giving licenses to the National Harrow Company in exchange for shares. National Harrow then licensed a package of patents to these and other firms to manufacture floating spring-tooth harrows, which were the state of the art in agricultural technology. One license provision required the manufacturers to sell at prices stipulated by National Harrow. In upholding that provision against an antitrust challenge, the Court reasoned that implicit in the Patent Act are both the right to make a patented article and the right to set its price. The firm could either do both of these things itself, or it could license away the right to make the article, while retaining the right to set the price.[13]

The Court's logic was bizarre. If Ford owns three automobile production plants, it has the legal right both to produce cars in the plants and to set their price. But it does not follow that Ford could sell one of the plants to Chrysler while "retaining" the right to set the price on the cars that Chrysler made in that plant. Once the plant had passed into Chrysler's hands, any attempt by Ford to set the price of Chrysler cars would be naked price-fixing.

A quarter century later the Supreme Court extended the *National Har-*

row holding in *General Electric (GE)*, a controversial decision that approved a price-fixing agreement between two lightbulb manufacturers, provided that the agreement was contained in a patent license.[14] GE, which owned the most successful patents on the incandescent lightbulb, licensed Westinghouse to make bulbs in competition with GE. The Court approved a license provision that specified the price Westinghouse must charge for the lightbulbs.

Under the *GE* rule two firms can fix the price of a good provided that the price fix is stipulated in a patent license to make that good. The Court reasoned that the owner of a patent covering a lightbulb could manufacture all the bulbs itself, and would presumably produce the monopoly amount. So a firm should be free to license another and produce that amount between the two of them, which they could do by agreeing on either the amount to be produced or the price to be charged. The *GE* case presents a true conflict between antitrust and patent policy. Price-fixing is the most serious antitrust offense. Nevertheless, the Patent Act expressly permits the patentee to license others to employ the patent, and inherent in the concept of a license is the right to specify an amount. So GE clearly could license Westinghouse to make "10,000 bulbs per week" under a patent license. Many cartel agreements are in fact output restriction agreements. GE could accomplish everything a cartel could simply by specifying the amount that licensees could make, and then adding enough of its own output to reach the monopoly amount.

While *GE* does expose a true antitrust/IP conflict, subsequent decisions made the conflict relatively narrow. Suppose, for example, that the patent covers only a small portion of a good—for example, a wiper blade on an automobile. The *GE* rule would not permit Ford to give Chrysler a license to produce Ford's patented wiper blade, and also let Ford stipulate the price at which the entire automobile bearing that blade is sold.[15] Or suppose the patent covers a process for making a good but not the good itself. For example, DuPont might develop a patent for mixing paint very thoroughly so that the heavier components of the paint will not settle to the bottom of the can. The paint itself is unpatented. Notwithstanding *GE*, DuPont could not license Glidden to use the process and specify the price of the mixed paint.[16] These licensing restrictions are not authorized by the Patent Act, so there is no conflict to resolve. Any resulting price fixes are illegal per se.

GE's consequences are particularly troublesome when a patent's validity is doubtful or there are good alternatives to the patented technology. Then the *GE* rule can condone blatant collusion while not furthering any interest in encouraging innovation. When faced with uncertainty over the validity or coverage of IP rights, competing firms have every incentive to negotiate a *GE*-style price-fixing agreement rather than determine whether a patent is valid or a rival's technology infringes. If litigation determines that the patent is invalid, the firms will no longer have a cloak for their collusion. By the same token, firms with indisputably valid patent rights would be less likely to impose price-fixing provisions and more likely to use higher license fees. Both types of provisions raise the licensee's price, but the higher license fee gives the excess to the patentee, while simple price-fixing gives it to the licensee.[17] So *GE*-style price-fixing is more likely to occur in precisely the circumstances where it does the most social harm.

To return to the *National Harrow* case, suppose that several firms claim patents on various mechanisms that can be used to make an agricultural harrow. Some of the patents are valid, but many may not be. Furthermore, while some of the patents contain claims that overlap, or "block," one another, many do not. The dilemma the firms face is this: the more dubious the patents, the more likely that this market will simply become competitive as a result of litigation. For example, if all the patents were declared invalid, the claimants as well as others would simply end up making harrows in competition with one another. So as the patents become more doubtful the firms acquire a greater incentive to "settle" and employ *GE*-style price-fixing licenses. The result could be a legally enforceable cartel.

Market division agreements rest on a little different footing than price-fixing agreements because some of them are explicitly authorized by the Patent Act. The statute expressly permits a patentee to grant a license to the "whole or any specified part of the United States."[18] Domestic territorial division agreements are legal, as when the patentee of a computer component licenses another to make and sell it east of the Mississippi while reserving west of the Mississippi to itself. As with price-fixing there are boundary problems, such as when the patent covers only a small part of the finished good and the territorial division covers the entire good. To return to a previous example, Ford's wiper blade patent gives Ford the power to tell Chrysler, its licensee, where blades produced under the patent may be sold. But Ford may not use that license to specify where entire Chrysler automobiles may be sold.

Patent "pools," or cross-licensing arrangements that do not involve price-fixing or market division, present fewer problems. First of all, patent claims sometimes overlap, meaning that for either patentee to practice its patent would constitute an infringement of the other person's patent. Closely related is the situation where complementary patents are both necessary to produce a marketable product. For example, I may own a patent on an application process for a certain road surface, but it works only with a certain emulsion, and you own the patent on the emulsion. In that case cross-licenses would permit both of us, separately or jointly, to market both the emulsion and the process.

Cross-licensing with price-fixing restrictions raises the same problems as the Supreme Court confronted in *GE,* and cross-licenses can also include market division agreements. In addition, even cross-licensing without price or market restrictions can be anticompetitive to the extent that it reduces firms' incentives to challenge patents.[19] When a patent is declared invalid the whole world can enter the market, while cross-licensing reserves it to the parties to the license agreement. Once again, the agreements are more threatening to competition as the validity of the patents is more doubtful.

Horizontal agreements licensing patents remain the one area where IP/antitrust conflicts are real in the sense that genuinely anticompetitive results are possible, but there are also serious IP rights that must be taken into account. For a court, the best way to resolve such conflicts is, first, to determine that there is a viable threat to competition; and if so, whether the conduct at issue is expressly authorized by the Patent Act, or seems reasonably necessary to carry out a purpose that the Patent Act recognizes as valid. Second, if threats to competition seem significant, it may become important to find out whether the parties reasonably believed their IP rights were valid at the time they made their agreement.

False Conflicts: IP and Vertical Restraints

Vertical restraints, the subject of Chapter 8, are contracts with manufacturers or suppliers limiting the ways in which retailers, franchisees, or other dealers can sell the supplier's product. Very few such restraints are anticompetitive.[20] The first significant vertical restraint cases before the Supreme Court also involved IP rights. In *Dr. Miles* (1911) the Court condemned resale price maintenance, or manufacturer stipulation of the retailer's resale price. Dr. Miles defended its practice by noting that its medicine was protected by a trade secret. The Court replied that while secret processes could be protected, that did not give the plaintiff the right to control the "entire trade." Stipulating the price does nothing to protect the secrecy of the process.[21]

While the Court was wrong to condemn resale price maintenance under a per se rule, *Dr. Miles* does stand for the important proposition that there is no conflict between IP and antitrust if the challenged practice does nothing to protect the IP right. For example, stipulating the resale price of a book does not further any interest that the publisher might have in protecting its copyright.

A publisher might have a financial interest in other kinds of limitations, however, such as restrictions on subsequent uses of the book. It might wish to prevent the book's buyer from lending it to others, thus forcing would-be borrowers to purchase a copy for themselves. However, the Supreme Court had already concluded in its *Bobbs-Merrill* decision three years before *Dr. Miles* that copyright law did not permit a publisher to impose such limitations. Under the "first sale" doctrine applied in that decision, any IP rights that the publisher had in the physical book itself were exhausted when the book was sold. As a result the copyright laws did not permit publishers to stipulate such things as resale prices or the extent to which a book may be shared.

In reaching its decision the *Bobbs-Merrill* Court observed that "there is no claim in this case of [a] contract limitation . . . controlling the subsequent sales of the book."[22] This observation has inspired some companies, such as software producers, to get around the "first sale" rule by using shrink-wrap license restrictions. Most courts treat these restrictions as purely private contracts between the seller of the software and a particular buyer; they are not copyright claims that can be asserted against anyone.[23] For example, a software manufacturer might license its software to be used on one computer and not shared with others—the equivalent of prohibiting a book's owner from lending it out. But in the shrink-wrap cases the contracts are just what they are: contracts. Interpreting them does not require courts to defer to IP rights, for none are at issue. So if a contract provision contained in a shrink-wrap license is anticompetitive, the copyright laws would not limit the court's ability to apply antitrust.

Tying arrangements historically provoked most of the conflicts that courts imagined to exist between antitrust and IP rights.[24] Nearly all the conflicts were false, although some troublesome doctrine still lingers. The first tying case that came to the Supreme Court was *A. B. Dick* (1912). The defendant conditioned the sale of its patented mimeograph, or copy, machine (the "tying" product) on the user's purchase of its ink and paper (the "tied" product). Nothing in the Patent Act either expressly permitted or prohibited a license agreement that tied a patented good to unpatented supplies in this way,[25] and the agreement did not fall within the traditional definition of agreements in restraint of trade. The Court found the licensing restriction lawful. Two years later Congress passed the Clayton Act with a tying provision that explicitly included patented goods. Soon after, in the *Motion Picture Patents* case (1917), the Supreme Court condemned the defendant's sale of movie projectors subject to a licensing restriction that only the defendant's films could be shown in them. The defendant was attempting to monopolize the entire movie industry by using its technologically superior projector as a bottleneck through which it could control the films that were exhibited.[26]

Ever since *A. B. Dick* and *Motion Picture Patents* the antitrust law of tying has been closely allied to disputes about the appropriate scope of IP rights. Most litigated tying cases have involved products protected by patents, copyrights, or trademarks. The "leverage" theory under which so many patent ties were condemned was believed to create a significant antitrust/patent conflict. For example, in *Carbice* (1931) the Supreme Court concluded that a tying arrangement was anticompetitive because it permitted a patentee to "extend" its patent monopoly from the patented product (in that case, an ice box) to an unpatented tied product (dry ice), and thereby increase its monopoly profits.[27] The per se rule against tying was a direct consequence of the leverage theory, as well as the presumption that mere ownership of a patent conferred enough market power to make the tie competitively harmful.[28] In the 1960s the Supreme Court extended this presumption to copyrights, and a few lower courts even extended it to trademarks.[29] The presumption has been severely criticized, and at this writing the Supreme Court has agreed to revisit it.[30] There is little question that the origins of this idiosyncratic and seriously overdeterrent rule originated in the Supreme Court's broad hostility toward patents in the 1940s.

As Chapter 2 explains, the traditional "leverage" theory of tying made no economic sense. When goods must be used together, the profit-maximizing price must be based on what the buyer is willing to pay for the combination. If A. B. Dick is already selling its mimeograph machine at the profit-maximizing price, it could charge a monopoly price for ink only by reducing the price of the machine. Once this basis for challenging ties is ruled out, all remaining tying claims should be addressed under the rule of reason—although in fact the per se rule remains alive and well.

The discredited leverage theory of ties was the *only* one that saw ties as inherently anticompetitive, improperly expanding the scope of a patent, and thus creating an IP/antitrust conflict. For the remaining theories of tying an IP right sometimes gives a procompetitive explanation of what the seller is doing, and in a few cases an IP right may contribute to a firm's market power. But none of the remaining tying theories recognize any kind of conflict between the IP laws and the antitrust laws. The absence of IP rights does not serve to condemn a tie that is not anticompetitive in the first place. And the presence of an IP right rarely serves to exonerate an anticompetitive tie.

Many patent ties are in fact price discrimination devices, and when used for this purpose most are competitively benign. For example, by tying ink to its mimeograph machine A. B. Dick took advantage of the fact that high-intensity users valued the machine more highly than low-intensity users. A. B. Dick then put a substantial portion of its markup in the ink rather than the machine and was able to obtain differential returns from users based on the volume of ink they consumed.[31] Under the same principle, ties can permit a franchisor or other IP owner to meter its royalties. For example, by requiring franchisees to purchase its pizza dough at an above-market price, Domino's uses pizza dough sales to monitor franchise sales and compute the franchise fee.

Using a tied product for price discrimination or royalty computation is not explicitly protected by the IP laws, but neither is it likely to be anticompetitive. The IP owner who cannot compute royalties via tying will probably revert to an alternative system, such as measuring sales directly, or placing a use meter on the machine. As a result tying does not make purchasers or licensees worse off. Furthermore, rivals are no worse off because such uses of tying almost invariably occur in competitive markets where nothing is foreclosed. The ink suppliers unable to sell their ink for use in A. B. Dick's mimeograph machines still have thousands of other purchasers, and Domino's controls only a trivial share of the flour, salt, oil, and water that go into aggregate sales of pizza dough.[32]

Tying arrangements are anticompetitive only in the rare situations when tying denies rivals access to markets. For example, by tying its Internet browser, Internet Explorer (IE), to its Windows operating system Microsoft severely constrained the options Netscape had for getting into the market. But in cases such as this it seldom matters that either the tying or tied product is patented or copyrighted. In *Microsoft* the appellate court held that the rule of reason should be applied to the Windows/IE tie because a per se rule could operate as an irrational restraint on efficiency and innovation, which often consists in combining functions or products that previously were separate.[33] While the court is correct, what it said about the relationship between tying and efficiency is true of most ties, whether or not IP rights are involved. That is why all ties should be addressed under the rule of reason.

One place where the presence of IP rights might be thought to create an antitrust conflict concerns computer code and tying law's requirement that there be "separate" tying and tied products. A great deal of software innovation (as well as innovation generally) consists in bundling things together that were formerly sold separately. If two goods are widely available separately, tying law considers them to be separate products.[34] Many of the collateral programs that have been incorporated into Microsoft Windows and other computer operating systems were initially sold separately. That is certainly true of Internet browsers, but it is also true of the little calculator and even the Solitaire game that Microsoft bundles into Windows. Under the traditional per se rule for tying, when products are separate and the defendant has market power in the tying product, then there is a prima facie violation of the antitrust laws.

In that case don't we have a conflict between antitrust policy and the need to encourage innovation in computer operating systems? No, the problem results entirely from the way that an irrational per se rule for tying has led to the development of the "separate products" requirement. The requirement ceases to be important once ties are analyzed, as they should be, under the rule of reason. The separate products test developed historically as a screen to deal with the fact that otherwise the per se rule would condemn many competitively harmless ties, such as refusing to sell new cars without their tires, bundling a computer with an operating system, or selling shoes only in pairs.

Applying the rule of reason to ties permits us to get straight to the policy question: is this bundle anticompetitive because it unreasonably excludes rivals? If the products are *widely* available separately, then the answer to that question will be no, but we do not need any "separate products" metaphysics to get us to that answer. Widespread availability of alternatives indicates that no one is foreclosed by the tie. By contrast, if the two products are not widely available separately, we need to look further for signs of anticompetitive foreclosure. In the case of a monopolist they might not be available separately because the monopolist designed them that way in the first place. The union might also be justified because the resulting product is better or cheaper, and the customer could not create the union herself.

Courts should not be in the business of substituting their product designs for those generated by the market. Nevertheless, often a court can determine whether a bundle is unreasonably exclusionary under the circumstances. Software bundling raises unusual issues because of the nearly infinite plasticity of software code. Almost any program can be merged into any other one. If Microsoft wanted to bundle an income tax program or party planning software into its Windows operating system it could readily do so. While some of these bundles might be anticompetitive, the fact that the code is copyrighted or patented is largely irrelevant to the inquiry. If significant and unreasonable foreclosure results—for example, if the Windows/Internet Explorer bundle unreasonably excludes Netscape from a properly defined market and if Microsoft could easily have configured the products to work as well separately—then the fact that the software is protected by IP rights would not save it. By contrast, if foreclosure is not established, then the invalidity of any claimed IP right would not matter.

The first proposition is illustrated by the *Microsoft* case. The court found that Microsoft's blending, or "commingling," of platform and browser code violated the monopolization provision of §2 of the Sherman Act. Included in that finding was a conclusion that there was no reasonable business justification for merging the two codes together.[35] No one was disputing the validity of Microsoft's IP claims.

One other subset of tying cases involves "pure" IP rights in the sense that both the "tying" and "tied" products are IP licenses. The practices are package licensing, blanket licensing, and block booking. Package licensing occurs when a patent owner has several patents and is willing to license them only as a group. The principal explanation for package licensing is transaction cost savings. In *Automatic Radio*, the leading Supreme Court decision, Hazeltine owned several hundred patents on various small circuits that could be incorporated into radios.[36] The circuits served overlapping purposes, and often it was difficult to tell from examining a radio which of the patents a radio manufacturer had actually used. The cost of licensing a patent that already exists is nearly zero, so it cost Hazeltine no more to license its entire inventory of patents than to license any subset. Furthermore, if it licensed only a subset, it would have been required to monitor its licensees continuously to make sure that they were using only the patents they had licensed. There would undoubtedly have been many costly disputes. The result is one that is fairly unique to intellectual property rights: licensing all the patents at once is actually less costly than licensing a few.

Blanket licensing serves a very similar function, albeit in copyrights. The thousands of authors and composers who own copyrights to recorded music issue nonexclusive licenses to organizations such as BMI, which groups them into a single "blanket license" that entitles the licensee to play anything in the BMI inventory. If WCBS has a blanket license and gets a special request to play "Heartbreak Hotel" on the air, it can do so immediately without calling in advance or negotiating a price. The blanket license has already taken care of that. But suppose the Triple Nickel Country and Western Bar really doesn't care to have all of the Mozart, Enya, and Snoop Dogg in the BMI library. It wants to play nothing but old-fashioned country. BMI is in the same position as Hazeltine in the package licensing case. It costs no more to license the entire BMI library than it costs to license a subset. Moreover, licensing the subset imposes high transaction costs. Someone must define what goes into the category of "country" and what doesn't, as well as monitor the Triple Nickel to make sure that its juke box plays only songs from the authorized category. The Triple Nickel's complaint did not depend at all on the validity or scope of the defendant's IP rights.[37]

The one exception to antitrust toleration for IP packages is "block booking," which occurs when the owner of copyrights in movies, television shows, or similar productions licenses them only in blocks. The Supreme Court has condemned block booking twice. In its 1962 *Loew's* decision the Supreme Court rested its condemnation on the presumption that a copyrighted movie conferred market power. It then analogized the practice to tying. A likely explanation for block booking is also transaction cost savings. At the time theaters lease films they do not know how strong the demand for a particular film will be. By leasing in blocks suppliers can give theaters a steady supply of films so that another one will always be available on short notice if the audiences for the current film become too small.[38]

While all these practices are readily defended as reducing transactions costs, the defense is unnecessary when there is no harm to competition in the first place. As a general matter, these practices foreclose no one. The recipient of a package license of patents, or the Triple Nickel buying its blanket license of recorded music, is not complaining that rivals are foreclosed from selling it certain products. It simply wants a smaller product than the one that the seller is offering. But that is not an injury to competition. Package and blanket licensing are simply the IP equivalent of the wholesaler who sells office supplies only in full carton lots, or the land developer that refuses to subdivide before selling. It is not antitrust's purpose to regulate the size of the products that sellers choose to sell. In sum, these licensing practices almost always fail to create any conflict between antitrust policy and IP law because there is no harm to competition.

An occasional licensing practice analogous to ties does foreclose. One example is the "per processor" licensing prohibited by the consent decree in the first round of *Microsoft* litigation.[39] Microsoft, whose Windows operating system dominated the market, contracted with computer makers requiring them to pay the licensing fee on a "per processor" rather than a "per Windows" basis. Suppose, for example, that a computer maker produced 1,000 computers in a month but wished to put Windows on 800 of them, leaving the others available for alternative operating systems such as IBM's OS/2 (a nearly defunct operating system that competed with Windows). Under its Microsoft agreement, however, the computer maker had to pay the license fee for each computer it made, whether or not that computer actually had Windows installed. As a result, if the computer was to have a different operating system than Windows, the license fee for that system would have to be paid on top of the Windows fee, thus making any computer with a non-Windows operating system more costly than a Windows-based system. This practice, which is somewhat more akin to exclusive dealing than tying, had the effect of raising the costs rival operating systems faced. Therefore, it is exclusionary and not merely the sale of a different package than a buyer preferred to purchase. But once again, there is no conflict between IP policy and the antitrust laws in this case because nothing in the IP laws authorizes or legitimizes per processor licensing practices. Indeed, the practice hinders rather than promotes innovation by suppressing the opportunities of smaller rivals who cannot realistically compete to have their operating systems installed on new computers. A practice that both excludes competition *and* impedes innovation presents no antitrust/IP conflict, particularly when it is not expressly authorized by the IP statutes.

Infringement Suits and Section 2 of the Sherman Act

Many claims of unlawful monopolization have been based on the theory that the defendant in the antitrust suit had previously filed an IP infringement suit that was improper, meaning that the patent owner knew or should have known that its patent had been obtained by fraud or was unenforceable for other reasons, or perhaps that the product really did not infringe. Variations of the doctrine have been applied to infringement suits under both the patent and the copyright laws. The Supreme Court recognized such claims in *Walker Process*, where the antitrust defendant allegedly had obtained a patent by fraud and then filed an infringement suit in order to keep a rival out of its market.[40] The decisions often contrast the patentee's legitimate interest in protecting its intellectual property through infringement suits against the competing rights of rivals and the public to be free of monopoly.

But the "intellectual property" content of *Walker Process* claims is easily exaggerated. The basis of the claim is that the antitrust defendant went to court or threatened to do so on a nonmeritorious claim. It in fact knew or should have known that the patent was invalid or unenforceable. These facts do not distinguish IP infringement suits from any of a variety of abusive litigation techniques that can keep rivals out of a market or raise their costs. For example, one firm in a market might file a frivolous objection before a court or regulatory agency in order to hold up a rival's license. Or one hospital may supply false information in a proceeding, objecting to a new entrant's request for a Certificate of Need, which the law requires before it can begin construction.[41]

The courts have tended to see improper IP infringement suits as distinctive from these other improper actions, largely because *Walker Process* spoke of the patent holder as having an "immunity" from the antitrust laws that the fraudulent lawsuit takes away. None of the cases that arise in other contexts use this "immunity" language, and the language itself was unfortunate. First, patentees have no antitrust "immunity." Second, just as any property owner, IP holders are entitled to go to court to defend their rights from a trespass, which in this case consists in unlawful copying.

The basic principle is clear: a firm that has a legal power to exclude, whether derived from the IP laws or elsewhere, has a right to enforce its power before a court or appropriate regulatory agency. However, it has no right to assert exclusionary powers that it does not have, to assert rights that are broader than the right that it actually has, or to assert claims against those who are not trespassing on its rights. Recognizing *Walker Process* claims does not create any conflict with IP rights, because the entire basis of the claim is that the IP "right" being asserted does not exist or is unenforceable.

When a firm asserts such rights improperly and should have known better, it is very likely guilty of the tort of malicious prosecution. And when the structural conditions for monopoly are present, it may also have violated the antitrust laws. Namely, it must be a dominant firm (or the improper litigation must threaten to make it dominant) and the lawsuit, if permitted to run its course, must realistically create, strengthen, or prolong the firm's monopoly power. Not many lawsuits meet those requirements, but among the small few that do, IP infringement actions are not distinctive.

Refusals to License IP Rights

The term "refusal to license" refers to simple or unconditional refusals. Most antitrust violations that involve IP licenses, however, also imply *conditional* refusals. For example, Microsoft's bundling of Windows and Internet Explorer entails a refusal to sell Windows without IE. Or a firm that imposes territorial division in a license would very likely have refused to license without it. Here, by contrast, we are speaking of the IP owner who simply chooses not to license the right to others.

Under the antitrust laws a firm, even a monopolist, has no general duty to sell to someone else.[42] The IP equivalent of the refusal to sell is the refusal to license. Is the duty to deal any broader when the thing that a rival wants to share is an IP license? If the answer is yes, then we might have one of those few situations where courts would have to balance IP and antitrust concerns.

The patent statute does not require compulsory licensing and even states that it is not patent "misuse" for a patentee to refuse to license.[43] Trademark law is generally hostile toward compulsory licensing because of its concern that the owners of trademarks be responsible for the quality of the goods that they represent. We don't want, say, Del Monte to license its trademark to any canner it wishes without being involved to at least some extent in that firm's food production.[44] While the Copyright Act contains a few compulsory licensing provisions, they are not of antitrust concern.

The compulsory licensing issue has come up mainly with respect to patents, and there the courts are almost unanimous in holding that a patentee has no duty to license its technology to a rival. One indefensible exception is the 1997 *Kodak* decision, which condemned Kodak for refusing to license its patented parts to firms that wanted to compete with Kodak in the repair of Kodak photocopiers. The court invented the theory that a patent may lawfully create a monopoly in only one market. The gist of the plaintiff's complaint was that Kodak had a monopoly in its aftermarket photocopier parts, which independent service technicians needed in order to repair the copiers. By refusing to sell these parts, the court concluded, Kodak was improperly creating a second monopoly in service, something the court believed the patent laws do not permit.[45]

This court thus claimed to find a true conflict between patent law and antitrust. But *Kodak* reflects a very serious misunderstanding of what a patent is and how it functions. Patent claims create exclusive rights in technologies, not in markets. In most cases a patent claim does not create a monopoly in anything because there are alternative routes to the same result. In some cases a patent may create a monopoly in a certain technology, and that technology may be of use in more than one market. For example, suppose that an inventor patented a process that was particularly good at mixing suspensions, or liquids that have heavier liquid or solid matter floating in them. Depending on the usability and superiority of this technology, it might create advantages in the markets for mixing paint, medical suspensions such as children's antibiotics, and salad dressings. Under the *Kodak* rule the patentee could choose one of these markets to keep its monopoly, but it would have to license its technology to rivals in the other two markets.

The court cited no source for this unique theory, and there is nothing in the Patent Act that hints at it. It was an attempt at resolving an imagined conflict between IP rights and the antitrust laws—namely, that the Patent Act should be interpreted so as to create some monopoly, but not too much. But imagining a conflict where none existed forced the court effectively to write a new provision into the Patent Act.

If we were to have an antitrust rule for compulsory licensing of IP rights, there is no reason it need be any broader than the rule for other business assets. For example, the essential facility doctrine described in Chapter 10 may require a monopolist to deal with a rival when not doing so is profitable only because it tends to perpetuate a monopoly.[46] Nearly all patentees, as most property owners in general, would pass that test because licensing technology to a rival would deprive the patentee of sales and that is always an adequate business justification. No law requires a firm to give up its own sales in order to wholesale a product to a rival. Even if the law did so, the monopolist would make those sales at the monopoly price unless the court also regulated the price. For IP rights as for everything else, a compulsory sales rule turns the defendant into a public utility and places the court in the indefensible position of price regulator. While price-regulated monopoly may sometimes be appropriate, that decision must be made by a legislature, and never via the antitrust laws.

The refusal to license as an antitrust offense must be distinguished from the compulsory license as an antitrust remedy. Once a firm has been found to violate the antitrust laws for other reasons, an IP license may be the only way competition can effectively be restored, particularly in technology-rich markets. For example, it would have done no good to break up AT&T as a consequence of the antitrust suit against it had AT&T not been required to license its thousands of patents and some copyrights to the Baby Bells that emerged from the breakup.[47] But such a remedy is not distinctive either. Forcing a firm to license a patent as part of an antitrust remedy is no different in principle from forcing a firm to divest itself of a plant or other productive assets. Such divestitures are fairly common in antitrust history.

Patent Acquisitions: Nonuse

Historically, patent law disfavored unworked, or purely "paper," patents. Courts did not necessarily invalidate patents simply because they were not used, but they did construe them narrowly or refuse to enjoin infringement.[48] At first glance that position seems logical: the purpose of the Patent Act is to further technological progress, but progress is not furthered by permitting someone to patent a device or process and then not use it, while denying others the right to do so.

But this logic ignores effects on incentives to innovate. For most inventive firms innovation is an ongoing process that produces uncertain results. Sometimes the results are immediately marketable and other times they are not. A firm that must use its own innovation immediately or else license it may be much more restrictive about what it innovates in the first place. So unused patents must be recognized. Nevertheless, there is some wisdom in the traditional rule that the proper remedy for infringement of an unused patent should be damages but not an injunction, at least if the period of nonuse is fairly long. That way a rival could use the technology that has not been used by the patentee by compensating the patentee for the loss that results. This is the equivalent of compulsory licensing.

In the *Paper Bag* case in 1908, during the heyday of broad patent expansionism, the Supreme Court repudiated the traditional rule and held that a patentee could obtain an injunction against infringement even if its patent was not being used.[49] Eighty years later that view was codified in amendments to the Patent Act.[50]

The statute does not distinguish internally developed from acquired patents. But nonuse of *acquired* IP rights can threaten competition, particularly when the acquired right is a substitute for the purchaser's current technology. Suppose a dominant firm is making widgets with process A and a different firm develops and patents a substitute process B, which is as good or better than A. Why would the first firm want to purchase an exclusive right to process B? Presumably, it might wish to change processes immediately, or employ both processes together. Then again, the firm may simply want to "shelve" process B so that others will not be able to use it. In the pure case—of the purchaser who intends *never* to use process B—the acquisition is a naked restraint. That is, the purchase does nothing to reduce the costs or enhance the output of the purchasing firm. The transaction is profitable only because of its success in suppressing the output of a rival.

Antitrust has only a limited role to play in the nonuse issue. A firm should be free to use or not to use patents that have been developed inside that firm. If we were writing on a clean slate, a wise rule would say that after a patent had been unused for, say, five years the remedy for infringement should be limited to damages rather than an injunction. But the Patent Act's express declaration protecting unused patents makes this impossible. In all events, this is a question of Patent Act interpretation.

Nonuse of acquired patents is a different issue. The acquisition itself can be an unlawful merger. Section 7 of the Clayton Act prevents anti-competitive asset acquisitions, and the courts have held that acquisitions of IP rights are covered by the statute.[51] Beyond that, strategic acquisition and nonuse of patents are unlawful monopolization if they restrain competition unreasonably.

"Misuse"

Patent "misuse" refers to improper acts committed by a patent or other IP holder. Historically, "misuse" referred mainly to licensing practices viewed by courts as attempts to extend the patent beyond its legally authorized boundaries. The *Motion Picture Patents* decision, where the Supreme Court first recognized the concept, concluded that a license provision that only the defendant's films could be shown in the defendant's projector was such an attempt.[52]

The concept of patent misuse is most often used to refer to *anti-competitive* practices that the Patent Act does not authorize. That raises an obvious question: if "misuse" means the same thing as an antitrust violation, then why bother having a separate concept of "misuse"? The patent/antitrust intersection is complicated enough as it stands. As Judge Posner once observed, the Supreme Court developed the doctrine of patent misuse before there was very much law on the relationship between IP and antitrust. When antitrust rules began to develop, the courts copied from the misuse cases. Furthermore, the concept of injury to competition is singular, in the sense that we don't have doctrinal alternatives. It would be meaningless to say that something constitutes misuse because it is an anticompetitive extension of an IP right, but also to hold that this practice does not violate the antitrust laws.[53]

One response to this argument is that the competition concerns of misuse doctrine cover the full range of competitive possibilities, and are not hemmed in by the statutory structure of the antitrust laws. Some practices may be anticompetitive in the economic sense, but fall between the legislative cracks, so to speak, because they are not precisely covered by any antitrust provision. This appears to be the view of the Federal Circuit Court of Appeals, which has exclusive jurisdiction over appeals involving patents.[54]

In the last three decades few cases have found misuse when there was clearly no violation of the antitrust laws.[55] Furthermore, the Federal Circuit's position seems incredible to someone familiar with the expansive body of antitrust doctrine. Section 1 of the Sherman Act reaches every agreement that restrains trade, and §2 reaches every act that monopolizes or dangerously threatens to do so. Without even getting to the more specific provisions of the Clayton Act, there seem to be very few cracks through which a practice could fall. As currently interpreted, the antitrust laws seem to reach every anticompetitive practice (except tacit collusion, which raises no "misuse" issues) and a few others that are not anticompetitive. Historically, nearly all of the expansionist applications of "misuse" have reached practices that were simply not anticompetitive under any definition. For example, the patent misuse doctrine has been used against patent ties even when the defendant clearly lacked market power;[56] or against contracts requiring payments after a patent expired, without any showing of anticompetitive effect;[57] or against discriminatory provisions in patent royalties even though price discrimination, particularly in IP licenses, is generally procompetitive or competitively harmless.[58] One decision found copyright misuse in a software license forbidding the licensee from developing a competing program, but without any showing of market power or anticompetitive effects.[59]

In 1952 and again in 1988 Congress amended the Patent Act to provide that certain practices are *not* misuse. In so doing, it intended to bring the concept of misuse more closely in line with antitrust principles. Under the amendments a patent owner does not commit misuse if it uses reasonable means to enforce a patent, refuses to license, requires licensees to purchase nonstaple goods (i.e., goods that can be used effectively only with the patent) from itself, or ties separate products when it lacks power in the primary product.[60]

"Misuse" may have a broader meaning if it refers to unfair or deceptive practices that have nothing to do with competition. For example, the patent applicant who engages in improper conduct during the application process is sometimes found guilty of misuse,[61] and courts have found misuse when a patent owner fraudulently attempts to obtain royalties from two parties at successive stages of production.[62] Fraud or unfair conduct rather than injury to competition is the perceived evil in these cases. Finding misuse simply declares that the IP statutes, *not* antitrust policy, are concerned with fraud, inequitable conduct, or other improper behavior quite aside from any impact on competition.

By the same token, misuse may be an appropriate vehicle for combating legislative capture of the IP law-making process, particularly in copyright. As noted earlier in this chapter, while the IP laws reflect significant special interest capture, antitrust is not the proper way for dealing with it. But misuse is fundamentally an IP doctrine and can be employed to prevent attempts to expand the scope of IP laws that are already too broad.[63]

Finally, misuse may have independent relevance even when its scope is limited to antitrust violations. The misuse remedial structure differs from the antitrust structure, making remedies available when antitrust remedies are not. For example, in *Microsoft* the indirect purchaser rule barred most damages actions by indirect purchasers, because passed-on damages would have to be computed, something that the indirect purchaser rule prohibits. One can only guess, but the amount that Microsoft actually paid in damages would appear to fall very far short of the amount needed to deter the conduct that was found unlawful. However, the misuse remedy is different, requiring no pass-on, or even the computation of damages. When the IP holder has misused its intellectual property right it can no longer maintain an infringement action against alleged infringers. Thinking of the consumer harm caused by antitrust violations involving IP rights as misuse could lead to a more effective set of remedies.[64]

Product Design as an Antitrust Violation: Strategic Creation of Incompatibility

A final exclusionary practice closely related to IP rights is anticompetitive product design, or situations where the way a product is configured is said to violate the antitrust laws. Antitrust must be particularly wary of such claims. Most product redesigns injure rivals because customers prefer the new design. Customer preference is a strong indication that a new or newly designed product is superior, and antitrust should not second-guess the judgment of consumers.

But what about a redesign that is not an improvement at all, but that merely makes rivals' complementary products incompatible? In *Berkey Photo* the Second Circuit wisely refused to condemn Kodak's simultaneous introduction of a newly designed camera (the pocket Instamatic) and the newly designed film cartridges that went with it. Purchasers of the camera were required to purchase their film from Kodak as well, for only these cartridges would fit the camera. By contrast, in *C. R. Bard* the court condemned the defendant's redesign of its biopsy gun, which takes small skin samples for medical analysis. The guns use disposable needles to obtain samples, and several firms had supplied needles for an older version of the gun. But the redesign was compatible only with the defendant's own needles. Such redesigns are sometimes called "technological ties," because they function like tying arrangements except that technological incompatibility serves the same function as a tying agreement. The camera-plus-film or gun-plus-needles are tied together by technological design.[65]

As a general matter, antitrust courts are not competent to second-guess decisions about product design. Furthermore, in most cases if the conduct is excessively exclusionary it is also self-deterring. Incompatibility can be expected to produce customer resistance, particularly if the redesigned good is no better than the old one. Innovation is a high-risk enterprise and the costs, once invested, cannot be recovered. If a predatory price is not working the defendant can quickly raise its prices once again, but once an innovation is brought to market the investment has been made. As a result the market itself provides strong discipline for innovations that customers reject. This suggests that truly anticompetitive product redesigns are uncommon.

Nevertheless, there are a few cases in which firms select technologies simply because of their impact on rivals and not because the technology is superior or more desirable in consumers' eyes. *C. R. Bard* may have been such a case, although *Berkey Photo* certainly was not—the pocket Instamatic camera and accompanying Kodacolor II film went on to become two of the great successes of amateur photography. *Microsoft*, discussed in the next chapter, provides a good example of anticompetitive product design decisions, but these were made in the context of a network industry where competitive concerns for product compatibility are particularly strong.

In all events, a firm should never be condemned of anticompetitive product design unless it has very substantial market power, sufficient to exclude complementary products from the market. Moreover, the competitive injury caused by the selection of a particular technology must have been intended, and it must be greatly disproportionate to the benefits that the redesign produces for consumers. This is one area where a cautious search for less restrictive alternatives is important: assuming there was some consumer benefit from the redesign, could those benefits have been achieved by a less injurious route? In *Microsoft,* as the next chapter explains, the defendant took advantage of the fact that computer code can readily be configured in practically any fashion that programmers wish. Microsoft then "commingled" the code for the Windows operating system and its Internet Explorer web browser so as to require the two to be installed together. This placed rival browsers at a significant disadvantage and reduced the threat to Microsoft that rival operating systems could emerge. Furthermore, Microsoft was not able to show any "integrative benefit" that resulted from commingling the code.[66] In that case the likelihood of harm is considerable, and for benefits that not even the defendant could articulate.

There is no conflict between antitrust condemnation of anticompetitive product designs and the IP system. In that small subset of cases where true competitive harm is possible, the IP laws do not bar antitrust prosecution of practices that are not authorized by the IP laws themselves. Thus anticompetitive innovation practices belong in the same classification as price-fixing, tying, and other practices that can be unlawful even though the underlying IP rights are perfectly valid.

Conclusion

The so-called IP/antitrust conflict exists in two places. First, at a very high level of abstraction, is the theoretical conflict about how the value we place on competition should be tempered by our equal concern to encourage innovation. Second, the conflict enters legislative judgments about the rights and powers that Congress itself should give to owners of patents, copyrights, and trademarks. But these concerns rarely collide with the daily administration of the antitrust laws. The great majority of the conflicts that courts have seen have been illusions, the only significant exception being cases that involve licensing agreements among competitors.

12

Network Industries and Computer Platform Monopoly

A "network" is a market subject to economies of scale in consumption.[1] This means that the product or service becomes more valuable to consumers as more use is made of it. For example, a newspaper's classified advertising section or a telephone system is more valuable as the number of advertisements, telephones, or subscribers it links together increases. An ATM network permitting people to withdraw cash from their bank accounts is more valuable as the system connects more machines. Or a real estate brokers' multiple listing service has greater value to its users as the number of listed homes or participating brokers grows. The most valuable general multiple listing service would list every house for sale in a community, permitting any broker to sell any other broker's listing. Economists describe such markets as having "positive network externalities," which means that use by one person also benefits other users. In some networks, such as the real estate multiple listing services, the users are also the suppliers. A real estate broker adds value to the system by including her own listings, in exchange for which she has access to the listings of every other broker who is a member.

Scale economies in consumption can give networks one peculiar attribute: demand curves that actually slope upwards, at least for part of their range. Consider the telephone system. In any ordinary market the people who are willing to pay the most for telephones would purchase first. Output would grow only as increasingly marginal customers were brought in, which would require the price to decline. But network effects can offset this decline because the system itself acquires additional value as it grows in size. For example, the 1,000,000th purchaser of a telephone will likely value it by much more than the 100th purchaser, because a telephone system linking 1,000,000 subscribers is worth so much more than one that links only 100. The fact that a large network may be more valuable to consumers than a small one serves to make some network monopolies particularly durable and lucrative.

Networks and Competition

Some networks are natural monopolies in the sense that costs decline or the network becomes more desirable as it grows larger, to the point that a single network saturates the market. For example, if someone wanted to rent an apartment or buy a used car in St. Louis, the most valuable classified advertising section would be one that listed every available apartment or every used car. The same thing is true of the telephone system and the real estate multiple listing service. For each of these, a single network in the market is likely to have lower costs or be more attractive to customers than any combination of two or more networks.

Natural monopoly is not an inherent feature of networks, however. Some networks become more costly or less desirable if they grow too large. Consider sports leagues. A baseball team cannot play against itself, and seasons would be less interesting if the same two teams repeatedly competed against each other. So a network of teams is a good thing. But that does not mean that a 1,000-team network is better than a network of, say, 18 teams. At a certain number most of the value that accrues to increased size is saturated. Beyond that point the network simply becomes more cumbersome and costly to manage. The largest sports "league" in the United States is the NCAA, which has roughly 1,200 members, but the only way it can manage itself is by dividing into size classifications, as well as numerous conferences such as the Big Ten, Pac Eight, Ivy League, and so on. Only a small percentage of the teams in the NCAA actually play each other in a given season. For example, the typical NCAA football team plays fewer than a dozen other teams per year.

One reason some networks are not monopolies is product differentiation. For example, while a single classified section may be the best for offering and seeking employment generally, it may not be the best for specialized employment such as anesthesiologists or law professors. These groups have their own specialized employment networks. Franchises are good examples of product-differentiated, nonmonopoly networks. The McDonald's franchise system is valuable on the selling side because there are significant economies in management, store design, and large-quantity purchasing. A larger system is also valuable to consumers because they can visit more McDonald's locations outside their local area and be confident of a dining experience similar to their experience back home. The greater the proliferation of stores, the more significant this network effect. However, McDonald's is one of many fast-food franchises, and these franchises in turn compete with unfranchised restaurants.

Another reason some networks are not monopolies is that competition among networks can also increase value. In addition to food franchises, general purpose charge cards such as Visa and MasterCard are built on large networks of banks that issue the cards and transfer money from the accounts of participating card holders to the accounts of participating merchants. But Visa and MasterCard compete with each other as well as with free-standing networks of general purpose cards, such as American Express and Discover.

Networks have some distinctive properties that explain both their value and some of the competitive problems they can cause. Perhaps most important, they frequently force technological or rule choices on both suppliers and consumers. Consider the now dated but still surviving VHS tape used for recording and playing videos—everything from commercially printed Hollywood films to home birthday parties. The "format" for VHS is a network, because people attach value to compatibility. You want to be able to go to the movie store and rent a video, knowing that it will work in your home VHS machine. This happens, however, only because the tape is made to certain specifications; because recording is done at a given speed and resolution; and because your VHS player was manufactured according to a set of specifications that VHS recorder manufacturers share. There is no reason to assume that VHS was *inherently* the best format for videotapes. If networking were not a factor, inventors would continuously market new formats and consumers would pick and choose for the best price/performance ratio. But once a dominant network format is established, both manufacturers and consumers become "locked in" by the collective weight of their prior commitments. If I developed a cartridge that used ¾" tape rather than the current ½" VHS standard, or that was 6" wide rather than the VHS standard of 7½" wide, few people would buy my tape, even though I could show them that it performed better.

The illustration indicates that one strong feature of many networks is path dependence, which means that once a format or technology is adopted and attains widespread acceptance, anyone offering an alternative technology or format faces significant market resistance. For that reason VHS was the standard for many years, even though technological innovation in video recording progressed significantly during this period.

VHS was the dominant video recording format only because it won a "standards" battle with Sony in the 1980s, despite the fact that Sony's Betamax format was regarded by many as technologically superior. One significant reason why Sony lost was that it failed to appreciate the network value of videotaping. Sony developed the Betamax video recording technology thinking of it mainly as a way people could record off their own televisions and play the tapes later. As long as that was true, network effects were minor because there would not be widespread exchange of tapes. But Sony failed to foresee the dramatic rise of the market for rental videotapes of commercial movies. That market placed a premium on compatibility. For many years video stores tried to maintain a selection of Betamax tapes, but the consortium of manufacturers that had adopted the VHS standard eventually acquired a dominant installed base. At that point Betamax technology could no longer sustain itself, superior or not.[2]

Of course, VHS did not remain the dominant standard forever. Eventually the DVD began to replace it. But that did not happen until a very significant change in technology (the development of digital recording) highlighted VHS's obsolescence. The DVD standard was developed in the early 1990s by a consortium of producers, including Pioneer, Toshiba, Sony, and Phillips.

As the VHS/DVD story illustrates, change in networks defined by a common technology is frequently "lumpier" than it is in non-networked markets. As the technology for kitchen toasters or blenders improves you can pretty much dump the old appliance without worrying whether the new one will be compatible with your sliced bread or tomatoes. But when equipment based on a particular network standard is marketed and acquires a significant installed base, resistance to change becomes considerable and only a very large technological improvement will succeed in displacing the existing format.

Actually, the story is more complex than that: once a standard is adopted, innovation competition can proceed apace *within* the standard. For example, VHS players could be developed with new features, lower cost, increased reliability, and the like. The quality of tape could be improved and cartridges could have their mechanisms redesigned so that they would track better, *provided* that the resulting product was consistent with the VHS standard. But any innovation that was incompatible with the standard could not be adopted until the standard changed. For example, someone might be able to get a sharper picture either by changing the chemical composition of a tape's surface or else by increasing the tape's width. Once the VHS standard is adopted, the first innovation would be acceptable, assuming that existing tape-head technology read the new chemical surface. However, the wider tape would not be acceptable because tape cartridges and thus tape players would have to be changed. Today a great deal of innovation occurs within the digital recording market, but most of it occurs subject to the constraint that it be backwardly compatible with existing digital technologies.

Given the "quasi-permanent" status of many networks, the idea of competition *within* the network is critical if we are to avoid monopoly prices or restraints on innovation. As a result it becomes important to identify those elements of a product in which competition is possible. For example, the teams in a sports league may have to agree on the number of games in a season or the number of players who can be on the field. Although these agreements are output reductions, they are necessary to make the network operate. But the teams probably do not have to agree on ticket prices or coaches' salaries. Or the members of a real estate multiple listing service may have to agree on the physical size of a listing entry in the multiple listing book, and on the kinds of information that will be provided; but they do not have to agree on the commissions that brokers will charge for sales. One task of antitrust policy in network industries, then, is to sort out those practices that are essential to making the network function from those that are not essential *and* that pose a competitive threat.

These same features that make networks attractive also create the opportunity for anticompetitive practices. The considerable advantages that accrue to an established, market-dominating network create the possibility that those running the network can increase price or restrain innovation without causing excessive defections. The costs of being excluded from the network are simply too high. The increased threat applies to both collusion and exclusionary practices, and also to both concerted and unilateral activity. For example:

- To the extent network membership confers significant advantages, business firms inside the network may be able to fix prices without concern about competition from outside the network; for example, if the real estate firms that are members of the multiple listing service fix commission rates and use network membership to police the cartel, a nonmember may not be able to compete for their business because access to the network is so important.
- In the case of competitor-controlled networks, those in charge might make membership rules that exclude innovators who threaten to steal market share from existing members; to this extent, networks can operate to restrain competitive innovation.
- The monopoly controller of a market-dominating network might use exclusionary practices to prevent others from developing technology that is compatible with the network or that will place the network under competitive control.

Network Dominance versus Network Monopolization

The fact that a network is a natural monopoly does not mean that the network itself must be monopolized. The appellate court failed to see this in the *Microsoft* case when it wrote:

> In markets characterized by network effects, one product or standard tends towards dominance, because "the utility that a user derives from consumption of the good increases with the number of other agents consuming the good." . . . Once a product or standard achieves wide acceptance, it becomes more or less entrenched. Competition in such industries is "for the field" rather than "within the field."[3]

But many networks that monopolize their markets are owned and operated by groups of firms in competition with each other. Good examples are real estate multiple listing services, the Internet, and the telecommunications system. Each of these networks is very likely a natural monopoly, and a single network dominates each market in which they operate. However, each of them is also home to considerable competition among the firms that operate within it. In such cases we say that competition occurs *inside* the network rather than among multiple networks.

Networks can be owned and operated in a variety of ways, with differing amounts of competition. One way that is quite conducive to competition is government ownership, such as the public highway system. The "hardware" of that system plus a set of rules of the road permit competing truckers, moving companies, and taxicabs to go from point to point with relatively few conflicts. Another possibility is a mixture of government and private ownership by a variety of firms in competing and complementary markets. The Internet is an example. Most of the Internet "backbone" is owned by large telecommunications companies like Worldcom/MCI, AT&T, and Sprint. This backbone consists of high-speed data transmission lines, servers that relay information, and switches. Connected to the backbone are Internet service providers (ISPs), such as AOL or Prodigy or Earthlink. ISPs have large fast servers that link the Internet to individual users by phone or cable lines. Some ISPs such as AOL provide their own additional content to their members; others are little more than access points where consumers can enter the Internet. In addition to this, much of the Internet is "owned" by its individual participants whose web pages are made available to Internet users. Finally, the government retains significant control over Internet domain names through the National Science Foundation, which is a federal agency, and by a contract with Network Solutions, a private firm responsible for controlling the assignment of individual Internet names.

A few natural monopoly networks are owned by single firms. One traditional example is AT&T, which, before its 1983 breakup, owned nearly all of the basic telecommunications system in the United States. Many local public utilities also own monopoly networks. Most of these, however, accept price regulation as a condition of monopoly ownership. One important exception is Microsoft Windows, the dominant operating system for personal computers and related technology. Its prices are not regulated. In that case one firm owns the entire network and thus far has successfully resisted both market and legal attempts to make that network competitive.

For many networks the most efficient system is ownership by private parties who adhere to a common set of network rules, but compete with each other in all elements of their business where competition is possible. For example, the goal of the 1996 Telecommunications Act, described in Chapter 10, is an integrated single telecommunications network with a set of interconnection protocols and traffic rules. That statute contemplates that the network itself be owned and operated by a variety of companies that compete with each other on price as well as services that the network permits to be offered. The ATM system for automated banking is also such a network. Organizations such as Cirrus and Star operate ATM networks to which banks can interconnect their ATM machines, and these networks are also connected with each other. The networks themselves are privately owned, and member banks compete on service charges as well as the types of transactions they permit.

In the nineteenth century the United States railroad system developed under a competitive network model. Each line owned its own track, and most railroads were historically chartered to operate within a single state. They achieved a national railroad transportation system by means of interconnection agreements that permitted transfers of cargo and freight cars. This in turn necessitated a national standard on track gauges—a railroad car could not move from one line to another unless the rails were of the same type and the same distance apart. Otherwise cars would have to be unloaded and reloaded at the transfer point. Today the standard "gauge" or distance between rails is 4′8½″. During the first half of the nineteenth century, however, there was a significant problem of incompatible gauges. Most eastern railroads adopted the 4′8½″ standard, because it was already well established in England. But many southern railroads as well as some in California used 5′ gauges, Pennsylvania used 4′9″, and the Erie Railroad initially used 6′. This standards battle largely came to an end by government intervention. The Lincoln administration selected 4′8½″ as the standard for the Union Pacific Railroad, because it matched that of most of the eastern railroads that would be connected to it. Once that gauge became dominant, other lines were forced to comply or else they would be unable to connect to the network.[4]

Smooth transfers of railroad cargo also necessitated coordination of scheduling and, since freight rates were calculated by pencil, agreements on multiline freight rates so that a freight agent could readily determine shipping charges for a package that was to move along several lines. The Supreme Court ignored all these "network elements" in its *Trans-Missouri* decision, which condemned a railroad joint operating agreement as nothing more than naked price-fixing.[5] Both lower courts, which upheld the agreement, and the Interstate Commerce Commission, which supported it, realized that the patchwork system of railroads could not operate efficiently as a single network without agreements that enabled railroads to integrate their operations. To be sure, the agreements may have covered more elements than necessary. Nevertheless, the Court's analysis left no room for distinguishing the harmful from the beneficial portions of the arrangement. In the *Trans-Missouri* and *Joint Traffic* cases the Court granted the government's request to have the arrangement dissolved.

Antitrust in Network Markets

For the most part network markets do not require special antitrust rules. Instead, they demand some sensitivity to the fact that networks can both produce significant efficiencies and increased opportunities for the exercise of market power.

Some have argued that networks are inherently efficient—otherwise they would not exist. As a result antitrust should leave them alone or simply treat them as single firms.[6] But efficiencies are the source of a great deal of market power. Recall that market power is the power to profit by raising price above cost. Nothing does that more quickly than the ability to produce something at lower cost or to produce a better product at the same cost. But this observation is insufficient to justify keeping antitrust away. For example, railroads were much more efficient movers of parcels than horse-drawn wagons. While that fact prevents antitrust from interfering with railroad development, it does not serve to make price-fixing by railroads lawful unless price-fixing is essential to their effective operation. When it comes to efficiency, antitrust is greedy: it would prefer, where practical, *both* the technological efficiencies that railroads make possible and the economic efficiencies that flow from competition among railroads.

Unfortunately, as history makes clear, antitrust can quickly become a tool for retarding the development of efficient technologies. So antitrust policy must be careful to preserve maximum freedom for innovation consistent with the intellectual property (IP) laws, while restraining anticompetitive practices that those laws do not protect. Significantly, the IP laws do not permit every profit-increasing practice that takes advantage of an IP right. For example, the returns to a patent could include (1) profits from manufacturing under the patent; (2) royalties from licensing; (3) price-fixing with patentees of related technology; (4) boycotts directed at competing innovators; and (5) tying or exclusive dealing designed to move the market away from alternative technologies and toward one's own. While each of these practices could increase the returns to innovation, the intellectual property laws largely conclude that only the first two are "legitimate" returns to innovation, while the other three are not. Some, such as (4) and sometimes (5), are not merely anticompetitive; they are also contrary to the purpose of the IP laws because they retard rather than promote innovation.

An antitrust policy toward networks must simultaneously encourage all of the efficiencies that networks are capable of achieving, while eliminating "unreasonable" restrictions on competition, which are restrictions that are not necessary to make the network operate efficiently. With some notable exceptions, such as the government's failure to pursue the *Microsoft* litigation to a defensible outcome, antitrust has made remarkable progress in understanding network markets and attaining competitive solutions within them.

The balance of this chapter is divided into two general headings. The first concerns the use of the "contract, combination or conspiracy" language of §1 of the Sherman Act to pursue anticompetitive agreements within networks, or occasionally among the members of different networks. The second concerns the use of the monopolization provision of Sherman Act §2 to go after exclusionary practices by single firms that dominate networks.

Collaborative Networks

Anticompetitive agreements among firms in a network come in the same two forms as horizontal agreements generally. First, firms within a network might agree to reduce their own collective output and raise price. Second, firms may agree to exclude competing firms from the network, either to facilitate a price increase or else to suppress rival technologies.

Successful, market-dominating networks typically create significant advantages to their sellers by reducing costs or enabling them to produce a more desirable product. While these results are a good thing, they create an incentive for network participants to fix prices. For example, if the cost of stand-alone production is $10, but participation in a network reduces these costs to $7, those sharing the network can increase price to nearly $10 without worrying about competition from non-networked providers. To protect this cartel, members of the network must limit price cutting, either by forcing firms within the network to price in conformity with the network's rules, or else by expelling or denying membership to firms that threaten to undercut the network's prices. The same generally applies to innovation. Once the members of a network have a great deal invested in a particular technology, they may be in a position to use the network to keep threatening alternative technologies out. Excluded technologies may face higher costs and may not even survive. All of these problems have surfaced in antitrust cases involving collaboratively run networks.

At the same time, antitrust policy must understand the need for collaborative rules in networked markets. To illustrate, the blanket license agreement at issue in the *Broadcast Music* case required thousands of artists to agree on a royalty schedule so that radio stations and other licensees could play their recorded music without advance negotiation. Whether there actually was a price-fixing agreement among *competitors* is worth debating. In form, the blanket license consisted of several thousand royalty agreements between individual artists and a clearing house that set up the blanket license. But these were vertical agreements between licensors and a licensee who combined them and relicensed them as a single blanket license. Normally a large number of vertical agreements does not establish horizontal price-fixing. For example, when a factory owner hires 100 workers at $20 per hour, one cannot infer an agreement among the workers to charge that amount for their labor. Nevertheless, the basic point should not be lost. A blanket license works only because the ultimate licensee is able to play anything in the library without advance negotiation, and this can happen only if there is a prior agreement (or set of agreements) involving all of the artists about what that price will be.[7]

Collusion in Network Markets

Most network markets operate quite well without price-fixing, and close scrutiny should be given to claims that price-fixing is essential. One distinctive feature of networks that require price-fixing is that the "product" being sold is a result of joint production. The blanket license in the *Broadcast Music* case is not a series of individual licenses, but a right to play any music in the BMI library immediately and without additional payment—something that no single artist could have offered. The same thing is true of many physician-operated prepaid health plans. Suppose that 100 physicians from every specialty get together and offer to give a family its complete medical needs for $400 per month. *Ex ante,* this health plan cannot be viewed as the sale of a tonsillectomy, routine pregnancy care, the setting of a fracture, and so on. Rather, it is an uncertain package of services combined with the physicians' assumption of some risk. At the time the family makes this purchase it does not know what its medical needs will be. No single physician can supply the full range of services; rather, each exchanges a share of the compensation for provision of a quantity of services that will not be absolutely known until the contract period is over. There is no way this monthly fee can be computed unless the physicians agree among themselves on a formula for compensating each of them. This program should be distinguished from the one the Supreme Court struck down in the *Maricopa* case, where the physicians simply agreed on the maximum fees they would charge, but subscribers paid on a fee-for-service basis.[8]

The best response for antitrust is to identify those products or services that cannot be delivered efficiently without a price or output agreement and those that can be. In *NCAA* the Supreme Court considered an NCAA agreement limiting the number of times a team's football games could appear on national television.[9] While the Court condemned the agreement, it also held that *all* horizontal restraints in a competitively operated network should be addressed under the rule of reason, even if the restraint appears on its face to be naked. The Supreme Court reasoned that in a network operated by many sellers some form of cooperation would be necessary to deliver the product. But to conclude from this that every restraint created by the network is potentially ancillary is a non sequitur. There is no reason why the members of the NCAA should be permitted to fix the price of stadium hot dogs, or why the banks who participate in an ATM network should be permitted to fix interest rates in passbook savings accounts simply because that agreement occurs on the same piece of paper as the ATM agreement. Networks serve to legitimate *some* agreements among rivals. But agreements come in the full range from ancillary and essential to completely naked and without any redeeming virtue. When a court confronts one of the latter there is no reason why it should not apply the per se rule.

Standard Setting and Network Exclusion

Many network joint ventures are involved in the setting of standards. Indeed, standard setting is virtually essential to the functioning of networks, whether it be railroad track gauges or the protocols for long-distance communication providers to interconnect with the local telephone loop. Some joint ventures do very little more than standard setting.

In *Allied Tube* the defendants were manufacturers and others who had formed the National Fire Protection Association (NFPA), which developed and updated a model electric code, mainly for use by state and local governments in setting building code standards.[10] Standard setting of this kind is a network because both suppliers and consumers profit as a standard becomes more general. An effective common standard reduces consumption costs because the "consumers" of standards, such as local governments writing building codes, do not have to test products and develop such codes individually. They can simply enact the Association's code. The NFPA code was highly influential; many local governments adopted it virtually verbatim. Furthermore, many insurance companies refused to insure buildings that did not meet the code's requirements. Insurers also profit from a widespread common standard, because computing premiums requires good data on risk; the more common the standard, the more reliable the risk data become. If every community had its own idiosyncratic building code, insurers would have to compute risk separately for each one. Finally, common standards mean that manufacturers need produce only one variation of a product, such as a light switch or transformer, rather than many different variations that comply with conflicting standards.[11]

Electric conduit, the product at issue in *Allied Tube,* is a hard, weather-resistant tube through which electric wires are run in installations where the wire might be subjected to the elements or other adverse conditions. While conduit was traditionally made of steel, Indian Head, a relatively small firm, developed an alternative made of polyvinyl chloride (PVC). This PVC conduit was cheaper to make and easier to install. Furthermore, since it was made of a nonconductor, it was less susceptible to short circuits. When Indian Head attempted to have the PVC conduit approved in the NFPA's model code, the defendant makers of steel conduit "packed" the relevant NFPA meeting with their own agents and employees. Allied, a major manufacturer of steel building products, sent 155 people to the meeting, most of whom had no knowledge about the merits of PVC conduit but were simply instructed to vote against it. The new conduit was disapproved by a vote of 394 to 390.

Subsequent developments indicate that the rule excluding PVC conduit was inefficient: once the rule was changed, the new product overwhelmed the market. In that case the exclusion was also inconsistent with the economic interests of the venture as a whole. For example, if the venture had been a single firm wishing to maximize sales and profits of its various products, it would almost always profit from marketing a new, highly successful product, notwithstanding reduced demand for older alternatives. Likewise, the venture would maximize its total sales by approving safe, economically useful products and disapproving those that are unsafe. The inefficient exclusion occurs because the joint venture is not a single firm. Rather, some firms in the venture are dedicated to one technology or process, while other firms are dedicated to alternatives.

A significant problem for innovation in network ventures is that innovators are often in the voting minority—by definition, an innovator is doing something that others are not doing.[12] This is not so much a problem in traditional markets, where the innovator (or a small group of them) can go it alone and then seek out customers for their innovation. But successful innovations can threaten the market shares of the innovators' rivals. If the latter have effective control of the network, they can manipulate network rules so as to suppress the innovation.[13]

In sum, the structure and decision-making process of joint ventures is such that one cannot always expect that joint ventures will make decisions that maximize the output of the venture as a whole. A *single* firm does not violate the antitrust laws simply by failing to maximize, but a joint venture's failure to maximize has antitrust significance. We are willing to accept the anticompetitive risks of joint ventures only because they promise greater efficiency.

Equally important, the profitability of Allied Tube's exclusion of plastic does not depend on the existence of price-fixing among the steel conduit makers. Even if they are behaving competitively, the steel conduit makers stand to gain by excluding or limiting the growth of a new product that is likely to displace a sizable share of their market. PVC conduit threatened the steel conduit makers with lost sales, excess capacity, and probably higher costs. If specialized investments in steel conduit production were significant, then a substantial output reduction would entail large business losses even though current returns are no higher than the competitive level.

Does this mean that traditional concerns about market power are irrelevant? No, for two important reasons. *First,* the presence of market power increases the incentives to exclude. That is to say, if the steel conduit makers in the above illustration *were* colluding, the entry of plastic could cost the steel conduit makers even more than if they had been behaving competitively.

Second, even though the firms do not have the power to raise prices above marginal cost, they may have the "power to exclude," which is relevant to antitrust analysis. This power is measured not by focusing on the relationship between a firm's costs and prices, but rather by traditional antitrust formulations such as market share or access to some unique or essential input. The steel conduit makers' control of a market-dominating network enabled these manufacturers to exclude Indian Head through the administration of network rules, even though the firms were behaving competitively in other respects.

Anticompetitive consequences can emerge even if the internal structure of the venture makes monopoly pricing unlikely. For example, the many thousands of physicians in the AMA are probably too numerous to fix their fees, but this does not mean that the AMA's members cannot profit by excluding chiropractors from the market. As one court observed when it condemned this exclusion, the fear was not physician fee-fixing, but rather that consumers would turn to lower-cost health care alternatives.[14] Likewise, in the *Visa* case discussed in Chapter 6, the principal antitrust concern when competing credit cards were excluded from the bank network was not price-fixing in the terms of individual credit cards, but rather with suppression of innovative technologies.[15]

Monopolized Networks

When a network is controlled by a single firm, price-fixing inside the network disappears as an antitrust concern. Moreover, we have no "monopolization without fault" provision permitting courts to challenge a unilaterally set monopoly price. So unless the firm's prices are regulated, a single firm that controls a market-dominating network is free to charge whatever the market will bear. In any event, it would be counterproductive for antitrust to condemn a firm simply for developing a highly successful network. That would seriously reduce incentives to innovate.

Furthermore, our antitrust laws do not have a coherent doctrine of simple refusal to deal. For example, suppose that a single real estate broker controls nearly 100 percent of home listings in a community and operates its own multiple listing service permitting its agents to show and sell one another's listings. When a second brokerage firm enters the market, the dominant firm simply refuses to permit the second firm to share listings with the dominant firm. Customers will prefer the service with the most listings, and this may place the new firm at a fatal disadvantage. Nevertheless, there are good reasons for not using antitrust to force the dominant firm to share, provided that the refusal is its only offense. As Chapter 10 explains, forced sharing under these circumstances places the court in the position of a public utility regulator, a task for which it is very poorly suited.

When conduct goes beyond the simple refusal to share, however, increased antitrust scrutiny is appropriate. In general, network monopolists are governed by the same conduct standards as monopolists generally. That is, conduct is not unlawful unless it is reasonably capable of creating or prolonging monopoly. Moreover, the conduct must be "unreasonable" in the sense that it has no business justification, or the justification is disproportionate to the harm.[16]

While monopoly almost always imposes some social cost, monopolized networks can be more costly than traditional monopolies, and thus require closer scrutiny. There is of course the traditional cost of monopoly output reduction and pricing. But the path dependence that inheres in networks can impose additional costs in loss of innovation. As the previously stated example of VHS technology indicates, up to a point the controller of the network can dictate the avenues along which research will proceed. Finally, a traditional monopoly such as Alcoa in the aluminum market is protected by high entry barriers that make it difficult for firms to enter the market using similar technology. But in a market with significant network effects a monopolist can exclude even superior technologies, provided that the network is dominant and its owner can ensure that the rival technologies remain incompatible.

Computer Platform Monopoly and the Microsoft Case

As operating systems for personal computers have evolved, their network effects have steadily become more prominent. First, there are significant economies of scale in production, as there are for almost any product whose principal input is intellectual property. While it costs millions to design a single copy of Windows or Apple's MAC OS, producing copies is very cheap. As a result per copy costs decidedly decline as the number of users increases. Second, there are also significant economies of scale in development of applications software. The potential market for an applications program is clearly greater if the program is written for an operating system with, say, 70,000,000 users rather than 70,000 users. Software written for a program with a large installed base will typically cost far less than software written for more esoteric platforms. Third, computer users place a very high value on compatibility with other users, and much of this compatibility is facilitated by use of a common operating system. While the Internet has made it possible for users to exchange data and even some applications among different operating systems, exchanges among computers running the same system are still easier and faster, and can be performed over a wider range. Finally, a large installed base creates a considerable amount of path dependence, making sudden changes in operating systems extremely costly. Not only do all the computers in an office have to be retrofitted, but much software has to be replaced, operators have to be retrained, and links with others have to be revised. All these factors work together to make the Microsoft Windows operating system a rather strong network.

In addition, Microsoft has found a unique way to solve the monopoly durability problem. The monopolist of a durable good faces the problem of competing with its own used goods. To take an extreme example, a monopolist of land, which is a highly durable good, loses some of its market share with each sale. GM's new car production must compete against its own used cars, and Alcoa as a monopolist of new aluminum ingot had to compete against "secondary" ingot made from reclaimed aluminum.[17]

Software is inherently very durable and the installed base is finite. If that were the entire story, Microsoft's business would be relegated to a relatively small number of new or expansion users each year. But there is another sense in which software is not very durable at all: it becomes obsolete. Microsoft continuously upgrades its Windows software, adding new features and more complexity. Not all buyers require the latest software; their needs consist mainly of word processing, e-mail, and perhaps one or two other relatively simple applications. But Microsoft stops supporting older versions of its operating system a few years after a new version replaces it. This fairly quick withdrawal of support is very likely a consequence of monopoly. In competitive markets support continues as long as the revenue from support exceeds its costs. For example, one can still get parts and service for twenty-year-old automobiles and refrigerators. To be sure, at some point the installed base for an obsolete product is so small that support no longer generates sufficient revenue to keep it going. But the monopolist has the additional incentive that withdrawal of support shifts users to new versions. This phenomenon has been a real boon to computer manufacturers, because consistently upgraded operating systems have required corresponding increases in hardware capacity. Not uncommonly, a computer that has a functional life of ten or twelve years or more becomes obsolete after three or four years because it can no longer run the latest operating system.

If a single firm controls a market-dominating network, it will have a strong incentive to prevent rivals from developing technologies that enable them to get "on the network." That is basically the story of the government's case against Microsoft. The trial record contained an interesting intrafirm memorandum that Bill Gates sent in May 1995, entitled "The Internet Tidal Wave." In it he warned his employees that the combination of the Netscape browser and Java computing language could operate "to commoditize the underlying operating system."[18]

What Gates meant by "commoditizing" the operating system was throwing the network open to competition. The operating system engages application software through Application Programming Interfaces, or APIs, which are little blocks of computer code that enable applications to communicate with the computer via the operating system. By following the protocols specified for a particular API, a computer programmer can make his software engage the operating system and make the computer do what the program's user wishes, whether displaying text or graphics, making sounds, calculating numbers, and the like. The traditional Windows operating system was designed to make Windows a conduit for all applications software running on an Intel "IBM-compatible" computer. Windows contained nearly all of the APIs, while software applications merely ran on top of Windows.

Netscape threatened this vision by including some of its own APIs, permitting its program to communicate with the computer directly, and also by incorporating Sun Microsystems Java computing language. Java computing language also developed its own APIs, which engaged the computer through the Java "virtual machine," or JVM. The best way to think of the JVM is as a kind of software-generated "shadow" operating system sitting on top of the computer's existing operating system. The JVM acts as a multiplatform "interpreter" that permits software written in Java language to engage computers running a variety of operating systems.

Microsoft's fundamental concern was that Netscape, combined with Java multiplatform language, could "link" different operating systems together so seamlessly that software writers could write software for all operating systems at once. This could render computer users indifferent as to which operating system they used. As the court put it:

> If a consumer could have access to the applications he desired—regardless of the operating system he uses—simply by installing a particular browser on his computer, then he would no longer feel compelled to select Windows in order to have access to those applications; he could select an operating system other than Windows based solely upon its quality and price. In other words, the market for operating systems would be competitive.[19]

Perhaps the following illustration is helpful. Imagine a country with two telephone systems that currently cannot be connected together. One system has older technology but has been around longer and has 10,000,000 subscribers. The newer system has superior technology but only 1,000 subscribers. Notwithstanding its inferior technology, the large installed base gives the older firm a very significant advantage over the new firm, because consumers value interconnection with as many others as possible. As a result the larger system has little incentive to improve its technology or cut its price.

But suppose someone develops a switch that enables the two systems to be connected together, so that a subscriber to one system can readily talk to people on the other system, and vice versa. The network advantages can now be aggregated across the two systems, and there is no extra benefit to being on one system or the other. Now consumers can choose a telephone on the basis of factors such as which has the better technology, price, or service.

Java-enhanced Netscape threatened to produce the "switch" that would connect multiple operating systems, thus destroying Microsoft's significant network advantage over rival systems. The result would be the emergence of a traditional product-differentiated market in which one could choose a Microsoft or non-Microsoft operating system based entirely on price, features, speed, support, and so on. Compatibility with other users would not be a factor. The government's antitrust theory was that Microsoft did everything in its power to keep this switch from being deployed, and thus to preserve the inability of the different systems to become interconnected.

The antitrust laws could do very little if Microsoft had simply refused to, say, license its source code to rivals so they could develop compatible and competing operating systems. But the history of the Microsoft antitrust litigation shows far more, including efforts to pressure computer makers to deny access to alternative operating systems, to force Intel not to make a chip that would process Java multiplatform language efficiently, to quash Internet access technology that would have served to link multiple operating systems together, and to suppress a computer language that would have permitted developers to write software that would run on multiple operating systems.

The *Microsoft* case was widely publicized as a novel antitrust venture carrying the law deep into concerns about technology and innovation. In fact, most of the challenged practices have been recognized in antitrust cases for a century: pressuring of third parties not to support rival technologies, and contracts with software developers encouraging them to forgo support for competitors. The appellate court condemned Microsoft's restrictions that prevented computer manufacturers from favoring non-Microsoft applications on new computers. It also condemned various restrictions that required the manufacturers to produce an opening boot sequence to favor Microsoft's Internet Explorer over rival Netscape as the default browser, as well as agreements with Internet service or access providers that either required them to use Internet Explorer exclusively or else to favor it over Netscape.

Microsoft also entered agreements with developers whose software accessed the Internet, requiring them either to use Internet Explorer exclusively or else to favor it in their Help and other support offerings. Consumers who used this software had a much friendlier experience if they used Internet Explorer as their browser. The court condemned these agreements as well as others under which software developers would use Microsoft's version of the Java programming language. The all-important difference between Microsoft's Java and Sun Microsystem's Java is that the Microsoft version did not have multiplatform capability—that is, it was unable to meet the "write once, run anywhere" goal that Sun had envisioned because it ran only on Windows systems. Finally, the court condemned Microsoft's coercion of Intel not to develop a processor chip that was able to process multiplatform Java language more effectively.

The court sent back the claim that Microsoft unlawfully tied Internet Explorer to its Windows operating system, and the government subsequently dropped that claim. As explained in Chapter 8, tying doctrine has been in disrepute since the "leverage" theory was exploded in the 1950s. That theory argued, for example, that a monopoly seller of copying machines might create a second monopoly in ink cartridges or paper by requiring purchasers to buy them as a condition of getting the machine. But tying cannot increase a monopolist's power or profits, because the seller can exact an overcharge for the tied product only by offering a compensating price reduction in the tying product. That is, there is a single profit-maximizing price for a package of complementary goods that cannot be enlarged simply by bundling the goods together.

But a variation of the leverage theory acquires plausibility when the intellectual property right holder uses contracts to tie *successive* rather than complementary technologies together. In the market for computer operating systems the profitable life of a product covered by a copyright or patent is typically much, much shorter than the statutory duration of the intellectual property right itself. Furthermore, each successive generation of the product promises new competition. As a result the owner of a software computer operating system knows that while its copyrights and patents will all last for several decades, the product itself may last only a few years. To be sure, the operating system developer is continuously innovating and will always have a successor operating system to replace the current one. But so will others. Thus the intellectual property laws themselves do not give today's dominant firm a guarantee that today's monopoly will continue into the next generation.

A tie can help a dominant firm ensure that it can roll over its dominant position in today's computer operating system into a dominant position in the next-generation system.[20] It does this by bundling new elements into the existing system. That is, there is no discrete break between the first and the second operating systems, but only a rolling set of upgrades incorporating innovations as they are developed. In addition, the operating system developer may use contractual ties to ensure that buyers of the current operating system also purchase features that lock them into the successor system—or at least, that make their ability to switch systems more costly. Microsoft, fearing a world in which the Internet plus multiplatform languages would supplant Windows' network advantages, used tying to ensure that insofar as possible the Windows/Internet Explorer system would remain incompatible with alternative operating systems, thus preventing the network from being thrown open to competition.

The Microsoft *Remedy and Nonantitrust Alternatives*

The D.C. Circuit stated the goals for an antitrust remedy in *Microsoft*. It must

> seek to "unfetter a market from anticompetitive conduct," to "terminate the illegal monopoly, deny to the defendant the fruits of its statutory violation, and ensure that there remain no practices likely to result in monopolization in the future. . . ."[21]

At this writing, there is little reason to believe that the consent decree that the government negotiated with Microsoft will achieve any of these goals.[22] If so, the *Microsoft* case may prove to be one of the great debacles in the history of public antitrust enforcement, snatching defeat from the jaws of victory. The consent decree addresses several types of conduct that the appellate court had condemned. It permits computer manufacturers to use any middleware they want on top of the Windows operating system. "Middleware" refers to programs such as Netscape and Java, which in addition to being applications also have their own operating system capabilities. The decree also forbids Microsoft from discriminating among computer manufacturers for five years—that is, it cannot use price or other terms to retaliate against manufacturers who chose to install non-Microsoft technologies. Microsoft is also forbidden from entering any exclusive dealing arrangements with software developers; the latter must be free to support non-Microsoft platforms as well. Finally, Microsoft must license to computer and software producers at reasonable royalties any intellectual property rights they need to take advantage of these provisions. A three-member panel of computer experts will oversee Microsoft's compliance with these measures.

The decree does not prohibit all the practices that the circuit court expressly condemned. For example, the court found that commingling of the platform and browser code was an unlawful act of monopolization; however, Microsoft was permitted to continue shipping Windows XP with commingled code. In approving this element of the decree, the district court concluded that while the decree found the act of commingling to be unlawful, what the circuit court had really intended to condemn was Microsoft's attempts to prevent computer manufacturers from including rivals' middleware products, something the decree already covered. That finding appears to contradict district court findings that forced inclusion of Internet Explorer gave it a significant advantage over rival browsers. As of this writing there has been no significant move by computer manufacturers to feature and support a non-Microsoft browser, notwithstanding the introduction of highly competitive alternatives such as Mozilla, Opera, and a revitalized version of Netscape.

The government has very likely made the same mistake twice. In its earlier monopolization action, described in the previous chapter, the government had challenged Microsoft's use of "per processor" licensing as a device for excluding alternative operating systems, mainly IBM's now largely defunct OS/2.[23] Under a per processor licensing agreement a computer manufacturer was required to pay a Windows licensing fee for each computer it manufactured, whether or not that computer actually employed the Windows operating system. Microsoft entered into a consent decree that forbade per processor licensing, but by that time the damage was done—OS/2 was virtually dead and never recovered. Similarly, in the more recent round of litigation the computer manufacturers and software vendors have acquired a right to support Netscape, but not until after Netscape was virtually destroyed as a viable alternative to Internet Explorer (IE). The success of the remedy depends largely on the emergence of new rival browsers that are able to overcome the significant advantage that accrues from Windows/IE bundling. That may happen, but it has not happened yet.

Both rounds of *Microsoft* litigation illustrate an issue that has always vexed antitrust policy in dynamic, innovation-intensive markets. Antitrust law is cumbersome. Even when a case is well managed, as the *Microsoft* litigation was, the legal wheels turn far too slowly. By the time each round of *Microsoft* litigation had produced a "cure," the victim was already dead. This makes it vitally important that settlements such as the one in *Microsoft* contain a clause that permits a court to retain its jurisdiction and assess future developments. Furthermore, the point of assessment down the road is *not* to ensure that Microsoft has complied with the decree, but that the market is moving toward the competition that the court insisted should be the goals of an antitrust remedy in the first place. Unfortunately, compliance with the decree has come to define success. The government can subsequently proclaim victory by citing compliance with the decree, without ever asking whether the decree is doing anything to make the market more competitive.[24]

Nothing in the settlement permits the court to pursue more aggressive remedies later if the current settlement has not achieved the goals that the court of appeals set out for it—namely, to "terminate the illegal monopoly" and "ensure that there remain no practices likely to result in monopolization in the future." If the operating system network has not become workably competitive within a reasonable amount of time, say five years, after the remedy decree issues, then the decree has failed.

Finding the right remedy for antitrust violations is never easy, and we have never been particularly good at it. Remedies have tended to miss the mark on both sides. Some of them are overly aggressive and do more harm to competition or innovation than the violation itself did. Others, such as the *Microsoft* remedies, are too little, too late.

Early in the history of antitrust enforcement courts tended to favor "structural" remedies in cases involving significant §2 violations. A structural remedy is one that typically breaks the defendant firm into two or more pieces, hopefully in a way that forces the pieces to compete with each other. One famous example was the massive breakup in the *Standard Oil* case of 1911.[25] Standard of New Jersey was broken up into eleven large production and distribution companies, including such names as Standard of Ohio (Sohio), Atlantic Refining (ARCO), and Standard of New York (Socony). The decree also forced the spin-off of several smaller refining companies, pipeline companies, and even a tank car company. The main companies were broken up by region, however, and at least in the short run such breakups do not produce noticeably greater competition. That is, if distribution markets are fairly local, then breaking up a nationwide monopoly into a dozen regional firms simply creates a dozen monopolies, but does little to further competition *within* each region. However, one hopes that the firms will expand relatively quickly into each other's regions, thus creating new competition. This was also a criticism of the 1982 AT&T breakup, which created the seven regional Bell Operating Companies (BOCs) but for the most part forbade them from expanding into one another's territories.

The government's original breakup proposal in *Microsoft,* which the D.C. Circuit rejected, would have separated Microsoft into a platform division and an "applications" division. The latter would have owned Internet Explorer, but the platform division would have acquired a perpetual license to use it. That remedy suffers from the same problem as the *Standard Oil* and Bell remedies: if the source of monopoly is the operating system, then the breakup does nothing to destroy the monopoly. But here again, the hope was that the two firms would quickly expand into each other's markets. Other, more creative, Microsoft remedies never got beyond the discussion stage. One of these would have required Microsoft to auction off nonexclusive licenses of its Windows source code to four or five purchasers, each of which could then develop its own version of Windows, creating a competitive network environment.

In rejecting the government's proposal, the D.C. Circuit Court of Appeals cautioned against a breakup, noting that Microsoft was a unitary firm that was not the product of historical mergers, and that it operated out of a single facility in Redmond, Washington. These facts make a breakup particularly risky. The court was probably thinking of the poorly structured breakup in the *United Shoe Machinery* case. USM had long held a dominant position in the market for shoe making machinery. In this case the firm *had* been created by the merger a half century earlier of three smaller firms.[26] After USM lost a controversial antitrust case in the 1950s,[27] the court initially issued an order regulating the way that USM priced its machines. Fifteen years later, however, the Supreme Court decided that this decree was unsatisfactory and ordered the firm to be broken up.[28] Unfortunately, the firm produced virtually all of its machinery in a single plant in Beverly, Massachusetts, and there is no easy way to break up a unified industrial plant. A few years later USM closed the plant. Whether the Court's breakup decree was the principal or even a significant factor in the closure is hard to say. At the time USM was largely dedicated to shoe making technologies that had become obsolete. Moreover, the domestic shoe machinery market was being hard-hit by foreign shoe imports. Today USM Group is a much more diversified firm offering an array of shoe manufacturing machinery.

Unsatisfactory experiences with structural remedies have led to the current trend toward "regulatory," or conduct-oriented decrees, such as the one in *Microsoft*.[29] But our experience with conduct remedies has also not been satisfying, and there is little reason to think that such decrees work any better in monopolization cases. This unpromising history suggests that we may be setting ourselves up for yet another monopolization case against *Microsoft* in a few years, or perhaps we will simply bear the cost of network monopoly in the very significant portion of our economy that involves personal computers.

However, there are nonantitrust alternatives to the problem of computer platform monopoly. When it has the will the government can encourage competition through a variety of policies. One is through direct legislation, as in the 1996 Telecommunications Act discussed in Chapter 10. Another is through its own participation in the market as a purchaser or seller. A famous example of the latter was the destruction of the aluminum monopoly in the wake of the *Alcoa* decision. Judge Learned Hand issued a decree in that case in 1945 but made it effective after the termination of World War II.[30] At that time Alcoa owned roughly half of the productive capacity for aluminum in the United States and the government itself owned the other half, which it had used to make aircraft and other war equipment. After the war the government sold these plants under provisions of the Surplus Property Act, which required the government to consider the impact on competition whenever it sold a significant piece of government property to a private firm. Two competing companies, Kaiser and Reynolds, were permitted to bid for the government plants, but not Alcoa. The resulting market was considerably more competitive than it had been prior to the war.[31]

Today the government could do something similar by requiring its departments and agencies to use open-source software as an alternative to Microsoft products. Open source is software code that is produced and distributed subject to a license that makes it royalty-free and freely able to be copied, provided that those who modify it and pass it on make it royalty-free as well.[32] While the open-source movement has been accompanied by a good deal of missionary zeal and hostility toward commercialism, the movement itself does not necessarily contemplate that its products be either "free" or noncommercial. There is much more to software provision than writing code. Firms that make open-source software provide and charge for distribution services and, most important, technical and support services. However, the network effects of these services are not nearly as strong as they are for provision of the code itself. They can be provided competitively within the network. The main shortcoming of open-source software today is an excessively small installed base. But once major purchasers such as the government make a commitment, the installed base would grow very quickly.

One reason the government balks at moving to open-source software is myopia. While a government move to open source would lower the direct costs of software significantly, it would impose other short-run costs—first in making the switch and, second, in living with short-run inadequacies in technology. While these costs of making the transition are visible and "on budget," most of the billions of dollars in resource savings as the economy moves from a monopolized to a competitive computer platform network are not. But the stakes are high. At this writing (2005) several foreign governments are actively promoting increased use of open-source software code. If the United States is a laggard we may witness the emergence of competitive computer platform markets in foreign countries while we remain shackled to an expensive, innovation-stifling monopoly. That could threaten the position of the United States as leader in personal computer technology.

Governmental actions such as the one proposed are not unusual. For example, in July 2003, MCI Corporation was found to have unlawfully evaded federal access charges on certain long-distance connections by rerouting calls so that they could not be detected. The government immediately banned MCI from future government contracts for the types of services that MCI traditionally provides. In the *Microsoft* case the justification for such a move is much greater. The government would not merely be switching to a different supplier; it would be making the market as a whole more competitive. Such a transition should proceed first with those government offices and agencies that use well-established applications for which there are adequate open-source products. Later it could include government agencies with more demanding needs. Finally, the government should insist that private firms contracting with it also use open-source software in their government dealings. The states might do the same on their own schedule.

Microsoft need not be excluded from such a policy. It could submit its own open-source products if it wished, either by developing new products for this purpose or else by releasing the code on products that it already owns. No intellectual property rights would be trampled: the government does not have an obligation to purchase a higher-priced patented or copyrighted product when a suitable, more accessible product exists. Furthermore, there would continue to be a significant market both for innovation and for collateral services such as support, except that it would be competitive rather than monopolized. Microsoft excels in these areas and could be expected to be a strong contender—albeit as a competitor rather than a network monopolist.

Epilogue: Antitrust Reform

Antitrust has come a long way since its expansionist heyday in the 1960s and 1970s. The consumer welfare principle is now secure, and we no longer condemn practices because they reduce costs or benefit consumers in other ways. But much remains to be done. Antitrust today is too complex. It remains excessively dominated by treble damage actions. There are still too many per se rules, and cases under the rule of reason are too difficult to prove.

The handful of modifications proposed below could go a long way toward making antitrust a more manageable, effective discipline. Most of these reforms could be implemented by the federal courts, with the Supreme Court leading the way. A few, such as modification of antitrust's treble damages provision, would require new legislation.

1. THE USE OF TREBLE DAMAGES ACTIONS MUST BE REDUCED

Section 4 of the Clayton Act makes treble damages mandatory in all successful antitrust actions where damages can be proven. As a result this proposal requires a congressional amendment.

Multiple damages make sense for antitrust violations whose success depends on secrecy, such as naked price-fixing. In price-fixing cases actual damages measured by the overcharge are underdeterrent if there is a good probability that the price-fixers will not be caught. But damages multipliers make no sense at all when assessed for public acts, particularly when reasonable minds could differ about illegality. For example, a merger, a franchise tie, or an exclusive provision in a contract are known to the most immediate victims the moment they are created or enforced. In such cases actual damages should provide an adequate deterrent.[1]

2. THE INDIRECT PURCHASER RULE SHOULD BE ABANDONED

The indirect purchaser rule is judge-made and thus can be changed by the Supreme Court. Roughly half of the states have interpreted their own antitrust provisions to reject the federal rule. As explained in Chapter 3, the rationale for the indirect purchaser rule was the great difficulty in apportioning overcharge damages between direct and indirect purchasers—say, between a retailer that purchases from a price-fixing manufacturer, and the retailer's customers. In most cases the retailer "absorbs" part of the overcharge but passes the rest on to its own customers in the form of higher prices. Determining how much is absorbed and how much is passed on can be computed by someone who knows the supply and demand elasticities that downstream firms face. But producing these numbers in litigation usually involves a great deal of guesswork. The indirect purchaser rule responds by assigning the full damages award to the first purchaser in line.

This argument for the indirect purchaser rule has two serious flaws. *First,* the "overcharge" is not even the conceptually correct measure of the retailer's injury. The retailer may lose money because it reduces its markup in response to the higher wholesale price. In the great majority of cases, however, the retailer passes on most of the nominal overcharge but ends up selling fewer units of the manufacturer's good. In other cases the retailer may reduce its margin in order to absorb part of the overcharge, but it still charges a higher price and experiences some loss of volume. In sum, the retailer's injury is lost profits, which are typically less than the overcharge. About the only time the overcharge measures the retailer's injury is the very rare situation when the retailer absorbs the entire overcharge, passing none of it on. As a result granting an overcharge action to a retailer or other reseller is inconsistent with the mandate of §4 of the Clayton Act that a private plaintiff is entitled to damages measured by its own loss.[2]

Second, while apportioning passed-on damages is very difficult, the methodologies that we use for assessing overcharge damages rarely require apportioning. Indirect purchaser damages are typically estimated by comparing the price that the indirect purchaser paid before or after the violation (the "before and after" method) or the price that similarly situated purchasers in a different market paid (the "yardstick" method). Neither methodology typically requires apportioning.

The principal impact of the indirect purchaser rule is to assign the damage action to the wrong person, and for no good reason. Typically, the final consumer is the one most seriously injured by cartel or monopoly prices, while retailers and other intermediaries have relatively minor injuries caused by lost volume of sales. In addition, direct purchasing wholesalers, who have ongoing business relationships with sellers, are often reluctant to sue. When that happens, no one can obtain damages under federal law.

The proper measure of damages in a price-fixing or other overcharge case involving passed-on damages is to award lost profits to all purchasers who resold the product in question, and award end-use consumers the trebled overcharges that they actually paid.

3. TECHNICAL ASPECTS OF EXPERT TESTIMONY SHOULD NOT BE SUBMITTED TO JURIES

The distinction developed early in the nineteenth century between questions of fact (decided by a jury) and questions of law (decided by the judge) rested substantially on two premises. The first was that juries were not competent to decide technical issues. The second was that on certain matters consistency of treatment from one trial to the next is very important. Both of these rationales apply to many of the technical issues raised by expert testimony. A jury is no more qualified to decide whether a certain data point should have been excluded in a regression analysis than what the standard of care for negligence is. Furthermore, whatever the technical rules for determining when a regression analysis is faulty, these rules should be applied consistently from one case to another.

If a genuine dispute among experts arises on a technical issue and it seems likely to affect the outcome, the judge should decide the issue or else submit it to a court-appointed neutral expert. Often the criteria that the Supreme Court developed in the *Daubert* case, which is discussed in Chapter 4, will be sufficient to enable the judge to make that decision— for example, if a party's expert has used a novel, untested procedure or is unable to provide information about the error rate of the approach he has taken. When *Daubert* is not sufficient to guide the judge, then the only reasonable alternative may be to appoint a neutral expert.

4. THE PER SE RULE SHOULD BE TREATED AS A METHOD OF ANTI-TRUST ANALYSIS RATHER THAN A CLASSIFICATION OF PRACTICES

Recommendations 4 and 5 are driven by parallel concerns. First, antitrust needs fewer per se rules and the per se rule needs a more coherent definition. Second, rule of reason cases must be made more manageable and the burden on plaintiffs lightened. Today courts have overreacted to excessive uses of the per se rule by making the rule of reason so cumbersome that even highly dangerous restraints survive challenge.

Antitrust irrationally condemns two kinds of vertical restraints, resale price maintenance (RPM) and tying, under the per se rule. At the same time it applies the rule of reason to horizontal agreements that are far more likely to threaten competition. This is so because while antitrust has developed a system of analytic steps for determining when the rule of reason should apply to an agreement among competitors, it has not applied this analytic approach to RPM and tying.

One disturbing impact of the per se rule that counsels against its overuse is that it cuts off inquiry into the anticompetitive effects of a practice. Courts should never do this under the guise of applying the antitrust laws until they are sufficiently sure that further inquiry is not worthwhile. In the case of RPM, the Supreme Court condemned the practice summarily on its very first encounter (*Dr. Miles* in 1911). When the per se rule was applied to tying in the 1940s the practice was very poorly understood, and ever since relatively little of the case law has explored the true economic rationales for tying.

The proper use of the per se rule is to distinguish "naked" restraints that threaten reduced market output and higher prices. The sequence of steps outlined in Chapter 5 is designed to identify such restraints. But this same sequence should apply to *all* restraints, both horizontal and vertical. Under this approach the per se rule against resale price maintenance would be abolished. Tying and exclusive dealing would be subjected to essentially the same analysis, and both would be treated under the rule of reason. If the rule of reason were applied to tying and RPM today, only a small minority of instances would be condemned—a sure sign that these practices should never have been unlawful per se to begin with.

5. THE RULE OF REASON NEEDS MORE STRUCTURE

Ever since its articulation by Justice Brandeis in the *Chicago Board of Trade* case (1918), the rule of reason has been excessively cumbersome. Under it, parties have launched into wide-ranging discovery into all parts of a firm's business, often without a good idea of the underlying theory of the complaint. The rule of reason is not an open-ended inquiry into "reasonableness." Nor should it be interpreted to require a plaintiff to prove that a practice is anticompetitive without the benefit of any of the shortcuts that common sense indicates. Rather, the rule of reason should be understood as a series of presumptions. At each stage, the burden of proof should be assigned to the party with the less plausible claim. In this sense applying the rule of reason depends on judicial experience with particular types of agreements, just as much as application of the per se rule does. In the *California Dental* case, for example, the FTC proved a significant restraint on advertising created by a market-dominating group of competitors. Furthermore, the restraints were "exclusive" in the sense that membership in the dental association was valuable and all dentists in the association were required to adhere to the rules.

This combination of factors—(1) competitors in charge, (2) suspicious restraints, (3) power, and (4) exclusivity—indicated a restraint that was highly likely to be anticompetitive. Once the plaintiff had made these showings, the burden should have shifted to the defendants to prove that this particular restraint imposed under these circumstances actually served procompetitive ends.

Deciding when the plaintiff has offered enough to shift the burden of proof is not easy, because horizontal agreements come in so many varieties. The judge needs some knowledge of antitrust law and economics. The *California Dental* case does not seem particularly close, although five Justices of the Supreme Court saw it differently.

6. THE SUPREME COURT SHOULD OVERRULE *KODAK*

In *Kodak* (1992) the Supreme Court held that a competitive firm could have monopoly power in aftermarkets (such as replacement parts or service) if previous purchasers were "locked in" to those parts or service and could not reasonably have foreseen that the firm might later take advantage of their situation.

This is not the type of economic power that concerns the antitrust laws. People and firms are locked in all the time by prior decisions. Someone who buys a Chrysler is locked in to Chrysler aftermarket parts for the term of her ownership. Someone who signs a ten-year lease is locked in to 120 months of rental payments. In some cases buyers may not have examined long-term ownership costs carefully, and in some they may have been deceived by initial misrepresentations or by postpurchase changes in policies. But to turn these into antitrust problems transforms antitrust into a general economic engine for the reform of improvident contracts or long-term commitments gone bad.

Kodak also misunderstood what it means to "monopolize" and it failed to appreciate the limits of judicial power to correct monopoly by regulating price. Yes, a firm with specialized aftermarket parts might be able to take advantage of locked-in customers by charging high prices for repair parts. To correct *that* problem would require nothing less than turning firms with specialized aftermarket parts into price-regulated public utilities. But Kodak was not selling parts at high prices; it was refusing to sell aftermarket parts *at all,* except through its own technicians. That is not a rational monopolistic strategy. A monopolist would try to maximize its profits on parts sales. If rival repair technicians were more efficient than Kodak was itself, so much the better for Kodak: it could charge even more for parts.[3]

More practically, in the dozen years since *Kodak* was decided there has not been a single meritorious plaintiff's victory in a case basing market power on the *Kodak* theory. While lawyers have spent hundreds of millions of dollars litigating the theory, the lower courts have construed *Kodak* as narrowly as possible. The time has come for the Supreme Court to recognize that *Kodak* was a failed experiment in a type of economic engineering where antitrust has no place.

7. THE ROBINSON-PATMAN ACT SHOULD BE REPEALED; OR FAILING THAT, THE COURTS SHOULD READ IN A COMPETITIVE INJURY REQUIREMENT

The Robinson-Patman Act was born out of Depression-era hostility to vertical integration and organized distribution. Those views are hopelessly archaic, and the revolution in distribution is now seen as one of the twentieth century's great economic successes.

Any analysis of a supplier's price discrimination among its own competing dealers must begin with one premise: no supplier can profit by injuring its own distribution network. On the contrary, suppliers compete by making their distribution systems more efficient, and they do this by rewarding more successful dealers with lower prices or other concessions that too often become the grist for Robinson-Patman lawsuits.

The most appropriate thing to do with the Robinson-Patman Act is to repeal it. The Sherman and Clayton Acts are more than sufficient for condemning any anticompetitive distribution practices. But repeal seems highly unlikely, given the strength of small-business lobbying and Congress's failure to respond to dozens of similar pleas.

The courts, however, could go a substantial way toward rationalizing the Robinson-Patman Act by insisting that plaintiffs show that price discrimination injured competition, in the sense of reducing market output or making a distribution system work less efficiently. The only practice likely to fall into that category would be powerful wholesale purchasers' insistence, contrary to the independent will of suppliers, that rival dealers pay higher prices.

8. THE RELATIONSHIP BETWEEN ANTITRUST AND REGULATION SHOULD BE SIMPLIFIED

As developed in Chapter 10, antitrust law today uses three different sets of rules for determining when government regulation in our federal system ousts, or preempts, antitrust control. The so-called doctrine of implied immunity applies to federal regulation; the "state action" doctrine applies to regulation by state and local government; and the *Noerr-Pennington* doctrine applies to various petitions or presentations made to courts and regulatory agencies. While the immunity rules for these three situations are articulated in three different ways, all three involve the same pair of principles. First, before regulation preempts antitrust the sovereign must have declared a policy of regulating a market in a way that includes the challenged activity. Second, if the activity being challenged is that of a private firm, some government actor must have supervised or approved it. This pair of rules would create a unified relationship between antitrust and regulatory practice. The Supreme Court's recent *Trinko* decision could be an important first step in this direction: there, the Court paid little attention to the difference between state and federal regulators; rather, it asked whether this was a case in which anti-trust could make a significant improvement in competition above and beyond what the regulatory enterprise already provided.[4]

These measures, if adopted, would give antitrust enforcement consider-ably better results and at lower cost than we have today. They will not create a perfect antitrust enforcement policy: our institutions are simply too limited. Moreover, when significant uncertainty exists, courts and enforcement agencies should err on the side of caution. It would be a rare day that a court, not fully understanding what it is doing, could be a better facilitator of competition than the market itself.

Notes

Introduction

1. For summaries of the law and ideology, see Richard A. Posner, *Antitrust Law* (Cambridge, Mass.: Harvard University Press, 2001); Herbert Hovenkamp, *Federal Antitrust Policy: The Law of Competition and Its Practices* (3d ed., St. Paul, Minn.: Thomson/West, 2005); Lawrence A. Sullivan and Warren S. Grimes, *The Law of Antitrust: An Integrated Handbook* (St. Paul, Minn.: West Group, 2000).
2. E.g., Albrecht v. The Herald Co., 390 U.S. 145 (1968), which found it per se unlawful for a supplier to limit the maximum prices charged by its dealers; Brown Shoe Co. v. United States, 370 U.S. 294 (1962), which condemned a horizontal merger in a highly competitive market with easy entry, in part because the resulting firm would be able to undersell its rivals; and FTC v. Procter & Gamble, 386 U.S. 568 (1967), which condemned a conglomerate merger for creating efficiencies that rivals were unable to match.
3. Robert H. Bork, *The Antitrust Paradox: A Policy at War with Itself* 8 (New York: Basic Books, 1978; rev. ed., 1993).
4. United States v. Paramount Pictures, 334 U.S. 131, 156–159 (1948); United States v. Loew's, 371 U.S. 38 (1962); most recently applied in MCA Television Limited v. Public Interest Corp., 171 F.3d 1265, 1280 (11th Cir. 1999).
5. To be sure, there are other sources of conflict, including state antitrust laws, which sometimes differ from federal law, and the offices of the state attorneys general, who have authority to bring actions under both federal and state antitrust law. See 14 Herbert Hovenkamp, *Antitrust Law,* ch. 24 (2d ed., New York: Aspen, 2005).
6. See Arthur D. Hellman, "The Shrunken Docket of the Rehnquist Court," 1996 *Sup. Ct. Rev.* 403; David M. O'Brien, "The Rehnquist Court's Shrinking Plenary Docket," 80 *Judicature* 58 (1996).
7. See Margaret Meriwether Cordray and Richard Cordray, "The Su-

preme Court's Plenary Docket," 58 *Wash. & Lee L. Rev.* 737, 757 & n.115 (2001).
8. See Agostini v. Felton, 521 U.S. 223, 237 (1997).

Chapter 1. The Legal and Economic Structure of the Antitrust Laws

1. Arguably, price discrimination can be socially costly even though it increases the number of units sold. The costs of administering the price discrimination scheme might be higher than any output gains. In any event, I know of no good argument for using the antitrust laws to condemn an instance of price discrimination that is known to increase output. Other practices, such as predatory pricing, might increase output in the short run (during the predatory period); but their competitive effects must be analyzed by looking at the long run, which includes the postpredation period of monopoly prices. See Chapter 7.
2. For additional discussion of these issues, see any good text in microeconomics. Good choices are Robert S. Pindyck and Daniel L. Rubinfeld, *Microeconomics* (6th ed., Upper Saddle River, N.J.: Pearson/Prentice Hall, 2005); W. Kip Viscusi, John M. Vernon, and Joseph E. Harrington, Jr., *Economics of Regulation and Antitrust* (4th ed., Cambridge, Mass.: MIT Press, 2005). For a briefer treatment, but one focused on antitrust enforcement issues, see Herbert Hovenkamp, *Federal Antitrust Policy: The Law of Competition and Its Practice,* ch. 1 (3d ed., St. Paul, Minn.: Thomson/West, 2005).
3. William S. Jevons, *The Theory of Political Economy* 1–2 (3d ed., London: Macmillan, 1888); Alfred Marshall, *Principles of Economics* (London: Macmillan, 1890). Foremost among the early marginalists in the United States was John Bates Clark, *The Philosophy of Wealth* (Boston: Ginn, 1886). See Herbert Hovenkamp, "The First Great Law and Economics Movement," 42 *Stanford L. Rev.* 993 (1990).
4. On the wage-fund doctrine in the United States in the nineteenth and early twentieth centuries, see Herbert Hovenkamp, *Enterprise and American Law, 1836–1937,* at 193–198 (Cambridge, Mass.: Harvard University Press, 1991).
5. E.g., Kenneth J. Arrow and Frank H. Hahn, *Competitive Equilibrium Analysis* (San Francisco, Calif.: Holden-Day, 1971).
6. See Richard A. Posner, "The Social Costs of Monopoly and Regulation," 83 *J. Pol. Econ.* 807 (1975); William M. Landes and Richard A. Posner, *The Economic Structure of Intellectual Property Law* 17–18, 220–221 (Cambridge, Mass.: Harvard University Press, 2003).

7. See Gary S. Becker, "Crime and Punishment: An Economic Approach," 76 *J. Pol. Econ.* 169 (1968); Richard A. Posner, *Economic Analysis of Law* 215–248 (6th ed., New York: Aspen, 2003). In antitrust, see Hovenkamp, *Federal Antitrust Policy,* note 2, at §1.3.

8. See Judge Posner's suggestion in *Antitrust Law,* at 259–265 (Chicago: University of Chicago Press, 2001).

9. National Collegiate Athletic Ass'n (NCAA) v. Board of Regents of the University of Oklahoma, 468 U.S. 85 (1984).

10. Eastern States Retail Lumber Dealers' Ass'n v. United States, 234 U.S. 600 (1914).

11. See Ford Motor Co. v. United States, 405 U.S. 562 (1972) (condemning the merger); United States v. E. I. du Pont de Nemours & Co., 353 U.S. 586 (1957) (same).

12. Prominent examples include State Oil Co. v. Khan, 522 U.S. 3 (1997) (upsetting per se rule against maximum resale price maintenance); Business Electronics v. Sharp Electronics, 485 U.S. 717, 727–728 (1988) (making unlawful resale price maintenance harder to prove); Continental T.V. v. GTE Sylvania ("Sylvania"), 433 U.S. 36 (1977) (overruling harsh rule against vertical nonprice restraints); Jefferson Parish Hosp. Dist. No. 2 v. Hyde, 466 U.S. 2 (1984) (making unlawful tying harder to prove).

13. Oliver E. Williamson, "Economies as an Antitrust Defense: The Welfare Tradeoffs," 58 *Am. Econ. Rev.* 18, 21 (1968).

14. Williamson, id. at 27. On other limitations of the Williamson model, see 4A Phillip E. Areeda, Herbert Hovenkamp, and John Solow, *Antitrust Law* ¶970, at 34–35 (2d ed., New York: Aspen, 2006).

15. Broadcast Music v. Columbia Broadcasting System, 441 U.S. 1 (1979).

Chapter 2. The Design of Antitrust Rules

1. Robert H. Bork, *The Antitrust Paradox: A Policy at War with Itself* (New York: Basic Books, 1978).

2. For more fully developed accounts of the Chicago School position, see Herbert Hovenkamp, *Federal Antitrust Policy: The Law of Competition and Its Practice* §2.2b (3d ed., St. Paul, Minn.: Thomson/West, 2005); Frank H. Easterbrook, "Ignorance and Antitrust," in *Antitrust, Innovation, and Competitiveness,* at 119 (Thomas M. Jorde and David J. Teece, eds., New York: Oxford University Press, 1992); Frank H. Easterbrook, "The Limits of Antitrust," 63 *Texas L. Rev.* 1, 2 (1984); Edward Kitch, "The Fire of Truth: A Remembrance of Law and Economics at Chicago, 1932–70," 26 *J.L. & Econ.* 163 (1983); Richard A. Posner, "The Chicago School of Antitrust Analysis," 127 *U. Pa. L. Rev.* 925 (1979); Bork, *The Antitrust Paradox,* note

1; Harold Demsetz, "Barriers to Entry," 72 *Am. Econ. Rev.* 47 (1982); Herbert Hovenkamp, "Antitrust Policy after Chicago," 84 *Mich. L. Rev.* 213 (1985).

3. E.g., United States v. Von's Grocery Co., 384 U.S. 270 (1966) (condemning merger of medium-size grocery chains); Brown Shoe Co. v. United States, 370 U.S. 294 (1962) (condemning vertical merger into shoe retailing).

4. See, e.g., Richard A. Posner, "The Social Cost of Monopoly and Regulation," 83 *J. Pol. Econ.* 807 (1975).

5. See Ronald H. Coase, "The Federal Communications Commission," 2 *J.L. & Econ.* 1 (1959).

6. For example, see Judge Posner's opinion in Hospital Corp. of Am., 106 F.T.C. 361 (1985), aff'd, 807 F.2d 1381 (7th Cir. 1986), cert. denied, 481 U.S. 1038 (1987).

7. Carbice Corp. v. American Patents Development Corp., 283 U.S. 27, 31–32 (1931).

8. See Ward Bowman, "Tying Arrangements and the Leverage Problem," 67 *Yale L.J.* 19 (1957); see also Bork, *The Antitrust Paradox*, note 1, at 372–374, which popularized Bowman's position.

9. E.g., United States v. Topco Assocs., 405 U.S. 596 (1972) (condemning efficient joint venture by grocers who lacked market power). For a critique, see Robert H. Bork, "The Rule of Reason and the Per Se Concept: Price Fixing and Market Division, Part II," 75 *Yale L.J.* 373 (1966).

10. E.g., Brown Shoe Co. v. United States, 179 F. Supp. 721, 738 (E.D. Mo. 1959), aff'd, 370 U.S. 294, 344 (1962) (condemning merger because postmerger firm would be able to make better shoes for the same price as rivals, or else undersell them). For a critique, see Harold Demsetz, "Industry Structure, Market Rivalry, and Public Policy," 16 *J.L. & Econ.* 1 (1973). Other literature is summarized in Posner, "The Chicago School," note 2.

11. On the Harvard School approach to industrial organization theory and antitrust policy, see Hovenkamp, *Federal Antitrust Policy*, note 2, at §§1.7, 2.2a. See also Robert J. Larner and James W. Meehan, Jr., "The Structural School, Its Critics, and Its Progeny: An Assessment," in *Economics and Antitrust Policy* 179, 180–191 (Robert J. Larner and James W. Meehan, Jr., eds., New York: Quorum Books, 1989); Leonard W. Weiss, "The Structure-Conduct-Performance Paradigm and Antitrust," 127 *U. Pa. L. Rev.* 1104, 1104–1123 (1979); Oliver E. Williamson, "Antitrust Enforcement: Where It's Been, Where It's Going," 27 *St. Louis U. L.J.* 289, 290–292, 312–313 (1983).

12. See, e.g., Edward S. Mason, *Economic Concentration and the Monopoly Problem* (Cambridge, Mass.: Harvard University Press, 1957, but reprinting earlier articles); Joe S. Bain, *Barriers to New Competition* 155–156 (Cam-

bridge, Mass.: Harvard University Press, 1956); Joe S. Bain, *Industrial Organization* 179, 360–364, 381 (2d ed., New York: Wiley, 1968); Carl Kaysen and Donald F. Turner, *Antitrust Policy: An Economic and Legal Analysis* (Cambridge, Mass.: Harvard University Press, 1959); Carl Kaysen, *United States v. United Shoe Machinery Corporation: An Economic Analysis of an Antitrust Case* (Cambridge, Mass.: Harvard University Press, 1956); Donald F. Turner, "The Validity of Tying Arrangements under the Antitrust Laws," 72 *Harv. L. Rev.* 50 (1958). Earlier Harvard School work includes Edward Chamberlin, *The Theory of Monopolistic Competition* (Cambridge, Mass.: Harvard University Press, 1933).

13. Augustin A. Cournot, *Studies in the Mathematical Principles of the Theory of Wealth* (1838; N. Bacon, English trans., New York: Macmillan, 1897). For explanations of Cournot from a variety of perspectives, see Robert S. Pindyck and Daniel L. Rubinfeld, *Microeconomics* 441–447 (6th ed., Upper Saddle River, N.J.: Pearson/Prentice-Hall, 2005); Hovenkamp, *Federal Antitrust Policy*, note 2, at §4.2a; Carl Shapiro, "Theories of Oligopoly Behavior," 329, 331–337, in 1 *Handbook of Industrial Organization* (R. Schmalensee and R. Willig, eds., New York: North-Holland, 1989); Mark Blaug, *Economic Theory in Retrospect* (Cambridge: Cambridge University Press, 1978).

14. Notably, several of the people who championed the Chicago School approach were originally members of the Harvard School or sympathetic to its views. See George Stigler, *Memoirs of an Unregulated Economist* 97–100 (Chicago: University of Chicago Press, 2003); Ward S. Bowman, Jr., "Toward Less Monopoly," 101 *U. Pa. L. Rev.* 577, 589, 641 (1953). See Posner, "The Chicago School," note 2, at 933–935.

15. See 2 Phillip E. Areeda and Donald F. Turner, *Antitrust Law* ¶409 (Boston: Little, Brown, 1978) (entry barriers); 3 id., ¶725 (1978) (vertical integration, finding nearly all of it lawful and rejecting leverage theory); 4 id., ¶¶908–915 (1980) (relaxed merger standards). See Herbert Hovenkamp, "The Rationalization of Antitrust," 116 *Harv. L. Rev.* 917 (2003).

16. See Bork, *The Antitrust Paradox*, note 1; Richard A. Posner, *Antitrust Law: An Economic Perspective* (Chicago: University of Chicago Press, 1976; 2d ed., 2001).

17. See Phillip E. Areeda and Herbert Hovenkamp, *Antitrust Law: An Analysis of Antitrust Principles and Their Application* (18 volumes plus annual supplement, New York: Aspen, 1978–2006). Donald F. Turner was the original coauthor with Areeda of volumes 1–5 (1978–1980); Phillip Areeda was author or coauthor of volumes 1–10, and was an active participant in the treatise until shortly before his death in 1995; I am the original author of volumes 11–14, and author or coauthor of all revised and second edition

volumes and the annual supplement. Other contributors have included Roger D. Blair, Einer Elhauge, and John Solow.

18. See Hovenkamp, "Antitrust Policy after Chicago," note 2. Some of the more important writing in this area includes Jean Tirole, *The Theory of Industrial Organization* (Cambridge, Mass.: MIT Press, 1988); Thomas G. Krattenmaker and Steven C. Salop, "Anticompetitive Exclusion: Raising Rivals' Costs to Achieve Power over Price," 96 *Yale L.J.* 209 (1986); Michael H. Riordan and Steven C. Salop, "Evaluating Vertical Mergers: A Post-Chicago Approach," 63 *Antitrust L.J.* 513, 515 (1995); Jonathan B. Baker, "Recent Developments in Economics That Challenge Chicago School Views," 58 *Antitrust L.J.* 645, 655 (1989). Other literature is discussed in Herbert Hovenkamp, "Post-Chicago Antitrust: A Review and Critique," 2001 *Colum. Bus. L. Rev.* 257.

19. See, e.g., Michael A. Salinger, "Vertical Mergers and Market Foreclosure," 103 *Q.J. Econ.* 345 (May 1988); Michael Waterson, "Vertical Integration, Variable Proportions, and Oligopoly," 92 *Econ. J.* 129 (March 1982). See also Roger D. Blair and David Kaserman, *Law and Economics of Vertical Integration and Control* (New York: Academic Press, 1983); Michael Katz, "Vertical Contractual Relations," in *Handbook of Industrial Organization*, note 13, at 185–250.

20. E.g., Tirole, *Theory of Industrial Organization*, note 18, at 367–374.

21. E.g., Tirole, id.; Aaron S. Edlin, "Stopping Above-Cost Predatory Pricing," 111 *Yale L.J.* 941, 942 (2002); Patrick Bolton, Joseph F. Brodley, and Michael H. Riordan, "Predatory Pricing: Strategic Theory and Legal Policy," 88 *Georgetown L.J.* 2239 (2000); Oliver E. Williamson, "Predatory Pricing: A Strategic and Welfare Analysis," 87 *Yale L.J.* 284 (1977).

22. See Krattenmaker and Salop, "Anticompetitive Exclusion," note 18; Steven C. Salop and David T. Scheffman, "Raising Rivals' Costs," 73 *Am. Econ. Rev.* 267 (1983); Hovenkamp, *Federal Antitrust Policy,* note 2, at §7.10.

23. See, e.g., Jonathan B. Baker, "Contemporary Empirical Merger Analysis," 5 *Geo. Mason L. Rev.* 347 (1997); Jonathan B. Baker, "Unilateral Competitive Effects Theories in Merger Analysis," 11 *Antitrust* 21 (Spring 1997); Carl Shapiro, "Mergers with Differentiated Products," 10 *Antitrust* 23, 24 (Spring 1996).

24. E.g., Eastman Kodak Co. v. Image Technical Servs., 504 U.S. 451 (1992). See Steven C. Salop, "The First Principles Approach to Antitrust, Kodak, and Antitrust at the Millennium," 68 *Antitrust L.J.* 187 (2000); Robert H. Lande, "Chicago Takes It on the Chin: Imperfect Information Could Play a Crucial Role in the Post-*Kodak* World," 62 *Antitrust L.J.* 193 (1993); Hovenkamp, "Post-Chicago Antitrust," note 18, at 283–304.

25. See Carl Shapiro, "Exclusivity in Network Industries," 7 *Geo. Mason L. Rev.*

673 (1999); Herbert Hovenkamp, "Exclusive Joint Ventures and Antitrust Policy," 1995 *Colum. Bus. L. Rev.* 1.

26. Earl W. Kintner, *The Legislative History of the Antitrust Laws* (11 vols., New York: Chelsea House, 1978–1985).

27. Robert H. Bork, "Legislative Intent and the Policy of the Sherman Act," 9 *J.L. & Econ.* 7 (1966); Bork, "The Rule of Reason and the Per Se Concept: Price Fixing and Market Division, Part I," 74 *Yale L.J.* 775 (1965).

28. For example, Alfred Marshall's great *Principles of Economics* (London: Macmillan, 1890) was published the same year that the Sherman Act was passed. There is no evidence that any member of Congress that year had read it or even knew about it. See generally Herbert Hovenkamp, "The Marginalist Revolution in Legal Thought," 46 *Vand. L. Rev.* 305 (1993).

29. See Thomas W. Hazlett, "The Legislative History of the Sherman Act Re-examined," 30 *Econ. Inquiry* 263, 267 (1992). See also Clarence Ames Stern, *Republican Heyday: Republicanism through the McKinley Years* (Ann Arbor: University of Michigan Press, 1962).

30. See, e.g., Fred S. McChesney and William F. Shughart II, eds., *The Causes and Consequences of Antitrust: The Public-Choice Perspective* (Chicago: University of Chicago Press, 1995); William Baxter, *The Political Economy of Antitrust: Principal Paper by William Baxter* (Robert D. Tollison, ed., Lexington, Mass.: Lexington Books, 1980); Hazlett, "The Legislative History of the Sherman Act Re-examined," note 29; Thomas J. DiLorenzo, "The Origins of Antitrust: An Interest-Group Perspective," 5 *Int'l Rev. L. & Econ.* 73 (1985). See also Lester G. Telser, *A Theory of Efficient Cooperation and Competition* 28–29 (New York: Cambridge University Press, 1987). The literature is summarized in Hovenkamp, *Federal Antitrust Policy,* note 2, at §2.1a.

31. Robert H. Lande, "Wealth Transfers as the Original and Primary Concern of Antitrust: The Efficiency Interpretation Challenged," 34 *Hastings L.J.* 65 (1982).

32. Hazlett, "The Legislative History of the Sherman Act Re-examined," note 29, at 273; DiLorenzo, "The Origins of Antitrust," note 30, at 79–81. See also George Stigler, "The Origin of the Sherman Act," 14 *J. Legal Stud.* 1 (1985).

33. See Herbert Hovenkamp, "Antitrust's Protected Classes," 88 *Mich. L. Rev.* 1, 28 (1989); Telser, *A Theory of Efficient Cooperation and Competition,* note 30, at 28–29; Jeremiah W. Jenks and Walter E. Clark, *The Trust Problem* 108 (New York: Doubleday, Page & Co., 1929); George Gunton, "The Economic and Social Aspect of Trusts," 3 *Pol. Sci. Q.* 385, 394 (1888).

34. See William F. Shughart II, *Antitrust Policy and Interest Group Politics* 11–12 (New York: Quorum Books, 1990).

35. On these practices, see Ron Chernow, *Titan: The Life of John D. Rockefeller, Sr.* 113–117, 144–147, 443–444 (New York: Random House, 1998); Elizabeth Granitz and Benjamin Klein, "Monopolization by 'Raising Rivals' Costs': The Standard Oil Case," 39 *J.L. & Econ.* 1 (1996).

36. See Herbert Hovenkamp, *Enterprise and American Law: 1836–1937,* at 308–315 (Cambridge, Mass.: Harvard University Press, 1991); Thomas J. DiLorenzo and Jack C. High, "Antitrust and Competition, Historically Considered," 26 *Econ. Inquiry* 423 (1988); Sanford D. Gordon, "Attitudes toward Trusts Prior to the Sherman Act," 30 *S. Econ. J.* 156 (1963).

37. See Hovenkamp, *Enterprise and American Law,* note 36, at 246–247; Jack Blicksilver, *Defenders and Defense of Big Business in the United States, 1880–1900,* at 122–128 (New York: Garland, 1985).

38. See Hovenkamp, "Antitrust's Protected Classes," note 33, at 25–27.

39. On congressional intent and the Clayton and Federal Trade Commission Acts, see Herbert Hovenkamp, "Distributive Justice and the Antitrust Laws," 51 *Geo. Wash. L. Rev.* 1, 19 (1982); Eleanor Fox, "The Modernization of Antitrust: A New Equilibrium," 66 *Cornell L. Rev.* 1140, 1144 (1981). On the Robinson-Patman Act, see 14 Herbert Hovenkamp, *Antitrust Law* ¶2303 (2d ed., New York: Aspen, 2006). On the Cellar-Kefauver amendments to §7 of the Clayton Act, see 4 *Antitrust Law* ¶¶901–904 (2d ed., 2006); Derek C. Bok, "Section 7 of the Clayton Act and the Merging of Law and Economics," 74 *Harv. L. Rev.* 226 (1960); Herbert Hovenkamp, "Derek Bok and the Merger of Law and Economics," 21 *J.L. Reform* 515 (1988). On labor immunity, see 1A Phillip E. Areeda and Herbert Hovenkamp, *Antitrust Law* ¶¶255–257 (2d ed., 2000).

40. See Blanchard v. Bergeron, 489 U.S. 87, 98 (1989) (statutory language trumps legislative history); Public Citizen v. United States Dep't of Justice, 491 U.S. 440, 479 (1989) (same). See generally Nicholas Q. Rosenkranz, "Federal Rules of Statutory Interpretation," 115 *Harv. L. Rev.* 2085 (2002); Antonin Scalia, "Common Law Courts in a Civil Law System: The Role of United States Federal Courts in Interpreting the Constitution and Laws," in *A Matter of Interpretation* 29–37 (Amy Gutmann, ed., Princeton, N.J.: Princeton University Press, 1997).

41. See 15 U.S.C. §§7, 12, 14, 18.

42. See 1 Phillip E. Areeda and Herbert Hovenkamp, *Antitrust Law* ¶100b (2d ed., New York: Aspen, 2000).

43. E.g., Tirole, *Theory of Industrial Organization,* note 18.

44. E.g., Karl R. Popper, *The Logic of Scientific Discovery* (1935; Popper, J. Freed, and L. Freed, English trans., New York: Basic Books, 1959). Economics took up the mantle of falsification a generation later, in Milton

Friedman, "The Methodology of Positive Economics," in *Essays in Positive Economics* 4 (Chicago: University of Chicago Press, 1953).

45. See, e.g., Bruce H. Kobayashi, "Game Theory and Antitrust: A Post-Mortem," 5 *Geo. Mason L. Rev.* 411 (1997); Sam Peltzman, "The Handbook of Industrial Organization: A Review Article," 99 *J. Pol. Econ.* 201 (1991). The criticism is not unique to post-Chicago antitrust economics, but has been generalized to all of economics. See, e.g., Ronald H. Coase, "How Should Economists Choose?" 16 (Warren Nutter Memorial Lecture, American Enterprise Institute, 1982), reprinted in Ronald Coase, *Essays on Economics and Economists* 15 (Chicago: University of Chicago Press, 1994); Deborah A. Redman, *Economics and the Philosophy of Science,* esp. ch. 9 (New York: Oxford University Press, 1991); Alfred S. Eichner, ed., *Why Economics Is Not Yet a Science* (Armonk, N.Y.: M. E. Sharpe, 1983). See also the essays collected in Avery Weiner Katz, ed., *Foundations of the Economic Approach to Law* (New York: Foundation Press, 1998).

46. Matsushita Elec. Indus. Co. v. Zenith Radio Corp., 475 U.S. 574 (1986).

47. See, e.g., Edlin, "Stopping Above-Cost Predatory Pricing," note 21; Tirole, *Theory of Industrial Organization,* note 18. The theories are described in 3 Phillip E. Areeda and Herbert Hovenkamp, *Antitrust Law* ¶736 (2d ed., New York: Aspen, 2002).

48. E.g., Oliver W. Holmes, Jr., *The Common Law* 49–51, 108 (Boston: Little, Brown, 1881); Holmes, "The Theory of Torts," 7 *Am. L. Rev.* 652 (1873); Holmes, "Primitive Notions in Modern Law," Part I, 10 *Am. L. Rev.* 422 (1876); id., Part II, 11 *Am. L. Rev.* 641 (1877).

49. Oliver W. Holmes, Jr., "Privilege, Malice and Intent," 8 *Harv. L. Rev.* 1 (1894).

50. Bok, "Section 7 of the Clayton Act," note 39, at 228.

Chapter 3. The Promises and Hazards of Private Antitrust Enforcement

1. 15 U.S.C. §15. The British Statute of Monopolies, 21 Jac. I., ch. 3 (1623), which mainly prohibited government grants of exclusive privileges, provided that an aggrieved party "shall recover three times so much as the damages which he or they sustained by means or occasion of being so hindered, grieved, disturbed, or disquieted. . . ."

2. E.g., Edward A. Snyder and Thomas E. Kauper, "Misuse of the Antitrust Laws: The Competitor Plaintiff," 90 *Mich. L. Rev.* 551 (1991); cf. William H. Page, "Optimal Antitrust Penalties and Competitors' Injury," 88 *Mich.*

L. Rev. 2151 (1990); Frank H. Easterbrook, "Predatory Strategies and Counterstrategies," 48 *U. Chi. L. Rev.* 263 (1981).

3. These issues are discussed in 2 Phillip E. Areeda, Herbert Hovenkamp, and Roger D. Blair, *Antitrust Law* (2d ed., New York: Aspen, 2000).

4. For current data, see Judicial Business of the U.S. Courts, available at *http://www.uscourts.gov/library.* See also Richard A. Posner, "A Statistical Study of Antitrust Enforcement," 13 *J.L. & Econ.* 365 (1970); Steven C. Salop and Lawrence J. White, "Economic Analysis of Private Antitrust Litigation," 74 *Geo. L.J.* 1001 (1986); Harry First, "Delivering Remedies: The Role of the States in Antitrust Enforcement," 69 *Geo. Wash. L. Rev.* 1004 (2001).

5. See, e.g., Clifford A. Jones, *Private Enforcement of Antitrust Law in the EU, UK, and USA* 193–198 (Oxford: Oxford University Press, 1999); Jonathan Sinclair, "Damages in Private Antitrust Actions in Europe," 14 *Loyola Consumer L. Rev.* 547 (2002); Kumar Mehra, "Politics and Antitrust in Japan," 43 *Virginia J. Int'l L.* 303, 315–316 (2002); James E. Crawford, "The Harmonization of Law and Mexican Antitrust: Cooperation or Resistance," 4 *Indiana J. Global Legal Stud.* 407 (1997).

6. Here is a sampling of the many anticompetitive antitrust actions brought by one of the government enforcement agencies: United States v. United Shoe Machinery Co., 110 F. Supp. 295 (D. Mass. 1953), aff'd per curiam, 347 U.S. 521 (1954) (accepting government claim that defendant monopolized by leasing, but refusing to sell, its shoe machinery equipment); United States v. Von's Grocery Co., 384 U.S. 270 (1966) (condemning merger in unconcentrated market with low entry barriers, fearing a rising tide of concentration in the grocery industry); Brown Shoe Co. v. United States, 370 U.S. 294 (1962) (condemning merger in unconcentrated market, in part because it created efficiencies that injured smaller rivals); FTC v. Procter & Gamble Co., 386 U.S. 568 (1967) (condemning conglomerate merger, in part because resulting advertising economies gave firm an advantage over rivals); FTC v. Consolidated Foods Corp., 380 U.S. 592 (1965) (accepting FTC challenge to merger of sellers of complementary products on theory that they might engage in reciprocal buying with others); United States v. E. I. du Pont de Nemours & Co., 353 U.S. 586 (1957) (accepting government challenge to vertical merger on theory that acquired firm would favor its parent in purchasing inputs); United States v. Penn-Olin Chem. Co., 378 U.S. 158 (1964) (condemning a joint venture that expanded industry output because the Supreme Court could envision more competitive expansions than the one that actually occurred); In re Foremost Dairies, Inc., 60 F.T.C. 944, 1084 (1962) (condemning a merger because the resulting efficiencies gave the firm a "decisive advantage" over "smaller rivals"); United States v. Loew's, Inc., 371 U.S. 38 (1962) (con-

demning block, or group, licensing of motion pictures without any showing of market power); Times-Picayune Pub. Co. v. United States, 345 U.S.
594 (1953) (rejecting government challenge to newspaper's requirement that advertisers run same ads in morning and evening editions even
though justified by reduced type-setting costs); International Salt Co. v.
United States, 332 U.S. 392 (1947) (challenge to nonmonopolist's requirements that users of its salt injector also purchase its salt); FTC v. Brown
Shoe Co., 384 U.S. 316 (1966) (accepting government challenge to
Brown's practices of giving special services to retailers who favored Brown's
shoes); Ash Grove Cement Co. v. FTC, 577 F.2d 1368 (9th Cir.), cert. denied, 439 U.S. 982 (1978) (accepting FTC challenge to relatively small
ready-mix firm's acquisition of a cement supplier); United States v. White
Motor Co., 194 F. Supp. 562, 576–577 (N.D. Ohio 1961), rev'd on other
grounds, 372 U.S. 253, 256 n.2 (1963) (lower court accepted government
challenge to supplier setting maximum prices its dealers could charge; issue not appealed to Supreme Court); United States v. Arnold, Schwinn &
Co., 388 U.S. 365 (1967) (accepting government's request for per se rule
against vertically imposed territorial restraints); United States v. Topco
Assocs., Inc., 405 U.S. 596 (1972) (accepting government's request for per
se rule against efficient territorial restrictions by joint venture without significant market power); FTC v. Henry Broch & Co., 363 U.S. 166 (1960)
(highly anticompetitive decision condemning broker for reducing commission in order to make large sale); FTC v. Morton Salt Co., 334 U.S. 37
(1948) (accepting challenge to nonmonopoly salt seller's quantity discount program); Mid-South Distrib. v. FTC, 287 F.2d 512 (5th Cir.), cert.
denied, 368 U.S. 838 (1961) (condemning buying cooperative for obtaining low prices on auto parts for its members); FTC v. A. E. Staley Mfg. Co.,
324 U.S. 746 (1945) (virtually requiring competitors to verify one another's prices in order to avoid Robinson-Patman Act violation).
7. See Ellen E. Sward, *The Decline of the Civil Jury* 95–98 (Durham, N.C.:
Carolina Academic Press, 2001); Jonathan T. Molot, "An Old Judicial
Role for a New Litigation Era," 113 *Yale L.J.* 27, 78–82 (2003). On the ear-
liest history of the distinction in British common law, see Theodore F. T.
Plucknett, *A Concise History of the Common Law* 417–418 (5th ed., Boston:
Little, Brown, 1956).
8. Matsushita Elec. Indus. Co. v. Zenith Radio Corp., 475 U.S. 574 (1986).
See Areeda, Hovenkamp, and Blair, *Antitrust Law*, note 3, at ¶308; Stephen
Calkins, "Summary Judgment, Motions to Dismiss, and Other Examples
of Equilibrating Tendencies in the Antitrust System," 74 *Geo. L.J.* 1065,
1114–1127 (1986).
9. California v. American Stores, 495 U.S. 271 (1990).

10. See William E. Kovacic, "Designing Antitrust Remedies for Dominant Firm Misconduct," 31 *Conn. L. Rev.* 1285 (1999); William E. Kovacic, "Failed Expectations: The Troubled Past and Uncertain Future of the Sherman Act as a Tool for Deconcentration," 74 *Iowa L. Rev.* 1105 (1989).

11. 15 U.S.C. §§4, 15, 25, 26.

12. See Areeda, Hovenkamp, and Blair, *Antitrust Law,* note 3, at ¶303b, c.

13. 15 U.S.C. §4; see also FTC v. Brown Shoe Co., 384 U.S. 316 (1966), which held that the coverage of the Federal Trade Commission Act exceeds the coverage of the Sherman Act. See also Areeda, Hovenkamp, and Blair, *Antitrust Law,* note 3, at ¶302.

14. The text statements must be qualified: the cartel must reduce output and it has administrative costs, both of which reduce its profits. So if *all* of the cartel overcharges were recovered through actions for single damages, the cartel would be unprofitable. But it is unlikely that every purchaser will obtain damages for every purchase, even if the cartel is detected. On the relationship between detection probabilities and damage multipliers, see William Breit and Kenneth Elzinga, *Antitrust Penalty Reform: An Economic Analysis* 3–29 (Washington, D.C.: American Enterprise Institute, 1986); William M. Landes, "Optimal Sanctions for Antitrust Violations," 50 *U. Chi. L. Rev.* 652 (1983); Herbert Hovenkamp, "Treble Damages Reform," 33 *Antitrust Bull.* 233 (1988). The literature is summarized in Herbert Hovenkamp, *Federal Antitrust Policy: The Law of Competition and Its Practice* §§17.1–17.2 (3d ed., St. Paul, Minn.: Thomson/West, 2005).

15. See, e.g., Concord Boat Corp. v. Brunswick Corp., 34 F. Supp. 2d 1125, 1134 (E.D. Ark. 1998), rev'd, 207 F.3d 1039 (8th Cir.), cert. denied, 531 U.S. 979 (2000), where the district court condemned and awarded treble damages for a vertical merger that the government had reviewed but not challenged; the circuit court reversed because the statute of limitation had run.

16. Conwood Co. v. United States Tobacco Co., 290 F.3d 768 (6th Cir. 2002), cert. denied, 537 U.S. 1148 (2003). See Chapters 4 and 7.

17. For the relevant formulae, see William M. Landes and Richard A. Posner, "Should Indirect Purchasers Have Standing to Sue under the Antitrust Laws? An Economic Analysis of the Rule of *Illinois Brick,*" 46 *U. Chi. L. Rev.* 602 (1979).

18. For proof of this proposition, see Areeda, Hovenkamp, and Blair, *Antitrust Law,* note 3, at ¶395a.

19. Illinois Brick v. Illinois, 431 U.S. 720 (1977).

20. See Areeda, Hovenkamp, and Blair, *Antitrust Law,* note 3, at ¶343; Landes and Posner, "Should Indirect Purchasers Have Standing to Sue," note 17; William Landes and Richard A. Posner, "The Economics of Passing On:

A Reply to Harris and Sullivan," 128 *U. Pa. L. Rev.* 1274, 1275–1276 (1980) (arguing that actual measurement of pass-on is necessary, and that it "would be a costly and difficult undertaking"). See also Robert G. Harris and Lawrence A. Sullivan, "Passing on the Monopoly Overcharge: A Comprehensive Policy Analysis," 128 *U. Pa. L. Rev.* 269 (1979) (arguing against indirect purchaser rule, but also assuming that computation of pass-on would be necessary).

21. On state indirect purchaser provisions, see 14 Herbert Hovenkamp, *Antitrust Law* ¶2412d (2d ed., New York: Aspen, 2006). In California v. ARC Am. Corp., 490 U.S. 93 (1989), the Supreme Court approved state antitrust statutes with indirect purchaser provisions. See 1 Phillip E. Areeda and Herbert Hovenkamp, *Antitrust Law* ¶216c (2d ed., New York: Aspen, 2000).

Chapter 4. Expert Testimony and the Predicament of Antitrust Fact Finding

1. See Peter W. Huber, *Galileo's Revenge: Junk Science in the Courtroom,* 206–209 (New York: Basic Books, 1991). For a comprehensive study in a number of legal disciplines, including antitrust, see *Modern Scientific Evidence: The Law and Science of Expert Testimony* (David Faigman, David Kaye, Michael Saks, and Joseph Sanders, eds., 2d ed., St. Paul, Minn.: West Group, 2002). On the use of expert testimony in collusion cases, see Gregory J. Werden, "Economic Evidence on the Existence of Collusion: Reconciling Antitrust Law with Oligopoly Theory," 71 *Antitrust L.J.* 719 (2004).
2. Daubert v. Merrell Dow Pharmaceuticals, 509 U.S. 579, 592 (1993).
3. Quoting Michael Green, "Expert Witnesses and Sufficiency of Evidence in Toxic Substances Litigation: The Legacy of Agent Orange and Bendectin Litigation," 86 *Nw. U. L. Rev.* 643, 645 (1992).
4. Daubert v. Merrell Dow Pharmaceuticals, 43 F.3d 1311, 1315 (9th Cir.), cert. denied, 516 U.S. 869 (1995).
5. See Margaret Bull Kovera, Melissa B. Russano, and Bradley D. McAuliff, "Assessment of the Commonsense Psychology Underlying *Daubert*," 8 *Psychology, Public Policy, and Law* 180, 190 (2002); Jason Schklar and Sheri S. Diamond, "Juror Reactions to DNA Evidence: Errors and Expectancies," 23 *Law and Human Behavior* 159 (1999); Brian C. Smith, Steven D. Penrod, Amy L. Otto, and Roger C. Park, "Jurors' Use of Probabilistic Evidence," 20 *Law and Human Behavior* 49 (1996); R. E. Nisbett, *Rules for Reasoning* (Hillsdale, N.J.: Erlbaum, 1993). For a somewhat more optimistic assessment, see Neil Vidmar and Shari Seidman Diamond, "Juries and Expert Evidence," 66 *Brooklyn L. Rev.* 1121 (2001).

6. See, e.g., City of Tuscaloosa v. Harcros Chemicals, 158 F.3d 548, 566 (11th Cir. 1998), cert. denied, 528 U.S. 812 (1999), which concluded that a statistician's testimony was admissible because "his testimony regarding estimated damages, are the products of simple arithmetic and algebra and of multiple regression analysis, a methodology that is well-established as reliable."

7. The Figure is from Nobel Prize economist Daniel L. McFadden, Brief Amicus Curiae in Support of Defendant United States Tobacco Co., United States Court of Appeals, Sixth Circuit, #00-6267 (Dec. 11, 2000), at 25. See also David H. Kaye, "The Dynamics of *Daubert:* Methodology, Conclusions, and Fit in Statistical and Econometric Studies," 87 *Va. L. Rev.* 1933, 2012 (2001) ("This kind of failure to examine the impact of such an outlier would not be acceptable in an undergraduate econometrics class, let alone professional work"); Federal Judicial Center, *Reference Manual on Scientific Evidence* 137 (2d ed., Washington, D.C.: Federal Judicial Center, 2000).

8. Concord Boat Co. v. Brunswick Corp., 207 F.3d 1039 (8th Cir.), cert. denied, 531 U.S. 979 (2000). The expert based his damages model on the theory that in a Cournot oligopoly market the price is higher as the market shares of the firms are less equal. This point is perfectly captured by the Herfindahl-Hirschman Index (HHI) of market concentration, which is based on a strict Cournot model of behavior. The HHI equals the sum of the squares of the market shares of every firm in the market. As a result the HHI in a market of two equal-size firms is $.5^2 + .5^2$, or .5. By contrast, in a 70–30 market the HHI is $.7^2 + .3^2$, or .58. To use this formula to calculate damages one has to know the elasticity of demand facing the firms. In general, the markup of price over marginal cost as measured by the Lerner Index $((P - MC)/P)$ is equal to the HHI divided by the elasticity of demand. For example, if the elasticity of demand is 10 and the HHI is .5, then the Lerner Index would read 1/20, which would occur when the price was roughly 10 percent above marginal cost. An HHI reading of .58 would yield a Lerner Index reading roughly 16 percent higher.

Significantly, however, the formula works only if the firms are producing identical products, have the same costs, and are engaged in a Cournot oligopoly. If they produce identical products and are in a Bertrand oligopoly, where they match price rather than output, the market will perform competitively regardless of share distributions. Likewise, under competition price will be the same regardless of size differences among firms. And if the firms are colluding, the price will be at the same level as that of a single-firm monopoly, no matter what the size distribution of the two firms. The expert ignored all these alternative assumptions, notwithstanding good evidence of price leadership and matching, which suggests the cartel outcome rather than the Cournot outcome.

The other problem with the expert's methodology was that it produced an enormous number of false positives unless one believes that in every market with a small number of firms inequality of market shares is a sign of exclusionary practices. In fact, inequality of market shares is extremely common, and is found more often than not. See the market share tables on litigated merger cases printed in 4A Phillip E. Areeda, Herbert Hovenkamp, and John Solow, *Antitrust Law,* App. A (2d ed., New York: Aspen, 2006).

9. Bazemore v. Friday, 478 U.S. 385, 400 (1986).

10. In addition to the sources cited in Chapter 3, note 7, see Morton J. Horwitz, *The Transformation of American Law, 1780–1860,* at 143–153 (Cambridge, Mass.: Harvard University Press, 1977); Leon Green, *Judge and Jury* 268–279 (Kansas City, Mo.: Vernon Law Books, 1930); Ann Woolhandler and Michael G. Collins, "The Article III Jury," 87 *Va. L. Rev.* 587 (2001); Stephen A. Weiner, "The Civil Jury Trial and the Law-Fact Distinction," 54 *Cal. L. Rev.* 1867 (1966).

11. Conwood Co. v. United States Tobacco Co., 290 F.3d 768 (6th Cir. 2002), cert. denied, 537 U.S. 1148 (2003).

12. E.g., Blue Cross and Blue Shield United of Wisconsin v. Marshfield Clinic, 152 F.3d 588, 592 (7th Cir. 1998), cert. denied, 525 U.S. 1071 (1999).

13. Moore v. James H. Matthews & Co., 682 F.2d 830, 836–837 (9th Cir. 1982). The methodologies are discussed in more detail in Herbert Hovenkamp, *Federal Antitrust Policy: The Law of Competition and Its Practice,* ch. 17 (3d ed., St. Paul, Minn.: Thomson/West, 2005).

14. Under an alternative scenario, it would have grown at a rate of 5.7 percentage points in each state. The jury picked a number midway between the two.

15. See Frederic M. Scherer and David Ross, *Industrial Market Structure and Economic Performance* 90 (3d ed., Boston: Houghton Mifflin, 1990), which summarizes the literature. See also Michael Gort, "Analysis of Stability and Change in Market Shares," 71 *J. Pol. Econ.* 51 (1963), one of the earlier studies, which found highly stable market shares in oligopolies over a seven-year testing period.

16. See Daubert v. Merrell Dow Pharmaceuticals, 509 U.S. 579, 595 (1993); see also *Reference Manual on Scientific Evidence,* note 7, at 59–63; Joe S. Cecil and Thomas E. Willging, "Accepting *Daubert's* Invitation: Defining a Role for Court-Appointed Experts in Assessing Scientific Validity," 43 *Emory L.J.* 995 (1994).

17. Richard A. Posner, *Antitrust Law* 280 (2d ed., Chicago: University of Chi-

cago Press, 2001); High Fructose Corn Syrup (HFCS) Antitrust Litigation, 295 F.3d 651 (7th Cir. 2002), cert. denied, 537 U.S. 1188 (2003). See also Herbert Hovenkamp, "The Rationalization of Antitrust," 116 *Harv. L. Rev.* 917 (2003).

18. See R. E. Schulman, "Multicollinearity," in *Statistics in Plain English: With Computer Applications* (New York: Van Nostrand Reinhold, 1992).

19. The *Reference Manual on Scientific Evidence,* note 7, at 62, suggests that costs initially be split and ultimately assessed against the losing party.

Chapter 5. Unreasonable Exercises of Market Power

1. Abba Lerner, "The Concept of Monopoly and the Measurement of Monopoly Power," 1 *Rev. Econ. Stud.* 157, 169 (1934). On the development, meaning, and limitations of the Lerner Index, as well as alternatives, see Robert S. Pindyck and Daniel L. Rubinfeld, *Microeconomics* 339–357 (6th ed., Upper Saddle River, N.J.: Pearson/Prentice Hall, 2005).

2. See 2A Phillip E. Areeda, Herbert Hovenkamp, and John Solow, *Antitrust Law* ¶521 (2d ed., New York: Aspen, 2002). Many of the conceptual problems were worked out in William Landes and Richard A. Posner, "Market Power in Antitrust Cases," 94 *Harv. L. Rev.* 937 (1981). On the empirical methodologies, see Gregory J. Werden, "Demand Elasticities in Antitrust Analysis," 66 *Antitrust L.J.* 363 (1998); Jonathan B. Baker and Timothy F. Bresnahan, "Empirical Methods of Identifying and Measuring Market Power," 61 *Antitrust L.J.* 3 (1992); Timothy F. Bresnahan, "Empirical Studies of Industries with Market Power," in Richard Schmalensee and Robert D. Willig, eds., 1 *Handbook of Industrial Organization* 1011 (New York: North-Holland, 1989); Jonathan B. Baker and Timothy F. Bresnahan, "Estimating the Residual Demand Curve Facing a Single Firm," 6 *Int'l J. Industrial Organization* 283 (1988); and David T. Scheffman and Pablo T. Spiller, "Geographic Market Definition under the U.S. Department of Justice Merger Guidelines," 30 *J.L. & Econ.* 123 (1987).

3. E.g., United States v. Aluminum Co. of Am., 148 F.2d 416 (2d Cir. 1945).

4. Mt. Lebanon Motors, Inc. v. Chrysler Corp., 283 F. Supp. 453 (W.D. Pa. 1968), aff'd, 417 F.2d 622 (3d Cir. 1969) (approving a relevant market of "Dodge automobiles sold in Allegheny County," Pennsylvania); Israel Travel Advisory Serv. v. Israel Identity, 61 F.3d 1250, 1255 (7th Cir. 1995) (rejecting as "absurd" a relevant market of "Bar mitzvah tours of Israel by families who live in New Jersey or near Chicago or Boston").

5. Eastman Kodak Co. v. Image Technical Servs., 504 U.S. 451 (1992).

6. Image Technical Servs. v. Eastman Kodak Co., 125 F.3d 1195 (9th Cir. 1997), cert. denied, 523 U.S. 1094 (1998).

7. The literature is discussed in Herbert Hovenkamp, "Post-Chicago Antitrust: A Review and Critique," 2001 *Colum. Bus. L. Rev.* 257, 283–299. Case law includes SMS Systems Maintenance Serv. v. Digital Equip. Corp., 11 F. Supp. 2d 166 (D. Mass. 1998), aff'd, 188 F.3d 11 (1st Cir. 1999), cert. denied, 528 U.S. 1188 (2000); PSI Repair Servs. v. Honeywell, 104 F.3d 811, 821 (6th Cir.), cert. denied, 520 U.S. 1265 (1997); Digital Equip. Corp. v. Uniq Digital Techs., 73 F.3d 756, 763 (7th Cir. 1996).

8. E.g., Tampa Elec. Co. v. Nashville Coal Co., 365 U.S. 320 (1961) (competitive effects of long-term exclusive dealing contract to be tested in the relevant market for the product being sold, not in the grouping of sales covered by that particular contract); Jefferson Parish Hosp. Dist. No. 2 v. Hyde, 466 U.S. 2 (1984) (exclusive contract between anesthesiologist and hospital to be tested in overall market for patient admissions, and antitrust claim failed because defendant hospital accounted for only 30 percent of these).

9. Recent decisions rejecting the relational market power theory include Maris Distributing Co. v. Anheuser-Busch, 302 F.3d 1207 (11th Cir. 2002); Queen City Pizza v. Domino's Pizza, 922 F. Supp. 1055, 1061 (E.D. Pa. 1996), aff'd, 124 F.3d 430 (3d Cir. 1997), cert. denied, 523 U.S. 1059 (1998); George Lussier Enters., Inc. v. Subaru of New England, Inc., 286 F. Supp. 2d 86 (D.N.H. 2003). A few decisions have recognized the theory. E.g., Subsolutions v. Doctor's Assocs., 62 F. Supp. 2d 616 (D. Conn. 1999) (permitting franchise lock-in claim to proceed). See Areeda, Hovenkamp, and Solow, *Antitrust Law,* note 2, at ¶519.

10. See Collins v. Dairy Queen Int'l, 59 F. Supp. 2d 1312 (M.D. Ga. 1999), overruled by *Maris Distributing,* note 9.

11. Defending this analysis is Warren S. Grimes, "Market Definition in Franchise Antitrust Claims: Relational Market Power and the Franchisor's Conflict of Interest," 67 *Antitrust L.J.* 243 (1999); for a contrary view, see Benjamin Klein, "Market Power in Franchise Cases in the Wake of *Kodak:* Applying Post-Contract Hold-up Analysis to Vertical Relationships," 67 *Antitrust L.J.* 283 (1999).

12. Contract law may provide its own remedy. See Restatement (Second) Contracts §211(3) (terms in standardized contracts are not binding when the proponent of the contract "has reason to believe that the party manifesting such assent would not do so if he knew that the writing contained a particular term"); id. at §211 comment f (buyers "are not bound to unknown terms [in standardized contracts] which are beyond the range of reasonable expectation"). See Alan J. Meese, "Regulation of Franchisor Opportunism and Production of the Institutional Framework: Federal Monopoly or Competition between the States," 23 *Harv. J. L. & Pub. Pol'y* 61,

70–71 (1999); John E. Murray, Jr., "The Standard Agreement Phenomenon in the Restatement (Second) of Contracts," 67 *Cornell L. Rev.* 735, 765–779 (1982).

13. See, e.g., Little Caesar's Enter. v. Smith, 1998 WL 892675 (E.D. Mich. 1998) (tying requirements were either "generally known or easily knowable" to the plaintiffs when they originally signed their agreements).

14. Joe S. Bain, *Barriers to New Competition: Their Character and Consequences in Manufacturing Industries* 5 (Cambridge, Mass.: Harvard University Press, 1956).

15. George J. Stigler, *The Organization of Industry* 67 (Homewood, Ill.: R. D. Irwin, 1968).

16. See Areeda, Hovenkamp, and Solow, *Antitrust Law,* note 2, at ¶420a.

17. Standard Oil Co. (N.J.) v. United States, 221 U.S. 1 (1911).

18. Mainly United States v. Trans-Missouri Freight Ass'n, 166 U.S. 290 (1897), and United States v. Joint-Traffic Ass'n, 171 U.S. 505 (1898), which condemned railroad joint ventures under a per se rule.

19. Board of Trade of City of Chicago v. United States, 246 U.S. 231, 238 (1918).

20. E.g., California Dental Ass'n v. FTC, 526 U.S. 756 (1999).

21. See, e.g., C. Frederick Beckner III and Steven C. Salop, "Decision Theory and Antitrust Rules," 67 *Antitrust L.J.* 41 (1999).

22. The FTC approved the venture, subject to some restrictions. In re General Motors Corp., 103 F.T.C. 374 (1984). It was also unsuccessfully challenged by Chrysler. See Chrysler Corp. v. General Motors Corp., 589 F. Supp. 1182 (D.D.C. 1984).

23. See National Collegiate Athletic Ass'n (NCAA) v. Board of Regents of the University of Oklahoma, 468 U.S. 85 (1984) (condemning NCAA agreement restricting number of televised games); Law v. NCAA, 134 F.3d 1010 (10th Cir.), cert. denied, 525 U.S. 822 (1998) (condemning NCAA agreement capping the salaries of certain coaches).

24. Wilk v. American Medical Ass'n, 719 F.2d 207 (7th Cir. 1982); 895 F.2d 352 (7th Cir.), cert. denied, 496 U.S. 927 (1990).

25. E.g., Otter Tail Power Co. v. United States, 410 U.S. 366 (1973); Verizon Communications, Inc. v. Law Offices of Curtis Trinko, LLP, 540 U.S. 398 (2004). Unilateral refusals to deal are discussed in Chapter 10.

26. Some restraints may create power simply because they reduce costs. For example, the blanket license in Broadcast Music, Inc. v. Columbia Broadcasting System *(BMI),* 441 U.S. 1 (1979), reduced the defendants' costs so significantly that they almost certainly had a significant cost advantage over rivals. However, the profitability of the restraint did not *depend on* the ability to exercise market power, but on the cost reduction.

27. NCAA v. Board of Regents, 468 U.S. 85 (1984).
28. See *BMI*, 441 U.S. 1 (1979), which upheld such a blanket license against a price-fixing challenge.
29. Agostini v. Felton, 521 U.S. 223, 237 (1997).
30. California Dental Ass'n v. FTC, 526 U.S. 756, 779–781 (1999).
31. This maxim has been restated many times. See, e.g., *BMI*, 441 U.S. at 2 ("It is only after considerable experience with certain business relationships that courts classify them as per se violations of the Sherman Act," quoting United States v. Topco Assocs., 405 U.S. 596, 607–608 (1972). See also FTC v. Superior Court Trial Lawyers Ass'n, 493 U.S. 411, 433 (1990) ("Once experience with a particular kind of restraint enables the Court to predict with confidence that the rule of reason will condemn it, it has applied a conclusive presumption that the restraint is unreasonable," quoting Arizona v. Maricopa County Medical Soc'y, 457 U.S. 332, 344 (1982)); NCAA v. Board of Regents, 468 U.S. 85, 100–101 (1984) ("judicial experience" determines when per se rule should be applied).
32. Jefferson Parish Hosp. Dist. No. 2 v. Hyde, 466 U.S. 2, 9–10 (1984) ("It is far too late in the history of our antitrust jurisprudence to question the proposition that certain tying arrangements pose an unacceptable risk of stifling competition and therefore are unreasonable 'per se'").
33. United States v. Arnold, Schwinn & Co., 388 U.S. 365 (1967); White Motor Co. v. United States, 372 U.S. 253, 263 (1963). And see Continental T.V. v. GTE Sylvania, 433 U.S. 36, 59 & n.30 (1977) ("the importance of stare decisis is, of course, unquestioned").
34. International Salt Co. v. United States, 332 U.S. 392, 396 (1947).
35. Illustrating the point is the Supreme Court's more recent decision in NYNEX Corp. v. Discon, Inc., 525 U.S. 128 (1998), which applied the rule of reason to a purely vertical agreement characterized as a boycott.
36. State Oil Co. v. Khan, 522 U.S. 3, 21 (1997).
37. *Topco,* 405 U.S. at 609.
38. *Khan,* 522 U.S. at 4 (giving several examples).
39. *Topco,* 405 U.S. at 612–613 (Blackmun, J., concurring).
40. See Robert H. Bork, *The Antitrust Paradox: A Policy at War with Itself* 274–278 (New York: Basic Books, 1978); Rothery Storage & Van Co. v. Atlas Van Lines, 792 F.2d 210, 226 (D.C. Cir. 1986), cert. denied, 479 U.S. 1033 (1987) (suggesting that to the extent *Topco* says that "all horizontal restraints are illegal per se," it has been "effectively overruled"); Polk Bros. v. Forest City Enters., 776 F.2d 185, 188–191 (7th Cir. 1985) (applying rule of reason to clearly ancillary product division agreement).
41. Palmer v. BRG of Georgia, 498 U.S. 46, 49 (1990) (citing *Topco* for proposi-

tion that "agreements between competitors to allocate territories to minimize competition are illegal"). See also Business Electronics Corp. v. Sharp Electronics Corp., 485 U.S. 717, 733 (1988) (citing *Topco*; stating that horizontal agreement to divide territories is illegal per se).

42. Northern Pacific Rwy. Co. v. United States, 356 U.S. 1, 6 (1958), quoting Standard Oil Co. of California v. United States (Standard Stations), 337 U.S. 293, 305–306 (1949).

43. Monsanto Co. v. Spray-Rite Serv. Corp., 465 U.S. 752 (1984).

44. Business Electronics Corp. v. Sharp Electronics Corp., 485 U.S. 717 (1988).

45. Cf. 8 Phillip E. Areeda and Herbert Hovenkamp, *Antitrust Law* ch. 16B (2d ed., New York: Aspen, 2004); and see Richard Posner, "The Next Step in the Antitrust Treatment of Restricted Distribution: Per Se Legality," 48 *U. Chi. L. Rev.* 6, 9 (1981).

Chapter 6. Combinations of Competitors

1. United States v. Addyston Pipe & Steel Co., 85 F. 271 (6th Cir. 1898), modified and aff'd, 175 U.S. 211 (1899).

2. Matsushita Elec. Indus. Co. v. Zenith Radio Corp., 475 U.S. 574 (1986). On *Matsushita,* see 2 Phillip E. Areeda and Herbert Hovenkamp, *Antitrust Law* ¶308 (2d ed., New York: Aspen, 2001). On proving horizontal agreements in the wake of *Matsushita,* see id., 6 *Antitrust Law* ¶¶1416–1436 (2d ed. 2003).

3. E.g., In re Flat Glass Antitrust Litigation, 385 F.3d 350 (3d Cir. 2004); Blomkest Fertilizer v. Potash Corp. of Saskatchewan, 203 F.3d 1028, 1033 (8th Cir., en banc), cert. denied, 531 U.S. 815 (2000).

4. George J. Stigler, "A Theory of Oligopoly," 72 *J. Pol. Econ.* 44 (1964); Richard A. Posner, "Oligopoly and the Antitrust Laws: A Suggested Approach," 21 *Stan. L. Rev.* 1562 (1969), expanded and updated in Richard A. Posner, *Antitrust Law* (2d ed., Chicago: University of Chicago Press, 2001). See also Carl Shapiro, "Theories of Oligopoly Behavior," at 364, in 1 *Handbook of Industrial Organization,* ch. 6 (Richard Schmalensee and Robert D. Willig, eds., New York: North-Holland, 1989); Herbert Hovenkamp, "The Rationalization of Antitrust," 116 *Harv. L. Rev.* 917 (2003).

5. Posner, *Antitrust Law,* note 4, at 94.

6. E.g., Carlill v. Carbolic Smoke Ball Co., 1 Q.B. 256 (1893). See E. Allan Farnsworth, *Contracts* §3.10 (4th ed., New York: Aspen, 2004).

7. Interstate Circuit v. United States, 306 U.S. 208 (1939), recently followed in Toys"R"Us, 5 Trade Reg. Rptr. ¶24516 (F.T.C. 1998), aff'd, 221 F.3d 928 (7th Cir. 2000). See Areeda and Hovenkamp, 6 *Antitrust Law,* note 2, at ¶1426.

8. Under a Cournot output restriction each firm reduces output to the point that its own marginal cost equals its marginal revenue. In a cartel output restriction, the firms reduce output to the joint profit-maximizing level, which is the same as that of a monopolist. The cartel output reduction is more severe than the oligopoly reduction, and the difference increases as the number of firms in the market increases. See Herbert Hovenkamp, *Federal Antitrust Policy: The Law of Competition and Its Practice* §4.2b (3d ed., St. Paul, Minn.: Thomson/West, 2005).

9. U.C.C. §2-305(1) (if the price is "not settled" in the contract, it will be "a reasonable price at the time for delivery. . . ."). Contrast U.C.C. §2-201 (a "contract . . . is not enforceable . . . beyond the quantity of goods shown. . . ."). See Jessen Bros. v. Ashland Recreation Ass'n, 204 Neb. 19, 281 N.W.2d 210 (1979) (contract for sod unenforceable for lack of specific quantity term). On incomplete contracts, see Ian Ayres and Robert Gertner, "Strategic Contractual Inefficiency and the Optimal Choice of Legal Rules," 101 *Yale L.J.* 729 (1992); Sanford J. Grossman and Oliver D. Hart, "The Costs and Benefits of Ownership: A Theory of Vertical and Lateral Integration," 94 *J. Pol. Econ.* 691 (1986); Ian Ayres and Robert Gertner, "Filling Gaps in Incomplete Contracts: An Economic Theory of Default Rules," 99 *Yale L.J.* 87 (1989).

10. Posner, *Antitrust Law,* note 4, at 69–80. See also Gregory J. Werden, "Economic Evidence on the Existence of Collusion: Reconciling Antitrust Law with Oligopoly Theory," 71 *Antitrust L.J.* 719 (2004).

11. E.g., Catalano v. Target Sales, 446 U.S. 643 (1980) (condemning agreement fixing credit terms); Sugar Institute v. United States, 297 U.S. 553 (1936) (condemning agreement to post prices and adhere to them during posting period); C-O-Two Fire Equip. Co. v. United States, 197 F.2d 489 (9th Cir.), cert. denied, 344 U.S. 892 (1952) (condemning product standardization agreement used to facilitate collusion).

12. Posner, *Antitrust Law,* note 4, at 79–93.

13. See, e.g., Monsanto v. Spray-Rite Serv. Corp., 465 U.S. 752, 768 (1984) (requiring "direct or circumstantial evidence" of an unlawful agreement).

14. See *Matsushita,* 475 U.S. at 587 ("if the factual context renders respondents' claim implausible—if the claim is one that simply makes no economic sense—respondents must come forward with more persuasive evidence to support their claim than would otherwise be necessary").

15. Blomkest Fertilizer v. Potash Corp. of Saskatchewan, 203 F.3d 1028, 1032–1033, 1043–1045 (8th Cir., en banc), cert. denied, 531 U.S. 815 (2000). The firms also contacted each other to explain or apologize when they deviated from posted list prices. See also Williamson Oil Co. v. Philip Morris U.S.A., 346 F.3d 1287 (11th Cir. 2003), which interpreted "plus factors"

very narrowly, even concluding that a history of conspiracy violations did not make an agreement more likely.

16. In re High Fructose Corn Syrup Antitrust Litigation, 295 F.3d 651 (7th Cir. 2002), cert. denied, 537 U.S. 1188 (2003). Accord In re Flat Glass Antitrust Litigation, 385 F.3d 350 (3d Cir. 2004).

17. The law of mergers does include partial acquisitions of stock and assets, and evaluating these can pose unique difficulties. See 5 Phillip E. Areeda and Herbert Hovenkamp, *Antitrust Law* ¶¶1202–1203 (2d ed., New York: Aspen, 2003).

18. National Collegiate Athletic Association (NCAA) v. Board of Regents of the University of Oklahoma, 468 U.S. 85 (1984) (condemning limitation on televised games); Law v. NCAA, 902 F. Supp. 1394 (D. Kan. 1995), aff'd, 134 F.3d 1010 (10th Cir.), cert. denied, 525 U.S. 822 (1998) (condemning agreement limiting coaching salaries).

19. See General Motors Corp., 103 F.T.C. 374 (1984) (approving joint venture).

20. United States v. Topco Assocs., 405 U.S. 596 (1972) (incorrectly condemning ancillary territory division agreement under per se rule).

21. Allied Tube & Conduit Corp. v. Indian Head, 486 U.S. 492 (1988) (manufacturers of steel conduit agree to deny market access to maker of plastic conduit); American Soc'y of Mechanical Engineers v. Hydrolevel Corp., 456 U.S. 556 (1982) (agreement among members of accreditation association to suppress a superior valve technology).

22. E.g., American Column & Lumber Co. v. United States, 257 U.S. 377 (1921) (disapproving exchange of price and output information); L.C.L. Theaters v. Columbia Pictures, 421 F. Supp. 1090, 1106–1107 (N.D. Tex. 1976), rev'd on other grounds, 566 F.2d 494 (5th Cir. 1978) (motion picture distributors could lawfully exchange information concerning exhibitors' reporting of box office receipts). See 13 Herbert Hovenkamp, *Antitrust Law* ¶¶2110–2114 (2d ed., New York: Aspen, 2005).

23. FTC v. California Dental Ass'n (CDA), 526 U.S. 756 (1999) (approving the limitations).

24. United States v. Visa USA, 163 F. Supp. 2d 322 (S.D.N.Y.), modified, 183 F. Supp. 2d 613 (S.D.N.Y. 2001), aff'd, 344 F.3d 229 (2d Cir. 2003), cert. denied, 125 S. Ct. 45 (2004).

25. Northwest Wholesale Stationers v. Pacific Stationery & Printing Co., 472 U.S. 284 (1985) (approving the expulsion).

26. Arizona v. Maricopa County Medical Soc'y, 457 U.S. 332 (1982) (condemning the arrangement).

27. Broadcast Music, Inc. v. Columbia Broadcasting System (*BMI*), 441 U.S. 1 (1979) (approving blanket license arrangement).

28. Board of Trade of City of Chicago v. United States, 246 U.S. 231 (1918) (upholding agreement).

29. See Herbert Hovenkamp, *Enterprise and American Law, 1836–1937*, at chs. 12–13 (Cambridge, Mass.: Harvard University Press, 1991); Herbert Hovenkamp, "Regulatory Conflict in the Gilded Age: Federalism and the Railroad Problem," 97 *Yale L.J.* 1017 (1988).

30. United States v. Trans-Missouri Freight Ass'n, 53 F. 440 (C.C.D. Kan. 1892), aff'd, 58 F. 58 (8th Cir. 1893), rev'd, 166 U.S. 290 (1897).

31. *BMI*, 441 U.S. 1 (1979); *Maricopa*, 457 U.S. 332 (1982). See also In re Polygram Holding, Inc., 2003 WL 21770765 (F.T.C. 2003), where the FTC condemned a joint venture to produce a new music CD because the parties placed severe limitations on how they would market their separate competing products.

32. Eastern States Retail Lumber Dealers' Ass'n v. United States, 234 U.S. 600 (1914); United States v. General Motors Corp., 384 U.S. 127, 146 (1966). On naked boycotts, see Hovenkamp, 13 *Antitrust Law*, note 22, at ¶2203.

33. E.g., Mid-South Grizzlies v. NFL, 720 F.2d 772, 777 (3d Cir. 1983), cert. denied, 467 U.S. 1215 (1984).

34. E.g., Thompson v. Metropolitan Multi-List, 934 F.2d 1566 (11th Cir. 1991), cert. denied, 506 U.S. 903 (1992); United States v. Realty Multi-List, 629 F.2d 1351 (5th Cir. 1980).

35. See *Visa*, note 24.

36. See Bruce L. Hay and Kathryn E. Spier, "Burdens of Proof in Civil Litigation: An Economic Perspective," 26 *J. Legal Stud.* 413 (1997); Bruce L. Hay, "Allocating the Burden of Proof," 72 *Ind. L.J.* 651, 674–676 (1997).

37. FTC v. California Dental Assn. (CDA), 526 U.S. 756, 784 (1999).

Chapter 7. Dominant Firms and Exclusionary Practices

1. Darcy v. Allen, or The Case of Monopolies, 11 Co. Rep. 84b, 77 Eng. Rep. 1262 (K.B. 1603). The decision is discussed in P.S. Atiyah, *The Rise and Fall of Liberty of Contract* 118 (Oxford: Clarendon Press, 1979).

2. See 5 & 6 Edw. VI, c. 14 (1552), which forbade the engrossing (buying up), forestalling (cornering the market), and regrating (buying for the purpose of resale) of "corn, grain, butter, cheese, fish or other ded . . . victuals whatsoever. . . ." See Wendell Herbruck, "Forestalling, Regrating, and Engrossing," 27 *Mich. L. Rev.* 365, 378 (1929).

3. See 3 Phillip E. Areeda and Herbert Hovenkamp, *Antitrust Law* ¶651 (2d ed., New York: Aspen, 2002); Herbert Hovenkamp, "Exclusion and the Sherman Act," 72 *U. Chi. L. Rev.* 147 (2005).

4. See, e.g., Brief for the United States and the Federal Trade Commission

as Amici Curiae, Verizon Communications, Inc. v. Trinko, 540 U.S. 398 (2004), at 10–11 ("exclusionary conduct normally involves the sacrifice of short-term profits or goodwill in order to maintain or obtain long-term monopoly power." If a refusal to deal "involves a sacrifice of profits or business advantage and makes economic sense only because it softens or injures competition, it is 'exclusionary.'").

5. E.g., Steven C. Salop and David T. Scheffman, "Raising Rivals' Costs," 73 *Am. Econ. Rev.* 267 (1983); Thomas G. Krattenmaker and Steven C. Salop, "Anticompetitive Exclusion: Raising Rivals' Costs to Achieve Power over Price," 96 *Yale L.J.* 209, 238–240 (1986); Einer Elhauge, "Defining Better Monopolization Standards," 56 *Stan. L. Rev.* 253 (2003). For historical perspective, see Elizabeth Granitz and Benjamin Klein, "Monopolization by 'Raising Rivals' Costs': The Standard Oil Case," 39 *J.L. & Econ.* 1 (1996).

6. See Richard A. Posner, *Antitrust Law* 196–197 (2d ed., Chicago: University of Chicago Press, 2001).

7. Id. at 194–195.

8. See United States v. Aluminum Co. ("Alcoa"), 148 F.2d 416, 431 (2d Cir. 1945) ("we disregard any question of intent").

9. Standard Oil Co. v. United States, 221 U.S. 1, 58, 61 (1911).

10. *Alcoa,* note 8, 148 F.2d at 427–428, as interpreted by Judge Wyzanski in United States v. United Shoe Machinery Corp., 110 F. Supp. 295, 342 (D. Mass. 1953), aff'd per curiam, 347 U.S. 521 (1954).

11. The proposal is preserved in its entirety, mainly as an historical artifact, in 3 *Antitrust Law,* note 3, at ¶¶630–638.

12. Scale economies include any significant input or production factor whose costs decline as volume increases. This includes many intellectual property rights even where straight production costs are constant. For example, it might cost $100,000,000 to develop the first copy of Microsoft Office but only $1 per copy to manufacture subsequent copies. In that case, all else being equal, any firm with a large output of copies will have a significant cost advantage over firms with lower outputs. A few multifirm network markets may enjoy monopoly power even though *individual* production costs are constant. However, the economies of the network relate to the network as a whole rather than individual firms. For example, a real estate multiple listing service controlled by 80 percent of the firms in a market could have a decisive cost advantage over rivals even though each member's costs of producing listing information for the service are fairly constant. Entry as an individual realtor is easy, but duplicating the entire network would be dauntingly expensive.

13. Image Technical Servs. v. Eastman Kodak Co., 125 F.3d 1195, 1203 (9th Cir. 1997), cert. denied, 523 U.S. 1094 (1998): "The 'commercial reality'

faced by service providers and equipment owners is that a service provider must have ready access to all parts to compete in the service market. . . . [Thus] the relevant market for parts from the equipment owners' and service providers' perspective is composed of 'all parts' that are designed to meet Kodak photocopier and micrographics equipment specifications."

14. See Chapter 11.

15. See E. I. du Pont de Nemours & Co., 96 F.T.C. 653, 747 (1980), which refused to condemn the defendant for developing a superior process for making titanium dioxide, and then building a plant large enough to handle all anticipated world demand. The Commission concluded that it could not reliably distinguish an anticompetitive decision to build a large plant from aggressive, demand-creating competition.

16. See, e.g., Jean Tirole, *The Theory of Industrial Organization* 367–374 (Cambridge, Mass.: MIT Press, 1992); Frederic M. Scherer and David Ross, *Industrial Market Structure and Economic Performance* 356–366, 405–406 (3d ed., Boston: Houghton Mifflin, 1990); Joe S. Bain, *Industrial Organization* 269–276 (2d ed., New York: Wiley, 1968). See also 3 *Antitrust Law*, note 3, at ¶736.

17. For a generally contrary view, see Aaron S. Edlin, "Stopping Above-Cost Predatory Pricing," 111 *Yale L.J.* 941, 942 (2002).

18. See 3 *Antitrust Law*, note 3, at ¶723.

19. The AVC curve is generally U-shaped, as the Figure indicates, although the bottom may be fairly flat over a wide range, indicating that AVC is constant in that area. This suggests that AVC is higher when the plant is being used to produce an amount that is either too low or too high in relation to that plant's capacity. For example, if a GM plant is designed to produce 1,000 cars per week, it could produce 100 per week, but per unit costs would be higher. It might also be pushed to produce 2,000 cars per week, but error rates and equipment failure rates would rise, and once again costs would be higher. The average total cost, or average cost (AC) curve, is higher than AVC and tends to converge with AVC at high levels of output. This is because average cost also includes fixed costs, and fixed costs per unit decline as output increases. Significantly, a price below AVC is always "below cost" in the sense that the firm is not earning enough to cover all of its variable as well as fixed costs.

20. E.g., Oliver E. Williamson, "Predatory Pricing: A Strategic and Welfare Analysis," 87 *Yale L.J.* 284 (1977).

21. United States v. AMR Corp., 335 F.3d 1109 (10th Cir. 2003).

22. See William J. Baumol, "Predation and the Logic of the Average Variable Cost Test," 39 *J.L. & Econ.* 49, 70 (1996).

23. Brooke Group Ltd. v. Brown & Williamson Tobacco Corp., 509 U.S. 209 (1993).

24. E.g., Edlin, "Stopping Above-Cost Predatory Pricing," note 17, at 942; Einer Elhauge, "Why Above-Cost Price Cuts to Drive Out Entrants Are Not Predatory—and the Implications for Defining Costs and Market Power," 112 *Yale L.J.* 681, 697 n.51 (2003).

25. However, disciplinary price cuts need not be this drastic. Sometimes no more than a price cut to the competitive level will suffice to deter "cheaters" on the oligopoly price. See Ian Ayres, "How Cartels Punish: A Structural Theory of Self-Enforcing Collusion," 87 *Colum. L. Rev.* 295 (1987).

26. *Brooke Group,* note 23, 509 U.S. at 214–215.

27. See id. at 227–228.

28. Conwood Co. v. United States Tobacco Co., 290 F.3d 768, 784 (6th Cir. 2002), cert. denied, 537 U.S. 1148 (2003).

29. Concord Boat Co. v. Brunswick Corp., 207 F.3d 1039 (8th Cir.), cert. denied, 531 U.S. 979 (2000). On the expert testimony in *Concord Boat,* see Chapter 4.

30. LePage's v. 3M, 324 F.3d 141 (3d Cir. 2003) (en banc), cert. denied, 124 S. Ct. 2932 (2004). The decision has provoked considerable legal and economic debate, most of which concludes that we do not yet know enough about such practices to draw definite conclusions. See Daniel L. Rubinfeld, "3M's Bundled Rebates: An Economic Perspective," 72 *U. Chi. L. Rev.* 243 (2005) (suggesting several theories of competitive harm, but concluding that the record was not sufficiently developed to permit definite conclusions about any of them); Richard A. Posner, "Vertical Restraints and Antitrust Policy," 72 *U. Chi. L. Rev.* 229, 238–241 (2005) (brief discussion suggesting further study of the issue). And see the government's brief opposing Supreme Court review, arguing mainly that the issue had not been sufficiently developed in the lower courts. 2004 WL 1205191 (May 28, 2004).

The example in the text assumes that LePage's could not join forces with other firms that made Post-it notes and staples. In that case, this joint venture could match 3M's entire discount program. See Daniel A. Crane, "Multi-Product Discounting: A Myth of Non-Price Predation," 72 *U. Chi. L. Rev.* 27 (2005).

31. E.g., Multistate Legal Studies v. Harcourt Brace Jovanovich, 63 F.3d 1540 (10th Cir. 1995), cert. denied, 516 U.S. 1044 (1996). See 3 *Antitrust Law,* note 3, at ¶749.

32. See Richard A. Epstein, *Torts,* ch. 21 (New York: Aspen, 1999).

33. E.g., Tarleton v. McGawley, 170 E.R. 153 (K.B. 1793) (defendant fired weapons to scare local tribesmen so they would not purchase from a com-

petitor); International News Serv. v. Associated Press, 248 U.S. 215 (1918) (defendant copied AP news stories from East Coast and telegraphed them to West Coast in time to be run in morning newspapers); Mosler Safe Co. v. Ely-Norris Safe Co., 273 U.S. 132 (1927) (defendant designed its safe so as to suggest that it had a security feature found on a competitor's safe).

34. *Conwood,* note 28, 290 F.3d at 784.

35. See 3A *Antitrust Law* ¶782b (2d ed., New York: Aspen, 2002). A few months later the Sixth Circuit corrected itself and assessed these requirements in a different case, although one where the false information was directed at consumers rather than retailers. That juxtaposition is perverse: consumers presumably need more protection from false supplier information than retailers do. See American Council of Certified Podiatric Physicians v. American Board of Podiatric Surgery, 185 F.3d 606 (6th Cir. 2003).

36. *Brooke Group,* note 23, 509 U.S. at 225.

37. 15 U.S.C. §15; and see 3 *Antitrust Law,* note 3, at ¶657b.

38. See Edward Snyder and Thomas Kauper, "Misuse of the Antitrust Laws: The Competitor Plaintiff," 90 *Mich. L. Rev.* 551 (1991); Frank H. Easterbrook, "Predatory Strategies and Counterstrategies," 48 *U. Chi. L. Rev.* 263 (1981); Robert H. Bork, *The Antitrust Paradox: A Policy at War with Itself* 144–155 (New York: Basic Books, 1978; rev. ed., 1993).

Chapter 8. Antitrust and Distribution

1. On the history of various aspects of distribution in the United states, see Alfred S. Chandler, Jr., *The Visible Hand: The Managerial Revolution in American Business* (Cambridge, Mass.: Harvard University Press, 1977); Mansel G. Blackford and K. Austin Kerr, *Business Enterprise in American History* (3d ed., New York: Houghton Mifflin, 1994); Thomas S. Dicke, *Franchising in America: The Development of a Business Method, 1840–1980* (Chapel Hill: University of North Carolina Press, 1992).

2. Ronald H. Coase, "The Nature of the Firm," 4 *Economica* (n.s.) 386 (1937). See also Ronald H. Coase, *The Firm, the Market, and the Law* (Chicago: University of Chicago Press, 1988); Oliver E. Williamson and Sydney G. Winter, eds., *The Nature of the Firm: Origins, Evolution, and Development* (New York: Oxford University Press, 1991).

3. The classic exposition of the free rider problem is Lester Telser, "Why Should Manufacturers Want Fair Trade?" 3 *J.L. & Econ.* 86 (1960). See 8 Phillip E. Areeda and Herbert Hovenkamp, *Antitrust Law* ¶¶1611–1614 (2d ed., New York: Aspen, 2004).

4. See Areeda and Hovenkamp, *Antitrust Law,* id. at ¶1614f; Raymond Deneckere, Howard Marvel, and James Peck, "Demand Uncertainty, Inven-

tories, and Resale Price Maintenance," 111 *Q.J. Econ.* 885 (1996); see also David Butz, "Vertical Price Controls with Uncertain Demand," 40 *J.L. & Econ.* 433 (1997).

5. Areeda and Hovenkamp, *Antitrust Law,* note 3, at ¶1606.

6. Business Electronics Corp. v. Sharp Electronics Corp., 485 U.S. 717, 726–728 (1988).

7. Cf. Richard A. Posner, "The Next Step in the Antitrust Treatment of Restricted Distribution: Per Se Legality," 48 *U. Chi. L. Rev.* 6 (1981), with Robert Pitofsky, "In Defense of Discounters: The No-Frills Case for a *Per Se* Rule against Vertical Price Fixing," 71 *Geo. L.J.* 1487 (1983).

8. Dr. Miles Medical Co. v. John D. Park & Sons Co., 220 U.S. 373 (1911).

9. The cartel's work is recounted in Herbert Hovenkamp, *Enterprise and American Law, 1836–1937,* ch. 25 (Cambridge, Mass.: Harvard University Press, 1991). Other decisions recognizing various aspects of the cartel include Loder v. Jayne, 142 F. 1010 (C.C.E.D. Pa.), aff'd, 149 F. 21 (3d Cir. 1906); Dr. Miles Medical Co. v. Jayne's Drug Co., 149 F. 838 (C.C.D. Mass. 1906); John D. Park & Sons Co. v. National Wholesale Druggists Ass'n, 67 N.E. 136, 137 (1903).

10. Monsanto Co. v. Spray-Rite Serv. Corp., 465 U.S. 752 (1984).

11. *Business Electronics,* 485 U.S. at 736: "a vertical restraint is not illegal per se unless it includes some agreement on price or price levels."

12. Ben Elfman & Sons v. Criterion Mills, 774 F. Supp. 683 (D. Mass. 1991).

13. Garment District v. Belk Stores Servs., 799 F.2d 905, 908–909 (4th Cir. 1986), cert. denied, 486 U.S. 1005 (1988).

14. For some tentative conclusions, see Areeda and Hovenkamp, 8 *Antitrust Law,* note 3, at ¶1604.

15. Toys"R"Us v. FTC, 221 F.3d 928 (7th Cir. 2000).

16. E.g., Big Apple BMW v. BMW of N. Am., 974 F.2d 1358 (3d Cir. 1992) (plaintiff dealer claimed boycott orchestrated against it, a price cutter, by other dealers); Lovett v. General Motors Corp., 769 F. Supp. 1506, 1511–1512 (D. Minn. 1991), aff'd, 975 F.2d 518 (8th Cir. 1992) ("full price" dealers conspired to eliminate price-cutting dealer).

17. Albrecht v. The Herald Co., 390 U.S. 145 (1968), overruled by State Oil Co. v. Khan, 522 U.S. 3 (1997).

18. White Motor Co. v. United States, 372 U.S. 253 (1963); United States v. Arnold, Schwinn & Co., 388 U.S. 365 (1967); Continental T.V., Inc. v. GTE Sylvania, Inc., 433 U.S. 36 (1977). On the situation today, see Douglas H. Ginsburg, "Vertical Restraints: De Facto Legality under the Rule of Reason," 60 *Antitrust L.J.* 67 (1991); Herbert Hovenkamp, *Federal Antitrust Policy: The Law of Competition and Its Practice* §11.6b (3d ed., St. Paul, Minn.: West Group, 2005).

19. See the lower court decision that finally approved the restraint. Continental T.V. v. GTE Sylvania, 461 F. Supp. 1046, 1052 (N.D. Cal. 1978), aff'd, 694 F.2d 1132 (9th Cir. 1982).
20. See O.S.C. Corp. v. Apple Computer, 792 F.2d 1464, 1469–1470 (9th Cir. 1986), which accepted Apple's argument that its computers should be sold only via authorized dealers through face-to-face transactions.
21. E.g., Tripoli Co. v. Wella Corp., 425 F.2d 932 (3d Cir.), cert. denied, 400 U.S. 831 (1970); Matrix Essentials v. Emporium Drug Mart, 988 F.2d 587, 594 (5th Cir. 1993). Both decisions upheld restraints that limited the sale of a manufacturer's beauty products to licensed salons.
22. See Areeda and Hovenkamp, 8 *Antitrust Law,* note 3, at ¶1648d.
23. E.g., Ezzo's Investments v. Royal Beauty Supply, 243 F.3d 980 (6th Cir.), cert. denied, 534 U.S. 993 (2001), concluding that the defendant's policy of supplying its beauty products only to stores that obtained most of their revenue from hair care services rather than product sales was a nonprice restraint.
24. This is one reading of the facts of United States v. General Motors Corp., 384 U.S. 127, 146 (1966).
25. E.g., J. Truett Payne Co. v. Chrysler Motors Corp., 451 U.S. 557, 562 (1981). See also Reeder-Simco GMC, Inc. v. Volvo GM Heavy Truck Corp., 374 F.3d 701 (8th Cir. 2004), cert. granted, 125 S. Ct. 1596 (2005), which the Supreme Court has promised to review.
26. On the history, basic structure, and application of the Robinson-Patman Act, see 14 Herbert Hovenkamp, *Antitrust Law,* ch. 23 (2d ed., New York: Aspen, 2006). Package discounts are discussed in Chapter 7 and also in 10 Phillip E. Areeda and Herbert Hovenkamp, *Antitrust Law* ¶1758 (2d ed., New York: Aspen, 2004).
27. See, e.g., Portland 76 Auto/Truck Plaza, Inc. v. Union Oil Co. of California, 153 F.3d 938 (9th Cir. 1998), cert. denied, 526 U.S. 1064 (1999) (franchisor spent substantial monies to refurbish more successful truck stop but not less successful one).
28. See Hovenkamp, 14 *Antitrust Law,* note 26, at ¶¶2301b, 2312.
29. Chroma Lighting v. GTE Products Corp., 111 F.3d 653, 654 (9th Cir.), cert. denied, 522 U.S. 943 (1997) (emphasis added), which was relying on FTC v. Morton Salt, 334 U.S. 37, 46–47 (1948).
30. See H.R. Rep. No. 2287, pt. 1, 74th Cong., 2d Sess., at 8 (1936) (emphasis added): "This provision accomplishes a substantial broadening of a similar clause now contained in section 2 of the Clayton Act. The existing law has in practice been too restrictive in requiring a showing of general injury to competitive conditions in the line of commerce concerned, whereas the more immediately important concern is in injury to the competitor victim-

ized by the discrimination. *Only through such injury in fact can the larger, general injury result.*" See Herbert Hovenkamp, "The Robinson-Patman Act and Competition: Unfinished Business," 68 *Antitrust L.J.* 125 (2000).

31. A few examples include the Report of the Attorney General's National Committee to Study the Antitrust Laws 155–221 (1955); United States Dep't of Justice, Report on the Robinson-Patman Act (1977); Hugh C. Hansen, "Robinson-Patman Law: A Review and Analysis," 51 *Fordham L. Rev.* 1113 (1983); Richard A. Posner, *The Robinson-Patman Act: Federal Regulation of Price Differences* (Washington, D.C.: AEI, 1976); William Baxter, "A Parable," 23 *Stan. L. Rev.* 973 (1971); Hovenkamp, "Unfinished Business," note 30.

32. George Haug Co. v. Rolls Royce Motor Cars, 148 F.3d 136, 143 (2d Cir. 1998), quoting Coastal Fuels of Puerto Rico v. Caribbean Petroleum Co., 79 F.3d 182 (1st Cir.), cert. denied, 519 U.S. 927 (1996).

33. See the next chapter.

34. See the quotation from the House Report in note 30.

35. Statement of H. B. Teegarden, counsel for the United States Wholesale Grocers Association, who acted as Representative Patman's "right-hand man" as drafter, explainer, and analyst for the congressional hearings. Hearings on H.R. 4995, H.R. 5062, and H.R. 8442, Before the House Comm. on the Judiciary, 74th Cong., 1st Sess. 217 (1935). On Teegarden's role in the drafting of the statute, see Frederick M. Rowe, *Price Discrimination under the Robinson-Patman Act* 11–12 & n.38 (Boston: Little, Brown, 1962).

36. See H.R. Rep. No. 2287, note 30, at 17, continuing: ". . . and whether those economies are from more orderly processes of manufacture, or from the elimination of unnecessary salesmen, unnecessary travel expense, unnecessary warehousing, unnecessary truck or other forms of delivery, or other such causes—none of them are in the remotest degree disturbed by this bill."

37. On the historical concern with the buying power of powerful retailers, see Federal Trade Commission, Final Report on the Chain-Store Investigation, S. Doc. No. 4, 74th Cong., 1st Sess. (1935); Hovenkamp, 14 *Antitrust Law*, note 26, at ¶2302.

38. Falls City Indus. v. Vanco Beverage, 460 U.S. 428, 436 (1983). While the Robinson-Patman Act contains a buyer liability provision, the Supreme Court has made actions against buyers almost impossible to prove. See Great Atl. & Pac. Tea Co. v. FTC (A&P), 440 U.S. 69, 75–76 (1979); and Hovenkamp, 14 *Antitrust Law*, note 26, at ¶2361.

39. United States v. American Can Co., 230 F. 859 (D. Md. 1916), appeal dismissed, 256 U.S. 706 (1921). More recently, see United States v. Dentsply Int'l, 399 F.2d 181 (3d Cir. 2005).

40. See 9 Phillip E. Areeda and Herbert Hovenkamp, *Antitrust Law* ¶1720 (2d ed., New York: Aspen, 2004). On the highly technical "separate product" requirement, see 10, id., at ¶¶1741–1751 (2d ed. 2004).
41. Siegel v. Chicken Delight, 448 F.2d 43 (9th Cir. 1971), cert. denied, 405 U.S. 955 (1972).
42. Jefferson Parish Hosp. Dist. No. 2 v. Hyde, 466 U.S. 2 (1984).
43. Carbice Corp. v. American Patents Development Corp., 283 U.S. 27, 31–32 (1931).
44. Queen City Pizza v. Domino's Pizza, 124 F.3d 430 (3d Cir. 1997), cert. denied, 523 U.S. 1059 (1998) (pre-made pizza dough); *Siegel,* note 41, 448 F.2d at 46–47 (napkins, paper plates, spices); Collins v. International Dairy Queen, 980 F. Supp. 1252 (M.D. Ga. 1997) (Oreo cookies).
45. E.g., Subsolutions v. Doctor's Assocs., 62 F. Supp. 2d 616 (D. Conn. 1999) (tying of computerized cash register system for Subway franchisees).

Chapter 9. The National Policy on Business Mergers

1. See 4, 4A, and 5 Phillip E. Areeda and Herbert Hovenkamp, *Antitrust Law,* ch. 9 (horizontal mergers), ch. 10 (vertical mergers), and ch. 11 (conglomerate mergers) (2d ed., New York: Aspen, 2003, 2006).
2. United States v. General Dynamics Corp., 415 U.S. 486 (1974).
3. Agostini v. Felton, 521 U.S. 203, 237 (1997).
4. United States v. General Dynamics Corp., 415 U.S. 486 (1974); United States v. Phillipsburg Nat'l Bank & Trust Co., 399 U.S. 350 (1970).
5. The Rehnquist Court has addressed issues of private plaintiff standing and remedies in Cargill, Inc. v. Monfort of Colorado, Inc., 479 U.S. 104 (1986), and California v. American Stores Co., 495 U.S. 271 (1990). Neither case addressed merger standards or decided whether the merger at issue was anticompetitive.
6. United States v. Von's Grocery Co., 384 U.S. 270 (1966).
7. United States v. Brown Shoe Co., 179 F. Supp. 721, 738 (E.D. Mo. 1959), aff'd, 370 U.S. 294 (1962) (emphasis added).
8. Brief for Respondent at 60, 62–63, 74, In re Procter & Gamble, 63 F.T.C. 1465 (1963), quoted in Alan A. Fisher and Robert H. Lande, "Efficiency Considerations in Merger Enforcement," 71 *Cal. L. Rev.* 1580, 1582 & n.5 (1983).
9. Robert H. Bork, *The Antitrust Paradox: A Policy at War with Itself* 200–201 (New York: Basic Books, 1978).
10. United States v. Columbia Steel Co., 334 U.S. 495 (1948).
11. The current (1992) Horizontal Merger Guidelines are reprinted as Appendix A in the annual supplement to Phillip E. Areeda and Herbert Hovenkamp, *Antitrust Law.* All earlier Guidelines are collected in 4

Trade Reg. Rep. ¶¶13,101 et seq. (Chicago: Commerce Clearing House, 2005).

12. See FTC, Merger Challenges Data, Fiscal Years 1999–2003, available at *www.ftc.gov.* One recent exception is FTC v. Arch Coal, 329 F. Supp. 2d 109 (D.D.C. 2004), dismissed, 2004 WL 2066879 (D.C. Cir. Sept. 15, 2004, unpublished), where the court rejected a merger challenge after concluding that market concentration was just barely above the Guidelines' thresholds for illegality.

13. FTC v. H. J. Heinz Co., 116 F. Supp. 2d 190, 196 (D.D.C. 2000), rev'd on other grounds, 248 F.3d 708 (D.C. Cir. 2001).

14. Derek Bok, "Section 7 of the Clayton Act and the Merging of Law and Economics," 74 *Harv. L. Rev.* 226, 228 (1960).

15. Northern Securities Co. v. United States, 193 U.S. 197 (1904).

16. See, e.g., United States v. Interstate Bakers Corp., 1996-1 Trade Cas. ¶71,272, at 76,190 (N.D. Ill. 1995) (approving consent decree predicated on this theory). The theory is explained in more detail in Herbert Hovenkamp, *Federal Antitrust Policy: The Law of Competition and Its Practice* §12.3d (3d ed., St. Paul, Minn.: West Group, 2005).

17. For further discussion, see the excellent symposium in 5 *Geo. Mason L. Rev.* (1997). See also Jon Baker, "Unilateral Competitive Effects Theories in Merger Analysis," 11 *Antitrust* 21 (Spring 1997); Carl Shapiro, "Mergers with Differentiated Products," 10 *Antitrust* 23, 24 (Spring 1996); Christopher A. Vellturo, "Evaluating Mergers with Differentiated Products," 11 *Antitrust* 16 (Spring 1997).

18. See Edward J. Lopez, "New Anti-Merger Theories: A Critique," 20 *Cato Journal* no. 3 (Winter 2001).

19. The government's recent loss in the *Oracle* software merger case cited many of these critiques and will very likely force the government to rethink its unilateral effects policy. See United States v. Oracle Corp., 331 F. Supp. 2d 1098, 1116–1123 (N.D. Cal. 2004).

20. Oliver E. Williamson, "Economies as an Antitrust Defense: The Welfare Tradeoffs," 58 *Am. Econ. Rev.* 18 (1968).

21. This is roughly Judge Posner's position. See Richard A. Posner, *Antitrust Law* 133 (2d ed., Chicago: University of Chicago Press, 2001).

22. See Areeda and Hovenkamp, 4A *Antitrust Law,* note 1, ch. 9E.

23. The Government's Merger Guidelines take a similar position. Guidelines, note 11, at §4.0.

24. See Dimitri Giotakos, Laurent Petit, Gaelle Garnier, and Peter De Luyck, "*General Electric/Honeywell*—An Insight into the Commission's Investigation and Decision," 3 *EU Competition Policy Newsletter* 5, 10 (Oct. 2001). For the view of the Antitrust Division, stating the "throwback" conclusion,

see United States Dep't of Justice, Antitrust Division Submission for OECD Roundtable on Portfolio Effects in Conglomerate Mergers: Range Effects—The United States Perspective (10-12-2001), available at *http://www.usdoj.gov/atr/public/international/9550.pdf.*

One of the "throwback" decisions is Allis Chalmers Mfg. Co. v. White Consolidated Indus., 414 F.2d 506, 515–518 (3d Cir. 1969), cert. denied, 396 U.S. 1009 (1970) (condemning merger of firm that produced steel rolling mills and firm that made the electrical "harness," or hookup, for such mills, on theory that merger would give the firm a competitive advantage over rivals and raise entry barriers into rolling mill market).

25. FTC v. H. J. Heinz Co., 248 F.3d 708 (D.C. Cir. 2001).
26. The Guidelines note that "efficiencies are most likely to make a difference in merger analysis when the likely adverse competition effects, absent the efficiencies, are not great." Merger Guidelines, note 11, at §4.0.

Part III. Regulation, Innovation, and Connectivity

1. See Herbert Hovenkamp, *Enterprise and American Law, 1836–1937,* at chs. 10–13 (Cambridge, Mass.: Harvard University Press, 1991); William J. Novak, *The People's Welfare: Law and Regulation in Nineteenth-Century America* (Chapel Hill: University of North Carolina Press, 1996).
2. Henry v. A. B. Dick Co., 224 U.S. 1 (1912); Motion Picture Patents Co. v. Universal Film Mfg. Co., 243 U.S. 502 (1917). See Chapter 11.
3. United States v. Trans-Missouri Freight Ass'n, 166 U.S. 290 (1897).

Chapter 10. Antitrust under Regulation and Deregulation

1. See Richard H. K. Vietor, *Contrived Competition: Regulation and Deregulation in America* (Cambridge, Mass.: Harvard University Press, 1994).
2. See Judge Posner's lament that economic history has largely disappeared from the study of economics. Richard A. Posner, *Overcoming Law* 411 (Cambridge, Mass.: Harvard University Press, 1995).
3. See Jim Chen, "Regulatory Education and Its Reform," 16 *Yale J. Reg.* 145, 147–148 (1999) (book review); James Willard Hurst, *Law and Markets in United States History* 21 (Madison: University of Wisconsin Press, 1982).
4. George J. Stigler, "The Economics of Information," 69 *J. Pol. Econ.* 213 (1961).
5. On this point, see Steven P. Croley, "Theories of Regulation: Incorporating the Administrative Process," 98 *Colum. L. Rev.* 1 (1998).
6. See Herbert Hovenkamp, *Enterprise and American Law, 1836–1937* (Cambridge, Mass.: Harvard University Press, 1991).

7. On the history of regulatory policy, see John McMillan, *Reinventing the Bazaar: The Natural History of Markets* (New York: Norton, 2002); Vietor, *Contrived Competition,* note 1; Claudia Goldin and Gary D. Libecap, eds., *The Regulated Economy: A Historical Approach to Political Economy* (Chicago: University of Chicago Press, 1994); Herbert Hovenkamp, "The Rise of Regulated Industry," in *Enterprise and American Law,* note 6, at 105–170; Herbert Hovenkamp, "Regulatory Conflict in the Gilded Age: Federalism and the Railroad Problem," 97 *Yale L.J.* 1017 (1988); Thomas K. McCraw, *Prophets of Regulation* (Cambridge, Mass.: Harvard University Press, 1984); Stephen Breyer, *Regulation and Its Reform* (Cambridge, Mass.: Harvard University Press, 1982); Harold U. Faulkner, *The Decline of Laissez Faire, 1897–1917* (New York: Harper & Row, 1951).

8. See 1 Phillip E. Areeda and Herbert Hovenkamp, *Antitrust Law* ¶¶221–227 (2d ed., New York: Aspen, 2000).

9. See Herbert Hovenkamp, "Antitrust Violations in Securities Markets," 28 *J. Corp. L.* 607 (2003).

10. See Parker v. Brown, 317 U.S. 341 (1943) (state regulation); Community Communications Co. v. City of Boulder, 455 U.S. 40 (1982) (municipal regulation).

11. 15 U.S.C. §17. See 1A Phillip E. Areeda and Herbert Hovenkamp, *Antitrust Law* ¶¶255–257 (2d ed., New York: Aspen, 2000).

12. Stock Exchanges Options Trading Antitrust Litigation, 317 F.3d 134 (2d Cir. 2003).

13. See, e.g., Fisher v. City of Berkeley, 475 U.S. 115 (1986) (upholding rent control ordinance); California Retail Liquor Dealers Ass'n v. Midcal Aluminum, 445 U.S. 97 (1980) (liquor pricing); 324 Liquor Corp. v. Duffy, 479 U.S. 335 (1987) (posting of liquor prices); Southern Motor Carriers Rate Conference v. United States, 471 U.S. 48 (1985) (intrastate trucking); Town of Hallie v. City of Eau Claire, 471 U.S. 34 (1985) (sewage treatment); Community Communications Co. v. City of Boulder, 455 U.S. 40 (1982) (cable television); Campbell v. City of Chicago, 823 F.2d 1182 (7th Cir. 1987) (taxicabs); City of Columbia & Columbia Outdoor Advertising v. Omni Outdoor Advertising, 499 U.S. 365 (1991) (billboards); Ambulance Serv. of Reno v. Nevada Ambulance Servs., 819 F.2d 910 (9th Cir. 1987) (ambulance); FTC v. Ticor Title Ins. Co., 504 U.S. 621 (1992) (insurance).

14. On the two requirements, see *Midcal Aluminum,* note 13. The authorization requirement was developed more fully in *Southern Motor Carriers,* note 13, and the active supervision requirement in *Ticor Title,* note 13; Patrick v. Burget, 486 U.S. 94 (1988). See Areeda and Hovenkamp, 1 *Antitrust Law,* note 8, at ¶¶224–225 (authorization); id. at ¶¶226–227 (supervision).

15. E.g., *Columbia Outdoor Advertising,* note 13 (immunizing city council's passage of regulatory provision that favored signs of politically well-connected business owner while excluding those of competitor).

16. Eastern R.R. Presidents Conference v. Noerr Motor Freight, 365 U.S. 127 (1961); United Mine Workers v. Pennington, 381 U.S. 657 (1965).

17. In addition to the *Noerr* and *Pennington* cases cited above, see *Columbia Outdoor Advertising,* note 13.

18. E.g., Kottle v. Northwest Kidney Centers, 146 F.3d 1056 (9th Cir. 1998), cert. denied, 525 U.S. 1140 (1999).

19. On "sham" petitioning, see California Motor Transport Co. v. Trucking Unlimited, 404 U.S. 508 (1972); and Areeda and Hovenkamp, 1 *Antitrust Law,* note 8, at ¶¶204–208.

20. See Alfred E. Kahn, "Deregulation: Looking Backward and Looking Forward," 7 *Yale J. Reg.* 325 (1990); Stephen Breyer, "Antitrust, Deregulation, and the Newly Liberated Marketplace," 75 *Cal. L. Rev.* 1005 (1987); Thomas G. Krattenmaker, "Implications of Deregulation for Antitrust Policy," 53 *Antitrust L.J.* 211 (1984). For history, see E. Sanders, "The Regulatory Surge of the 1970s in Historical Perspective," in *Public Regulation: New Perspectives on Institutions and Policies* (Elizabeth Bailey, ed., Cambridge, Mass.: MIT Press, 1987); Richard D. Cudahy, "The Folklore of Deregulation (With Apologies to Thurman Arnold)," 15 *Yale J. Reg.* 427 (1998). On overall effects, see Richard A. Posner, "The Effects of Deregulation on Competition: The Experience of the United States," 23 *Fordham Int'l L.J.* 7 (2000).

21. On telecommunications, see Peter W. Huber, Michael K. Kellogg, and John Thorne, *Federal Telecommunications Law,* ch. 1 (2d ed., New York: Aspen, 1999); Jerry A. Hausman and J. Gregory Sidak, "A Consumer Welfare Approach to the Mandatory Unbundling of Telecommunications Networks," 109 *Yale L.J.* 417 (1997). On electric power, see Michael O. Wise, "Overview: Deregulation and Antitrust in the Electric Power Industry," 64 *Antitrust L.J.* 267 (1996); Lee A. Rau, "Open Access in the Power Industry: Competition, Cooperation, and Policy Dilemmas," 64 *Antitrust L.J.* 279 (1996); Herbert Hovenkamp, "The Takings Clause and Improvident Regulatory Bargains," 108 *Yale L.J.* 801 (1997).

22. Interestingly, this critique was developed both by writers on the political left and the right. E.g., Gabriel Kolko, *Railroads and Regulation, 1877–1916* (Princeton, N.J.: Princeton University Press, 1965) (New Left); George J. Stigler, "The Theory of Economic Regulation," 2 *Bell J. Econ. & Mgmt. Sci.* 3 (1971) (Chicago School).

23. E.g. Harvey Averch and Leland L. Johnson, "Behavior of the Firm under Regulatory Constraint," 52 *Am. Econ. Rev.* 1052 (1962).

24. James M. Landis, *The Administrative Process* (New Haven, Conn.: Yale Uni-

versity Press, 1938); James M. Landis, "Report on Regulatory Agencies to the President-Elect" (G.P.O. 1960). See Morton J. Horwitz, *The Transformation of American Law: The Crisis of Legal Orthodoxy, 1880–1960,* at 241 (New York: Oxford University Press, 1992). Landis had been a member of the Federal Trade Commission (1933–1934) and chair of the Securities and Exchange Commission (1935–1937), as well as dean of Harvard Law School (1937–1946). He later served as Special Counsel to President Kennedy.

25. James Buchanan and Gordon Tullock, *The Calculus of Consent* (Ann Arbor: University of Michigan Press, 1962); Mancur Olson, *The Logic of Collective Action: Public Goods and the Theory of Groups* (Cambridge, Mass.: Harvard University Press, 1965; 2d ed., 1971). A good survey of the literature on public choice is Daniel A. Farber and Philip P. Frickey, *Law and Public Choice: A Critical Introduction* (Chicago: University of Chicago Press, 1991).

26. See Herbert Hovenkamp, "Judicial Restraint and Constitutional Federalism: The Supreme Court's *Lopez* and *Seminole Tribe* Decisions," 96 *Colum. L. Rev.* 2213 (1996).

27. See Herbert Hovenkamp, "Legislation, Well-Being, and Public Choice," 57 *U. Chi. L. Rev.* 63, 99 (1990).

28. E.g., FTC v. Ticor Title Ins. Co., 504 U.S. 621 (1992).

29. See W. Viscusi, J. Vernon, and J. Harrington, *Economics of Regulation and Antitrust,* chs. 10–12 (4th ed., Cambridge, Mass.: MIT Press, 2005).

30. See Averch and Johnson, "Behavior of the Firm," note 23.

31. See Frank M. Machovec, *Perfect Competition and the Transformation of Economics* (London: Routledge, 1995); George J. Stigler, "Perfect Competition, Historically Contemplated," 65 *J. Pol. Econ.* 1 (1957).

32. The voluminous literature on "contestability" includes William J. Baumol, John C. Panzar, and Robert D. Willig, *Contestable Markets and the Theory of Industry Structure* (San Diego, Calif.: Harcourt Brace Jovanovich, 1982); Joseph F. Brodley, "Antitrust Policy under Deregulation: Airline Mergers and the Theory of Contestable Markets," 61 *Boston U. L. Rev.* 823 (1981); Harold Demsetz, "Why Regulate Utilities?" 11 *J.L. & Econ.* 55 (1968). For a critique, see William G. Shepherd, "'Contestability' vs. Competition," 74 *Am. Econ. Rev.* 572 (1984).

33. The classic piece on this problem is Oliver E. Williamson, "Franchise Bidding for Natural Monopolies—in General and with Respect to CATV," 7 *Bell J. Econ. & Mgmt. Sci.* 73 (1976).

34. See Elizabeth E. Bailey and John C. Panzar, "The Contestability of Airline Markets during the Transition to Deregulation," 44 *L. &. Contemp. Probs.* 125 (1981); David R. Graham, D. P. Kaplan, and David S. Sibley,

"Efficiency and Competition in the Airline Industry," 14 *Bell J. Econ. & Mgmt. Sci.* 118 (1983).

35. See Areeda and Hovenkamp, 1A *Antitrust Law*, note 11, at ¶251i. On the antitrust impact of deregulation in various industries, see id. at ¶241.
36. See Huber, Kellogg, and Thorne, *Federal Telecommunications Law*, note 21, at §1.3.
37. See Hush-A-Phone Corp. v. United States, 238 F.2d 266, 268 (D.C. Cir. 1956); Use of the Carterphone Device in Message Toll Telephone Servs., 13 F.C.C.2d 420, recon. denied, 14 F.C.C.2d 571 (1968). On the gradual demise of the AT&T monopoly, see Gerald W. Brock, *The Telecommunications Industry: The Dynamics of Market Structure,* ch. 9 (Cambridge, Mass.: Harvard University Press, 1981); Walter G. Bolter et al., *Transition to Competition: Telecommunications Policy for the 1980s* (Englewood Cliffs, N.J.: Prentice Hall, 1984); Philip L. Cantelon, *The History of MCI: The Early Years* (Dallas, Tex.: Heritage Press, 1993).
38. See United States v. AT&T, 552 F. Supp. 131, 143 (D.D.C. 1982), aff'd sub nom. Maryland v. United States, 460 U.S. 1001 (1983), which gave the Bell Operating Companies control over the local hardwired monopoly but denied them the right to engage in any "non-monopoly business."
39. See Huber, Kellogg, and Thorne, *Federal Telecommunications Law*, note 21, at §10.4.2.
40. See J. Gregory Sidak, "The Failure of Good Intentions: The Worldcom Fraud and the Collapse of American Telecommunications after Deregulation," 20 *Yale J. Reg.* 207 (2003); Jerry A. Hausman and J. Gregory Sidak, "A Consumer-Welfare Approach to the Mandatory Unbundling of Telecommunications Networks," 109 *Yale L.J.* 417 (1999).
41. Verizon Communications, Inc. v. Law Offices of Curtis Trinko, LLP, 540 U.S. 398 (2004).
42. The interconnection dispute arose on December 9, 1999, and was resolved by an FCC-approved consent decree in March of 2000, about three months later. Order, Bell Atlantic-New York Authorization, 15 F.C.C.R. 5413, 5416 (2000).
43. This was a significant error the Ninth Circuit made in Eastman Kodak Co. v. Image Technical Servs., 125 F.3d 1195 (9th Cir. 1997), cert. denied, 523 U.S. 1094 (1998). The court ordered Kodak to supply all repair parts to independent service organizations even though most of the parts were readily obtainable from other sources.
44. E.g., Delaware & Hudson Ry. Co. v. Consolidated Rail Corp., 902 F.2d 174 (2d Cir. 1990), cert. denied, 500 U.S. 928 (1991) (railroad track); Consolidated Gas Co. of Florida, Inc. v. City Gas Co. of Florida, 880 F.2d 297 (11th Cir. 1989) (gas pipeline); Fishman v. Wirtz, 807 F.2d 520, 539 (7th

Cir. 1986) (stadium); Hecht v. Pro-Football, 570 F.2d 982 (D.C. Cir. 1977), cert. denied, 436 U.S. 956 (1978) (stadium).

45. My own views are elaborated in 3A Phillip E. Areeda and Herbert Hovenkamp, *Antitrust Law* ¶771b, c (2d ed., New York: Aspen, 2003).

46. Aspen Skiing Co. v. Aspen Highlands Skiing Corp., 472 U.S. 585 (1985).

47. Otter Tail Power Co. v. United States, 410 U.S. 366 (1973).

Chapter 11. The Conflict between Antitrust and Intellectual Property Rights

1. United States Constitution, art. 1, §8.

2. Robert P. Merges, "One Hundred Years of Solicitude: Intellectual Property Law, 1900–2000," 88 *Cal. L. Rev.* 2187, 2223 (2000).

3. See, e.g., William M. Landes and Richard A. Posner, *The Economic Structure of Intellectual Property Law* (Cambridge, Mass.: Harvard University Press, 2003) at 220–221 (copyright), 407–415 (generally). Landes and Posner believe that copyright has produced the most instances of legislative capture. They also believe, id. at 417, that judge-made rules in IP law tend to be more public-regarding than legislatively created rules. On overuse of the patent system as stifling innovation, see Adam B. Jaffe and Josh Lerner, *Innovation and Its Discontents: How Our Broken Patent System Is Endangering Innovation and Progress, and What to Do about It* (Princeton, N.J.: Princeton University Press, 2005).

4. Eldred v. Ashcroft, 537 U.S. 186 (2003).

5. William F. Patry, "Copyright and the Legislative Process: A Personal Perspective," 14 *Cardozo Arts & Ent. L.J.* 139, 141 (1996). For good historical perspectives on special interest control of IP legislation, see Merges, "One Hundred Years of Solicitude," note 2; Siva Vaidhyanathan, *Copyrights and Copywrongs: The Rise of Intellectual Property and How It Threatens Creativity* (New York: New York University Press, 2001). See also Jessica D. Litman, *Digital Copyright* 1–10 (Amherst, N.Y.: Prometheus Books, 2001), who notes that in copyright there is a long history of permitting the principal market participants to draft legislative amendments.

6. See the discussion of public choice in the previous chapter, and Daniel A. Farber and Philip P. Frickey, *Law and Public Choice: A Critical Introduction* (Chicago: University of Chicago Press, 1991).

7. Cf. Dan L. Burk and Mark A. Lemley, "Policy Levers in Patent Law," 89 *Va. L. Rev.* 1575 (2003) (skeptical of different terms of coverage in different industries); Landes and Posner, *Economic Structure of Intellectual Property Law,* note 3, at 296–297, 314–315 (pharmaceutical patents); Richard Gilbert and Carl Shapiro, "Optimal Patent Length and Breadth," 21 *Rand J. Econ.* 106 (1990).

8. See William M. Landes and Richard A. Posner, "Indefinitely Renewable Copyright," 70 *U. Chi. L. Rev.* 471, 490 (2003). On the copyrightability of colorized black-and-white movies, see 37 C.F.R. §202.

9. Jared Diamond, *Guns, Germs, and Steel: The Fates of Human Societies* 244–245 (New York: W. W. Norton, 1997). Making similar arguments in the context of copyright is Siva Vaidhyanathan, *Copyrights and Copywrongs,* note 5.

10. For generally pessimistic views, see Lawrence Lessig, *The Future of Ideas: The Fate of the Commons in a Connected World* (New York: Random House, 2001); and Lawrence Lessig, "The Death of Cyberspace," 57 *Wash. & Lee L. Rev.* 337 (2000). Other good literature includes Robert P. Merges, "Intellectual Property Rights and the New Institutional Economics," 53 *Vand. L. Rev.* 1857 (2000); Michael A. Heller, "The Boundaries of Private Property," 108 *Yale L.J.* 1163 (1999); Michael A. Heller and Rebecca S. Eisenberg, "Can Patents Deter Innovation? The Anticommons in Biomedical Research," 280 *Science* 698 (1998); Michael A. Heller, "The Tragedy of Anticommons: Property in the Transition from Marx to Market," 111 *Harv. L. Rev.* 621, 621 (1998).

11. SCM Corp. v. Xerox Corp., 645 F.2d 1195, 1203 (2d Cir. 1981).

12. See 1 Herbert Hovenkamp, Mark D. Janis, and Mark A. Lemley, *IP and Antitrust: An Analysis of Antitrust Principles Applied to Intellectual Property Law,* chs. 1, 2 (New York: Aspen, 2002); Louis Kaplow, "The Patent-Antitrust Intersection: A Reappraisal," 97 *Harv. L. Rev.* 1813 (1984).

13. Bement v. National Harrow Co., 186 U.S. 70, 93 (1902).

14. United States v. General Electric Co., 272 U.S. 476 (1926).

15. See, e.g., Ethyl Gasoline Corp. v. United States, 309 U.S. 436 (1940) (patentee of Ethyl antiknock compound could not fix the price of gasoline containing the compound); Hovenkamp, Janis, and Lemley, 1 *IP and Antitrust,* note 12, at §§24.1c, 24.2d.

16. See, e.g., Cummer-Graham Co. v. Straight Side Basket Corp., 142 F.2d 646, 647 (5th Cir.), cert. denied, 323 U.S. 726 (1944) (patentee of basket-making machine part could not fix price of unpatented baskets made with the machine); American Equip. Co. v. Tuthill Bldg. Material Co., 69 F.2d 406 (7th Cir. 1934) (condemning agreement among brick makers fixing the price of unpatented brick made with patented brick-making machine).

17. On this point, see Landes and Posner, *Economic Structure of Intellectual Property Law,* note 3, at 384.

18. 35 U.S.C. §261. See Hovenkamp, Janis, and Lemley, 1 *IP and Antitrust,* note 12, at ch. 33.

19. See Landes and Posner, *Economic Structure of Intellectual Property Law,* note 3, at 383.

20. The fact that so few vertical agreements are anticompetitive explains

why the perceived "conflict" between antitrust and copyright is so much smaller than that between antitrust and patent. Except in the market for computer software, infringers of copyrights are much less frequently competitors of the holder. Most copyright licensing agreements are between suppliers and users rather than between competitors.

21. Dr. Miles Medical Co. v. John D. Park & Sons Co., 220 U.S. 373, 400–401 (1911).

22. Bobbs-Merrill Co. v. Straus, 210 U.S. 339, 350 (1908).

23. See, e.g., Bowers v. Baystate Technologies, 320 F.3d 1317 (Fed. Cir.), cert. denied, 539 U.S. 928 (2003); ProCD, Inc. v. Zeidenberg, 86 F.3d 1447, 39 U.S.P.Q.2d 1161 (7th Cir. 1996); Justin Graham, "Preserving the Aftermarket in Copyrighted Works: Adapting the First Sale Doctrine to the Emerging Technological Landscape," 2002 *Stan. Tech. L. Rev.* 1.

24. On the history of the close relation between tying law and patent licensing policy, see 9 Phillip E. Areeda and Herbert Hovenkamp, *Antitrust Law* ¶1701 (2d ed., New York: Aspen, 2004); 10, id., at ¶¶1781–1782.

25. In 1988 Congress amended the Patent Act to make clear that patent ties were not patent misuse unless the patentee had market power. 35 U.S.C. §271d.

26. Henry v. A. B. Dick Co., 224 U.S. 1 (1912); Motion Picture Patents Co. v. Universal Film Mfg. Co., 243 U.S. 502 (1917). See Michael Conant, *Antitrust in the Motion Picture Industry* 16–21, 77–80 (Berkeley: University of California Press, 1960); Lewis Jacobs, *The Rise of the American Film: A Critical History* 8, 81–85, 88, 164–165, 291–292 (New York: Harcourt, Brace, 1939).

27. Carbice Corp. of Am. v. American Patents Development Corp., 283 U.S. 27 (1931).

28. E.g., International Salt Co. v. United States, 332 U.S. 392 (1947).

29. See United States v. Loew's, 371 U.S. 38 (1962) (copyrighted movie); Siegel v. Chicken Delight, Inc., 448 F.2d 43 (9th Cir. 1971), cert. denied, 405 U.S. 955 (1972) (trademark).

30. Recently the Federal Circuit noted the severe criticism but felt constrained by Supreme Court precedent to adhere to the presumption. Independent Ink, Inc. v. Illinois Tool Works, Inc., 396 F.3d 1342 (Fed. Cir. 2005), cert. granted, 125 S.Ct. 2937 (2005). For critiques of the presumption, see Areeda and Hovenkamp, 9 *Antitrust Law*, note 24, at ¶1720; Herbert Hovenkamp, *Federal Antitrust Policy: The Law of Competition and Its Practice* §10.3 (3d ed., St. Paul, Minn.: Thomson/West, 2005).

31. See 9 *Antitrust Law*, note 24, at ¶1711; Landes and Posner, *Economic Structure of Intellectual Property Law*, note 3, at 374–376. For a contrary view, see Edmund W. Kitch, "Elementary and Persistent Errors in the Eco-

nomic Analysis of Intellectual Property," 53 *Vand. L. Rev.* 1727, 1734–1735 (2000).

32. See Queen City Pizza v. Domino's Pizza, 124 F.3d 430 (3d Cir. 1997), cert. denied, 523 U.S. 1059 (1998), which refused to condemn Domino's pizza dough tie.

33. United States v. Microsoft Corp., 253 F.3d 34, 84–90 (D.C. Cir.), cert. denied, 534 U.S. 952 (2001).

34. See Areeda and Hovenkamp, 10 *Antitrust Law,* note 24, at ¶¶1744–1745.

35. *Microsoft,* note 33. On tying, see 253 F.3d at 84–90. On "commingling" of Windows and Internet Explorer code as unlawful monopolization, see id. at 65–67.

36. Automatic Radio Mfg. Co. v. Hazeltine Research, Inc., 339 U.S. 827, 831 (1950).

37. See BMI, Inc. v. Moor-Law, Inc., 527 F. Supp. 758, 767–768 (D. Del. 1981), which approved the blanket license. On BMI, see *www.BMI.com.*

38. United States v. Loew's, 371 U.S. 38 (1962); United States v. Paramount Pictures, 334 U.S. 131, 156–159 (1948). The lower courts have condemned block booking as recently as 1999. MCA Television Limited v. Public Interest Corp., 171 F.3d 1265 (11th Cir. 1999). See F. Andrew Hanssen, "The Block Booking of Films Reexamined," 43 *J.L. & Econ.* 395 (2000).

39. The practice is described in United States v. Microsoft, 56 F.3d 1448, 1451 (D.C. Cir. 1995).

40. Walker Process Equip. v. Food Machinery & Chem. Corp., 382 U.S. 172 (1965). More recently, see Nobelpharma v. Implant Innovations, 141 F.3d 1059 (Fed. Cir.), cert. denied, 525 U.S. 876 (1998) (patent infringement). See also Professional Real Estate Investors v. Columbia Pictures Indus., 508 U.S. 49 (1993) (copyright infringement).

41. California Motor Transport v. Trucking Unlimited, 404 U.S. 508 (1972) (frivolous objections to rivals' requests for operating license); Clipper Exxpress v. Rocky Mountain Motor Tariff Bureau, 690 F.2d 1240, 1254 (9th Cir. 1982), cert. denied, 459 U.S. 1227 (1983) (similar); Kottle v. Northwest Kidney Centers, 146 F.3d 1056 (9th Cir. 1998), cert. denied, 525 U.S. 1140 (1999) (false information in Certificate of Need proceeding); St. Joseph's Hosp. v. Hospital Corp. of Am., 795 F.2d 948, 955 (11th Cir. 1986) (similar). See the discussion of the *Noerr-Pennington* doctrine in Chapter 10.

42. One modest qualification is the essential facility doctrine discussed in the previous chapter.

43. See 35 U.S.C. §271d. A 1970 amendment to the Clean Air Act, 42 U.S.C. §7608, does provide that the Attorney General can seek judicially supervised compulsory licensing of patented technology necessary to achieve

clean air standards, where such licensing might be needed to avoid giving the patentee a monopoly. The provision has never been used.

44. E.g., Beanstalk Group, Inc. v. AM General Corp., 283 F.3d 856, 861 (7th Cir. 2002) ("a trademark is an identifier, not a freestanding piece of intellectual property; hence the rule that a trademark cannot be sold in gross, that is, without the assets that create the product that it identifies").

45. Eastman Kodak Co. v. Image Technical Servs., 125 F.3d 1195, 1218–1219 (9th Cir. 1997), cert. denied, 523 U.S. 1094 (1998).

46. The Supreme Court's recent decision in Verizon Communications, Inc. v. Law Offices of Curtis Trinko, LLP, 540 U.S. 398 (2004), severely narrowed the essential facility doctrine but refused to abolish it.

47. See United States v. AT&T, 552 F. Supp. 131, 136 (D.D.C. 1982), aff'd mem. sub nom. Maryland v. United States, 460 U.S. 1001 (1983), discussed in Chapter 10, which required AT&T to license its many patents and copyrights to the spun-off companies. See also 3 Phillip E. Areeda and Herbert Hovenkamp, *Antitrust Law* ¶710 (2d ed., New York: Aspen, 2002).

48. E.g., Westinghouse Elec. & Mfg. Co. v. Toledo, 172 F. 371, 372 (6th Cir. 1909) (narrow construction for unused patent); Electric Smelting & Aluminum Co. v. Carborundum Co., 189 F. 710 (C.C.W.D. Pa. 1900) (denying injunction as remedy for infringement). See Merges, "One Hundred Years of Solicitude," note 2, at 2219.

49. Continental Paper Bag Co. v. Eastern Paper Bag Co., 210 U.S. 405 (1908).

50. 35 U.S.C. §271(d).

51. See 5 Phillip E. Areeda and Herbert Hovenkamp, *Antitrust Law* ¶1202f (2d ed., New York: Aspen, 2003).

52. Motion Picture Patents Co. v. Universal Film Mfg. Co., 243 U.S. 502 (1917). On IP misuse generally, see Hovenkamp, Janis, and Lemley, 1 *IP and Antitrust,* note 12, at ch. 3.

53. USM Corp. v. SPS Technologies, 694 F.2d 505, 510–513 (7th Cir. 1982), cert. denied, 462 U.S. 1107 (1983).

54. C. R. Bard, Inc. v. M3 Systems, Inc., 157 F.3d 1340, 1372 (Fed. Cir. 1998), cert. denied, 526 U.S. 1130 (1999): "Patent misuse is viewed as a broader wrong than antitrust violation because of the economic power that may be derived from the patentee's right to exclude. Thus misuse may arise when the conditions of antitrust violation are not met." See also Virginia Panel Corp. v. MAC Panel Co., 133 F.3d 860, 872 (Fed. Cir. 1997) ("violation of the antitrust laws . . . requires more exacting proof than suffices to demonstrate patent misuse").

55. One exception is Scheiber v. Dolby Laboratories, 293 F.3d 1014 (7th Cir. 2002), cert. denied, 537 U.S. 1109 (2003).

56. E.g., Morton Salt Co. v. G. S. Suppiger Co., 314 U.S. 488 (1942); Mercoid Corp. v. Mid-Continent Investment Co. (*Mercoid I*), 320 U.S. 661 (1943).

57. Brulotte v. Thys Co., 379 U.S. 29 (1964); recently followed by Judge Posner, under protest, in *Scheiber,* note 55.

58. Laitram Corp. v. King Crab, 244 F. Supp. 9, modified, 245 F. Supp. 1019 (D. Ala. 1965).

59. Lasercomb America v. Reynolds, 911 F.2d 970, 973, 979 (4th Cir. 1990).

60. 35 U.S.C. §271(d). For fuller treatment, see Hovenkamp, Janis, and Lemley, 1 *IP and Antitrust,* note 12, at §3.3.

61. See, e.g., Argus Chem. Corp. v. Fibre Glass-Evercoat Co., 812 F.2d 1381, 1384 (Fed. Cir. 1987).

62. PSC, Inc. v. Symbol Technologies, 26 F. Supp. 2d 505 (W.D.N.Y. 1998).

63. See, e.g., Assessment Technologies v. Wiredata, Inc., 350 F.3d 640 (7th Cir. 2003); 361 F.3d 434 (7th Cir. 2004). The infringement plaintiff owned a copyrighted database program that public tax assessors used to collect data about real property, and that local governments used to store and organize the data. The infringement defendant wanted the raw data for use by real estate brokers and when it attempted to download that data, the plaintiff claimed copyright infringement. While the database itself was copyrightable, the raw data clearly were not. Judge Posner found misuse, viewing the infringement action as an attempt by the copyright holder to "sequester" the uncopyrighted data in its copyrighted database, for the data were not practically available in any form other than in the database. However, there was no showing that any relevant market was threatened with monopoly. Such an application of misuse resembles tort law more than antitrust. See also Chamberlain Group v. Skylink Technologies, Inc., 381 F.3d 1178 (Fed. Cir. 2004) (refusing to construe Digital Millennium Copyright Act so as to permit garage door manufacturer to deny access to uncopyrighted information necessary for making a universal remote control, where such a denial would otherwise constitute copyright misuse).

64. See United States v. Microsoft Corp., 253 F.3d 34, 49 (D.C. Cir.), cert. denied, 534 U.S. 952 (2001), discussed in the next chapter. On the indirect purchaser rule, see Chapter 3.

65. On tying arrangements, see Chapter 8. See also Berkey Photo v. Eastman Kodak Co., 603 F.2d 263, 287 (2d Cir. 1979), cert. denied, 444 U.S. 1093 (1980); C. R. Bard v. M3 Systems, 157 F.3d 1340 (Fed. Cir. 1998), cert. denied, 526 U.S. 1130 (1999). On technological ties, see 3A Phillip E. Areeda and Herbert Hovenkamp, *Antitrust Law* ¶776 (2d ed., New York: Aspen,

2002) (treated as monopolization); and 10, id., at ¶1757 (2d ed., 2004) (treated as tying).
66. *Microsoft*, 253 F.3d at 66–67.

Chapter 12. Network Industries and Computer Platform Monopoly

1. See Richard A. Posner, *Antitrust Law* 246 (2d ed., Chicago: University of Chicago Press, 2001). While some writers distinguish between "standards" and "networks," many standards either create networks or implicitly recognize networks that already exist. The illustrations in this chapter of railroad track gauge and VHS tape architecture bear this out.
2. See "The Format War," *Video Magazine* (April 1988), at 50–54; "VHS Meets Beta," *Popular Electronics* (Aug. 1981), at 43; "Even Sony Can't Avoid the Price War in VCRs," *Business Week* (Sept. 6, 1982), at 33–34; "Sony Isn't Mourning the 'Death' of Betamax," *Business Week* (Jan. 25, 1988), at 37; "Goodbye Beta," *Time* (Jan. 25, 1988), at 52.
3. United States v. Microsoft Corp., 253 F.3d 34, 49 (D.C. Cir.), cert. denied, 534 U.S. 952 (2001) (citations omitted).
4. George W. Hilton, "A History of Track Gauge," *Trains* (2002), Internet edition available at *www.trains.com;* George W. Hilton, *American Narrow Gauge Railroads* (Stanford, Calif.: Stanford University Press, 1995).
5. United States v. Trans-Missouri Freight Ass'n, 53 F. 440 (C.C.D. Kan. 1892), aff'd, 58 F. 58 (8th Cir. 1893), rev'd, 166 U.S. 290 (1897); and United States v. Joint-Traffic Ass'n, 171 U.S. 505 (1898).
6. E.g., Donald I. Baker, "Compulsory Access to Network Joint Ventures under the Sherman Act: Rules or Roulette," 1993 *Utah L. Rev.* 999.
7. Broadcast Music, Inc. v. Columbia Broadcasting System, 441 U.S. 1 (1979); and see 13 Phillip E. Areeda and Herbert Hovenkamp, *Antitrust Law* ¶2132c (2d ed., New York: Aspen, 2005).
8. Arizona v. Maricopa County Medical Soc'y, 457 U.S. 332 (1982).
9. NCAA v. Board of Regents of the University of Oklahoma, 468 U.S. 85 (1984).
10. Allied Tube & Conduit Corp. v. Indian Head, 486 U.S. 492 (1988).
11. See the lower court's opinion, 817 F.2d at 945 (2d Cir. 1987).
12. In the most typical venture arrangements voting rights are given one to each member, or the members elect a board of directors who vote on all important decisions. Alternatively, venture members may have voting rights in proportion to their ownership interests. For example, if the venture is incorporated and the venturers own shares, they may have one vote

per share. See Steven R. Salbu and Richard A. Brahm, "Strategic Considerations in Designing Joint Venture Contracts," 1992 *Colum. Bus. L. Rev.* 253.

13. See Herbert Hovenkamp, "Exclusive Joint Ventures and Antitrust Policy," 1995 *Colum. Bus. L. Rev.* 1.

14. Wilk v. American Medical Ass'n, 719 F.2d 207 (7th Cir. 1982); 735 F.2d 217 (7th Cir. 1984); 895 F.2d 352 (7th Cir.), cert. denied, 496 U.S. 927 (1990).

15. United States v. Visa USA, 163 F. Supp. 2d 322 (S.D.N.Y.), modified, 183 F. Supp. 2d 613 (S.D.N.Y. 2001), aff'd, 344 F.3d 229 (2d Cir. 2003), cert. denied, 125 S. Ct. 45 (2004).

16. See Chapter 7.

17. United States v. Aluminum Co. of Am. (Alcoa), 148 F.2d 416, 424 (2d Cir. 1945). See Ronald H. Coase, "Durability and Monopoly," 15 *J.L. & Econ.* 143 (1972); John Wiley, Eric Rasmusen, and J. Mark Ramseyer, "The Leasing Monopolist," 37 *UCLA L. Rev.* 693 (1990); Jean Tirole, *The Theory of Industrial Organization* 72–92 (Cambridge, Mass.: MIT Press, 1988).

18. See United States v. Microsoft, 84 F. Supp. 2d 9, 29 (D.D.C. 1999).

19. *Microsoft,* note 3, 253 F.3d at 60.

20. Perhaps the issue can be addressed legislatively by drastic shortening of the duration of IP rights, at least in markets subject to rapid innovation. See Lawrence Lessig, *The Future of Ideas: The Fate of the Commons in a Connected World* (New York: Random House, 2001). See also Mark A. Lemley and David McGowan, "Legal Implications of Network Economic Effects," 86 *Cal. L. Rev.* 479 (1998); M. L. Katz and Carl Shapiro, "Network Externalities, Competition, and Compatibility," 75 *Am. Econ. Rev.* 424 (1985).

21. United States v. Microsoft Corp., 253 F.3d 34, 103 (D.C. Cir.), cert. denied, 534 U.S. 952 (2001), quoting and citing Ford Motor Co. v. United States, 405 U.S. 562, 577 (1972); United States v. United Shoe Machinery Corp., 391 U.S. 244, 250 (1968); United States v. Grinnell Corp., 384 U.S. 563, 577 (1966).

22. In a later decision approving the consent decree the D.C. Circuit did not consider whether it met the goals it had initially articulated, and made only one fleeting reference to the objection that the decree did nothing to terminate the unlawful monopoly. See Massachusetts v. Microsoft Corp., 373 F.3d 1199, 1242 (D.C. Cir. 2004).

23. See United States v. Microsoft, 56 F.3d 1448, 1451 (D.C. Cir. 1995).

24. Subsequent evaluation has focused entirely on whether Microsoft is in compliance with the decree. See, e.g., "Judge Satisfied with Microsoft's Antitrust Case Compliance," *New York Times,* Jan. 24, 2004; "Judge Praises Microsoft Compliance in Antitrust Settlement," *Mercury News,* July 24, 2003.

25. Standard Oil Co. of N.J. v. United States, 221 U.S. 1, 46 (1911); and see Ron Chernow, *Titan: The Life of John D. Rockefeller, Sr.* (New York: Random House, 1998).

26. United States v. Sidney W. Winslow, 227 U.S. 202 (1913). The uniting firms were not competitors, but rather made complementary shoe making equipment.

27. United States v. United Shoe Machinery Co., 110 F. Supp. 295, 340, 341 (D. Mass. 1953), aff'd per curiam, 347 U.S. 521 (1954). For contrary views of the case, see S. Masten and E. Snyder, "*United States v. United Shoe Machinery Corp.:* On the Merits," 36 *J.L. & Econ.* 33 (1993), and J. F. Brodley and C. Albert Ma, "Contract Penalties, Monopolizing Strategies, and Antitrust Policy," 45 *Stan. L. Rev.* 1161, 1211 (1993).

28. United States v. United Shoe Machinery, 391 U.S. 244, 249–252 (1968). For criticism of the decree, see W. Kovacic, "Designing Antitrust Remedies for Dominant Firm Misconduct," 31 *Conn. L. Rev.* 1285 (1999).

29. See E. Thomas Sullivan, "The Antitrust Division as a Regulatory Agency: An Enforcement Policy in Transition," 64 *Wash. U. L.Q.* 997 (1986).

30. United States v. Aluminum Co. of Am., 148 F.2d 416, 445–448 (2d Cir. 1945).

31. The transaction is recounted in 2 Simon N. Whitney, *Antitrust Policies: American Experience in Twenty Industries* 95–98 (New York: Twentieth Century Fund, 1958); and Merton J. Peck, *Competition in the Aluminum Industry, 1945–1958,* at 11–19 (Cambridge, Mass.: Harvard University Press, 1961). Judge Hand, writing about three years before the transfer took place, had indicated that the breadth of the court's breakup decree might depend on whether Alcoa or one of its rivals purchased the plants; he also noted the policy of the Surplus Property Act to discourage "monopolistic practices" and to sell to smaller buyers when they were available. United States v. Aluminum Co. of Am., 148 F.2d at 446.

32. For a basic description, see *http://www.opensource.org.*

Epilogue

1. See the discussion in Chapter 3. Recent legislation provides for single damages against cartel members who turn themselves in to the Justice Department and disclose their cartel. The statute expands the DOJ's "corporate leniency" program, which was designed to detect cartels by giving firms an incentive to blow the whistle. Historically, the incentive was limited to immunity from criminal prosecution for nonringleader cartel members. See H.R. 1086, Title II (signed June 23, 2004), codified in 15 U.S.C. §1.

2. 15 U.S.C. §15 provides that a person may recover treble the damages "by him sustained" because of an antitrust violation.

3. Assume that a Kodak technician had a labor cost of $100 for a repair and a part cost of $50. Suppose that the technicians working for competing service companies had labor costs of only $90. Kodak could charge them $60 for the part and the package price would be the same.

4. Verizon Communications, Inc. v. Law Offices of Curtis Trinko, LLP, 540 U.S. 398 (2004).

Index

A. B. Dick. See Henry v. A. B. Dick
Addyston Pipe & Steel Co., United States v.,
   125
Administrability, 50–56; limits, 50, 53–54;
   subjective v. objective standard, 50, 61;
   vertical restraints and, 190–191
Administrative Process, The (James M.
   Landis), 239
Alcoa. See Aluminum Co. of Am.
Allied Tube & Conduit Corp. v. Indian Head,
   289–291
Aluminum Co. of Am. v. United States, 156,
   302
American Airlines. See AMR
American Can Co., United States v., 199
AMR, United States v., 165–167
Antitrust Division, Department of Justice,
   58, 60–61, 64, 208, 209
Antitrust economics: average cost, 163–167;
   consumer welfare, 14, 31–32, 39, 305;
   deadweight loss, 19, 27–28; decision making by judicial system, 46–47, 78–91;
   drawbacks of complex economic theories,
   45–49; "efficiency" as defense, 40; jury interpretation of economic evidence, 47–48;
   marginal cost curve, 15–20, 27–20
Antitrust goals, 1–2, 7–10, 21–25; common
   law origins, 44; consumer welfare, 14, 31–
   32, 39, 305; horizontal restraints, 22–23;
   legislative history, 39–44; network industries in, 281; unilateral exclusionary practices, 23–24; vertical practices, 24–25. See
   also Clayton Act; Robinson-Patman Act;
   Sherman Act
Antitrust Law (Richard Posner), 90
Antitrust Law treatise, 37, 90
Antitrust Paradox, The (Robert H. Bork), 209

Areeda, Philip E., 116, 156, 163
Areeda-Turner test, 163–167. See also Preda-
   tory pricing
Arizona v. Maricopa County Med. Ass'n, 142,
   288
Arnold, Schwinn & Co., United States v., 118–
   119, 189
AT&T, United States v., 244–45, 300–301
Automatic Radio Mfg. Co. v. Hazeltine Re-
   search, 264
Average variable cost, 163–167

Bain, Joe S., 102
Barriers to entry, 14, 33, 36, 102–104
Bement v. Nat'l Harrow Co., 256–259
Berkey Photo, Inc. v. Eastman Kodak Co., 275
Blanket licenses, 29, 265–267, 287–288
Block booking, 265
Blomkest Fertilizer v. Potash Corp of Saskatch-
   ewan, 135–136
BMI. See Broadcast Music
Bobbs-Merrill Co. v. Straus, 260
Bok, Derek, 53
Bork, Robert H., 5, 37, 39–40, 43; The Anti-
   trust Paradox, 5, 9, 209
Boycotts, 20–22; Sherman Act, §1, regulation
   of, 21
Brandeis, Justice, 33, 105–106, 149, 201, 309
Broadcast Music, Inc. v. Columbia Broadcasting
   System, Inc. (BMI), 29–30, 142, 265–266,
   287
Brooke Group Ltd. v. Brown & Williamson To-
   bacco Corp., 167–170, 178
Brown Shoe Co. v. United States, 209–210
Brunswick Corp. v. Pueblo Bowl-O-Mat, Inc.,
   83–84
Buchanan, James, 239

363